Legal Principles in WTO Disputes

Principles play a crucial role in any dispute settlement system, and the World Trade Organization (WTO) is no exception. However, WTO Panels and the Appellate Body have been too timid in using principles, sometimes avoiding their use when appropriate and at other times using them without fully acknowledging that they are doing so. Perhaps more worryingly, these bodies often fail to delve deeply enough into principles. They tend to overlook key questions such as the legal basis for using a given principle, whether the principle is being used in an interpretative manner or as applicable law, and the meaning of the principle in public international law. This book establishes a framework for addressing these questions. The use of such a framework should allay fears and misconceptions about the use of principles and ensure that they are used in a justifiable manner, improving the quality of dispute settlement in the WTO.

ANDREW D. MITCHELL is a Senior Lecturer at Melbourne Law School. Previously he was a solicitor with Allens Arthur Robinson in Australia. He has also worked in the Trade Directorate of the Organisation for Economic Co-operation and Development (OECD), the intellectual Property Division of the World Trade Organization (WTO), and the Legal Department of the International Monetary Fund (IMF).

CAMBRIDGE STUDIES IN INTERNATIONAL AND COMPARATIVE LAW

Established in 1946, this series produces high-quality scholarship in the fields of public and private international law and comparative law. Although these are distinct legal sub-disciplines, developments since 1946 confirm their interrelation.

Comparative law is increasingly used as a tool in the making of law at national, regional and international levels. Private international law is now often affected by international conventions, and the issues faced by classical conflicts rules are frequently dealt with by substantive harmonisation of law under international auspices. Mixed international arbitrations, especially those involving state economic activity, raise mixed questions of public and private international law, while in many fields (such as the protection of human rights and democratic standards, investment guarantees and international criminal law) international and national systems interact. National constitutional arrangements relating to 'foreign affairs', and to the implementation of international norms, are a focus of attention.

The Board welcomes works of a theoretical or interdisciplinary character, and those focusing on the new approaches to international or comparative law or conflicts of law. Studies of particular institutions or problems are equally welcome, as are translations of the best work published in other languages.

A list of books in the series can be found at the end of this volume.

Legal Principles in WTO Disputes

Andrew D. Mitchell

CAMBRIDGE
UNIVERSITY PRESS

CAMBRIDGE UNIVERSITY PRESS
Cambridge, New York, Melbourne, Madrid, Cape Town, Singapore,
São Paulo, Delhi, Dubai, Tokyo, Mexico City

Cambridge University Press
The Edinburgh Building, Cambridge CB2 8RU, UK

Published in the United States of America by Cambridge University Press, New York

www.cambridge.org
Information on this title: www.cambridge.org/9780521873260

First published 2008

A catalogue record for this publication is available from the British Library

Library of Congress Cataloguing in Publication data
Mitchell, Andrew D.
Legal principles in WTO disputes / Andrew D. Mitchell,
p. cm. – (Cambridge studies in international and comparative law ; [61])
Includes bibliographical references and index.
ISBN 978-0-521-87326-0 (hardback)
1. World Trade Organization. 2. Foreign trade regulation.
3. Tariff–Law and legislation. 4. Dispute resolution (Law) I. Title.
II. Series.
K4610.M58 2008
382′.92–dc22 2008028689

ISBN 978-0-521-87326-0 Hardback

To my wife and best friend, Tania
and to my son, Max

Contents

Detailed chapter outline

Table of WTO Agreements

Table of WTO cases

Table of general abbreviations

Short title	Full citation
Anti-Dumping Agreement	Agreement on Implementation of Article VI of the GATT 1994
ATC	Agreement on Textiles and Clothing
BISD	Basic Instruments and Selected Documents
CDSOA	*Continued Dumping and Subsidy Offset Act of 2000*, Pub L No 106–387, 114 Stat 1549, 1001–1003 (2001) (US)
covered agreements	The Agreements listed in Annex 1 of the Understanding on Rules and Procedures Governing the Settlement of Disputes
Doha Declaration	WTO Ministerial Conference, *Ministerial Declaration*, WT/MIN(01)/DEC/1 (20 November 2001)
Doha Declaration on TRIPS and Public Health	WTO Ministerial Conference, *Declaration on the TRIPS Agreement and Public Health*, WT/MIN(01)/DEC/2 (20 November 2001)
Doha Implementation Decision	WTO Ministerial Conference, *Implementation-Related Issues and Concerns - Decision of 14 November 2001*, WT/MIN(01)/17 (20 November 2001)
DSB	Dispute Settlement Body
DSU	Understanding on Rules and Procedures Governing the Settlement of Disputes (Dispute Settlement Understanding)
EC	European Communities
ECJ	European Court of Justice
Enabling Clause	Decision on Differential and More Favourable Treatment, Reciprocity, and Fuller Participation

	of Developing Countries, GATT Document L/4903, 28 November 1979, BISD 26S/203
GATS	General Agreement on Trade in Services
GATT	General Agreement on Tariffs and Trade
GSP	Generalised System of Preferences
HS	Harmonized Commodity Description and Coding System (Harmonized System)
ICJ	International Court of Justice
ILC Articles	International Law Commission's Articles on Responsibility of States for Internationally Wrongful Acts: General Assembly, UN, *Report of the International Law Commission*, A/56/10 (SUPP) (1 October 2001)
IMF	International Monetary Fund
July Package	WTO General Council, *Decision Adopted by the General Council on 1 August 2004*, WT/L/579 (2 August 2004)
LDC	Least-developed country
Marrakesh Agreement	Marrakesh Agreement Establishing the World Trade Organization
MFN	Most Favoured Nation
Multilateral Trade Agreements	The Agreements and associated legal instruments included in Annexes 1, 2 and 3 to the Marrakesh Agreement Establishing the World Trade Organization
NAFTA	North American Free Trade Agreement
OECD	Organisation for Economic Co-operation and Development
PCIJ	Permanent Court of International Justice
Plurilateral Trade Agreements	The Agreements and associated legal instruments included in Annex 4 to the Marrakesh Agreement Establishing the World Trade Organization
Rules of Conduct	DSB, *Rules of Conduct for the Understanding on Rules and Procedures Governing the Settlement of Disputes*, WT/DSB/RC/1 (11 December 1996)
S&D	Special and differential treatment
SCM Agreement	Agreement on Subsidies and Countervailing Measures
SPS Agreement	Agreement on the Application of Sanitary and Phytosanitary Measures

SPS measure	Sanitary or phytosanitary measure
TBT Agreement	Agreement on Technical Barriers to Trade
TRIMS Agreement	Agreement on Trade-Related Investment Measures
TRIPS Agreement	Agreement on Trade-Related Aspects of Intellectual Property Rights
UN	United Nations
UN Charter	Charter of the United Nations
UNCTAD	United Nations Conference on Trade and Development
VCLT	Vienna Convention on the Law of Treaties, opened for signature on 23 May 1969, 1155 UNTS 331 (entered into force 27 January 1980)
Working Procedures for Appellate Review	Appellate Body, *Working Procedures for Appellate Review*, WT/AB/WP/5 (4 January 2005)
WTO	World Trade Organization
WTO agreements	The Marrakesh Agreement and the documents contained in its four annexes
WTO Tribunals	WTO Arbitral Bodies, Panels, and the Appellate Body

Table of WTO award and report abbreviations

Short Title	Full citation
Argentina – Ceramic Tiles	Panel Report, *Argentina – Definitive Anti-Dumping Measures on Imports of Ceramic Floor Tiles from Italy*, WT/DS189/R, adopted 5 November 2001, DSR 2001:XII, 6241
Argentina – Footwear (EC)	Appellate Body Report, *Argentina – Safeguard Measures on Imports of Footwear*, WT/DS121/AB/R, adopted 12 January 2000, DSR 2000:I, 515
Argentina – Footwear (EC)	Panel Report, *Argentina – Safeguard Measures on Imports of Footwear*, WT/DS121/R, adopted 12 January 2000, as modified by Appellate Body Report, WT/DS121/AB/R, DSR 2000:II, 575
Argentina – Hides and Leather	Panel Report, *Argentina – Measures Affecting the Export of Bovine Hides and Import of Finished Leather*, WT/DS155/R and Corr.1, adopted 16 February 2001, DSR 2001:V, 1779
Argentina – Hides and Leather	Award of the Arbitrator, *Argentina – Measures Affecting the Export of Bovine Hides and Import of Finished Leather – Arbitration under Article 21.3(c) of the DSU*, WT/DS155/10, 31 August 2001, DSR 2001:XII, 6013
Argentina – Poultry Anti-Dumping Duties	Panel Report, *Argentina – Definitive Anti-Dumping Duties on Poultry from Brazil*, WT/DS241/R, adopted 19 May 2003
Argentina – Preserved Peaches	Panel Report, *Argentina – Definitive Safeguard Measure on Imports of Preserved Peaches*, WT/DS238/R, adopted 15 April 2003

Argentina – Textiles and Apparel	Appellate Body Report, *Argentina – Measures Affecting Imports of Footwear, Textiles, Apparel and Other Items*, WT/DS56/AB/R and Corr.1, adopted 22 April 1998, DSR 1998:III, 1003
Argentina – Textiles and Apparel	Panel Report, *Argentina – Measures Affecting Imports of Footwear, Textiles, Apparel and Other Items*, WT/DS56/R, adopted 22 April 1998, as modified by Appellate Body Report, WT/DS56/AB/R, DSR 1998:III, 1033
Australia – Automotive Leather II	Panel Report, *Australia – Subsidies Provided to Producers and Exporters of Automotive Leather*, WT/DS126/R, adopted 16 June 1999, DSR 1999:III, 951
Australia – Automotive Leather II (Article 21.5 – US)	Panel Report, *Australia – Subsidies Provided to Producers and Exporters of Automotive Leather – Recourse to Article 21.5 of the DSU by the United States*, WT/DS126/RW and Corr.1, adopted 11 February 2000, DSR 2000:III, 1189
Australia – Salmon	Appellate Body Report, *Australia – Measures Affecting Importation of Salmon*, WT/DS18/AB/R, adopted 6 November 1998, DSR 1998:VIII, 3327
Australia – Salmon	Panel Report, *Australia – Measures Affecting Importation of Salmon*, WT/DS18/R and Corr.1, adopted 6 November 1998, as modified by Appellate Body Report, WT/DS18/AB/R, DSR 1998:VIII, 3407
Australia – Salmon	Award of the Arbitrator, *Australia – Measures Affecting Importation of Salmon – Arbitration under Article 21.3(c) of the DSU*, WT/DS18/9, 23 February 1999, DSR 1999:I, 267
Australia – Salmon (Article 21.5 – Canada)	Panel Report, *Australia – Measures Affecting Importation of Salmon – Recourse to Article 21.5 of the DSU by Canada*, WT/DS18/RW, adopted 20 March 2000, DSR 2000:IV, 2031
Brazil – Aircraft	Appellate Body Report, *Brazil – Export Financing Programme for Aircraft*, WT/DS46/AB/R, adopted 20 August 1999, DSR 1999:III, 1161
Brazil – Aircraft	Panel Report, *Brazil – Export Financing Programme for Aircraft*, WT/DS46/R, adopted 20 August 1999,

	as modified by Appellate Body Report, WT/DS46/AB/R, DSR 1999:III, 1221
Brazil – Aircraft (Article 21.5 – Canada)	Appellate Body Report, *Brazil – Export Financing Programme for Aircraft – Recourse by Canada to Article 21.5 of the DSU*, WT/DS46/AB/RW, adopted 4 August 2000, DSR 2000:VIII, 4067
Brazil – Aircraft (Article 21.5 – Canada)	Panel Report, *Brazil – Export Financing Programme for Aircraft – Recourse by Canada to Article 21.5 of the DSU*, WT/DS46/RW, adopted 4 August 2000, as modified by Appellate Body Report, WT/DS46/AB/RW, DSR 2000:IX, 4093
Brazil – Aircraft (Article 21.5 – Canada II)	Panel Report, *Brazil – Export Financing Programme for Aircraft – Second Recourse by Canada to Article 21.5 of the DSU*, WT/DS46/RW/2, adopted 23 August 2001, DSR 2001:X, 5481
Brazil – Aircraft (Article 22.6 – Brazil)	Decision by the Arbitrators, *Brazil – Export Financing Programme for Aircraft – Recourse to Arbitration by Brazil under Article 22.6 of the DSU and Article 4.11 of the SCM Agreement*, WT/DS46/ARB, 28 August 2000, DSR 2002:I, 19
Brazil – Desiccated Coconut	Appellate Body Report, *Brazil – Measures Affecting Desiccated Coconut*, WT/DS22/AB/R, adopted 20 March 1997, DSR 1997:I, 167
Brazil – Desiccated Coconut	Panel Report, *Brazil – Measures Affecting Desiccated Coconut*, WT/DS22/R, adopted 20 March 1997, as upheld by Appellate Body Report, WT/DS22/AB/R, DSR 1997:I, 189
Brazil – Retreaded Tyres	Panel Report, *Brazil – Measures Affecting Imports of Retreaded Tyres*, WT/DS332/R, 12 June 2007
Brazil – Retreaded Tyres	Appellate Body Report, *Brazil – Measures Affecting Imports of Retreaded Tyres*, WT/DS332/AB/R, adopted 17 December 2007
Canada – Aircraft	Appellate Body Report, *Canada – Measures Affecting the Export of Civilian Aircraft*, WT/DS70/AB/R, adopted 20 August 1999, DSR 1999:III, 1377
Canada – Aircraft	Panel Report, *Canada – Measures Affecting the Export of Civilian Aircraft*, WT/DS70/R, adopted 20 August 1999, as upheld by Appellate Body Report, WT/DS70/AB/R, DSR 1999:IV, 1443

Canada – Aircraft (Article 21.5 – Brazil)	Appellate Body Report, *Canada – Measures Affecting the Export of Civilian Aircraft – Recourse by Brazil to Article 21.5 of the DSU*, WT/DS70/AB/RW, adopted 4 August 2000, DSR 2000:IX, 4299
Canada – Aircraft (Article 21.5 – Brazil)	Panel Report, *Canada – Measures Affecting the Export of Civilian Aircraft – Recourse by Brazil to Article 21.5 of the DSU*, WT/DS70/RW, adopted 4 August 2000, as modified by Appellate Body Report, WT/DS70/AB/RW, DSR 2000:IX, 4315
Canada – Aircraft Credits and Guarantees	Panel Report, *Canada – Export Credits and Loan Guarantees for Regional Aircraft*, WT/DS222/R and Corr.1, adopted 19 February 2002, DSR 2002:III, 849
Canada – Aircraft Credits and Guarantees (Article 22.6 – Canada)	Decision by the Arbitrator, *Canada – Export Credits and Loan Guarantees for Regional Aircraft – Recourse to Arbitration by Canada under Article 22.6 of the DSU and Article 4.11 of the SCM Agreement*, WT/DS222/ARB, 17 February 2003
Canada – Autos	Appellate Body Report, *Canada – Certain Measures Affecting the Automotive Industry*, WT/DS139/AB/R, WT/DS142/AB/R, adopted 19 June 2000, DSR 2000:VI, 2985
Canada – Autos	Panel Report, *Canada – Certain Measures Affecting the Automotive Industry*, WT/DS139/R, WT/DS142/R, adopted 19 June 2000, as modified by Appellate Body Report, WT/DS139/AB/R, WT/DS142/AB/R, DSR 2000:VII, 3043
Canada – Autos	Award of the Arbitrator, *Canada – Certain Measures Affecting the Automotive Industry – Arbitration under Article 21.3(c) of the DSU*, WT/DS139/12, WT/DS142/12, 4 October 2000, DSR 2000:X, 5079
Canada – Dairy	Appellate Body Report, *Canada – Measures Affecting the Importation of Milk and the Exportation of Dairy Products*, WT/DS103/AB/R, WT/DS113/AB/R and Corr.1, adopted 27 October 1999, DSR 1999:V, 2057
Canada – Dairy	Panel Report, *Canada – Measures Affecting the Importation of Milk and the Exportation of Dairy Products*, WT/DS103/R, WT/DS113/R, adopted 27 October 1999, as modified by Appellate Body

	Report, WT/DS103/AB/R, WT/DS113/AB/R, DSR 1999:VI, 2097
Canada – Dairy (Article 21.5 – New Zealand and US)	Appellate Body Report, *Canada – Measures Affecting the Importation of Milk and the Exportation of Dairy Products – Recourse to Article 21.5 of the DSU by New Zealand and the United States*, WT/DS103/AB/RW, WT/DS113/AB/RW, adopted 18 December 2001, DSR 2001:XIII, 6829
Canada – Dairy (Article 21.5 – New Zealand and US)	Panel Report, *Canada – Measures Affecting the Importation of Milk and the Exportation of Dairy Products – Recourse to Article 21.5 of the DSU by New Zealand and the United States*, WT/DS103/RW, WT/DS113/RW, adopted 18 December 2001, as reversed by Appellate Body Report, WT/DS103/AB/RW, WT/DS113/AB/RW, DSR 2001:XIII, 6865
Canada – Dairy (Article 21.5 – New Zealand and US II)	Appellate Body Report, *Canada – Measures Affecting the Importation of Milk and the Exportation of Dairy Products – Second Recourse to Article 21.5 of the DSU by New Zealand and the United States*, WT/DS103/AB/RW2, WT/DS113/AB/RW2, adopted 17 January 2003
Canada – Dairy (Article 21.5 – New Zealand and US II)	Panel Report, *Canada – Measures Affecting the Importation of Milk and the Exportation of Dairy Products – Second Recourse to Article 21.5 of the DSU by New Zealand and the United States*, WT/DS103/RW2, WT/DS113/RW2, adopted 17 January 2003, as modified by Appellate Body Report, WT/DS103/AB/RW2, WT/DS113/AB/RW2
Canada – Patent Term	Appellate Body Report, *Canada – Term of Patent Protection*, WT/DS170/AB/R, adopted 12 October 2000, DSR 2000:X, 5093
Canada – Patent Term	Panel Report, *Canada – Term of Patent Protection*, WT/DS170/R, adopted 12 October 2000, as upheld by Appellate Body Report, WT/DS170/AB/R, DSR 2000:XI, 5121
Canada – Patent Term	Award of the Arbitrator, *Canada – Term of Patent Protection – Arbitration under Article 21.3(c) of the DSU*, WT/DS170/10, 28 February 2001, DSR 2001:V, 2031

Canada – Periodicals	Appellate Body Report, *Canada – Certain Measures Concerning Periodicals*, WT/DS31/AB/R, adopted 30 July 1997, DSR 1997:I, 449
Canada – Periodicals	Panel Report, *Canada – Certain Measures Concerning Periodicals*, WT/DS31/R and Corr.1, adopted 30 July 1997, as modified by Appellate Body Report, WT/DS31/AB/R, DSR 1997:I, 481
Canada – Pharmaceutical Patents	Panel Report, *Canada – Patent Protection of Pharmaceutical Products*, WT/DS114/R, adopted 7 April 2000, DSR 2000:V, 2289
Canada – Pharmaceutical Patents	Award of the Arbitrator, *Canada – Patent Protection of Pharmaceutical Products – Arbitration under Article 21.3(c) of the DSU*, WT/DS114/13, 18 August 2000, DSR 2002:I, 3
Canada – Wheat Exports and Grain Imports	Appellate Body Report, *Canada – Measures Relating to Exports of Wheat and Treatment of Imported Grain*, WT/DS276/AB/R, adopted 27 September 2004
Canada – Wheat Exports and Grain Imports	Panel Report, *Canada – Measures Relating to Exports of Wheat and Treatment of Imported Grain*, WT/DS276/R, adopted 27 September 2004, as upheld by Appellate Body Report, WT/DS276/AB/R
Chile – Alcoholic Beverages	Appellate Body Report, *Chile – Taxes on Alcoholic Beverages*, WT/DS87/AB/R, WT/DS110/AB/R, adopted 12 January 2000, DSR 2000:I, 281
Chile – Alcoholic Beverages	Panel Report, *Chile – Taxes on Alcoholic Beverages*, WT/DS87/R, WT/DS110/R, adopted 12 January 2000, as modified by Appellate Body Report, WT/DS87/AB/R, WT/DS110/AB/R, DSR 2000:I, 303
Chile – Alcoholic Beverages	Award of the Arbitrator, *Chile – Taxes on Alcoholic Beverages – Arbitration under Article 21.3(c) of the DSU*, WT/DS87/15, WT/DS110/14, 23 May 2000, DSR 2000:V, 2583
Chile – Price Band System	Appellate Body Report, *Chile – Price Band System and Safeguard Measures Relating to Certain Agricultural Products*, WT/DS207/AB/R, adopted 23 October 2002, DSR 2002:VIII, 3045
Chile – Price Band System	Panel Report, *Chile – Price Band System and Safeguard Measures Relating to Certain Agricultural Products*,

	WT/DS207/R, adopted 23 October 2002, as modified by Appellate Body Report, WT/DS207AB/R, DSR 2002:VIII, 3127
Chile – Price Band System	Award of the Arbitrator, *Chile – Price Band System and Safeguard Measures Relating to Certain Agricultural Products – Arbitration under Article 21.3 (c) of the DSU*, WT/DS207/13, 17 March 2003
Dominican Republic – Import and Sale of Cigarettes	Appellate Body Report, *Dominican Republic – Measures Affecting the Importation and Internal Sale of Cigarettes*, WT/DS302/AB/R, adopted 19 May 2005
Dominican Republic – Import and Sale of Cigarettes	Panel Report, *Dominican Republic – Measures Affecting the Importation and Internal Sale of Cigarettes*, WT/DS302/R, adopted 19 May 2005, as modified by Appellate Body Report, WT/DS302/AB/R
EC – Asbestos	Appellate Body Report, *European Communities – Measures Affecting Asbestos and Asbestos-Containing Products*, WT/DS135/AB/R, adopted 5 April 2001, DSR 2001:VII, 3243
EC – Asbestos	Panel Report, *European Communities – Measures Affecting Asbestos and Asbestos-Containing Products*, WT/DS135/R and Add.1, adopted 5 April 2001, as modified by Appellate Body Report, WT/DS135/AB/R, DSR 2001:VIII, 3305
EC – Bananas III	Appellate Body Report, *European Communities – Regime for the Importation, Sale and Distribution of Bananas*, WT/DS27/AB/R, adopted 25 September 1997, DSR 1997:II, 591
EC – Bananas III (Ecuador)	Panel Report, *European Communities – Regime for the Importation, Sale and Distribution of Bananas, Complaint by Ecuador*, WT/DS27/R/ECU, adopted 25 September 1997, as modified by Appellate Body Report, WT/DS27/AB/R, DSR 1997:III, 1085
EC – Bananas III (Guatemala and Honduras)	Panel Report, *European Communities – Regime for the Importation, Sale and Distribution of Bananas, Complaint by Guatemala and Honduras*, WT/DS27/R/GTM, WT/DS27/R/HND, adopted 25 September 1997, as modified by Appellate Body Report, WT/DS27/AB/R, DSR 1997:II, 695

EC – Bananas III (Mexico)	Panel Report, *European Communities – Regime for the Importation, Sale and Distribution of Bananas, Complaint by Mexico*, WT/DS27/R/MEX, adopted 25 September 1997, as modified by Appellate Body Report, WT/DS27/AB/R, DSR 1997:II, 803
EC – Bananas III (US)	Panel Report, *European Communities – Regime for the Importation, Sale and Distribution of Bananas, Complaint by the United States*, WT/DS27/R/USA, adopted 25 September 1997, as modified by Appellate Body Report, WT/DS27/AB/R, DSR 1997:II, 943
EC – Bananas III	Award of the Arbitrator, *European Communities – Regime for the Importation, Sale and Distribution of Bananas – Arbitration under Article 21.3(c) of the DSU*, WT/DS27/15, 7 January 1998, DSR 1998:I, 3
EC – Bananas III (Article 21.5 – EC)	Panel Report, *European Communities – Regime for the Importation, Sale and Distribution of Bananas – Recourse to Article 21.5 of the DSU by the European Communities*, WT/DS27/RW/EEC and Corr.1, 12 April 1999, DSR 1999:II, 783
EC – Bananas III (Article 21.5 – Ecuador)	Panel Report, *European Communities – Regime for the Importation, Sale and Distribution of Bananas – Recourse to Article 21.5 of the DSU by Ecuador*, WT/DS27/RW/ECU, adopted 6 May 1999, DSR 1999: II, 803
EC – Bananas III (Ecuador) (Article 22.6 – EC)	Decision by the Arbitrators, *European Communities – Regime for the Importation, Sale and Distribution of Bananas – Recourse to Arbitration by the European Communities under Article 22.6 of the DSU*, WT/DS27/ARB/ECU, 24 March 2000, DSR 2000:V, 2237
EC – Bananas III (US) (Article 22.6 – EC)	Decision by the Arbitrators, *European Communities – Regime for the Importation, Sale and Distribution of Bananas – Recourse to Arbitration by the European Communities under Article 22.6 of the DSU*, WT/DS27/ARB, 9 April 1999, DSR 1999:II, 725
EC – Bed Linen	Appellate Body Report, *European Communities – Anti-Dumping Duties on Imports of Cotton-Type Bed Linen from India*, WT/DS141/AB/R, adopted 12 March 2001, DSR 2001:V, 2049

EC – Bed Linen	Panel Report, *European Communities – Anti-Dumping Duties on Imports of Cotton-Type Bed Linen from India*, WT/DS141/R, adopted 12 March 2001, as modified by Appellate Body Report, WT/DS141/AB/R, DSR 2001:VI, 2077
EC – Bed Linen (Article 21.5 – India)	Appellate Body Report, *European Communities – Anti-Dumping Duties on Imports of Cotton-Type Bed Linen from India – Recourse to Article 21.5 of the DSU by India*, WT/DS141/AB/RW, adopted 24 April 2003
EC – Bed Linen (Article 21.5 – India)	Panel Report, *European Communities – Anti-Dumping Duties on Imports of Cotton-Type Bed Linen from India – Recourse to Article 21.5 of the DSU by India*, WT/DS141/RW, adopted 24 April 2003, as modified by Appellate Body Report, WT/DS141/AB/RW
EC – Biotech	Panel Report, *European Communities – Measures Affecting the Approval and Marketing of Biotech Products*, WT/DS291, 292, 293/R, adopted 21 November 2006
EC – Chicken Cuts	Appellate Body Report, *European Communities – Customs Classification of Frozen Boneless Chicken Cuts*, WT/DS269/AB/R, WT/DS286/AB/R, 12 September 2005
EC – Chicken Cuts (Brazil)	Panel Report, *European Communities – Customs Classification of Frozen Boneless Chicken Cuts, Complaint by Brazil*, WT/DS269/R, 30 May 2005
EC – Chicken Cuts (Thailand)	Panel Report, *European Communities – Customs Classification of Frozen Boneless Chicken Cuts, Complaint by Thailand*, WT/DS286/R, 30 May 2005
EC – Commercial Vessels	Panel Report, *European Communities – Measures Affecting Trade in Commercial Vessels*, WT/DS301/R, adopted 20 June 2005
EC – Computer Equipment	Appellate Body Report, *European Communities – Customs Classification of Certain Computer Equipment*, WT/DS62/AB/R, WT/DS67/AB/R, WT/DS68/AB/R, adopted 22 June 1998, DSR 1998:V, 1851
EC – Computer Equipment	Panel Report, *European Communities – Customs Classification of Certain Computer Equipment*, WT/DS62/R, WT/DS67/R, WT/DS68/R, adopted

	22 June 1998, as modified by Appellate Body Report, WT/DS62/AB/R, WT/DS67/AB/R, WT/DS68/AB/R, DSR 1998:V, 1891
EC – Countervailing Measures on DRAM Chips	Panel Report, *European Communities – Countervailing Measures on Dynamic Random Access Memory Chips from Korea*, WT/DS299/R, adopted 3 August 2005
EC – Export Subsidies on Sugar	Appellate Body Report, *European Communities – Export Subsidies on Sugar*, WT/DS265/AB/R, WT/DS266/AB/R, WT/DS283/AB/R, adopted 19 May 2005
EC – Export Subsidies on Sugar (Australia)	Panel Report, *European Communities – Export Subsidies on Sugar, Complaint by Australia*, WT/DS265/R, adopted 19 May 2005, as modified by Appellate Body Report, WT/DS265/AB/R, WT/DS266/AB/R, WT/DS283/AB/R
EC – Export Subsidies on Sugar (Brazil)	Panel Report, *European Communities – Export Subsidies on Sugar, Complaint by Brazil*, WT/DS266/R, adopted 19 May 2005, as modified by Appellate Body Report, WT/DS265/AB/R, WT/DS266/AB/R, WT/DS283/AB/R
EC – Export Subsidies on Sugar (Thailand)	Panel Report, *European Communities – Export Subsidies on Sugar, Complaint by Thailand*, WT/DS283/R, adopted 19 May 2005, as modified by Appellate Body Report, WT/DS265/AB/R, WT/DS266/AB/R, WT/DS283/AB/R
EC – Hormones	Appellate Body Report, *EC Measures Concerning Meat and Meat Products (Hormones)*, WT/DS26/AB/R, WT/DS48/AB/R, adopted 13 February 1998, DSR 1998:I, 135
EC – Hormones (Canada)	Panel Report, *EC Measures Concerning Meat and Meat Products (Hormones), Complaint by Canada*, WT/DS48/R/CAN, adopted 13 February 1998, as modified by Appellate Body Report, WT/DS26/AB/R, WT/DS48/AB/R, DSR 1998:II, 235
EC – Hormones (US)	Panel Report, *EC Measures Concerning Meat and Meat Products (Hormones), Complaint by the United States*, WT/DS26/R/USA, adopted 13 February 1998, as modified by Appellate Body Report, WT/DS26/AB/R, WT/DS48/AB/R, DSR 1998:III, 699

EC – Hormones	Award of the Arbitrator, *EC Measures Concerning Meat and Meat Products (Hormones) – Arbitration under Article 21.3(c) of the DSU*, WT/DS26/15, WT/DS48/13, 29 May 1998, DSR 1998:V, 1833
EC – Hormones (Canada) (Article 22.6 – EC)	Decision by the Arbitrators, *European Communities – Measures Concerning Meat and Meat Products (Hormones), Original Complaint by Canada – Recourse to Arbitration by the European Communities under Article 22.6 of the DSU*, WT/DS48/ARB, 12 July 1999, DSR 1999:III, 1135
EC – Hormones (US) (Article 22.6 – EC)	Decision by the Arbitrators, *European Communities – Measures Concerning Meat and Meat Products (Hormones), Original Complaint by the United States – Recourse to Arbitration by the European Communities under Article 22.6 of the DSU*, WT/DS26/ARB, 12 July 1999, DSR 1999:III, 1105
EC – Poultry	Appellate Body Report, *European Communities – Measures Affecting the Importation of Certain Poultry Products*, WT/DS69/AB/R, adopted 23 July 1998, DSR 1998:V, 2031
EC – Poultry	Panel Report, *European Communities – Measures Affecting the Importation of Certain Poultry Products*, WT/DS69/R, adopted 23 July 1998, as modified by Appellate Body Report, WT/DS69/AB/R, DSR 1998:V, 2089
EC – Sardines	Appellate Body Report, *European Communities – Trade Description of Sardines*, WT/DS231/AB/R, adopted 23 October 2002, DSR 2002:VIII, 3359
EC – Sardines	Panel Report, *European Communities – Trade Description of Sardines*, WT/DS231/R and Corr.1, adopted 23 October 2002, as modified by Appellate Body Report, WT/DS231/AB/R, DSR 2002:VIII, 3451
EC – Scallops (Canada)	Panel Report, *European Communities – Trade Description of Scallops – Request by Canada*, WT/DS7/R, 5 August 1996, DSR 1996:I, 89
EC – Scallops (Peru and Chile)	Panel Report, *European Communities – Trade Description of Scallops – Requests by Peru and Chile*, WT/DS12/R, WT/DS14/R, 5 August 1996, DSR 1996:I, 93

EC – Tariff Preferences	Appellate Body Report, *European Communities – Conditions for the Granting of Tariff Preferences to Developing Countries*, WT/DS246/AB/R, adopted 20 April 2004
EC – Tariff Preferences	Panel Report, *European Communities – Conditions for the Granting of Tariff Preferences to Developing Countries*, WT/DS246/R, adopted 20 April 2004, as modified by Appellate Body Report, WT/DS/246/AB/R
EC – Tariff Preferences	Award of the Arbitrator, *European Communities – Conditions for the Granting of Tariff Preferences to Developing Countries – Arbitration under Article 21.3(c) of the DSU*, WT/DS246/14, 20 September 2004
EC – Trademarks and Geographical Indications (Australia)	Panel Report, *European Communities – Protection of Trademarks and Geographical Indications for Agricultural Products and Foodstuffs, Complaint by Australia*, WT/DS290/R, adopted 20 April 2005
EC – Trademarks and Geographical Indications (US)	Panel Report, *European Communities – Protection of Trademarks and Geographical Indications for Agricultural Products and Foodstuffs, Complaint by the United States*, WT/DS174/R, adopted 20 April 2005
EC – Tube or Pipe Fittings	Appellate Body Report, *European Communities – Anti-Dumping Duties on Malleable Cast Iron Tube or Pipe Fittings from Brazil*, WT/DS219/AB/R, adopted 18 August 2003
EC – Tube or Pipe Fittings	Panel Report, *European Communities – Anti-Dumping Duties on Malleable Cast Iron Tube or Pipe Fittings from Brazil*, WT/DS219/R, adopted 18 August 2003, as modified by Appellate Body Report, WT/DS219/AB/R
Egypt – Steel Rebar	Panel Report, *Egypt – Definitive Anti-Dumping Measures on Steel Rebar from Turkey*, WT/DS211/R, adopted 1 October 2002, DSR 2002:VII, 2667
Guatemala – Cement I	Appellate Body Report, *Guatemala – Anti-Dumping Investigation Regarding Portland Cement from Mexico*, WT/DS60/AB/R, adopted 25 November 1998, DSR 1998:IX, 3767
Guatemala – Cement I	Panel Report, *Guatemala – Anti-Dumping Investigation Regarding Portland Cement from*

	Mexico, WT/DS60/R, adopted 25 November 1998, as modified by Appellate Body Report, WT/DS60/AB/R, DSR 1998:IX, 3797
Guatemala – Cement II	Panel Report, *Guatemala – Definitive Anti-Dumping Measures on Grey Portland Cement from Mexico*, WT/DS156/R, adopted 17 November 2000, DSR 2000:XI, 5295
India – Autos	Appellate Body Report, *India – Measures Affecting the Automotive Sector*, WT/DS146/AB/R, WT/DS175/AB/R, adopted 5 April 2002, DSR 2002:V, 1821
India – Autos	Panel Report, *India – Measures Affecting the Automotive Sector*, WT/DS146/R, WT/DS175/R and Corr.1, adopted 5 April 2002, DSR 2002:V, 1827
India – Patents (EC)	Panel Report, *India – Patent Protection for Pharmaceutical and Agricultural Chemical Products, Complaint by the European Communities*, WT/DS79/R, adopted 22 September 1998, DSR 1998:VI, 2661
India – Patents (US)	Appellate Body Report, *India – Patent Protection for Pharmaceutical and Agricultural Chemical Products*, WT/DS50/AB/R, adopted 16 January 1998, DSR 1998:I, 9
India – Patents (US)	Panel Report, *India – Patent Protection for Pharmaceutical and Agricultural Chemical Products, Complaint by the United States*, WT/DS50/R, adopted 16 January 1998, as modified by Appellate Body Report, WT/DS50/AB/R, DSR 1998:I, 41
India – Quantitative Restrictions	Appellate Body Report, *India – Quantitative Restrictions on Imports of Agricultural, Textile and Industrial Products*, WT/DS90/AB/R, adopted 22 September 1999, DSR 1999:IV, 1763
India – Quantitative Restrictions	Panel Report, *India – Quantitative Restrictions on Imports of Agricultural, Textile and Industrial Products*, WT/DS90/R, adopted 22 September 1999, as upheld by Appellate Body Report, WT/DS90/AB/R, DSR 1999:V, 1799
Indonesia – Autos	Panel Report, *Indonesia – Certain Measures Affecting the Automobile Industry*, WT/DS54/R, WT/DS55/R, WT/DS59/R, WT/DS64/R and Corr.1, 2, 3, and 4, adopted 23 July 1998, DSR 1998:VI, 2201

Indonesia – Autos	Award of the Arbitrator, *Indonesia – Certain Measures Affecting the Automobile Industry – Arbitration under Article 21.3(c) of the DSU*, WT/DS54/15, WT/DS55/14, WT/DS59/13, WT/DS64/12, 7 December 1998, DSR 1998:IX, 4029
Japan – Agricultural Products II	Appellate Body Report, *Japan – Measures Affecting Agricultural Products*, WT/DS76/AB/R, adopted 19 March 1999, DSR 1999:I, 277
Japan – Agricultural Products II	Panel Report, *Japan – Measures Affecting Agricultural Products*, WT/DS76/R, adopted 19 March 1999, as modified by Appellate Body Report, WT/DS76/AB/R, DSR 1999:I, 315
Japan – Alcoholic Beverages II	Appellate Body Report, *Japan – Taxes on Alcoholic Beverages*, WT/DS8/AB/R, WT/DS10/AB/R, WT/DS11/AB/R, adopted 1 November 1996, DSR 1996:I, 97
Japan – Alcoholic Beverages II	Panel Report, *Japan – Taxes on Alcoholic Beverages*, WT/DS8/R, WT/DS10/R, WT/DS11/R, adopted 1 November 1996, as modified by Appellate Body Report, WT/DS8/AB/R, WT/DS10/AB/R, WT/DS11/AB/R, DSR 1996:I, 125
Japan – Alcoholic Beverages II	Award of the Arbitrator, *Japan – Taxes on Alcoholic Beverages – Arbitration under Article 21.3(c) of the DSU*, WT/DS8/15, WT/DS10/15, WT/DS11/13, 14 February 1997, DSR 1997:I, 3
Japan – Apples	Appellate Body Report, *Japan - Measures Affecting the Importation of Apples*, WT/DS245/AB/R, adopted 10 December 2003
Japan – Apples	Panel Report, *Japan – Measures Affecting the Importation of Apples*, WT/DS245/R, adopted 10 December 2003, as upheld by Appellate Body Report, WT/DS245/AB/R
Japan – Apples (Article 21.5 – US)	Panel Report, *Japan – Measures Affecting the Importation of Apples, Recourse to Article 21.5 of the DSU by the United States*, WT/DS245/RW, adopted 20 July 2005
Japan – Film	Panel Report, *Japan – Measures Affecting Consumer Photographic Film and Paper*, WT/DS44/R, adopted 22 April 1998, DSR 1998:IV, 1179

Korea – Alcoholic Beverages	Appellate Body Report, *Korea – Taxes on Alcoholic Beverages*, WT/DS75/AB/R, WT/DS84/AB/R, adopted 17 February 1999, DSR 1999:I, 3
Korea – Alcoholic Beverages	Panel Report, *Korea – Taxes on Alcoholic Beverages*, WT/DS75/R, WT/DS84/R, adopted 17 February 1999, as modified by Appellate Body Report, WT/DS75/AB/R, WT/DS84/AB/R, DSR 1999:I, 44
Korea – Alcoholic Beverages	Award of the Arbitrator, *Korea – Taxes on Alcoholic Beverages – Arbitration under Article 21.3(c) of the DSU*, WT/DS75/16, WT/DS84/14, 4 June 1999, DSR 1999:II, 937
Korea – Commercial Vessels	Panel Report, *Korea – Measures Affecting Trade in Commercial Vessels*, WT/DS273/R, adopted 11 April 2005
Korea – Dairy	Appellate Body Report, *Korea – Definitive Safeguard Measure on Imports of Certain Dairy Products*, WT/DS98/AB/R, adopted 12 January 2000, DSR 2000: I, 3
Korea – Dairy	Panel Report, *Korea – Definitive Safeguard Measure on Imports of Certain Dairy Products*, WT/DS98/R and Corr.1, adopted 12 January 2000, as modified by Appellate Body Report, WT/DS98/AB/R, DSR 2000:I, 49
Korea – Procurement	Panel Report, *Korea – Measures Affecting Government Procurement*, WT/DS163/R, adopted 19 June 2000, DSR 2000:VIII, 3541
Korea – Various Measures on Beef	Appellate Body Report, *Korea – Measures Affecting Imports of Fresh, Chilled and Frozen Beef*, WT/DS161/AB/R, WT/DS169/AB/R, adopted 10 January 2001, DSR 2001:I, 5
Korea – Various Measures on Beef	Panel Report, *Korea – Measures Affecting Imports of Fresh, Chilled and Frozen Beef*, WT/DS161/R, WT/DS169/R, adopted 10 January 2001, as modified by Appellate Body Report, WT/DS161/AB/R, WT/DS169/AB/R, DSR 2001:I, 59
Mexico – Anti-Dumping Measures on Rice	Panel Report, *Mexico – Definitive Anti-Dumping Measures on Beef and Rice, Complaint with Respect to Rice*, WT/DS295/R, 6 June 2005
Mexico – Corn Syrup	Panel Report, *Mexico – Anti-Dumping Investigation of High Fructose Corn Syrup (HFCS) from the United*

	States, WT/DS132/R and Corr.1, adopted 24 February 2000, DSR 2000:III, 1345
Mexico – Corn Syrup (Article 21.5 – US)	Appellate Body Report, *Mexico – Anti-Dumping Investigation of High Fructose Corn Syrup (HFCS) from the United States – Recourse to Article 21.5 of the DSU by the United States*, WT/DS132/AB/RW, adopted 21 November 2001, DSR 2001:XIII, 6675
Mexico – Corn Syrup (Article 21.5 – US)	Panel Report, *Mexico – Anti-Dumping Investigation of High Fructose Corn Syrup (HFCS) from the United States – Recourse to Article 21.5 of the DSU by the United States*, WT/DS132/RW, adopted 21 November 2001, as upheld by Appellate Body Report, WT/DS132/AB/RW, DSR 2001:XIII, 6717
Mexico – Telecoms	Panel Report, *Mexico – Measures Affecting Telecommunications Services*, WT/DS204/R, adopted 1 June 2004
Thailand – H-Beams	Appellate Body Report, *Thailand – Anti-Dumping Duties on Angles, Shapes and Sections of Iron or Non-Alloy Steel and H-Beams from Poland*, WT/DS122/AB/R, adopted 5 April 2001, DSR 2001:VII, 2701
Thailand – H-Beams	Panel Report, *Thailand – Anti-Dumping Duties on Angles, Shapes and Sections of Iron or Non-Alloy Steel and H-Beams from Poland*, WT/DS122/R, adopted 5 April 2001, as modified by Appellate Body Report, WT/DS122/AB/R, DSR 2001:VII, 2741
Turkey – Textiles	Appellate Body Report, *Turkey – Restrictions on Imports of Textile and Clothing Products*, WT/DS34/AB/R, adopted 19 November 1999, DSR 1999:VI, 2345
Turkey – Textiles	Panel Report, *Turkey – Restrictions on Imports of Textile and Clothing Products*, WT/DS34/R, adopted 19 November 1999, as modified by Appellate Body Report, WT/DS34/AB/R, DSR 1999:VI, 2363
US – 1916 Act	Appellate Body Report, *United States – Anti-Dumping Act of 1916*, WT/DS136/AB/R, WT/DS162/AB/R, adopted 26 September 2000, DSR 2000:X, 4793
US – 1916 Act (EC)	Panel Report, *United States – Anti-Dumping Act of 1916, Complaint by the European Communities*, WT/DS136/R and Corr.1, adopted 26 September

	2000, as upheld by Appellate Body Report, WT/DS136/AB/R, WT/DS162/AB/R, DSR 2000:X, 4593
US – 1916 Act (Japan)	Panel Report, *United States – Anti-Dumping Act of 1916, Complaint by Japan*, WT/DS162/R and Add.1, adopted 26 September 2000, as upheld by Appellate Body Report, WT/DS136/AB/R, WT/DS162/AB/R, DSR 2000:X, 4831
US – 1916 Act	Award of the Arbitrator, *United States – Anti-Dumping Act of 1916 – Arbitration under Article 21.3(c) of the DSU*, WT/DS136/11, WT/DS162/14, 28 February 2001, DSR 2001:V, 2017
US – 1916 Act (EC) (Article 22.6 – US)	Decision by the Arbitrators, *United States – Anti-Dumping Act of 1916, Original Complaint by the European Communities – Recourse to Arbitration by the United States under Article 22.6 of the DSU*, WT/DS136/ARB, 24 February 2004
US – Anti-Dumping Measures on Oil Country Tubular Goods	Panel Report, *United States – Anti-Dumping Measures on Oil Country Tubular Goods (OCTG) from Mexico*, WT/DS282/R, 20 June 2005
US – Carbon Steel	Appellate Body Report, *United States – Countervailing Duties on Certain Corrosion-Resistant Carbon Steel Flat Products from Germany*, WT/DS213/AB/R and Corr.1, adopted 19 December 2002, DSR 2002:IX, 3779
US – Carbon Steel	Panel Report, *United States – Countervailing Duties on Certain Corrosion-Resistant Carbon Steel Flat Products from Germany*, WT/DS213/R and Corr.1, adopted 19 December 2002, as modified by Appellate Body Report, WT/DS213/AB/R and Corr.1, DSR 2002:IX, 3833
US – Certain EC Products	Appellate Body Report, *United States – Import Measures on Certain Products from the European Communities*, WT/DS165/AB/R, adopted 10 January 2001, DSR 2001:I, 373
US – Certain EC Products	Panel Report, *United States – Import Measures on Certain Products from the European Communities*, WT/DS165/R and Add.1, adopted 10 January 2001, as modified by Appellate Body Report, WT/DS165/AB/R, DSR 2001:II, 413

US – Corrosion-Resistant Steel Sunset Review	Appellate Body Report, *United States – Sunset Review of Anti-Dumping Duties on Corrosion-Resistant Carbon Steel Flat Products from Japan*, WT/DS244/AB/R, adopted 9 January 2004
US – Corrosion-Resistant Steel Sunset Review	Panel Report, *United States – Sunset Review of Anti-Dumping Duties on Corrosion-Resistant Carbon Steel Flat Products from Japan*, WT/DS244/R, adopted 9 January 2004, as modified by Appellate Body Report, WTDS244/AB/R
US – Cotton Yarn	Appellate Body Report, *United States – Transitional Safeguard Measure on Combed Cotton Yarn from Pakistan*, WT/DS192/AB/R, adopted 5 November 2001, DSR 2001:XII, 6027
US – Cotton Yarn	Panel Report, *United States – Transitional Safeguard Measure on Combed Cotton Yarn from Pakistan*, WT/DS192/R, adopted 5 November 2001, as modified by Appellate Body Report, WT/DS192/AB/R, DSR 2001:XII, 6067
US – Countervailing Duty Investigation on DRAMS	Appellate Body Report, *United States – Countervailing Duty Investigation on Dynamic Random Access Memory Semiconductors (DRAMS) from Korea*, WT/DS296/AB/R, adopted 20 July 2005
US – Countervailing Duty Investigation on DRAMS	Panel Report, *United States – Countervailing Duty Investigation on Dynamic Random Access Memory Semiconductors (DRAMS) from Korea*, WT/DS296/R, adopted 20 July 2005, as modified by Appellate Body Report, WT/DS296/AB/R
US – Countervailing Measures on Certain EC Products	Appellate Body Report, *United States – Countervailing Measures Concerning Certain Products from the European Communities*, WT/DS212/AB/R, adopted 8 January 2003
US – Countervailing Measures on Certain EC Products	Panel Report, *United States – Countervailing Measures Concerning Certain Products from the European Communities*, WT/DS212/R, adopted 8 January 2003, as modified by Appellate Body Report, WT/DS212/AB/R
US – Countervailing Measures on Certain EC	Panel Report, *United States – Countervailing Measures Concerning Certain Products from the European Communities, Recourse to Article 21.5 of the DSU by*

Products (Article 21.5 – EC)	*the European Communities*, WT/DS212/RW, 17 August 2005
US – DRAMS	Panel Report, *United States – Anti-Dumping Duty on Dynamic Random Access Memory Semiconductors (DRAMS) of One Megabit or Above from Korea*, WT/DS99/R, adopted 19 March 1999, DSR 1999:II, 521
US – DRAMS (Article 21.5 – Korea)	Panel Report, *United States – Anti-Dumping Duty on Dynamic Random Access Memory Semiconductors (DRAMS) of One Megabit or Above from Korea – Recourse to Article 21.5 of the DSU by Korea*, WT/DS99/RW, 7 November 2000
US – Export Restraints	Panel Report, *United States – Measures Treating Exports Restraints as Subsidies*, WT/DS194/R and Corr.2, adopted 23 August 2001, DSR 2001:XI, 5767
US – FSC	Appellate Body Report, *United States – Tax Treatment for "Foreign Sales Corporations"*, WT/DS108/AB/R, adopted 20 March 2000, DSR 2000: III, 1619
US – FSC	Panel Report, *United States – Tax Treatment for "Foreign Sales Corporations"*, WT/DS108/R, adopted 20 March 2000, as modified by Appellate Body Report, WT/DS108/AB/R, DSR 2000:IV, 1675
US – FSC (Article 21.5 – EC)	Appellate Body Report, *United States – Tax Treatment for "Foreign Sales Corporations" – Recourse to Article 21.5 of the DSU by the European Communities*, WT/DS108/AB/RW, adopted 29 January 2002, DSR 2002:I, 55
US – FSC (Article 21.5 – EC)	Panel Report, *United States – Tax Treatment for "Foreign Sales Corporations" – Recourse to Article 21.5 of the DSU by the European Communities*, WT/DS108/RW, adopted 29 January 2002, as modified by Appellate Body Report, WT/DS108/AB/RW, DSR 2002:I, 119
US – FSC (Article 22.6 – US)	Decision by the Arbitrator, *United States – Tax Treatment for "Foreign Sales Corporations" – Recourse to Arbitration by the United States under Article 22.6 of the DSU and Article 4.11 of the SCM Agreement*, WT/DS108/ARB, 30 August 2002, DSR 2002:VI, 2517

US – Gambling Appellate Body Report, *United States – Measures Affecting the Cross-Border Supply of Gambling and Betting Services*, WT/DS285/AB/R, adopted 20 April 2005

US – Gambling Panel Report, *United States – Measures Affecting the Cross-Border Supply of Gambling and Betting Services*, WT/DS285/R, adopted 20 April 2005, as modified by Appellate Body Report, WT/DS285/AB/R

US – Gasoline Appellate Body Report, *United States – Standards for Reformulated and Conventional Gasoline*, WT/DS2/AB/R, adopted 20 May 1996, DSR 1996:I, 3

US – Gasoline Panel Report, *United States – Standards for Reformulated and Conventional Gasoline*, WT/DS2/R, adopted 20 May 1996, as modified by Appellate Body Report, WT/DS2/AB/R, DSR 1996:I, 29

US – Hot-Rolled Steel Appellate Body Report, *United States – Anti-Dumping Measures on Certain Hot-Rolled Steel Products from Japan*, WT/DS184/AB/R, adopted 23 August 2001, DSR 2001:X, 4697

US – Hot-Rolled Steel Panel Report, *United States – Anti-Dumping Measures on Certain Hot-Rolled Steel Products from Japan*, WT/DS184/R, adopted 23 August 2001 as modified by Appellate Body Report, WT/DS184/AB/R, DSR 2001:X, 4769

US – Hot-Rolled Steel Award of the Arbitrator, *United States – Anti-Dumping Measures on Certain Hot-Rolled Steel Products from Japan – Arbitration under Article 21.3(c) of the DSU*, WT/DS184/13, 19 February 2002, DSR 2002:IV, 1389

US – Lamb Appellate Body Report, *United States – Safeguard Measures on Imports of Fresh, Chilled or Frozen Lamb Meat from New Zealand and Australia*, WT/DS177/AB/R, WT/DS178/AB/R, adopted 16 May 2001, DSR 2001:IX, 4051

US – Lamb Panel Report, *United States – Safeguard Measures on Imports of Fresh, Chilled or Frozen Lamb Meat from New Zealand and Australia*, WT/DS177/R, WT/DS178/R, adopted 16 May 2001, as modified by

	Appellate Body Report, WT/DS177/AB/R, WT/DS178/AB/R, DSR 2001:IX, 4107
US – Lead and Bismuth II	Appellate Body Report, *United States – Imposition of Countervailing Duties on Certain Hot-Rolled Lead and Bismuth Carbon Steel Products Originating in the United Kingdom*, WT/DS138/AB/R, adopted 7 June 2000, DSR 2000:V, 2595
US – Lead and Bismuth II	Panel Report, *United States – Imposition of Countervailing Duties on Certain Hot-Rolled Lead and Bismuth Carbon Steel Products Originating in the United Kingdom*, WT/DS138/R and Corr.2, adopted 7 June 2000, as upheld by Appellate Body Report, WT/DS138/AB/R, DSR 2000:VI, 2623
US – Line Pipe	Appellate Body Report, *United States – Definitive Safeguard Measures on Imports of Circular Welded Carbon Quality Line Pipe from Korea*, WT/DS202/AB/R, adopted 8 March 2002, DSR 2002:IV, 1403
US – Line Pipe	Panel Report, *United States – Definitive Safeguard Measures on Imports of Circular Welded Carbon Quality Line Pipe from Korea*, WT/DS202/R, adopted 8 March 2002, as modified by Appellate Body Report, WT/DS202/AB/, DSR 2002:IV, 1473
US – Line Pipe	Report of the Arbitrator, *United States – Definitive Safeguard Measures on Imports of Circular Welded Carbon Quality Line Pipe from Korea – Arbitration under Article 21.3(c) of the DSU*, WT/DS202/17, 26 July 2002, DSR 2002:V, 2061
US – Offset Act (Byrd Amendment)	Appellate Body Report, *United States – Continued Dumping and Subsidy Offset Act of 2000*, WT/DS217/AB/R, WT/DS234/AB/R, adopted 27 January 2003
US – Offset Act (Byrd Amendment)	Panel Report, *United States – Continued Dumping and Subsidy Offset Act of 2000*, WT/DS217/R, WT/DS234/R, adopted 27 January 2003, as modified by Appellate Body Report, WT/DS217/AB/R, WT/DS234/AB/R
US – Offset Act (Byrd Amendment)	Award of the Arbitrator, *United States – Continued Dumping and Subsidy Offset Act of 2000 – Arbitration under Article 21.3(c) of the DSU*, WT/DS217/14, WT/DS234/22, 13 June 2003

US – Offset Act (Byrd Amendment) (Brazil) (Article 22.6 – US)	Decision by the Arbitrator, *United States – Continued Dumping and Subsidy Offset Act of 2000, Original Complaint by Brazil – Recourse to Arbitration by the United States under Article 22.6 of the DSU*, WT/DS217/ARB/BRA, 31 August 2004
US – Offset Act (Byrd Amendment) (Canada) (Article 22.6 – US)	Decision by the Arbitrator, *United States – Continued Dumping and Subsidy Offset Act of 2000, Original Complaint by Canada – Recourse to Arbitration by the United States under Article 22.6 of the DSU*, WT/DS234/ARB/CAN, 31 August 2004
US – Offset Act (Byrd Amendment) (Chile) (Article 22.6 – US)	Decision by the Arbitrator, *United States – Continued Dumping and Subsidy Offset Act of 2000, Original Complaint by Chile – Recourse to Arbitration by the United States under Article 22.6 of the DSU*, WT/DS217/ARB/CHL, 31 August 2004
US – Offset Act (Byrd Amendment) (EC) (Article 22.6 – US)	Decision by the Arbitrator, *United States – Continued Dumping and Subsidy Offset Act of 2000, Original Complaint by the European Communities – Recourse to Arbitration by the United States under Article 22.6 of the DSU*, WT/DS217/ARB/EEC, 31 August 2004
US – Offset Act (Byrd Amendment) (India) (Article 22.6 – US)	Decision by the Arbitrator, *United States – Continued Dumping and Subsidy Offset Act of 2000, Original Complaint by India – Recourse to Arbitration by the United States under Article 22.6 of the DSU*, WT/DS217/ARB/IND, 31 August 2004
US – Offset Act (Byrd Amendment) (Japan) (Article 22.6 – US)	Decision by the Arbitrator, *United States – Continued Dumping and Subsidy Offset Act of 2000, Original Complaint by Japan – Recourse to Arbitration by the United States under Article 22.6 of the DSU*, WT/DS217/ARB/JPN, 31 August 2004
US – Offset Act (Byrd Amendment) (Korea) (Article 22.6 – US)	Decision by the Arbitrator, *United States – Continued Dumping and Subsidy Offset Act of 2000, Original Complaint by Korea – Recourse to Arbitration by the United States under Article 22.6 of the DSU*, WT/DS217/ARB/KOR, 31 August 2004
US – Offset Act (Byrd Amendment) (Mexico) (Article 22.6 – US)	Decision by the Arbitrator, *United States – Continued Dumping and Subsidy Offset Act of 2000, Original Complaint by Mexico – Recourse to Arbitration by the United States under Article 22.6 of the DSU*, WT/DS234/ARB/MEX, 31 August 2004

US – Oil Country Tubular Goods Sunset Reviews	Appellate Body Report, *United States – Sunset Reviews of Anti-Dumping Measures on Oil Country Tubular Goods from Argentina*, WT/DS268/AB/R, adopted 17 December 2004
US – Oil Country Tubular Goods Sunset Reviews	Panel Report, *United States – Sunset Reviews of Anti-Dumping Measures on Oil Country Tubular Goods from Argentina*, WT/DS268/R and Corr.1, adopted 17 December 2004, as modified by Appellate Body Report, W/DS/268/AB/R
US – Oil Country Tubular Goods Sunset Reviews	Award of the Arbitrator, *United States – Sunset Reviews of Anti-Dumping Measures on Oil Country Tubular Goods from Argentina – Arbitration under Article 21.3(c) of the DSU*, WT/DS268/12, 7 June 2005
US – Section 110(5) Copyright Act	Panel Report, *United States – Section 110(5) of the US Copyright Act*, WT/DS160/R, adopted 27 July 2000, DSR 2000:VIII, 3769
US – Section 110(5) Copyright Act	Award of the Arbitrator, *United States – Section 110 (5) of the US Copyright Act – Arbitration under Article 21.3(c) of the DSU*, WT/DS160/12, 15 January 2001, DSR 2001:II, 657
US – Section 110(5) Copyright Act (Article 25.3)	Award of the Arbitrators, *United States – Section 110(5) of the US Copyright Act – Recourse to Arbitration under Article 25 of the DSU*, WT/DS160/ARB25/1, 9 November 2001, DSR 2001:II, 667
US – Section 129(c)(1) URAA	Panel Report, *United States – Section 129(c)(1) of the Uruguay Round Agreements Act*, WT/DS221/R, adopted 30 August 2002, DSR 2002:VII, 2581
US – Section 211 Appropriations Act	Appellate Body Report, *United States – Section 211 Omnibus Appropriations Act of 1998*, WT/DS176/AB/R, adopted 1 February 2002, DSR 2002:II, 589
US – Section 211 Appropriations Act	Panel Report, *United States – Section 211 Omnibus Appropriations Act of 1998*, WT/DS176/R, adopted 1 February 2002, as modified by Appellate Body Report, WT/DS176/AB/R, DSR 2002:II, 683
US – Section 301 Trade Act	Panel Report, *United States – Sections 301–310 of the Trade Act of 1974*, WT/DS152/R, adopted 27 January 2000, DSR 2000:II, 815
US – Shrimp	Appellate Body Report, *United States – Import Prohibition of Certain Shrimp and Shrimp Products*,

	WT/DS58/AB/R, adopted 6 November 1998, DSR 1998:VII, 2755
US – Shrimp	Panel Report, *United States – Import Prohibition of Certain Shrimp and Shrimp Products*, WT/DS58/R and Corr.1, adopted 6 November 1998, as modified by Appellate Body Report, WT/DS58/AB/R, DSR 1998:VII, 2821
US – Shrimp (Article 21.5 – Malaysia)	Appellate Body Report, *United States – Import Prohibition of Certain Shrimp and Shrimp Products – Recourse to Article 21.5 of the DSU by Malaysia*, WT/DS58/AB/RW, adopted 21 November 2001, DSR 2001:XIII, 6481
US – Shrimp (Article 21.5 – Malaysia)	Panel Report, *United States – Import Prohibition of Certain Shrimp and Shrimp Products – Recourse to Article 21.5 of the DSU by Malaysia*, WT/DS58/RW, adopted 21 November 2001, as upheld by Appellate Body Report, WT/DS58/AB/RW, DSR 2001:XIII, 6529
US – Softwood Lumber III	Panel Report, *United States – Preliminary Determinations with Respect to Certain Softwood Lumber from Canada*, WT/DS236/R, adopted 1 November 2002, DSR 2002:IX, 3597
US – Softwood Lumber IV	Appellate Body Report, *United States – Final Countervailing Duty Determination with Respect to Certain Softwood Lumber from Canada*, WT/DS257/AB/R, adopted 17 February 2004
US – Softwood Lumber IV	Panel Report, *United States – Final Countervailing Duty Determination with Respect to Certain Softwood Lumber from Canada*, WT/DS257/R and Corr.1, adopted 17 February 2004, as modified by Appellate Body Report, WT/DS257/AB/R
US – Softwood Lumber IV (Article 21.5 – Canada)	Panel Report, *United States – Final Countervailing Duty Determination with Respect to Certain Softwood Lumber from Canada, Recourse by Canada to Article 21.5 of the DSU*, WT/DS257/RW, 1 August 2005
US – Softwood Lumber V	Appellate Body Report, *United States – Final Dumping Determination on Softwood Lumber from Canada*, WT/DS264/AB/R, adopted 31 August 2004

US – Softwood Lumber V	Panel Report, *United States – Final Dumping Determination on Softwood Lumber from Canada*, WT/DS264/R, adopted 31 August 2004, as modified by Appellate Body Report, WT/DS264/AB/R
US – Softwood Lumber V	Report of the Arbitrator, *United States – Final Dumping Determination on Softwood Lumber from Canada – Arbitration under Article 21.3(c) of the DSU*, WT/DS264/13, 13 December 2004
US – Softwood Lumber VI	Panel Report, *United States – Investigation of the International Trade Commission in Softwood Lumber from Canada*, WT/DS277/R, adopted 26 April 2004
US – Stainless Steel	Panel Report, *United States – Anti-Dumping Measures on Stainless Steel Plate in Coils and Stainless Steel Sheet and Strip from Korea*, WT/DS179/R, adopted 1 February 2001, DSR 2001:IV, 1295
US – Steel Plate	Panel Report, *United States – Anti-Dumping and Countervailing Measures on Steel Plate from India*, WT/DS206/R and Corr.1, adopted 29 July 2002, DSR 2002:VI, 2073
US – Steel Safeguards	Appellate Body Report, *United States – Definitive Safeguard Measures on Imports of Certain Steel Products*, WT/DS248AB/R, WT/DS249AB/R, WT/DS251AB/R, WT/DS252AB/R, WT/DS253AB/R, WT/DS254AB/R, WT/DS258AB/R, WT/DS259AB/R, adopted 10 December 2003
US – Steel Safeguards	Panel Report, *United States – Definitive Safeguard Measures on Imports of Certain Steel Products*, WT/DS248, WT/DS249, WT/DS251, WT/DS252, WT/DS253, WT/DS254, WT/DS258, WT/DS259, adopted 10 December 2003, as modified by Appellate Body Report, WT/DS248AB/R, WT/DS249AB/R, WT/DS251AB/R, WT/DS252AB/R, WT/DS253AB/R, WT/DS254AB/R, WT/DS258AB/R, WT/DS259AB/R
US – Textiles Rules of Origin	Panel Report, *United States – Rules of Origin for Textiles and Apparel Products*, WT/DS243/R and Corr.1, adopted 23 July 2003

US – Underwear	Appellate Body Report, *United States – Restrictions on Imports of Cotton and Man-made Fibre Underwear*, WT/DS24/AB/R, adopted 25 February 1997, DSR 1997:I, 11
US – Underwear	Panel Report, *United States – Restrictions on Imports of Cotton and Man-made Fibre Underwear*, WT/DS24/R, adopted 25 February 1997, as modified by Appellate Body Report, WT/DS24/AB/R, DSR 1997:I, 31
US – Upland Cotton	Appellate Body Report, *United States – Subsidies on Upland Cotton*, WT/DS267/AB/R, adopted 21 March 2005
US – Upland Cotton	Panel Report, *United States – Subsidies on Upland Cotton*, WT/DS267/R, and Corr.1, adopted 21 March 2005, as modified by Appellate Body Report, WT/DS267/AB/R
US – Wheat Gluten	Appellate Body Report, *United States – Definitive Safeguard Measures on Imports of Wheat Gluten from the European Communities*, WT/DS166/AB/R, adopted 19 January 2001, DSR 2001:II, 717
US – Wheat Gluten	Panel Report, *United States – Definitive Safeguard Measures on Imports of Wheat Gluten from the European Communities*, WT/DS166/R, adopted 19 January 2001, as modified by Appellate Body Report, WT/DS166/AB/R, DSR 2001:III, 779
US – Wool Shirts and Blouses	Appellate Body Report, *United States – Measure Affecting Imports of Woven Wool Shirts and Blouses from India*, WT/DS33/AB/R and Corr.1, adopted 23 May 1997, DSR 1997:I, 323
US – Wool Shirts and Blouses	Panel Report, *United States – Measure Affecting Imports of Woven Wool Shirts and Blouses from India*, WT/DS33/R, adopted 23 May 1997, as upheld by Appellate Body Report, WT/DS33/AB/R, DSR 1997:I, 343

Foreword

In *Legal Principles in WTO Disputes*, Dr Mitchell addresses one of the most important and challenging questions raised by contemporary WTO jurisprudence and scholarship. That question is how the WTO, as an institution with its own body of rules, interacts with public international law. It is clear from reading this work that Dr Mitchell has an impressive understanding of both public international law and of the workings and nature of the WTO, and he combines these two areas of knowledge with flair in *Legal Principles in WTO Disputes*, making a number of insightful and original points.

The dispute settlement processes of the WTO have always been an important focus of the scholarly debate on how the WTO interacts with public international law. Often Panels and the Appellate Body are faced with questions of how to interpret ambiguous provisions of the covered agreements or how to proceed when those agreements are silent, and frequently public international law is suggested as an answer to these problems. The dispute settlement processes of the WTO are also central to the functioning of the institution. The importance placed on these processes by Members is perhaps most clearly and simply indicated by how frequently the dispute settlement system is used. At the end of 2006, over 350 complaints had been made to the Dispute Settlement Body, and over 100 Panel and Appellate Body Reports had been adopted.

Yet, until this book, there has been no detailed study of the role that legal principles play in dispute settlement in the WTO. A few commentators have evaluated the use of certain individual principles, but none has undertaken such a systematic study of the nature of principles and the bases upon which they can and should be used by WTO

Panels and the Appellate Body. *Legal Principles in WTO Disputes* is thus filling an important void in the literature.

Part II of this book provides a detailed study of four particular principles and their application in the WTO (good faith, due process, proportionality, and special and differential treatment), but a particular strength of *Legal Principles in WTO Disputes* is that Dr Mitchell does not limit his analysis to how principles have been applied in WTO disputes. Instead, he uses his knowledge of public international law with finesse in Part I of this book to provide a vital theoretical and conceptual framework. He examines the definition and meaning of 'principles', as distinguished from 'rules', at international law, and carefully analyses three alternative sources of principles: WTO law, customary international law, and general principles of law. This categorisation aids the identification of principles that could be used in WTO disputes. It also provides the basis for Dr Mitchell's compelling explanation of the role and limitations of different kinds of principles in WTO disputes, both in interpreting the covered agreements and as sources of substantive rights and obligations of Members.

With this detailed work on principles and their use within WTO disputes, Dr Mitchell has made a significant contribution to the ongoing debate about the interaction of the WTO and public international law, which is a valuable and accessible resource for general international lawyers and trade specialists alike.

Dr Gabrielle Marceau
Counsellor, Office of the WTO Director General
Professor, Faculty of Law, University of Geneva
Geneva

Acknowledgements

This book is based on my PhD thesis, which I began in August 2001, spending the first two years in Cambridge and the next two in Geneva. During this time I completed a fellowship at the Institute of International Economic Law at Georgetown University Law Center, as well as working for the Organisation for Economic Co-operation and Development in Paris, the World Trade Organization in Geneva, and the International Monetary Fund in Geneva and Washington, DC. I benefited greatly from this exposure to different aspects of trade law and policy.

I would like to thank my supervisor, Daniel Bethlehem, for his assistance in choosing this topic and for his guidance and encouragement. Susan Marks provided me with helpful feedback on my first-year paper. Mary Footer and Guglielmo Verdirame were wonderful examiners for my PhD. I am grateful to Gonville & Caius College, in particular for providing me with the financial support to undertake this research as a WM Tapp Scholar, and to my Director of Studies, Pippa Rogerson, for her good humour and assistance. Thanks also to Alison Hirst for her continuous aid. The librarians at the Squire Law Library at the University of Cambridge, the Legal Resource Centre at the University of Melbourne, the Georgetown Law Library at the Georgetown University Law Center, the World Trade Organization, the Graduate Institute of International Studies, Geneva, and the Peace Palace Library were very helpful to me. I would also like to thank the following people, who read earlier drafts of various chapters and provided useful comments and suggestions: Kerry Allbeury, Erica Badocco, Gavin Goh, Matthew Harding, David Heaton, Gabrielle Marceau, Katie Mitchell, Hunter Nottage, Ana Novik, Alexander Orakhelashvili, Fernando Piérola, Arun Venkataraman, Tania Voon,

Alan Yanovich, and Werner Zdouc. I thank Melbourne Law School for providing research support funds in the final stages of my work, which permitted me to hire Elizabeth Sheargold, who provided enormous assistance with Chapter 6 and, together with Stephanie Chu, ensured that the book manuscript was finally dispatched to Cambridge University Press. I corrected the proofs while Scholar-in-Residence at the International Arbitration Department of Wilmer Cutler Pickering Hale and Dorr LLP (London) and thank the partners for their support. Stephanie Chu did an incredible job helping me again at this stage. However, any errors or omissions are mine.

Parts of Chapter 2 and Chapter 3 were first published by Oxford University Press as 'The Legal Basis for Using Principles in WTO Disputes' (2007) 10(4) *Journal of International Economic Law* 795–835. Parts of Chapter 4 were first published as 'Good Faith in WTO Dispute Settlement' (2006) 7(2) *Melbourne Journal of International Law* 339–71. Parts of Chapter 5 were first published as 'Fair Crack of the Whip: Examining Procedural Fairness in WTO Disputes Using an Australian Administrative Law Framework' in WTO Trade Law Branch, DFAT (eds.), *Ten Years of WTO Dispute Settlement: Australian Perspectives* (Canberra: DFAT, 2006) 45–69 (ISBN 1 921244 08 9) and 'Due Process in WTO Disputes' in Rufus Yerxa and Bruce Wilson (eds.), *Key Issues in WTO Dispute Settlement: The First Ten Years* (Cambridge: WTO/Cambridge University Press, 2005) 144–60 (ISBN 0521861594). Parts of Chapter 6 were first published by Oxford University Press as 'Proportionality as a Principle of WTO Dispute Settlement' (2006) 17(5) *European Journal of International Law* 985–1008. Finally, parts of Chapter 7 were first published by Cambridge University Press as 'A Legal Principle of Special and Differential Treatment for WTO Disputes?' (2006) 5(3) *World Trade Review* 445–70.

Finally, I would like to thank my family for their constant love and support, and especially my wife, Tania, without whom I could never have done this.

1 Introduction

> [C]an we refer to a rule of general international law such as good faith? Can we have a legal system without the rule of good faith?...Can there be any system of law that can work without a reasonable concept of proportionality?
>
> Professor Georges Abi-Saab, Appellate Body member, World Trade Organization[1]

1.1 Beyond the ostensible

Having passed its thirteenth anniversary, the World Trade Organization (WTO) has become one of the most important international organisations in existence. As the only global intergovernmental organisation concerned with the rules of trade between nations, it is the leading forum for trade negotiations and for the resolution of trade disputes. Its dispute settlement system has attracted enormous interest because of its binding, rule-oriented nature and its well-established appeals system, both a rarity at the international level. More than 360 disputes have been brought to the WTO since its creation in January 1995,[2] and the recommendations of WTO Panels and the Appellate Body frequently generate intense controversy. These recommendations often require Members to change their measures[3] to bring them into

[1] Georges Abi-Saab, 'The WTO Dispute Settlement and General International Law' in Rufus Yerxa and Bruce Wilson (eds.), *Key Issues in WTO Dispute Settlement: The First Ten Years* (2005) 7, 11.

[2] WTO Secretariat, *Update of WTO Dispute Settlement Cases*, WT/DS/OV/31 (22 August 2007) ii.

[3] 'In principle, any act or omission attributable to a WTO Member can be a measure of that Member for purposes of dispute settlement proceedings': Appellate Body Report, *US – Corrosion-Resistant Steel Sunset Review*, [81]. See generally Alan Yanovich and Tania Voon, 'What Is the Measure at Issue?' in Andrew Mitchell (ed.), *Challenges and Prospects for the WTO* (2005) 115.

compliance with WTO obligations, which may have significant economic consequences for companies, consumers and workers, as well as major political implications for governments. Panel and Appellate Body reports are therefore carefully scrutinised, and WTO Members and academics alike are quick to pounce on perceived failures in the resolution of disputes under the Dispute Settlement Understanding (DSU).

The Appellate Body has traditionally adopted a conservative approach to interpreting and applying the WTO agreements, perhaps in view of the vigorous debates surrounding its decisions and in order to maintain legitimacy of the organisation in the minds of the various WTO players. Several years ago, Weiler referred to the 'almost obsessive attempts of the Appellate Body to characterize wherever possible... wide-ranging, sophisticated, multifaceted and eminently legitimate interpretations of the Agreement as "textual" resulting from the ordinary meaning of words'.[4]

However, no complex legal system can provide clear textual answers to every issue or dispute that falls within its scope as time goes by. Like any other such system, the WTO agreements contain some provisions that are ambiguous, contradictory, or silent on particular questions. This is becoming increasingly apparent. In early 2005, the first dissenting opinion of an Appellate Body member appeared in *US – Upland Cotton*, in relation to whether Article 10.2 of the Agreement on Agriculture exempts export credit guarantee programmes from export subsidy disciplines.[5] The dissenting member stated: 'I recognize that the language of this provision is not free from ambiguity. As noted by my colleagues on the Division, the drafters could have – dare I say, should have – made their intentions even more plain.'[6] With the expiry of the peace clause,[7] the number, scale and complexity of disputes about

[4] Joseph Weiler, 'The Rule of Lawyers and the Ethos of Diplomats – Reflections on the Internal and External Legitimacy of WTO Dispute Settlement' (2001) 35 *Journal of World Trade* 191, 206.

[5] Appellate Body Report, *US – Upland Cotton*, [631]–[641] ('separate opinion'). Previously, one Appellate Body member had issued a 'concurring statement' in Appellate Body Report, *EC – Asbestos*, [149]–[154]. Such opinions have been more common at the Panel level. See, e.g., Panel Report, *EC – Tariff Preferences*, [9.1]–[9.21]; Panel Report, *US – Softwood Lumber V*, [9.1]–[9.24]; Panel Report, *EC – Poultry*, [289]–[292].

[6] Appellate Body Report, *US – Upland Cotton*, [634].

[7] Agreement on Agriculture, art. 13; Appellate Body Report, *US – Upland Cotton*, [310], n. 311; Richard Steinberg and Timothy Josling, 'When the Peace Ends: The Vulnerability of EC and US Agricultural Subsidies to WTO Legal Challenge' (2003) 6 *Journal of International Economic Law* 369.

agricultural products of vital interest to developed and developing countries are set to grow. Other recent disputes also demonstrate the absence of textual answers to every issue, particularly in interpreting Members' schedules (which do not necessarily adopt uniform language or concepts),[8] or where the negotiating history is unclear.[9]

In addition to explicit legal rules, broader principles regularly embody fundamental rights and obligations and provide critical guidance in understanding individual legal provisions, particularly where the text is silent or ambiguous. An understanding of legal principles that underlie or influence the WTO system is therefore essential to enable Panels and the Appellate Body to discharge their function. Furthermore, the consistency and 'correctness' of Panel and Appellate Body decisions can be better evaluated against a backdrop of principles, which should themselves be subject to critical scrutiny. In 2000, Howse suggested that the Appellate Body had increased coherence and integrity in the interpretation of WTO provisions by using the treaty text 'as the necessary beginning point for an interpretative exercise that includes teleological dimensions', taking into account the 'diverse, and possible competing, values' of the WTO agreements rather than assuming that the prevailing value is 'free trade',[10] as some General Agreement on Tariffs and Trade (GATT) and WTO panels had a tendency to do.[11] As discussed further in Chapter 3, the provisions of the DSU provide a legal basis for a teleological approach to interpretation, creating one path through which 'principles' may enter WTO dispute settlement. Specifically, principles may assist in identifying and balancing the various interests affected by international trade.

Frequently, the most relevant and valid principles in WTO disputes will be derived partly or wholly from sources of law beyond the WTO agreements themselves. For example, the Appellate Body was recently asked to address 'the principle of good faith', 'the principle of estoppel', and the 'principle of judicial economy' in *EC – Export Subsidies on Sugar*.[12]

[8] See, e.g., Appellate Body Report, *EC – Chicken Cuts*, [142]–[147]; Appellate Body Report, *EC – Export Subsidies on Sugar*, [173]–[174], [186]; Appellate Body Report, *US – Gambling*, [176], [179], [182].

[9] See, e.g., Appellate Body Report, *EC – Export Subsidies on Sugar*, [223]; Appellate Body Report, *US – Upland Cotton*, [623], [636].

[10] Robert Howse, 'Adjudicative Legitimacy and Treaty Interpretation in International Trade Law: The Early Years of WTO Jurisprudence' in Joseph Weiler (ed.), *The EU, the WTO and the NAFTA: Toward a Common Law of International Law* (2000) 35, 54.

[11] Ibid. 52–3. [12] Appellate Body Report, *EC – Export Subsidies on Sugar*, [304], [307], [321].

For Members such as the United States, the inclusion of non-WTO law in WTO disputes may raise longstanding fears of overreaching by Panels and the Appellate Body. In the Special Session of the Dispute Settlement Body (DSB), which is dedicated to improving the DSU, the United States has recently identified several issues on which it suggests Members could 'provid[e] some form of additional guidance to WTO adjudicative bodies'.[13] These issues include: the role of WTO Tribunals in interpreting the WTO agreements, particularly where the agreements are silent on an issue; whether WTO Tribunals can use 'public international law other than customary rules of interpretation'; and the content of public international law that could be so used.[14] As explained further below, the use of principles from various sources of law and the continued integration of the WTO dispute settlement system into the general framework of public international law will in fact increase the legitimacy of the system and provide greater consistency and transparency to decision-making.

Remarkably little has been written on the use of principles in WTO dispute settlement. An exploratory article by Hilf in 2001 is perhaps the most significant. In this article, Hilf describes a number of principles that could be used in WTO disputes, dividing the principles into three broad categories: principles internal to the WTO; principles of public international law that are external to the WTO; and '[p]rinciples common to the internal legal regimes of WTO Members'.[15] This article provides a useful overview of a variety of principles and introduces some of the theoretical issues surrounding their use. However, it does not examine any of the principles in depth; nor does it offer a detailed analysis of the legal basis for WTO Tribunals to use principles in WTO disputes or the manner in which they could do so. In the same year, Cameron and Gray also wrote an article on principles in WTO disputes. This article is essentially a catalogue of previous dispute settlement decisions in which WTO Tribunals have used 'principles of international law'.[16] Certain other articles and other works have examined individual concepts that may be principles

[13] DSB Special Session, *Contribution by the United States*, TN/DS/W/74 (15 March 2005) 1.

[14] Ibid. 2–3.

[15] Meinhard Hilf, 'Power, Rules and Principles – Which Orientation for WTO/GATT Law?' (2001) 4 *Journal of International Economic Law* 111, 124.

[16] James Cameron and Kevin Gray, 'Principles of International Law in the WTO Dispute Settlement Body' (2001) 50 *International and Comparative Law Quarterly* 248.

relevant to WTO dispute settlement, including good faith,[17] due process,[18] proportionality,[19] special and differential treatment,[20] the

[17] Marion Panizzon, *Good Faith in the Jurisprudence of the WTO* (2006); Helge Zeitler, '"Good Faith" in the WTO Jurisprudence - Necessary Balancing Element or an Open Door to Judicial Activism' (2005) 8 *Journal of International Economic Law* 721; Durval De Noronha Goyos, 'Brazil: Duty of Good Faith in International Services Negotiations' (2005) 11 *International Trade Law & Regulation* N15; Yenkong Ngangjoh, '*Pacta Sunt Servanda* and Complaints in the WTO Dispute Settlement' (2004) 1 *Manchester Journal of International Economic Law* 76; Donald Regan, 'Do WTO Dispute Settlement Reports Affect the Obligations of Non-Parties?' (2003) 37 *Journal of World Trade* 883; Youngjin Jung and Sun Hyeong Lee, 'The Legacy of the Byrd Amendment Controversies: Rethinking the Principle of Good Faith' (2003) 37 *Journal of World Trade* 921; Aditi Bagchi, 'Compulsory Licensing and the Duty of Good Faith in TRIPS' (2003) 55 *Stanford Law Review* 1529; Thomas Cottier and Krista Schefer, 'Good Faith and the Protection of Legitimate Expectations in the WTO' in Marco Bronckers and Reinhard Quick (eds.), *New Directions in International Economic Law: Essays in Honour of John H Jackson* (2000) 47.

[18] Panagiotis Delimatsis, 'Due Process and "Good" Regulation Embedded in the GATS - Disciplining Regulatory Behaviour in Services through Article VI of the GATS' (2007) 10 *Journal of International Economic Law* 13; Ana Frischtak, 'Balancing Judicial Economy, State Opportunism, and Due Process Concerns in the WTO' (2005) 26 *Michigan Journal of International Law* 947; John Gaffney, 'Due Process in the World Trade Organization: The Need for Procedural Justice in the Dispute Settlement System' (1999) 14 *American University International Law Review* 1173; David Palmeter, 'The Need for Due Process in WTO Proceedings' (1997) 31 *Journal of World Trade* 51.

[19] Thomas Sebastian, 'World Trade Organization Remedies and the Assessment of Proportionality: Equivalence and Appropriateness' (2007) 48 *Harvard International Law Journal* 337; Mads Andenas and Stefan Zleptnig, 'Proportionality and Balancing in WTO Law: A Comparative Perspective' (2007) 20 *Cambridge Review of International Affairs* 71; Facundo Perez-Aznar, *Countermeasures in the WTO Dispute Settlement System: An Analysis of Their Characteristics and Procedure in the Light of General International Law* (2006); Federico Ortino, 'From "Non-Discrimination" to "Reasonableness": A Paradigm Shift in International Economic Law?' (Working Paper No 01/05, Jean Monnet Centre for International and Regional Economic Law & Justice, 2005); Federico Ortino, *Basic Legal Instruments for the Liberalisation of Trade: A Comparative Analysis of EC and WTO Law* (2004) ch 4; Jan Neumann and Elisabeth Türk, 'Necessity Revisited: Proportionality in World Trade Organization Law after *Korea - Beef*, *EC - Asbestos* and *EC - Sardines*' (2003) 37 *Journal of World Trade* 199; Meinhard Hilf and Sebastian Puth, 'The Principle of Proportionality on Its Way into WTO/GATT Law' in Armin von Bogdandy, Petros Mavroidis and Yves Mény (eds.), *European Integration and International Co-Ordination: Studies in Transnational Economic Law in Honour of Claus-Dieter Ehlermann* (2002) 199; D. A. Osiro, 'GATT/WTO Necessity Analysis: Evolutionary Interpretation and its Impact on the Authority of Domestic Regulation' (2002) 29 *Legal Issues of Economic Integration* 123; Axel Desmedt, 'Proportionality in WTO Law' (2001) 4 *Journal of International Economic Law* 441.

[20] Amin Alavi, 'On the (Non-)Effectiveness of the World Trade Organization Special and Differential Treatments in the Dispute Settlement Process' (2007) 41 *Journal of World Trade* 319; Alexander Keck and Patrick Low, 'Special and Differential Treatment in the WTO: Why, When and How?' in Simon Evenett and Bernard Hoekman (eds.), *Economic Development & Multilateral Trade Cooperation* (2006) 147; William Kerr, 'Special and

precautionary principle,[21] and non-discrimination.[22] Primarily, these focus on the principles within the WTO while paying little attention to their definition or their meaning under international law, and they are largely concerned with the operation of the principle in question rather than its implications for the use of principles in WTO dispute settlement more generally.

This book goes beyond the two previous studies of the use of principles in WTO disputes by defining and critically examining the categories of principles addressed. It also includes a thorough assessment of the legal basis for using different types of principles in WTO disputes, and the limitations on such use. Rather than merely describing the ways in which WTO Tribunals have used principles in their decisions to date, it evaluates these decisions in light of the principles used, the basis for using them, and the meaning of these principles outside the WTO. It also considers how principles could have been used in some decisions to confirm the result reached or to reach a better result. The four individual principles addressed in detail are assessed in terms of their meaning, validity, and scope. This analysis is conducted not only to understand these particular principles but also to provide a solid foundation for envisaging how WTO Tribunals could use principles more frequently, accurately, and legitimately in future.

I now turn to examine in more detail the nature of legal principles as distinct from rules.

Differential Treatment: A Mechanism to Promote Development?' (2005) 6 *Estey Centre Journal of International Law and Trade Policy* 84; Bernard Hoekman, 'Operationalizing the Concept of Policy Space in the WTO: Beyond Special and Differential Treatment' (2005) 8 *Journal of International Economic Law* 405.

[21] Ilona Cheyne, 'Gateways to the Precautionary Principle in WTO Law' (2007) 19 *Journal of Environmental Law* 155; Ilona Cheyne, 'Risk and Precaution in World Trade Organization Law' (2006) 40 *Journal of World Trade* 837; Gabrielle Marceau, 'La jurisprudence sur le principe de précaution dans le droit de l'OMC' (Paper presented at the Inaugural Professorial Lecture, Faculty of Law, University of Geneva, 19 May 2005); Christiane Gerstetter and Matthais Leonhard Maier, 'Legalise It, or Criticise It? Debating the Precautionary Principle in and around the WTO' (Working Paper, Universität Bremen, 2004); Jan Bohanes, 'Risk Regulation in WTO Law: A Procedure-Based Approach to the Precautionary Principle' (2002) 40 *Columbia Journal of Transnational Law* 323.

[22] T. Srinivasan, 'Nondiscrimination in GATT/WTO: Was There Anything to Begin with and Is There Anything Left?' (2005) 4 *World Trade Review* 69; WTO Secretariat, 'The Fundamental WTO Principles of National Treatment, Most-Favoured-Nation Treatment and Transparency', WT/WGTCP/W/114 (14 April 1999).

1.2 The nature of principles

1.2.1 Distinguishing principles from rules

The existence of principles of law as distinct from rules is widely recognised, both in jurisprudential thought and in the standard legal methodologies of academics, judges, and lawyers.[23] Both principles and rules are species of norms (standards for how one ought to act).[24] Typically, principles are seen as general, basic or underlying assumptions or precepts.[25] They embody fundamental regulatory purposes or values and provide a broad guide for the development of legal rules, which are directed towards specific behaviour and can be used to resolve particular problems.[26] Thus, principles are the 'intellectual foundations of any legal order',[27] while rules are the precise laws that implement them and are explicit in the legal corpus.[28] Put differently, a 'rule answers the question "what": a principle in effect answers the question "why".'[29] This distinction seems more useful than one focusing simply on the breadth of the law in question. As Hart points out, the suggestion that principles are expressed in general or abstract terms is unhelpful, because all laws have a core of settled meaning and an uncertain penumbra.[30] The content of principles may not be as

[23] Larry Alexander and Ken Kress, 'Against Legal Principles' (1997) 82 *Iowa Law Review* 739, 745–54.

[24] Joseph Raz, *Practical Reason and Norms* (rev. edn, 1999) ch 1; Brian H. Bix, *A Dictionary of Legal Theory* (2004) 149.

[25] '5. a. A fundamental truth or proposition, on which many others depend; a primary truth comprehending, or forming the basis of, various subordinate truths; a general statement or tenet forming the (or a) ground of, or held to be essential to, a system of thought or belief; a fundamental assumption forming the basis of a chain of reasoning': John Simpson and Edmund Weiner (eds.), *The Oxford English Dictionary* (2nd edn, 1989) vol. XII, 499.

[26] Neil MacCormick, *Legal Reasoning and Legal Theory* (1994).

[27] Sujit Choudhry, 'Globalization in Search of Justification: Toward a Theory of Comparative Constitutional Interpretation' (1999) 74 *Indiana Law Journal* 819, 843. See also Antonio Cassese, *International Law* (2nd edn, 2005) 46: 'Principles are the pinnacle of the legal system and are intended to serve as basic guidelines for the life of the whole community.'

[28] See also Fallon who uses the terms 'first principles' and 'doctrine': Richard Fallon, 'Foreword: Implementing the Constitution' (1997) 111 *Harvard Law Review* 54, 60–1.

[29] Gerald Fitzmaurice, 'The General Principles of International Law Considered from the Standpoint of the Rule of Law' (1957-II) *Recueil des Cours* 1, 7.

[30] H. L. A. Hart, *The Concept of Law* (1961) 120. The view that all law has a settled core and an uncertain penumbra has been taken further in Timothy A. O. Endicott, *Vagueness in Law* (2000). Endicott argues that all rules are radically indeterminate owing to the vagueness of legal language and concepts.

'narrow' as rules, but this does not mean that they are without a definable content.[31]

Dworkin suggests that rules generally operate in a binary manner.[32] When the conditions for the application of a given rule have been satisfied, the rule operates to provide a determinative result to the legal problem; when the conditions for the application of the rule have not been satisfied, the rule has no operation.[33] Principles do not have this kind of binary operation.[34] A principle cannot lead to a determinative result or solution, because it must be applied together with other principles and taking account of the particular situation in dispute. In some circumstances, this may involve balancing and weighing different principles.[35] In other circumstances, principles may represent values that are incommensurable and unable to be weighed against each other, for example liberty and equality.[36] Thus, Eckhoff and Sundby state that rules either apply or do not apply, whereas principles are guidelines that are more or less relevant and persuasive in determining the preferable solution.[37]

However defined, it is clear that the categories of principles and rules overlap to some extent, and it is often difficult to determine where a principle ends and a rule begins. In many circumstances the line drawn between principles and rules may be somewhat subjective and dependent on the language used to describe the relevant laws. For example, one might contend that a principle of equality exists in

[31] Robert Kolb, 'Principles as Sources of International Law' (2006) 53 *Netherlands International Law Review* 1, 7.

[32] Ronald Dworkin, *Taking Rights Seriously* (1977) 24–8.

[33] 'A "rule" . . . "is essentially practical and, moreover, binding . . .; there are rules of art as there are rules of government" while principle "expresses a general truth, which guides our action, serves as a theoretical basis for the various acts of our life, and the application of which to reality produces a given consequence."': The Umpire in the *Gentini Case* of the Italian-Venezuelan Mixed Claims Commission (H Ralston and W Doyle, *Venezuelan Arbitrations of 1903, etc* (1904) 720, 725) quoted in Bin Cheng, *General Principles of Law as Applied by International Courts and Tribunals* (1987) 376.

[34] Ronald Dworkin takes a different view in *Law's Empire* (1986), but this is not widely shared.

[35] Dworkin, *Taking Rights Seriously*, 24–8.

[36] On the incommensurability of values, see generally: Isaiah Berlin, *Four Essays on Liberty* (1969) ch 3; Joseph Raz, *The Morality of Freedom* (1986) ch 13; Ruth Chang (ed.), *Incommensurability, Incomparability and Practical Reason* (1997); William Lucy, 'Adjudication' in Jules Coleman and Scott Shapiro (eds.), *The Oxford Handbook of Jurisprudence & Philosophy of Law* (2002) 206, 234–47.

[37] See Martti Koskenniemi, *General Principles: Reflexions on Constructivist Thinking in International Law* (1985) 135.

European Union law. This principle is reflected in certain rules of the Treaty of Rome such as Article 12, which prohibits discrimination on the basis of nationality, and Article 141, which requires equal pay for equal work by men and women. Based on this description, the difference between the underlying principle and the implementing rules seems fairly clear. However, is the notion in Anglo-American contract law that a binding contract requires consideration – that is, something of value flowing from the promisee to the promisor – better characterised as a principle or a rule? On one hand, it seems like a principle, in that it provides the context for more specific rules, such as the rule that past consideration (consideration that passed before the relevant promise was made) is inadequate. On the other hand, as it can be expressed not as a purpose but as a specific legal requirement, perhaps it could also be called a rule.

The distinction between principles and rules may be even harder to apply in international law. O'Connor states that a 'principle is a common denominator for a number of related rules and a principle functions through the application of rules singly or in combination to relevant situations'.[38] In national law, a given principle is often reflected in numerous detailed rules.[39] But the customary international law principle of non-intervention, for example, is not reflected in any more detailed rules. As will be discussed, the International Court of Justice (ICJ) has often looked for principles only when it cannot find rules to resolve a particular case.[40] However, the fact that the ICJ has used principles at all suggests that they may be useful in understanding or interpreting international law (including WTO law).[41] For instance, the ICJ may be seen as balancing several principles to find an equitable solution to a continental shelf delimitation problem.[42]

For the purpose of this book, I need not offer any new way of distinguishing between principles and rules in the abstract. Instead, in Chapter 2 I identify three broad types of principles that may be particularly useful in WTO disputes. These three types, at least, are capable of fairly precise definition and justification. In the following section,

38 J. O'Connor, *Good Faith in International Law* (1991) 122.

39 Koskenniemi, *General Principles*, 132.

40 See, e.g., Fisheries *(United Kingdom v. Norway)* [1951] ICJ Rep 116.

41 Principles 'do not normally entail rights and obligations; rather, they are to be considered in the interpretation of rules': Albrecht Randelzhofer, 'Article 2' in Bruno Simma (ed.), *The Charter of the United Nations: A Commentary* (2nd edn, 2002) vol. I, 63.

42 Koskenniemi, *General Principles*, 135.

I put the distinction between different types of principles to one side and explain certain generic ways in which principles may be used in understanding legal systems such as the WTO.

1.2.2 Normative and descriptive aspects of principles

Two different theories about principles can help explain their relevance and potential use in dispute settlement. The first is a normative theory, under which principles are norms or standards used to judge or direct human conduct.[43] Principles are higher norms that influence the rest of the legal system, including other norms such as rules. Principles are distinguished 'from "ordinary" norms through some criteria, for example their general character, their binding nature or their position in a norm hierarchy'.[44] According to this theory, principles can justify rules, but rules cannot justify principles.[45] Seen in this light, principles 'guide State behaviour and ... explain judicial decision-making'.[46] Under a normative theory, principles are determined through a process of deduction from a set of premises. The set of premises may be based on, for example, the nature of legal systems or natural law.

The second theory of principles is a descriptive theory, under which principles are simply inductive generalisations of rules (that is, inferences from particular to general). In other words, principles are descriptions of groups of rules. While principles in this sense may have useful systematic or didactic purposes and may help promote coherence, they do not possess any independent legal content.[47] Thus, Schwarzenberger maintains that principles are only 'abstractions and generalizations from legal rules or individual cases'.[48] For him, at least in the context of international law, 'rules ... are the only legally binding norms'.[49]

These two theories are not necessarily mutually exclusive. In the chapters that follow, I identify certain principles using both theories. For example, in Chapter 7, I address the principle of special and differential treatment in WTO law, which is reflected both in the express

[43] Ted Honderich (ed.), *The Oxford Companion to Philosophy* (1995) 626.
[44] Koskenniemi, *General Principles*, 128.
[45] Stephen Perry, 'Two Models of Legal Principles' (1997) 82 *Iowa Law Review* 787, 787–8.
[46] Koskenniemi, *General Principles*, 128. See also David Walker, *The Oxford Companion to Law* (1980) 989–90.
[47] Koskenniemi, *General Principles*, 126.
[48] Georg Schwarzenberger, *The Inductive Approach to International Law* (1965) 50.
[49] Georg Schwarzenberger and E. D. Brown, *A Manual of International Law* (6th edn, 1976) 17.

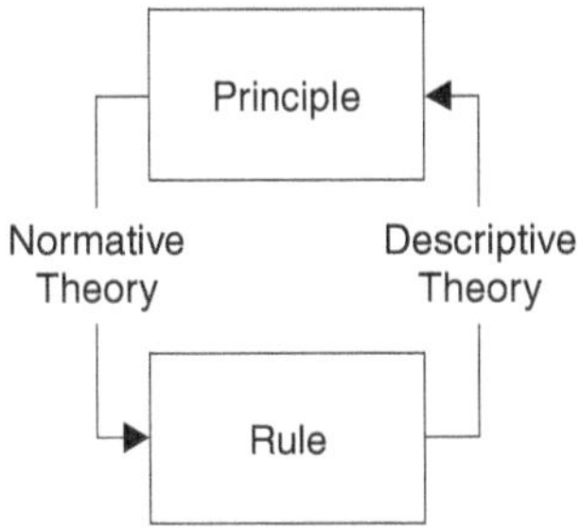

Figure 1 Two views of the relationship between principles and rules

purposes of the WTO (in a normative sense) and in specific WTO rules (in a descriptive sense). Furthermore, whether principles are identified from a normative or descriptive perspective, they can be used to explain the coherence or structure of a given legal system and the way the rules interact. This is because legal systems are almost invariably composed of competing principles and exceptions to principles, such that specific legal rules may represent a compromise between opposing principles.[50] Kolb suggests that principles can be seen as 'elements of law-creation and of law-creativity, inspiring as much the legislator as the law-applier'.[51] MacCormick suggests that principles could be used to help determine the answer in 'hard cases' (that is, where there is not a relevant, clear, and unambiguous proposition of law applicable to the case). In particular, arguments that resonate more clearly with the principles of the legal system are often preferred over others, on the assumption 'that the multitudinous rules of a developed legal system should "make sense" when taken together'.[52] Under both theories, principles may be used to illuminate the underlying logic in particular rules and decisions that might otherwise seem illogical.

Nevertheless, the two theories of principles may be more or less useful depending on the particular legal system under examination. For example, in the European civil law tradition, domestic constitutions are often seen as embodying identifiable normative principles. From that perspective, the normative theory may be more appropriate in understanding principles in the WTO if the WTO agreements are characterised as constitutional (as discussed further in Chapter 3). Similarly,

[50] Hilf, 'Power, Rules and Principles', 111–12.
[51] Kolb, 'Principles as Sources of International Law', 7.
[52] Neil MacCormick, *Legal Reasoning and Legal Theory* (1978, rev. edn 1994) 152.

principles themselves may be of more or less use depending on which theory is adopted. Under a strictly descriptive theory of principles, principles are of limited use in assessing the legitimacy of a given legal system (such as the WTO). In contrast, under the normative theory, if the system's principles are justified morally, economically or socially, this lends legitimacy to the system as a whole. In addition, if principles are normative rather than purely descriptive, they may assist in interpreting specific legal rules in situations where the meaning of the rule is unclear from the text, or where the rule does not point definitively to any particular outcome. In other words, as mentioned earlier, principles can support a teleological reading of a given legal provision.[53]

In this book, I use principles in both a normative and descriptive manner. As norms, principles may assist in guiding or evaluating decisions by Panels and the Appellate Body. As descriptions of groups of WTO rules, principles may also assist in interpreting specific provisions. The next section explains the importance of principles in interpretation given the frequent gaps and ambiguities found in all legal texts.

1.2.3 Inherent uncertainty of legal texts

In legal jurisprudence generally, some definitions of the interpretation process draw a distinction between interpretation and construction.[54] For example, some definitions propose that interpretation is only required in 'difficult cases', and not where the text is 'clear'.[55] Some commentators define interpretation as the process of giving meaning to the text, and construction as the process of creating one where there is no discoverable meaning.[56] This book adopts a broader definition of interpretation in accordance with standard usage: interpretation is the process of determining the meaning of the text.[57] This definition draws no distinction between interpretation and construction, given that the object of both is to determine meaning. It also treats as an

[53] Panel Report, *US – Section 301 Trade Act*, [7.92].

[54] Bryan A. Garner, *A Dictionary of Modern Legal Usage* (2nd edn, 1995) 462.

[55] Brian H. Bix, *Dictionary of Legal Theory*, 103.

[56] Francis Lieber, *Legal and Political Hermeneutics, or Principles of Interpretation and Construction in Law and Politics, with Remarks on Precedents and Authorities* (1839); Joel Trachtman, 'The Domain of WTO Dispute Resolution' (1999) 40 *Harvard International Law Journal* 333, 339; Keith E Whittington, *Constitutional Interpretation: Textual Meaning, Original Intent, and Judicial Review* (1999) 5–10.

[57] Walker, *Oxford Companion*, 644.

interpretative exercise every attempt to give meaning to text, no matter how 'clear' that text might be.[58]

An underlying problem of interpreting legal texts is that they are inherently incomplete and imprecise. Therefore, several of the problems of interpretation in the WTO context also arise in interpreting non-WTO treaties, domestic constitutions, statutes, and private contracts. The experience of courts and tribunals in these areas, and theories of interpretation based on this experience, may provide useful guidance for WTO disputes. At the same time, one must keep in mind that legal texts operating at different levels (for example, public/private, and domestic/international) serve different purposes and therefore may entail different considerations in connection with interpretation.

The 'incomplete contracts' and 'rules and standards' literature in the field of law and economics explains some of the reasons for the uncertainty of legal texts. Very briefly, the incomplete contracts literature considers that contracts (like all legal texts) are necessarily incomplete in their capacity to specify rules that will apply to every type of conduct.[59] The reasons for this include the limits of human foresight, the ambiguities of language, and the high costs of preparing detailed rules. However, this incompleteness may be desirable, for example, when the subject of the agreement is complex and a court can fill in the agreement at a lower cost than the parties.[60] In filling in the gaps in an agreement, the court may use certain 'default rules', except to the extent that the parties have expressly stated that these rules do not apply. As discussed further below, principles may play a gap-filling role in the WTO, subject to certain limits imposed by the WTO agreements.

The 'rules and standards' literature describes laws as lying somewhere between the extremes of rules (whose content is determined *ex ante*) and standards (whose content is determined *ex post*).[61] Thus, the content of a rule (such as a law specifying several chemicals that cannot be traded) is clearly ascertainable when the rule is made. In contrast,

[58] Harvard Research in International Law, 'Draft Convention on the Law of Treaties' (1935) 29 *American Journal of International Law (Supp)* 697, 938.

[59] Trachtman, 'WTO Dispute Resolution', 334.

[60] George Cohen, 'Implied Terms and Interpretation in Contract Law' in Boudewijn Bouckaert and Gerrit De Geest (eds.), *Encyclopedia of Law and Economics* (2000) vol. III, 78.

[61] Louis Kaplow, 'General Characteristics of Rules' in Boudewijn Bouckaert and Gerrit De Geest (eds.), *Encycopedia of Law and Economics* (2000) vol. V, 502.

the content of a standard (such as a law stating that 'hazardous' chemicals cannot be traded) is established only through adjudication. In an international legal system that includes a binding dispute settlement mechanism, such as the WTO, standards involve a transfer of power from states to the dispute resolution body, whereas rules reserve states' power.[62] States may consciously and willingly decide to use standards in order to relieve themselves of the difficulty of resolving hard problems and issues, to mask disagreement, or to reduce the transparency of international agreements.[63] Alternatively, in the absence of extensive experience in a particular area, states might settle on a standard as an interim measure and establish rules after the dispute settlement body has developed detailed jurisprudence.[64]

The WTO agreements include provisions that could be described as rules (such as Article 16.1 of the DSU, which states that reports of Panels 'shall not be considered for adoption by the DSB until 20 days after the date they have been circulated to the Members') and others that could be described as standards (such as Article XX(a) of GATT 1994, which provides an exception for measures 'necessary to protect public morals'). Interpretation may be more difficult and controversial in relation to standards, and therefore the use of principles may become more important. However, the line between rules and standards is blurred, and ambiguities may arise in relation to both.

Sir Hersch Lauterpacht contends that a given legal text can have only one legally correct meaning.[65] At the other extreme, some critical legal scholars argue that all text is inherently indeterminate,[66] such that an interpreter's declared reasons for a particular interpretation simply disguise a particular subjective response. In my view, the answer lies somewhere in between these positions. As a result of the imprecision in legal texts, different actors interpreting the same legal text may make reasonable competing arguments about its meaning.[67] This explains the possibility envisaged in Article 17.6(ii) of the Anti-Dumping

[62] Trachtman, 'WTO Dispute Resolution', 335. [63] Ibid. 352.

[64] Louis Kaplow, 'Rules versus Standards: An Economic Analysis' (1992) 42 *Duke Law Journal* 557.

[65] Hersch Lauterpacht, 'Restrictive Interpretation and the Principle of Effectiveness in the Interpretation of Treaties' (1949) 26 *British Yearbook of International Law* 48, 81–2.

[66] David Kennedy, 'Theses about International Legal Discourse' (1980) 23 *German Yearbook of International Law* 353.

[67] Kent Greenawalt, 'Constitutional and Statutory Interpretation' in Jules Coleman and Scott Shapiro (eds.), *The Jurisprudence and Philosophy of Law* (2002) 268, 277; Hans Kelsen, *Pure Theory of Law* (Max Knight trans., 2nd rev. edn, 1967) 351.

Agreement that the application of the 'customary rules of interpretation of public international law' to a WTO provision could lead to 'more than one permissible interpretation' (even though Panels have rarely used this provision to admit a 'permissible' interpretation).[68] It also explains why judges in domestic and international courts often issue concurring or dissenting opinions. In these circumstances, principles may provide a useful and legitimate basis for choosing between available meanings.

1.3 Need for principles in WTO disputes

1.3.1 Interpretation and evaluation

The drafters of the WTO agreements did not foresee and could not have foreseen every possible dispute or circumstance that might arise in the future concerning the text. Furthermore, in some instances, the drafters may have deliberately left matters open or ambiguous due to an absence of agreement. Once this is accepted, it is clear that WTO Tribunals cannot always simply declare the law as set out in specific WTO rules. Rather, they will need to decipher the intentions of the drafters as reflected in the text through a careful process of interpretation, in which not only rules but also principles may play a role. The principles that are most likely to be relevant in WTO disputes are those that are reflected in the WTO agreements themselves and recognised as such by WTO Tribunals. These kinds of principles can operate in a normative or descriptive manner to assist in interpreting WTO provisions and in evaluating decisions by WTO Tribunals.

Article 3.2 of the DSU provides for WTO Tribunals to interpret the WTO agreements in accordance with customary rules of interpretation of public international law, which means principally the rules contained in Articles 31 and 32 of the Vienna Convention on the Law of Treaties (VCLT). The Appellate Body's report in *EC – Chicken Cuts* highlights the intricacy of these rules of interpretation when it comes to applying them to a given provision.[69] As explained further below,[70] Article 31(1) of the VCLT has led to a heavy reliance by WTO Tribunals on the text, context, and object and purpose in interpreting WTO provisions. Through these three crucial paths, principles drawn from the WTO agreements as a whole may play a vital role in interpretation,

[68] But see Panel Report, *Argentina – Poultry Anti-Dumping Duties*, [7.341], n. 223.

[69] Appellate Body Report, *EC – Chicken Cuts*, [170]–[346].

[70] See below in section 3.2.3.

so as to 'clarify' the existing provisions and thereby provide 'security and predictability to the multilateral trading system'.[71] Such principles may also be reflected in the preparatory work of the WTO and therefore provide a subsidiary means of interpretation under Article 32 of the VCLT.

In addition to their role in interpreting the WTO agreements, principles of WTO law provide a means of assessing WTO dispute settlement decisions. Where WTO Tribunals refer expressly to principles in resolving disputes, the content and relevance of these principles can be investigated to determine if their use was justified and accurate. Where WTO Tribunals make decisions on matters relating to certain principles without making any reference to them, the decisions can still be examined against the background of these principles to see if the reasoning and results reflect a coherent view of the WTO agreements that will prove correct when different circumstances arise in the future.

The following section looks beyond the principles contained in the framework of the WTO agreements themselves to consider the extent to which principles drawn from broader international law may be relevant to WTO disputes. This involves an analysis of whether the WTO is an institution within the scope of public international law and the extent to which public international law applies in the WTO.

1.3.2 The WTO within the framework of public international law

As mentioned earlier, the second sentence of Article 3.2 of the DSU states that the dispute settlement system of the WTO 'serves to preserve the rights and obligations of Members under the covered agreements, and to clarify the existing provisions of those agreements in accordance with customary rules of interpretation of public international law'. In its very first appeal, *US – Gasoline* in 1996, the Appellate Body stated that this 'direction reflects a measure of recognition that the *General Agreement* is not to be read in clinical isolation from public international law'.[72] This statement met with general approval, and few Members would dispute the relevance of public international law in interpreting the WTO provisions, based on the reference in Article 3.2 to customary rules of interpretation.[73]

[71] DSU, art. 3.2. [72] Appellate Body Report, *US – Gasoline*, 17.

[73] See, e.g., DSB, *Minutes of Meeting Held on 20 May 1996*, WT/DSB/M/17 (6 June 1996) 2 (United States); Gabrielle Marceau, 'A Call for Coherence in International Law – Praise for the Prohibition against "Clinical Isolation" in WTO Dispute Settlement' (1999) 33 *Journal of World Trade* 87.

In 2000, the Panel in *Korea – Procurement* concluded that 'the relationship of the WTO Agreements to customary international law is broader than this'.[74] The Panel also indicated that it saw 'no basis' in Article 3.2 of the DSU 'for an *a contrario* implication that rules of international law other than rules of interpretation do not apply',[75] as discussed further below.[76] This decision was adopted by the DSB without appeal,[77] which means that it carries legal weight in relation to the dispute at issue,[78] but it cannot be regarded as having the endorsement of the Appellate Body.[79] Moreover, several Members expressed disagreement with the Panel's use of international law in that case.[80]

This highlights a key area of contention among governments and academics alike, namely the extent to which the WTO falls within the established architecture of public international law. Speaking generally, McLachlan states that 'treaties are themselves creatures of international law. However wide their subject matter, they are all nevertheless limited in scope and are predicated for their existence and operation on being part of the international law system'.[81] Article 2(1) of the VCLT defines a treaty as 'an international agreement concluded between states in written form and governed by international law, whether embodied in a single instrument or in two or more related instruments and whatever its particular designation'. In the specific context of the WTO, Marceau thus contends that '[t]he conclusion of the WTO Agreement as a formal treaty and the creation of the World Trade Organization as an international organization are developments that had the effect of subjecting the WTO fully to international law'.[82] Similarly, Pauwelyn maintains that the WTO agreements 'derive from a treaty'; therefore, '[t]hat WTO rules are

[74] Panel Report, *Korea – Procurement*, [7.96]. [75] Ibid. n. 753.

[76] See below section 3.3.3.

[77] DSB, *Minutes of Meeting Held on 19 June 2000*, WT/DSB/M/84 (24 July 2000) [71]–[72].

[78] Appellate Body Report, *Japan – Alcoholic Beverages II*, 14.

[79] Appellate Body Report, *Canada – Periodicals*, n. 28.

[80] DSB, *Minutes of Meeting Held on 19 June 2000*, WT/DSB/M/84 (24 July 2000) [58]–[59] (Korea), [64] (Philippines), [69] (India).

[81] Campbell McLachlan, 'The Principle of Systemic Integration and Article 31(3)(c) of the Vienna Convention' (2005) 54 *International and Comparative Law Quarterly* 279, 280.

[82] Gabrielle Marceau, 'Conflicts of Norms and Conflicts of Jurisdictions: The Relationship between the WTO Agreement and MEAs and Other Treaties' (2001) 35 *Journal of World Trade* 1081, 1081. See also Abi-Saab, 'WTO Dispute Settlement', 10.

legally binding rules part of international law must . . . stand beyond doubt'.[83]

On this issue, it is worth noting that Article 3.2 of the DSU and the corresponding Article 17.6(ii) of the Anti-Dumping Agreement are not the only provisions in the WTO agreements that refer to public international law.[84] For instance, the Trade Related Aspects of Intellectual Property Rights (TRIPS) Agreement incorporates several obligations from existing intellectual property conventions, with Article 9.1 requiring Members to comply with certain provisions of the Berne Convention for the Protection of Literary and Artistic Works.[85] Article 3.4 of the Sanitary and Phytosanitary Measures (SPS) Agreement requires Members to 'play a full part, within the limits of their resources, in . . . the Codex Alimentarius Commission, the International Office of Epizootics, and the international and regional organizations operating within the framework of the International Plant Protection Convention'. Trebilcock and Howse correctly point out that:

> [t]he coherence of the international legal system would be put at risk if WTO panels and the [Appellate Body] were to apply or interpret provisions of other agreements referenced in WTO Agreements in abstraction from the practice surrounding those agreements, including dispute rulings, views of the institutional organs associated with the treaty and the opinions of jurists.[86]

In summary, as Broude explains, the 'contention that WTO obligations are part of public international law . . . is . . . , for international lawyers, quite obvious'.[87] The real debate concerns whether WTO Tribunals may apply substantive international law (rather than merely customary rules of interpretation) in resolving WTO disputes or otherwise use such law in interpreting the WTO agreements. I discuss this issue in

[83] Joost Pauwelyn, *Conflict of Norms in Public International Law: How WTO Law Relates to Other Rules of International Law* (2003) 27.

[84] See David Palmeter and Petros Mavroidis, *Dispute Settlement in the World Trade Organization: Practice and Procedure* (2nd edn, 2004) 69–73.

[85] Opened for signature 14 July 1967, 828 UNTS 221 (entered into force 29 July 1970).

[86] Michael J. Trebilcock and Robert Howse, *The Regulation of International Trade* (3rd edn, 2005) 128.

[87] Tomer Broude, *International Governance in the WTO: Judicial Boundaries and Political Capitulation* (2004) 267–8. See also Pauwelyn, *Conflict of Norms*, 25–6; Debra Steger, 'Jurisdiction of the WTO' (2004) 98 *American Society of International Law Proceedings* 142, 143; Peter van den Bossche, *The Law and Policy of the World Trade Organization: Text, Cases and Materials* (2005) 57.

detail in Chapter 3.[88] As background to that discussion, it is necessary to identify the various sources of international law that could possibly be relevant to WTO disputes. I begin with Article 38(1) of the ICJ Statute, which sets out the law that the ICJ is to apply.

According to Jennings, 'it is an open question whether [Article 38(1)] is now of itself a sufficient guide to the content of modern international law'.[89] For Fitzmaurice, Article 38(1) does not even profess to set out the formal sources of international law; it simply directs the Court as to what law it should apply in deciding cases brought before it.[90] Pauwelyn argues that, as Article 38(1) is itself merely a treaty provision, it forms part of international law rather than defining international law. He identifies unilateral acts of states and decisions of international organisations as additional sources of international law.[91] While it is important to keep these criticisms in mind, most commentators would accept that Article 38(1) does contain a list of sources of international law, although perhaps not an exhaustive statement of such sources. It therefore provides a valid basis for considering the principles derived from international law that might play a role in WTO disputes.

Article 38(1) of the ICJ Statute reads:

> The Court, whose function is to decide in accordance with international law such disputes as are submitted to it, shall apply:
>
> (a) international conventions, whether general or particular, establishing rules expressly recognized by the contesting States;
> (b) international custom, as evidence of a general practice accepted as law;
> (c) the general principles of law recognized by civilized nations;
> (d) subject to the provisions of Art. 59, judicial decisions and the decisions of the most highly qualified publicists of the various nations, as subsidiary means for the determination of rules of law.

No hierarchy exists between the three main sources of international law identified in Article 38(1) of the ICJ Statute, namely treaties, customary international law, and general principles of law.[92] And although Article 38(1)(d) refers to 'judicial decisions' as 'subsidiary means for the

[88] See especially below sections 3.2.3(B)(iv) and 3.3.3.

[89] Robert Jennings, 'What Is International Law and How Do We Tell It When We See It?' (1981) 37 *Schweizerisches Jahrbuch für Internationales Recht* 59, 61.

[90] Gerald Fitzmaurice, 'Some Problems Regarding the Formal Sources of International Law' [1958] *Symbolae Verzijl* 153, 173.

[91] Pauwelyn, *Conflict of Norms*, 90.

[92] Cheng, *General Principles of Law*, 20.

determination of rules of law', Jennings wrote in 1981 that '[t]here has long been no room for doubt that international law has become very much a case law' and, '[p]aradoxically, the subsidiary means are now . . . of the first importance'.[93] This is so even though Article 38(1)(d) is expressed as being subject to Article 59 of the ICJ Statute, which states that '[t]he decision of the Court has no binding force except between the parties and in respect of that particular case'. (A similar rule applies to decisions by Panels and the Appellate Body,[94] although it is not set out expressly in the DSU.)

According to Palmeter and Mavroidis, 'all of the subparagraphs of Article 38(1) are potential sources of law to be drawn on in WTO dispute settlement'.[95] This is a highly contested statement, and I do not propose to explore this question in such broad terms. However, in this book I conclude that, at a minimum, WTO Tribunals would be justified in resorting to general principles of law (in the sense of Article 38(1)(c) of the ICJ Statute) and principles abstracted from customary international law (under Article 38(1)(b) of the ICJ Statute) in resolving WTO disputes, in the following manner.

As an aid to interpreting WTO provisions, general principles of law and principles of customary international law may assist the WTO dispute settlement system in enhancing security and predictability in international trade, as envisaged by Article 3.2 of the DSU. This is in addition to the principles of WTO law discussed in the previous section, which could be seen as a subset of conventional international law as described in Article 38(1)(a) of the ICJ Statute. Even when not reflected in any WTO principles or individual WTO provisions, principles drawn from international law have a recognised role in treaty interpretation to the extent that they encompass 'relevant rules of international law between the parties' under Article 31(3)(c) of the VCLT. As highlighted by Article 38(1)(d) of the ICJ Statute, judicial decisions from within and outside the WTO may also assist in identifying and understanding principles of WTO law, general principles of law, and principles of customary international law. Certain principles that could be described as general principles of law or principles of customary international law could also play a role beyond interpretation, either in the exercise of the inherent jurisdiction of WTO Tribunals to resolve procedural

[93] Jennings, 'What Is International Law', 73, 77.

[94] See, e.g., Appellate Body Report, *Japan – Alcoholic Beverages II*, 14.

[95] Palmeter and Mavroidis, *Dispute Settlement*, 50.

matters, or (in the case of 'due process' in particular) as claims falling within the subject matter jurisdiction of WTO Tribunals.

Explicit consideration by WTO Tribunals of general principles of law and principles of customary international law, in appropriate circumstances, would serve to locate the WTO more clearly within the framework of public international law, enhance the authority and legitimacy of WTO dispute settlement decisions, and reduce the incidence and effects of conflicts with non-WTO law. Interpreting WTO provisions in a manner consistent with such principles would avoid some potential conflicts and provide answers to questions on which the WTO agreements are silent or unclear. That is not to say that the WTO agreements are necessarily subject to all other international law. The resolution of conflicts between norms of public international law, including WTO norms, is addressed extensively elsewhere.[96] The question of conflicts between the WTO agreements and other treaties falls outside the scope of this book, which examines only certain principles and not the entire body of international law as it relates to the WTO. For reasons presented in Chapter 3, general principles of law and principles of customary international law form part of the applicable law in WTO disputes only to the extent that they are reflected in provisions of the WTO agreements. Accordingly, the possibility of conflict between such principles and WTO provisions does not arise.

Principles have been a relatively neglected area not only of WTO law, as highlighted earlier, but also of international law more generally. Limited literature exists on the distinction between principles and rules in international law.[97] General principles of law have not been widely explored, although two outstanding contributions on this field are Lauterpacht's *Private Law Sources and Analogies of International Law* of 1927 and Cheng's *General Principles of Law as Applied by International Courts and Tribunals* of 1953.

1.3.3 *Problems with principles*

One argument against the use of 'broad principles' rather than 'detailed rules' in any legal setting is that the former may 'descend into an intuitive and unpredictable form of justice that ultimately involves

[96] Pauwelyn, *Conflict of Norms*.
[97] Humberto Ávila, *Theory of Legal Principles* (2007); Koskenniemi, *General Principles*.

abandonment of the rule of law'.[98] The 'axiomatic simplicity and familiarity' of certain principles (such as good faith and due process) could also contribute to their 'uncritical acceptance' without proper consideration of their 'nature, scope and function'.[99]

This book does not suggest that principles should prevail over rules or that they should be accepted uncritically. Indeed, as shown in Part II, before using a principle in dispute settlement, WTO Tribunals should carefully inspect the principle in order to ensure that: the principle has sufficient clarity and coherence to be of value; a concrete legal basis exists to validate the use of the principle; and the principle is not being used to contradict the plain meaning of the text of the WTO agreements. To date, these criteria have not always been met.

Some Members contend that they only agreed to be bound by the express words of the WTO agreements, and deference to national sovereignty means that the gap-filling role played by judges employing principles in the domestic sphere is inappropriate for WTO Tribunals. Panels and the Appellate Body are to follow the sovereign will of the Members as expressed in the WTO agreements, and leave everything not expressed in the WTO agreements to the Members to decide for themselves. In particular, some might point to the prohibition in Articles 3.2 and 19.2 of the DSU on adding to or diminishing the rights and obligations in the covered agreements as evidence that amorphous, unwritten 'principles' can play no part in resolving WTO disputes.

As explained earlier, gap-filling is an essential part of the adjudicative process given the inherent ambiguity of language. Moreover, interpreting the WTO agreements in accordance with the customary rules of international law, as mandated by Article 3.2, does not add to or diminish the rights or obligations of WTO Members. The application of policy and principle, at least in hard cases, is necessary to ensure equity and justice.[100] It is also preferable to refer explicitly to the principles that inform a decision rather than refusing to acknowledge the

[98] M. P. Ellinghaus and E. W. Wright, 'The Common Law of Contracts: Are Broad Principles Better than Detailed Rules? An Empirical Investigation' (2005) 11 *Texas Wesleyan Law Review* 399, 400.

[99] O'Connor, *Good Faith*, 1.

[100] See Francis Jacobs, 'Varieties of Approach to Treaty Interpretation: With Special Reference to the Draft Convention on the Law of Treaties Before the Vienna Diplomatic Conference' (1969) 18 *International and Comparative Law Quarterly* 318, 343; Jeff Waincymer, *WTO Litigation: Procedural Aspects of Formal Dispute Settlement* (2002) 390.

underlying principles or pretending that the text contains all the answers.

It could also be argued that the WTO system is fragile[101] and that WTO Tribunals must refrain from the use of principles to avoid adding further pressures. Established in 1995, it is true that the WTO is a comparatively young international organisation. Its Members are in some respects only just beginning to understand the system as a whole, and some face considerable pressure from industry, labour groups, and NGOs about its operation. The issues dealt with by its dispute settlement system, such as quarantine laws, restrictions on genetically modified organisms, and measures to protect industries from 'unfair' competition, are extremely controversial. The power of an international body in Geneva to determine such issues is highly contested. Furthermore, no international tribunal can 'fully reflect the value diversities of all States subject to it, [so] it can never receive the degree of acceptance and confidence bestowed on domestic courts'.[102]

These concerns should not be overstated. The WTO has suffered setbacks on several occasions in the past, and the success or failure of the institution as a whole is likely to depend more on the ability of negotiators to reach agreement at each stage than on the approach taken by WTO Tribunals. Furthermore, the suggestion that international tribunals are less effective than domestic tribunals in managing competing values and goals rests on the mistaken assumption that domestic polities are necessarily largely heterogeneous in their values and goals.[103] If anything, the WTO dispute settlement system is working better than the rest of the system and, through its extensive body of case law, has become highly respected and authoritative. Although critics are not shy in attacking individual decisions (as occurs in many other legal systems), the DSB has never decided by consensus not to adopt a Panel or Appellate Body report, and no Member has ever declared an intention not to comply with a recommendation or ruling of the DSB.

[101] See, e.g., Supachai Panitchpakdi, 'Why Cancún Matters', (Speech delivered at the Second International Conference on Globalisation, Leuven, 26 November 2002), www.wto.org/english/news_e/spsp_e/spsp08_e.htm.

[102] Ian Johnstone, 'Treaty Interpretation: The Authority of Interpretive Communities' (1991) 12 *Michigan Journal of International Law* 371.

[103] Howse, 'Adjudicative Legitimacy', 41.

1.4 Structure and content of the book

In Part I of this book, I establish a framework for the use of principles in WTO disputes, which I then rely on in examining four specific examples of principles in Part II. Chapter 2 begins by outlining three types of principles that may be particularly relevant to the WTO, namely principles of WTO law, principles of customary international law, and general principles of law. This chapter provides some examples of principles that WTO Tribunals have used or could use in WTO disputes, aside from the four principles examined in Part II. These examples provide some insight into the various debates surrounding particular principles and the potential scope for further research in this area. Chapter 3 explains the legal basis for WTO Tribunals to use the three types of principles in WTO disputes, either to interpret WTO provisions or on a more substantive basis. The use of different types of principles may be justified on different grounds, and in Part II I rely on these conclusions to narrow the ways in which particular principles can play a valid role.

WTO Tribunals have explicitly recognised the four principles addressed in Part II, namely the 'principle of good faith',[104] the 'principle of due process',[105] the 'principle of proportionality',[106] and the 'principle of special and differential treatment'.[107] At the outset, this provides a good reason to use them as case studies of the role of principles in WTO dispute settlement. The four principles are also all reflected in various rules of the WTO agreements rather than deriving solely from judicial pronouncements within the WTO or sources external to the WTO. At the same time, none is clearly delineated within the text of the agreements, so their existence, meaning and use may be more problematic than explicit WTO rules. Finally, these principles are useful in highlighting different aspects of WTO law and

[104] See, e.g., Appellate Body Report, *EC – Export Subsidies on Sugar*, [319]; Appellate Body Report, *US – Offset Act (Byrd Amendment)*, [296]–[297]; Appellate Body Report, *US – FSC*, [166].

[105] Decision by the Arbitrator, *Canada – Aircraft Credits and Guarantees (Article 22.6 – Canada)*, n. 112. Parties have made arguments concerning the 'principle of due process' in several cases: see, e.g., Panel Report, *EC – Tariff Preferences*, [6.17].

[106] Appellate Body Report, *US – Cotton Yarn*, [120], [122]; Appellate Body Report, *US – Line Pipe*, [256]; Decision by the Arbitrators, *EC – Bananas III (US) (Article 22.6 – EC)*, [6.16].

[107] Panel Report, *India – Quantitative Restrictions*, [5.157], [7.6]. See also the European Communities' arguments in Appellate Body Report, *EC – Tariff Preferences*, [14], [27], [93].

different issues that arise in WTO disputes (both procedural and substantive), as well as the relevance of the relationship between WTO law and international law more generally.

Chapter 4 considers 'good faith', which several WTO agreements expressly mention, most notably Articles 3.10 and 4.3 of the DSU, which impose an obligation on Members to engage in WTO dispute settlement procedures in good faith.[108] Article 31(1) of the VCLT also requires the interpretation of treaty provisions in good faith. This principle is therefore particularly important in relation to WTO disputes, although it may also impose substantive obligations on Members. The WTO agreements do not define 'good faith' or spell out what it requires in the context of WTO disputes or otherwise. Accordingly, it may assist in interpreting or applying good faith in the WTO to understand its possible status as a general principle of law or a principle of customary international law. Despite its rather vague scope, the legal significance of good faith should not be underestimated. In his authoritative treatise on general principles of law, Cheng devoted more than fifty pages to the principle of good faith.[109]

Chapter 5 concerns the principle of due process, which addresses some of the same concerns as good faith and partially overlaps with that principle. An examination of WTO Tribunals' decisions on these two principles to date suggests that they could be better clarified and distinguished. It therefore makes sense to address both of these principles in Part II. Like good faith, due process has characteristics that suggest it could be a general principle of law[110] or a principle of customary international law. Moreover, due process is the most obvious principle that WTO Tribunals may use to resolve procedural matters in the exercise of inherent jurisdiction, showing how principles may help resolve a myriad of unforeseeable circumstances that specific rules cannot address. Due process is also one of the chief grounds on which a Member may claim that a Panel failed to fulfil its function under the DSU,[111] providing a rare example of a general principle of law or a principle of customary international law that would likely fall within the subject matter jurisdiction of the Appellate Body even if it were not incorporated in any WTO provisions. Finally, in addition to governing

[108] See also TRIPS Agreement, arts. 24.4, 24.5, 48.2, 58(c); Understanding on the Interpretation of Article XXIV of the General Agreement on Tariffs and Trade 1994 [5].

[109] Cheng, *General Principles of Law*, 105–60. [110] Ibid. 279–98.

[111] See, e.g., Appellate Body Report, *US – Gambling*, [270]–[273].

WTO dispute settlement proceedings, due process is a source of substantive obligations imposed on Members in the context of their own judicial or administrative systems. The principle of due process may therefore inform WTO Tribunals' conduct of dispute settlement proceedings as well as their interpretation of substantive WTO provisions.

Two specific forms of the principle of proportionality are the focus of Chapter 6, namely the relationship between a particular offence or undesirable conduct and the allowable penalty, and the relationship between an exception and the rule. This is the only purely substantive principle addressed in Part II, in the sense that it has nothing to do with dispute settlement procedures (the other three principles have both substantive and procedural implications). Along with good faith,[112] proportionality is also one of the few 'principles' to have been analysed as such in the context of the WTO.[113] In relation to exceptions, the principle of proportionality can be found in public international law and the notion of proportionality is reflected in the WTO agreements through language such as 'proportionate', 'necessary', 'less trade restrictive' and 'commensurate'. The need for proportionality in imposing penalties is also reflected in various ways in different WTO provisions, although not always in a manner consistent with proportionality in non-WTO contexts. This demonstrates the potential flexibility of principles and the possibility that a principle within the WTO might conflict with or involve a modification of a principle in international law more generally.

The final substantive chapter of this book concerns the principle of special and differential treatment. This principle is of primary consequence for the present troubled Doha Round of negotiations, in which the Ministerial Conference has 'reaffirm[ed] that provisions for special and differential treatment are an integral part of the WTO Agreements' and agreed that such provisions 'shall be reviewed with a view to strengthening them and making them more precise, effective and operational'.[114] Unlike the other three principles in Part II, special and differential treatment finds no real counterpart in the general principles of law or the principles of customary international law. This principle is largely internal to the WTO system. Accordingly, it is harder to draw from non-WTO sources in understanding its meaning or

[112] See, e.g., Cottier and Schefer, 'Protection of Legitimate Expectations'.
[113] Hilf, 'Power, Rules and Principles', 120–1; Desmedt, 'Proportionality in WTO Law'.
[114] Doha Declaration, [44].

appraising its use by WTO Tribunals. Within the WTO, as discussed further in Chapter 2, one of the prevailing economic principles of the WTO is the principle of non-discrimination, to which special and differential treatment represents a major exception. Special and differential treatment is thus of special interest in showing how principles within a single treaty may conflict or need to be balanced. Special and differential treatment has both substantive aspects (in that it varies the usual WTO disciplines in relation to international trade for certain Members) and procedural aspects (in that developing countries may deserve different treatment in the course of dispute settlement proceedings).

In summary, the four principles I have chosen to address in Part II of the book are all of major significance in WTO law but have been scarcely analysed as principles in relation to WTO dispute settlement. Together, they display the breadth and depth of questions and concerns that may arise in using principles in WTO disputes, including the initial puzzle of how to identify and define 'principles'. The first three principles are obvious candidates for consideration by WTO Tribunals, as exhibited by previous decisions, and they demonstrate nicely the interplay between WTO law and public international law more generally. The inclusion of special and differential treatment underscores the troublesome aspects of relying in dispute settlement on trade-centred principles that have no obvious equivalent in other legal systems, whose economic implications are disputed, and that are subject to negotiation among WTO Members. The better strategy in these circumstances (which could apply to several other principles of WTO law mentioned in Chapter 2) is for WTO Tribunals to base their decisions on the specific rules embodying such principles rather than seeking guidance from the principles themselves in some more expansive sense.

In Chapter 8, I draw together the conclusions from the case studies in Part II and suggest that principles may come to play an increasingly important role in guiding, legitimising and evaluating dispute settlement in the WTO.

PART I · A FRAMEWORK FOR PRINCIPLES

2 Principles of particular relevance to the WTO

> It has sometimes been complained that the decisions of the World Court have been unpredictable. But the outcome of any case worth litigating must be to a serious degree unpredictable. The problem lies deeper and is more serious than that: it is that the *choice* of legal principles to be applied and upon which the decision will be made is itself often unpredictable . . .[1]

2.1 Introduction

A common feature of legal principles is that they are uncertain in scope and meaning. This problem is compounded by the fact that principles are often described in imprecise and conflicting ways in the relevant literature and decisions of the WTO Tribunals and other international tribunals. This chapter therefore sets out to define clearly three categories of principles that may be of particular relevance to WTO disputes: principles of WTO law, principles of customary international law, and general principles of law.

These categories are not intended to be rigid, mutually exclusive, or exhaustive. Thus, a given principle may fall within more than one category, and other principles relevant to the WTO (or international law more generally) may fall within none of these categories. Moreover, the examination of international law in this book focuses on principles, although other types of international law may well be relevant or applicable in WTO disputes. Of potential significance, for instance, are obligations under non-WTO treaties such as multilateral environmental agreements[2] and interpretative maxims such as *expressio unius est exclusio*

[1] Robert Jennings, 'What Is International Law and How Do We Tell It When We See It?' (1981) 37 *Schweizerisches Jahrbuch fur Internationales Recht* 59, 59–60.

[2] See, e.g., Appellate Body Report, *US – Shrimp*, [130]–[132]; Gabrielle Marceau, 'Conflicts of Norms and Conflicts of Jurisdictions: The Relationship between the WTO Agreement and MEAs and Other Treaties' (2001) 35 *Journal of World Trade* 1081.

alterius (the express inclusion of one thing implies the exclusion of the other)[3] which could be described as principles of logic or common sense. The three categories I have chosen nevertheless provide a useful guide to certain types of principles that are likely to arise in WTO disputes. By anchoring principles within this framework, it is possible to assess their authenticity and value, and to compare their use in different legal systems. In addition, the general categorisation set out in this chapter facilitates the detailed examination in Chapter 3 of the legal basis for using principles in WTO disputes, which differs according to the type of principle in question.

This chapter investigates the legitimacy of each category of principle by assessing the ease and assurance with which a principle can be identified under each category and the normative basis for doing so. It also considers the various ways in which principles may develop, including the role of WTO Tribunals in creating, defining or adopting certain principles. Finally, this chapter identifies examples of principles that could fall within each category, apart from the four principles of good faith, due process, proportionality, and special and differential treatment, which are reserved for detailed discussion in Part II of this book. The examples provided in this chapter offer a good introduction to the ways in which principles could be and have been used in WTO disputes, and some of the concerns surrounding such use.

2.2 Principles of WTO law

2.2.1 Defining principles of WTO law

A. Principles derived from the WTO agreements

Principles of WTO law derive primarily from treaty law, in the sense of Article 38(1)(a) of the ICJ Statute, but they concern only one particular international agreement, being that contained in the WTO agreements. Moreover, the principles of WTO law for the purpose of this book encompass not all WTO rules but only certain 'principles' within the WTO agreements. Thus, although this category of principles relates to a written treaty, the specific principles themselves may be unwritten and therefore must be ascertained using the normative or descriptive approach to identifying principles, as explained in Chapter 1.

[3] See, e.g., Appellate Body Report, *US – Hot-Rolled Steel*, [22] (argument by Japan).

The concept of principles drawn from an international agreement is sometimes explicitly recognised. For example, Article 7(2) of the UN Convention on Contracts for the International Sale of Goods (CISG), provides: 'Questions concerning matters governed by this Convention which are not expressly settled in it are to be settled in conformity with the general principles on which it is based.' Magnus argues that these principles in the CISG can be determined from: (1) provisions which explicitly claim that they apply to the entire convention; (2) analogy; (3) provisions containing concepts subject to generalisation; and (4) an overall context indicating the implicit assumption of a particular rule.[4]

Adopting a normative approach to identifying principles of WTO law, one could examine the preamble of the Marrakesh Agreement (or individual WTO agreements), as the preambles of multilateral treaties often set out the motives for such treaties and their object and purpose. One could also analyse the objectives or values that best justify the rules contained in the WTO agreements and guide decision-making by Panels and the Appellate Body. This process should identify the key intellectual foundations of the WTO. Adopting a descriptive approach to identifying principles, one would begin with the WTO rules themselves, grouping them together and summarising the operation of these groups. The key question under this approach would be: what abstractions or generalisations from the legal rules best explain those rules?

These two approaches would not necessarily lead to the identification of different principles of WTO law, but the choice of approach has a significant impact on the use of these principles. In particular, it affects whether principles of WTO law play a normative role in the application of WTO rules, or simply have useful systematic or didactic purposes. In Chapter 3, I consider in more detail the way in which principles could be used in the WTO. For the purposes of the present chapter, I therefore use aspects of both approaches to identify possible examples of principles of WTO law. In any event, in WTO dispute settlement, principles derived from the WTO agreements will, by definition, have the most concrete legal basis and the strongest claim to legitimacy of the types of principles addressed in this book.

[4] Quoted in Troy Keily, 'Good Faith & The Vienna Convention on Contracts for the International Sale of Goods (CISG)' (1999) 3 *Vindobona Journal of International Commercial Law & Arbitration* 15, n. 59.

B. Principles derived from judicial decisions

The reasoning and decisions of WTO Tribunals (that is, 'judicial decisions' within the meaning of Article 38(1)(d) of the ICJ Statute) may provide evidence or confirmation of the existence of particular principles of WTO law contained in the WTO agreements; they could also serve as an independent source of such principles even if they were not set out in the WTO agreements. I have decided not to treat principles derived from decisions of WTO Tribunals as 'principles of WTO law' in Part II of this book, although I examine these decisions to assist in identifying and exploring such principles.

Several factors explain this decision. First, Article IX:2 of the Marrakesh Agreement makes clear that the 'Ministerial Conference and the General Council shall have the exclusive authority to adopt interpretations of this Agreement and of the Multilateral Trade Agreements', which can be done by a three-fourths majority decision of Members. In addition, Article 3.9 of the DSU specifies that the DSU provisions 'are without prejudice to the rights of Members to seek authoritative interpretation of provisions of a covered agreement through decision-making' under the Marrakesh Agreement. Thus, WTO Tribunals' interpretations of WTO provisions in the course of disputes are not authoritative, although the recommendations and rulings flowing from those interpretations are binding on the parties to the dispute upon adoption by the DSB. Second, no formal principle of *stare decisis* operates in WTO dispute settlement, meaning that WTO Tribunals' decisions are strictly binding only in relation to the dispute at issue.[5] Third, decisions of WTO Tribunals do not constitute subsequent practice within the meaning of Article 31(3)(b) of the VCLT,[6] as mentioned in Chapter 3.[7] 'Subsequent practice' is used to demonstrate the 'intention' of the parties as to how the relevant treaty provision should be interpreted.[8] While these reports are adopted by all WTO Members, this adoption does not necessarily represent acceptance as to how the WTO provisions should be interpreted. In the DSB meetings where Panel and Appellate Body reports are adopted, Members frequently disagree with particular interpretations yet still adopt the report. A clear

[5] See, e.g., Appellate Body Report, *Japan – Alcoholic Beverages II*, 14. [6] Ibid. 12–15.

[7] See below, section 3.2.3(B).

[8] *Corfu Channel Case (Assessment of the Amount of Compensation Due from the People's Republic of Albania)* [1949] ICJ Rep 4, 25.

example of this was the adoption of the Panel Report in *Australia – Automotive Leather II (Article 21.5–US)*. Even the US, which benefited from the rulings in the report, told the DSB that it did not 'agree with every word of the Panel Report' but 'nevertheless' sought its adoption in order to end the dispute.[9] A range of Members, including Japan, Canada, the European Communities, Brazil, and Australia, strongly criticised the Panel's interpretation of the phrase 'withdraw the subsidy' in Article 4.7 of the Subsidies and Countervailing Measures (SCM) Agreement.[10] The DSB adopted the Panel report despite these criticisms, but it seems unlikely that the Members would have intended for the Panel's interpretation of Article 4.7 to be authoritative. Moreover, 'subsequent practice' under Article 31(3)(b) of the VCLT requires 'a sequence of facts or acts and cannot in general be established by one isolated fact or act or even by several individual applications'.[11] The adoption of one (or even a few) report of WTO Tribunals may not be sufficient to establish such a sequence of facts.

Finally, and perhaps most importantly, in order to gauge the correctness of and justification for particular decisions by WTO Tribunals, whether or not they rely on particular principles, it is necessary to have a benchmark of principles that exists separately from the jurisprudence. Accordingly, Part II of this book considers the implications of WTO Tribunals' decisions to recognise certain principles, and also assesses the extent to which those decisions accord with underlying principles of WTO law or other types of principles.

2.2.2 Possible examples of principles of WTO law

A. Clues from Marrakesh and Doha: a broad range of principles

In this section, I provide some examples of principles of WTO law that could be used in WTO disputes, other than the principles of good faith, due process, proportionality, and special and differential treatment (which are covered in Part II of this book). The Preamble to the Marrakesh Agreement provides a useful starting point for identifying the principles of WTO law, at least as they were conceived upon

[9] DSB, *Minutes of Meeting Held on 11 February 2000*, WT/DSB/M/75 (1 February 2000) 5 (United States).

[10] Ibid. 5–9.

[11] Ian Sinclair, *The Vienna Convention on the Law of Treaties* (2nd edn, 1984) 137.

establishment.[12] The Preamble indicates that the WTO Members are '[d]etermined to preserve the basic principles and further the objectives underlying this multilateral trading system',[13] indicating that the drafters were aware that the WTO system is more than a collection of rules. This statement also raises the issue of the difference between principles and objectives. An objective is typically understood as an aim or goal.[14] In contrast, a principle could be understood as referring to a means of achieving an objective or a number of objectives by providing the basis for a series of more detailed rules. However, this distinction may be stronger under a descriptive approach to identifying principles than a normative approach.

The Marrakesh Agreement does not go on to list the principles to which the Preamble refers. This does not mean that such principles do not exist. Indeed, the use of the word 'underlying' in the Preamble (referring to the principles underlying the multilateral trading system) suggests that the principles may be 'present and important but not immediately obvious'.[15] The Preamble does list a number of objectives such as 'raising standards of living, ensuring full employment', increasing 'real income and effective demand', 'expanding the production of and trade in goods and services', 'optimal use of the world's resources in accordance with ... sustainable development', and ensuring that developing countries 'share in the growth in international trade'.[16] The Preamble notes that WTO Members will contribute to these objectives through, amongst other things, 'reciprocal and mutually advantageous arrangements directed to the substantial reduction of tariffs and other barriers to trade and to the elimination of

[12] The Appellate Body has held that the preambular language 'must add colour, texture and shading to our interpretation of the agreements annexed to the WTO Agreement': Appellate Body Report, *US – Shrimp*, [153].

[13] Emphasis omitted.

[14] An objective can be aspirational and not have legal effect. For example, SPS Agreement, art. 5.5 (which refers to 'the objective of achieving consistency in the application of the concept of appropriate level of sanitary or phytosanitary protection') has not been interpreted as establishing a legal obligation of consistency of appropriate levels of protection: Appellate Body Report, *EC – Hormones*, [213].

[15] Definition of 'underlying' in Microsoft, *Encarta World English Dictionary* (2007) http://encarta.msn.com/dictionary_1861707761/underlying.html/.

[16] Similar objectives of the IMF include to 'facilitate the expansion and balanced growth of international trade, and to contribute thereby to the promotion and maintenance of high levels of employment and real income and to the development of the productive resources of all members as primary objectives of economic policy': Articles of Agreement of the International Monetary Fund, 27 December 1945, art. 1.

discriminatory treatment in international trade relations'. These statements suggest that trade liberalisation, reciprocity, and non-discrimination could be principles of WTO law.

The Doha Declaration offers a valuable insight into more recent thinking of WTO Members on the objectives of and challenges faced by the organisation. The Doha Declaration reiterates the centrality of WTO principles. There, Members state that they 'strongly reaffirm the principles and objectives set out in the [Marrakesh Agreement]'.[17] They go on to refer explicitly to the 'principle of special and differential treatment for developing and least-developed countries'.[18] In relation to the work programme on the Interaction between Trade and Competition Policy, the Doha Declaration refers to: 'core principles, including transparency, non-discrimination and procedural fairness'.[19] The work programme on WTO rules states that, while 'clarifying and improving disciplines', Members will preserve basic concepts and principles.[20] As well as identifying possible WTO principles, these statements reflect a recognition within the WTO membership of the significance of principles in the future development of the WTO.

Together, the Doha Declaration and the Preamble to the Marrakesh Agreement suggest that the principles of WTO law might include: trade liberalisation, transparency, non-discrimination, reciprocity, procedural fairness, and special and differential treatment for developing and least-developed countries. Other principles may also exist within WTO law. For example, the WTO Secretariat has suggested as principles predictable policies and encouraging competition.[21] Hilf has suggested as principles of WTO law: sovereignty and national deference, sustainable development, cooperation and multilateralism, and the rule of law.[22] In Part II, I address four potential principles of WTO law, but it is not possible in this book to address all these possible principles.

B. Trade liberalisation, non-discrimination, reciprocity

Three principles of particular importance to the WTO have their roots in GATT/WTO law rather than any external source of law, namely trade liberalisation, non-discrimination, and reciprocity. Hilf and Goettsche argue that these three principles are part of a series of 'classical' GATT/

[17] Doha Declaration, [1]. [18] Ibid. [50]. [19] Ibid. [25]. [20] Ibid. [28].

[21] WTO, *Principles of the Trading System*, www.wto.org/english/thewto_e/whatis_e/tif_e/fact2_e.htm.

[22] Meinhard Hilf, 'Power, Rules and Principles - Which Orientation for WTO/GATT law?' (2001) 4 *Journal of International Economic Law* 111, 117–21.

WTO principles that can be traced to the 'interregional commerce of ancient and medieval times' but that were given legal form for the first time in the GATT 1947.[23] While these principles may be reflected in the text of the WTO agreements, and thus can be considered principles of WTO law (as well as economic principles), their origins and the purpose of their inclusion in the WTO agreements are primarily economic. I introduce these principles below due to their importance in the WTO, but I do not analyse them further in Part II of this book, largely because they are closely related to trade issues and are of greater interest from an economic perspective than from a legal perspective.

As foreshadowed earlier, Howse contends that dispute settlement under GATT (and in the early WTO Panel proceedings) was focused on trade liberalisation:

> Normatively, the GATT elite embraced economic liberalism – the notion that everyone could be better off, or more prosperous as a consequence of freer trade – as the substantive telos of the system . . . The tendency of panels to assume they understood the general purpose of a provision, and to give sense to it in light of that purpose, without regard to the individual words and phrases, almost always resulted in rulings tilted towards one particular value among the competing values at stake, namely that of liberal trade – since the purpose invariably understood by the panel was the greatest possible discipline on barriers to trade.[24]

Today, WTO Tribunals are far less likely to give explicit primacy to free trade in their decisions, although some argue that they are still biased in this direction.[25] Non-trade values and Members' rights to regulate and determine their own policies and interests are recognised in the Preamble to the Marrakesh Agreement and many other WTO provisions, such as Article XX of GATT 1994, the Preamble to the General Agreement on Trade in Services (GATS), and Article 2.1 of the SPS Agreement. Moreover, WTO Tribunals appear particularly sensitive to criticism that they are interfering unduly in Members' sovereign decision-making,[26] granting insufficient deference to decisions of

[23] Meinhard Hilf and Goetz J. Goettsche, 'The Relation of Economic and Non-Economic Principles in International Law' in Stefan Griller (ed.), *International Economic Governance and Non-Economic Concerns: New Challenges for the International Legal Order* (2003) 15–17.

[24] Robert Howse, 'Adjudicative Legitimacy and Treaty Interpretation in International Trade Law: The Early Years of WTO Jurisprudence' in Joseph Weiler (ed.), *The EU, the WTO and the NAFTA: Toward a Common Law of International Law* (2000) 35, 38, 52–3.

[25] Consultative Board, WTO, *The Future of the WTO: Addressing Institutional Challenges in the New Millennium* (2004) [248].

[26] See, e.g., Award of the Arbitrator, *EC – Tariff Preferences*, [30].

domestic authorities,[27] or leaving too little policy space.[28] In these circumstances, WTO Tribunals would have great difficulty justifying a trade-liberal bias.

In the appeal in *EC – Chicken Cuts*, the European Communities argued that the Panel erred by relying on an 'interpretative principle directing Panels to bias towards the reduction of tariff commitments'.[29] The Appellate Body concluded that the Panel did not rely 'on trade expansion and tariff reduction as an interpretative principle'.[30] Nevertheless, the Appellate Body stated that it agreed with the Panel's statement that 'the security and predictability of "the reciprocal and mutually advantageous arrangements directed to the substantial reduction of tariffs and other barriers to trade" is an object and purpose of the [Marrakesh] Agreement, generally, as well as of the GATT 1994'.[31] Thus, trade liberalisation is unlikely to serve as an independent principle in WTO disputes, although it may be reflected in WTO provisions and thus play a role as one of the objects and purposes of the WTO agreements.

I turn now to the principle of non-discrimination in the WTO. Broadly speaking, this principle means that Members may not discriminate against other Members' products in favour of domestic products (the national treatment obligation), against other Members' products in favour of any non-Member's products, or between the products of other Members (the most favoured nation or MFN obligation). Non-discrimination is justified by its important trade-liberalising effect: it forces Members to extend their most trade-liberal measures to all goods and services. The principle of non-discrimination is reflected in a series of specific WTO provisions, in various forms. For example, a national treatment obligation is contained in Article III of GATT 1994, Article XVII of GATS, Article 3 of the TRIPS Agreement, and Article 2 of the Agreement on Trade-Related Investment Measures (TRIMS); an MFN

27 See generally William Davey, 'Has the WTO Dispute Settlement System Exceeded Its Authority? A Consideration of Deference Shown by the System to Member Government Decisions and Its Use of Issue-Avoidance Techniques' in Thomas Cottier and Petros Mavroidis (eds.), *The Role of the Judge in International Trade Regulation: Experience and Lessons for the WTO* (2003) vol. IV, 43; James Durling, 'Deference, but Only When Due: WTO Review of Anti-Dumping Measures' (2003) 6 *Journal of International Economic Law* 125.

28 See generally Olivier Cattaneo, 'Has the WTO Gone Too Far or Not Far Enough? Some Reflections on the Concept of "Policy Space"' in Andrew Mitchell (ed.), *Challenges and Prospects for the WTO* (2005) 55.

29 Appellate Body Report, *EC – Chicken Cuts*, [243]. 30 Ibid. [243].

31 Ibid. (quoting Panel Reports, *EC – Chicken Cuts*, [7.318]).

obligation is contained in Article I of GATT 1994, Article II of GATS, Article 4 of the TRIPS Agreement, Article 9.2 of the Anti-Dumping Agreement, and Article 2.2 of the Agreement on Safeguards. Indeed, the recent 'Future of the WTO' report describes 'unconditional MFN as the defining principle of the GATT'.[32]

Exceptions to the principle of non-discrimination exist. For example, contrary to the MFN obligation under GATT, Article XXIV allows WTO Members to provide more favourable treatment to other WTO Members with which they have entered free-trade areas or customs unions.[33] Another exception to the MFN obligation is found in the Enabling Clause, which allows Members to 'accord differential and more favourable treatment to developing countries' alone, subject to certain conditions.[34] This exception illustrates the tension between the principle of non-discrimination and the principle of special and differential treatment, which is discussed below in Chapter 7. However, even the Enabling Clause requires that tariff preferences to developing countries be 'non-discriminatory',[35] which the Appellate Body has read to mean that a developed country Member granting tariff preferences to developing countries pursuant to a Generalized System of Preferences (GSP) scheme 'must make available identical tariff preferences to all similarly-situated beneficiaries'.[36]

Non-discrimination provisions have a long history in international treaties and have been traced back to the Middle Ages.[37] From this history, and the principle of equality of states, it might be argued that a principle of non-discrimination exists in customary international law or as a general principle of law. However, this would be difficult to establish. No general rule of non-discrimination has developed to the extent that it demands strict equality in the treatment of states and

[32] Consultative Board, *Future of the WTO* (2005) [59].

[33] See generally Nicolas Lockhart and Andrew Mitchell, 'Regional Trade Agreements under GATT 1994: An Exception and Its Limits' in Andrew Mitchell (ed.), *Challenges and Prospects for the WTO* (2005) 217.

[34] Enabling Clause, [1].

[35] Enabling Clause, n. 3; Appellate Body Report, *EC – Tariff Preferences*, [146]–[148].

[36] Appellate Body Report, *EC – Tariff Preferences*, [154]. Compare Robert Howse, 'India's WTO Challenge to Drug Enforcement Conditions in the European Community Generalized System of Preferences: A Little Known Case with Major Repercussions for "Political" Conditionality in US Trade Policy' (2003) 4 *Chicago Journal of International Law* 385, 395.

[37] Endre Ustor, 'Most-Favoured-Nation Clause' in Rudolf Bernhardt (ed.), *Encyclopaedia of Public International Law* (2003) vol. III, 468, 468.

their nationals.[38] Such '[o]bligations of equal treatment or non-discrimination arise only on the basis of specific rules and provisions and within the limited scope of their application',[39] such as within WTO law or in human rights law with respect to individuals.

In many respects, the principle of non-discrimination in the WTO is similar to the principle of special and differential treatment (outlined in Chapter 7). Both of these principles are trade centred, and each is reflected in a range of provisions in the WTO agreements. However, these provisions often embody different standards for enforcing each of these principles. For example, Article III:2 of GATT 1994 provides that imports 'shall not be subject, directly or indirectly, to internal taxes or other internal charges of any kind in excess of those applied, directly or indirectly, to like domestic products', while Article III:4 of the same agreement provides that imports 'shall be accorded treatment no less favourable than that accorded to like products of national origin in respect of all laws, regulations and requirements'. The difference in these two standards can be seen through their interpretation by the Appellate Body. In relation to Article III:2 the Appellate Body held in *Chile – Alcoholic Beverages* that the principle of non-discrimination was violated even when the tax measure imposed by Chile was based on alcohol content rather than the foreign origin of goods (this was 'indirectly' imposing taxes on imports).[40] In contrast, in *Dominican Republic – Cigarettes*, the Appellate Body held that a detrimental effect on imported cigarettes from Honduras did not violate Article III:4 of GATT 1994 because it could be explained by 'factors or circumstances unrelated to the foreign origin of the product'[41] (the measure at issue was a requirement that a bond be paid by cigarette producers to ensure their taxation obligations were met, and Honduras alleged that the per-unit cost of the bond was higher for foreign producers than for domestic producers because imported cigarettes had lower sales).

Even within a single WTO article, the Appellate Body sometimes applies substantially different standards for 'non-discrimination'. Thus, the application of non-discrimination in WTO disputes is closely linked to the wording of particular provisions. As I argue in Chapter 7 in

[38] Ibid.

[39] Günther Jaenicke, 'States, Equal Treatment and Non-Discrimination' in Rudolf Bernhardt (ed.), *Encyclopaedia of Public International Law* (2003) vol. IV, 660, 661.

[40] Appellate Body Report, *Chile – Alcoholic Beverages*, [49]–[54].

[41] Appellate Body Report, *Dominican Republic – Cigarettes*, [96].

relation to special and differential treatment, this is the correct approach to economic principles that have been incorporated in a range of different provisions in the WTO agreements. These economic principles, while central to the WTO, have been subject to negotiation among WTO Members and their exact scope is often disputed. For this reason, interpretation of the provisions that embody the principle of non-discrimination should continue to depend largely on the wording of the particular provision, rather than a broad principle.

Another possible example of a principle of WTO law is reciprocity or balance of concessions. In the WTO, reciprocity means that Members exchange similar or comparable trade-liberalising commitments. Members typically 'bind' their commitments, providing a degree of predictability in trade. On this basis, Members seek to achieve a balance of concessions, meaning an approximate equality between the value of what is given (their own market liberalising commitments) and what is obtained (others' market liberalising commitments). Thus, Hoekman writes that '[r]eciprocity is the engine of the WTO, the means through which to obtain concessions from trading partners'.[42]

Unlike the principle of non-discrimination, the text of the WTO agreements makes little reference to reciprocity, and this principle is not expressly contained in any WTO rule. The key reference to the principle is in the Preamble of the Marrakesh Agreement, which refers to 'entering into reciprocal and mutually advantageous arrangements directed to the substantial reduction of tariffs and other barriers to trade and to the elimination of discriminatory treatment in international trade relations', largely repeating the wording of the Preamble to GATT.[43] According to the Appellate Body, 'the security and predictability of "the reciprocal and mutually advantageous arrangements directed to the substantial reduction of tariffs and other barriers to trade" is an object and purpose of the WTO Agreement, generally, as well as of the GATT 1994'.[44]

The notion of reciprocity in the WTO may have a tremendous impact on trade negotiations, not as a legal principle but as a matter of practice and policy, in the sense that Members will generally aim to achieve a

[42] Bernard Hoekman, 'Operationalizing the Concept of Policy Space in the WTO: Beyond Special and Differential Treatment' (2005) 8 *Journal of International Economic Law* 405, 409.

[43] See also GATT 1994, art. XXVIII:2.

[44] Appellate Body Report, *EC – Computer Equipment*, [82].

balance of trade concessions granted and obtained from others in the bargaining process.[45] Thus, the Appellate Body has recognised that '[t]ariff negotiations are a process of reciprocal demands and concessions, of "give and take" '.[46] However, reciprocity has certain limitations as a theoretical principle. First, the general rationale for a Member to liberalise trade in the WTO is that the Member itself will benefit along with its trading partners. Thus, it may be inappropriate to emphasise the idea of 'concessions' or the need to ensure that one gets as much as one gives up. Second, since the WTO agreements form a 'single undertaking'[47] and rely heavily on the general MFN obligation, Members must typically extend any 'concessions' granted to one WTO Member to all other Members. In this sense, the result may not necessarily be reciprocal. Third, reciprocity has a counterpart in what could be described as a principle of non-reciprocity,[48] whereby developing countries need not always make reciprocal commitments, in view of their special situation. Thus reciprocity, like trade liberalisation, is unlikely to arise as an independent principle in WTO disputes.

2.3 Principles of customary international law

2.3.1 Introduction

Paragraph (b) of Article 38(1) of the ICJ Statute describes one of the three sources of law as 'international custom, as evidence of a general practice accepted as law'. Based on the word 'custom', this source gives rise to what is known as 'customary international law'. The essential idea behind customary international law is that states, by their conduct, can implicitly consent to the creation of international legal rules. The creation of customary international law is classically understood as requiring two elements, both of which are reflected in Article 38(1)(b): an objective element – the established, widespread and consistent *practice* on the part of states; and a subjective element – a belief that

[45] See Michael Finger, 'A Diplomat's Economics: Reciprocity in the Uruguay Round Negotiations' (2005) 4 *World Trade Review* 27, 29–30, 35–6.

[46] Appellate Body Report, *EC – Computer Equipment*, [109].

[47] See below section 3.2.3, second para. beginning 'The WTO agreements comprise a "single undertaking" . . .'.

[48] See, e.g., GATT 1994, art. XXXVI:8; Howse, 'India's WTO Challenge', 396. See also Enabling Clause, n. 3; Consultative Board, *Future of the WTO* (2005) [93].

this practice is required (or permitted)[49] by law (the *opinio juris sive necessitatis*, normally shortened to *opinio juris*). The judgment of the ICJ in the *North Sea Continental Shelf Case* summarises these two elements:[50]

> Not only must the acts concerned amount to a settled practice, but they must also be such, or be carried out in such a way, as to be evidence of a belief that this practice is rendered obligatory by the existence of a rule of law requiring it. The need for such a belief, i.e. the existence of a subjective element, is implicit in the very notion of the *opinio juris sive necessitatis*.[51]

Similarly, the *Third Restatement of the Foreign Relations Law of the United States* describes customary international law as resulting from 'a general and consistent practice of states followed by them from a sense of legal obligation.'[52] While customary international law is generally binding on all states, some customary international law may be regional (in which case its application is limited to a particular region), and some customary international law will not bind states that have contentiously objected to it (the continuous objector rule).[53]

In this book, I focus on the potential relevance for WTO disputes of principles abstracted from customary international law. The following sections elaborate on the definition of customary international law and certain conceptual difficulties with that definition, which may affect its utility or validity in WTO law, before describing certain principles of customary international law that might be particularly relevant in the context of WTO dispute settlement. Notwithstanding academic critiques of the definition of customary international law,[54] it is generally acknowledged as a binding source of law. It has been accepted by states and most writers, and it is regularly applied by international tribunals, including the ICJ and others. The uncertainties surrounding its exact scope and nature are insufficient to discard it as a legitimate concern in the WTO. Rather, these uncertainties should be taken into account in using customary international law in the WTO in any given instance.

[49] In the case of permissive rules of customary international law.

[50] The Court was discussing the process by which treaty law could generate customary international law, but the process is the same for customary international law generally.

[51] *North Sea Continental Shelf (Federal Republic of Germany v. Denmark; Federal Republic of Germany v. Netherlands)* [1969] ICJ Rep 3, [77].

[52] American Law Institute, *Restatement of the Law Third: The Foreign Relations Law of the United States* (1987) art. 102.

[53] See, e.g., *Asylum Case (Colombia v. Peru)* [1950] ICJ Rep 266, 268–9, 277–8.

[54] See, e.g., J Patrick Kelly, 'The Twilight of Customary International Law' (2000) 40 *Virginia Journal of International Law* 449; Vladimir Degan, *Sources of International Law* (1997) 146.

2.3.2 *Dissecting the meaning of customary international law*

A. What state practice counts?

Assuming that customary international law is accepted as a useful source of international law, disagreement remains about what forms of behaviours, manifested in a particular material source, are relevant.[55] Many material sources have been used as evidence of state practice in establishing customary international law. They include: diplomatic correspondence, policy statements, the opinions of official legal advisers, official manuals on legal questions, legislation, international and national decisions, recitals in international instruments, patterns of treaties in the same form, and resolutions relating to legal questions in the United Nations General Assembly.[56] Brownlie acknowledges that 'the value of these sources varies and much depends on the circumstances'.[57]

Some consider that only acts, and not statements, can constitute state practice. So, for example, to prevent the development of the right of satellite overflight, states would have had to take action against satellites or otherwise retaliate against the states that launched them.[58] This approach clearly favours powerful states over weaker ones. Others consider that any type of state behaviour, including statements and omissions, can constitute customary international law.[59] The better view is that a combination of acts and statements/omissions is required, so that statements/omission alone cannot constitute sufficient state practice to generate a norm of customary international law.

For some commentators, the flexibility in identifying and evaluating relevant state practice is troubling because it may allow state practice to be used to support any particular value judgement.[60] For example, on the one hand, it could be said that customary international law requires full compensation for expropriation of foreign-owned property, as this standard is contained in several bilateral investment treaties.[61] Conversely, one might argue that the frequent inclusion of this standard in

[55] Michael Byers, *Custom, Power and the Power of Rules: International Relations and Customary International Law* (1999) 133–4.

[56] Ian Brownlie, *Principles of Public International Law* (6th edn, 2003) 6. [57] Ibid.

[58] Anthony D'Amato, *The Concept of Custom in International Law* (1971).

[59] Michael Akehurst, 'Custom as a Source of Law' (1974) 47 *British Yearbook of International Law* 1, 10.

[60] Kelly, 'Twilight of Customary International Law', 503.

[61] Davis Robinson, 'Expropriation in the Restatement (Revised)' (1984) 78 *American Journal of International Law* 176.

such treaties provides evidence of a conflicting customary international law rule, which governments consider it necessary to contract out of.[62] The fact that governments sometimes make lump-sum payments to compensate for expropriation at less than full value could also indicate that customary international law simply requires national treatment in compensating for expropriation.[63] This example shows how state practice could be used selectively in an attempt to establish customary international law on a question about which no consensus has been reached.[64] It also shows how identifying customary international law can be changed from an empirical to a normative exercise, dependent on the views of the person or body engaged in this process.[65] These are real dangers that should be considered in recognising any particular rule of customary international law.

Some of the material sources that are used to establish state practice are contested. For example, Kelly argues:

> decisions of national courts are of minimal value in determining CIL [customary international law]. Domestic courts generally lack an understanding of how to determine CIL. In particular, they do not undertake a detailed analysis of state practice in other cultures, are prone to accept the values of their own culture or the political positions of their own governments as CIL, and overestimate the role of judges in the customary law process.[66]

Like other sources of state practice, the value of national decisions is likely to vary considerably according to the particular approach used.[67] However, in appropriate circumstances these decisions can provide useful indirect evidence of state practice in a given jurisdiction and also a thorough explanation of the law.[68] Further, surely the actions of the judiciary must be included as state practice, along with the legislature and the executive, since they are all equally significant.

Another contested material source is treaties. McGinnis notes that treaties provide 'opportunities for trade-offs and deals in which one party concedes a provision in return for another country's concession'.[69]

62 Jennings, 'What is International Law', 65.
63 Bernard Kishoiyian, 'The Utility of Bilateral Investment Treaties in the Formulation of Customary International Law' (1994) 14 *Northwestern Journal of International Law and Business* 327.
64 Kelly, 'Twilight of Customary International Law', 503. 65 Ibid. 458. 66 Ibid. 506.
67 Brownlie, *Principles of Public International Law*, 22. 68 Ibid.
69 John McGinnis, 'The Appropriate Hierarchy of Global Multilateralism and Customary International Law: The Example of the WTO' (2003) 44 *Virginia Journal of International Law* 229, 240.

This is certainly true in the WTO: '[d]eadlocks that have blocked progress in international organizations ... are resolved in the WTO because here governments can make package deals.'[70] Where a provision is only accepted as part of a quid pro quo, a state cannot be said to have consented to a principle reflecting that provision in a broader international context, in particular without reciprocal concessions from other states.

One significant limitation in identifying relevant state practice is that much useful material is not published, and much of the relevant published material originates in Western developed countries.[71] Often, it will be inappropriate or impossible to use this kind of material to draw general conclusions about state practice in other countries.[72] Nevertheless, in some cases enough material from different countries will be available to constitute a solid basis of state practice. If possible, Western material should be balanced with appropriate material from non-Western countries. Sources such as resolutions of the United Nations General Assembly may be useful in this regard, given the high proportion of developing countries within that body.[73] Where the available material is restricted to particular countries or groups of countries, particular care should be taken in relying on it as evidence of broader practice.

B. Divergent state practice

No positive standard exists as to the degree of uniformity required in state practice in establishing customary international law or changes to that law. The general rule is that the practice need only be consistent and widespread to contribute to the creation of customary international law. In the *Asylum Case*, the ICJ stated that a rule of customary

[70] Marco Bronckers, 'Better Rules for a New Millennium: A Warning against Undemocratic Developments in the WTO' (1999) 2 *Journal of International Economic Law* 547, 548.

[71] See, e.g., *Australian Yearbook of International Law*; *British Yearbook of International Law*; *Canadian Yearbook of International Law*; *Finnish Yearbook of International Law*; *German Yearbook of International Law*; *Italian Yearbook of International Law*; *Netherlands Yearbook of International Law*; *Polish Yearbook of International Law*; *Schweizerisches Jahrbuch für Internationales Recht*. However, see also: *Palestine Yearbook of International Law*; *South African Yearbook of International Law*; *African Yearbook of International Law*; *Asian Yearbook of International Law*.

[72] Kelly, 'Twilight of Customary International Law', 468.

[73] See Stephen Schwebel, 'The Effect of Resolutions of the UN General Assembly on Customary International Law' (1979) 73 *American Society of International Law Proceedings* 301.

international law must be based on 'a constant and uniform usage'.[74] In the *Nicaragua* case, the ICJ stated:

> It is not to be expected that in the practice of States the application of the rules in question should have been perfect, in the sense that States should have refrained, with complete consistency, from the use of force or from intervention in each other's internal affairs. The Court does not consider that, for a rule to be established as customary, the corresponding practice must be in absolutely rigorous conformity with the rule. In order to deduce the existence of customary rules, the Court deems it sufficient that the conduct of States should, in general, be consistent with such rules, and that instances of State conduct inconsistent with a given rule should generally have been treated as breaches of that rule, not as indications of recognition of a new rule.[75]

This passage leaves uncertain the degree of compliance with a rule required in order to prove a norm of customary international law. The ICJ has never articulated any numerical approach to the question of state practice. Nor could it do so, as customary international law cannot be reduced to calculations of the percentage of states whose practice is consistent with a particular rule.[76] Furthermore, the ICJ has indicated that the practice of 'specially affected states' may be given more weight, which also defeats any attempt at a precise formula for assessing whether a sufficient level of state practice has been demonstrated. Goldsmith and Posner suggest that customary international law 'is usually based on a highly selective survey of state practice that includes only major powers and interested nations'.[77]

Clearly, demonstrating sufficient state practice to prove a norm of customary international law is not a scientific exercise. It can involve questions of fact and degree. But this does not mean it is impossible. It merely means that, in some areas, proof of a norm may be difficult. The numerous examples of satisfactory proof of norms of customary international law suggest that these difficulties are not insurmountable.

[74] *Asylum Case (Colombia* v. *Peru)* [1950] ICJ Rep 266, 276.

[75] *Military and Paramilitary Activities in and against Nicaragua (Nicaragua* v. *United States of America) (Merits)* [1986] ICJ Rep 14, [186].

[76] *North Sea Continental Shelf (Federal Republic of Germany* v. *Denmark; Federal Republic of Germany* v. *Netherlands)* [1969] ICJ Rep 3, [74].

[77] Jack Goldsmith and Eric Posner, 'A Theory of Customary International Law' (1999) 66 *University of Chicago Law Review* 1113, 1117.

C. Opinio juris

It is clearly difficult to identify in the abstract the beliefs or intentions of a state. The ICJ has therefore tended to infer *opinio juris* from state acts or omissions,[78] academic consensus, or previous determinations of international tribunals.[79] Significantly, in the three situations where the International Court adopted a more rigorous approach, demanding direct evidence of *opinio juris*,[80] the evidence was held to be inadequate to establish the *opinio juris* element of customary international law.

Obviously, if state practice is held to comprise both acts and statements, then using it to determine *opinio juris* seems to render superfluous this element of customary international law. Byers refers to this as the epistemological circle.[81] One pragmatic way of resolving this problem is to recognise the 'sliding scale' identified by Kirgis:

> [V]ery frequent, consistent state practice establishes a customary rule without much (or any) affirmative showing of an *opinio juris*, so long as it is not negated by evidence of non-normative intent. As the frequency and consistency of the practice decline in any series of cases, a stronger showing of *opinio juris* is required. At the other end of the scale, a clearly demonstrated *opinio juris* establishes a customary rule without much (or any) affirmative showing that governments are consistently behaving in accordance with the asserted rule.[82]

The extent that one element can be used in place of the other depends on the activity in question and on the reasonableness of the asserted customary rule.[83] Tasioulas explains Kirgis' sliding scale using Dworkin's interpretative theory of law, balancing theories that adequately fit past action and choosing the one that is morally the

[78] Peter Malanczuk, *Akehurst's Modern Introduction to International Law* (7th edn, 1997) 44.

[79] Brownlie, *Principles of Public International Law*, 8.

[80] SS Lotus *(France* v. *Turkey)* [1927] PCIJ (ser A) No 10; *Military and Paramilitary Activities in and against Nicaragua (Nicaragua* v. *United States of America) (Merits)* [1986] ICJ Rep 14; *North Sea Continental Shelf (Federal Republic of Germany* v. *Denmark; Federal Republic of Germany* v. *Netherlands) (Merits)* [1969] ICJ Rep 3: cited in Brownlie, *Principles of Public International Law*, 9–10.

[81] Byers, *Custom, Power and the Power of Rules*, 136.

[82] Fredric Kirgis, 'Custom on a Sliding Scale' (1987) 81 *American Journal of International Law* 146, 149.

[83] 'The more destabilizing or morally distasteful the activity – for example, the offensive use of force or the deprivation of fundamental human rights – the more readily international decision makers will substitute one element for the other, provided that the asserted restrictive rule seems reasonable': ibid.

best.[84] However, Roberts notes two important limitations on the sliding-scale approach. First, finding custom purely on the basis of state practice gives strong states enormous power in law-making, and finding custom purely from *opinio juris* can create international laws completely removed from reality. Second, international tribunals do not appear to consider the moral nature of the activity addressed by the law in a symmetrical manner. Rather, the nature of the activity seems mainly 'to arise in situations where the problems with it concern a lack of affirming state practice rather than a lack of *opinio juris*'.[85]

To some extent, the two extremes of Kirgis' sliding scale represent what Roberts terms 'traditional custom' and 'modern custom'. Traditional custom 'is evolutionary and is identified through an *inductive* process in which a general custom is derived from specific instances of state practice'.[86] Modern custom is 'derived by a *deductive* process that begins with general statements of rules rather than particular instances of practice'.[87] Therefore, traditional custom emphasises state practice and develops slowly, while modern custom emphasises *opinio juris* and can develop quickly. Roberts notes that emphasising *opinio juris* is potentially more democratic, since all states can participate in the process of making treaties and declarations.[88]

Another difficulty with using state practice to determine *opinio juris* is that states can adopt a consistent pattern of behaviour unrelated to a belief in the existence of a legal norm requiring such behaviour. Goldsmith and Posner have used game theory[89] to suggest that states' consistent patterns of behaviour also occur in different strategic situations: coincidence of interest,[90] coercion,[91] bilateral repeat prisoner's

[84] John Tasioulas, 'In Defence of Relative Normativity: Communitarian Values and the Nicaragua Case' (1996) 16 *Oxford Journal of Legal Studies* 85, 113.

[85] Anthea Roberts, 'Traditional and Modern Approaches to Customary International Law: A Reconciliation' (2001) 95 *American Journal of International Law* 757, 773.

[86] Ibid. 758 (original emphasis, footnotes omitted). [87] Ibid. [88] Ibid. 768.

[89] Game theory is a branch of economics concerned with 'the study of interacting decision makers'. In particular, it is concerned with a player's optimal strategy (that is, one that maximises their pay-offs) in situations of competition or conflict: Robert Beynon (ed.), *The Routledge Companion to Global Economics* (2001) 214–15.

[90] Coincidence of interest is where 'states engage in behavioral regularities simply because each obtains private advantages from a particular action (which happens to be the same action taken by the other state) irrespective of the action of the other': Goldsmith and Posner, 'Theory of Customary International Law', 1122.

[91] Coercion is where '[o]ne state, or a coalition of states with convergent interests, forces other states to engage in actions that serve the interest of the first state or states': ibid. 1123.

dilemma,[92] and bilateral coordination.[93] In each case, this pattern of behaviour results from states acting in their own interests rather than from a sense of legal obligation.[94]

In view of the difficulties concerning the relationship between state practice and *opinio juris*, Koskenniemi argues that customary international law theory is indeterminate in its application:

> Attempting to identify the presence of the psychological element, [the theory of customary international law] draws inferences (presumptions) on the basis of material practice. To ascertain what acts of material practice are relevant for formation, it makes reference to the psychological element (ie. 'those acts count which express the *opinio juris*'.) The psychological element is defined by the material and *vice versa*.[95]

Although *opinio juris* may not always be easily distinguishable from state practice, the former element does play an important part in defining customary international law. Sometimes *opinio juris* will be clear and valuable in supporting state practice, for example where states have expressly recognised a legal obligation or expressly condemned particular action as illegal.

2.3.3 Possible examples of relevant principles of customary international law

A. Interpretative principles: in dubio mitius, effectiveness

Having outlined some of the theoretical difficulties with customary international law and the limits to its legitimacy, I now consider some of the principles that could be extracted from customary international law that might be of relevance to WTO disputes, apart from good faith, due process, and proportionality (as discussed in Part II of this book). In particular, I address here the principles of *in dubio mitius* and

92 Bilateral repeat prisoner's dilemma is where two states are involved in an indefinite series of games where, for each game, it pays an individual state to behave in a particular way, even through it would pay both states to behave in some other way: ibid. 1127.

93 Bilateral coordination is where two 'states' interests converge, as in the case of coincidence of interest; but unlike the other case, each state's best move depends on the move of the other state': ibid. See also Jack Goldsmith and Eric Posner, 'Understanding the Resemblance between Modern and Traditional Customary International Law' (2000) 40 *Virginia Journal of International Law* 639.

94 Goldsmith and Posner, 'Theory of Customary International Law'.

95 Martii Koskenniemi, *From Apology to Utopia* (1989) 363.

effectiveness (which are primarily principles that could be used to interpret WTO provisions), as well as the principle of precaution (which could be used to interpret WTO provisions and also, perhaps, as a principle imposing substantive rights and obligations). These illustrate how WTO Tribunals have used certain principles in their decisions so far, as well as certain potential difficulties in defining and using principles within the WTO dispute settlement system.

Beginning with *in dubio mitius*, the Appellate Body referred to this principle for the first and only time to date in *EC – Hormones*. The Panel in that dispute had found that Article 3.1 of the SPS Agreement, which generally requires Members to 'base their sanitary or phytosanitary measures on international standards, guidelines or recommendations', obliges Members to ensure that their SPS measures *conform to* relevant international standards, guidelines, or recommendations.[96] The Appellate Body rejected this interpretation by the Panel, which it understood as indicating that 'based on' means the same thing as 'conform to'.[97] The Appellate Body stated: 'We cannot lightly assume that sovereign states intended to impose upon themselves the more onerous, rather than the less burdensome, obligation by mandating *conformity or compliance* with such standards, guidelines and recommendations',[98] and added in a footnote:

> The interpretative principle of *in dubio mitius*, widely recognized in international law as a 'supplementary means of interpretation', has been expressed in the following terms:
>
> 'The principle of *in dubio mitius* applies in interpreting treaties, in deference to the sovereignty of states. If the meaning of a term is ambiguous, the meaning is to be preferred which is less onerous to the party assuming an obligation, or which interferes less with the territorial and personal supremacy of a party, or involves less general restrictions upon the parties.'[99]

In support of the existence of this principle in international law, the Appellate Body cited several decisions of international tribunals[100] and several legal texts (all of which might be said to fall within Article 38(1)(d) of the ICJ Statute). Yet several commentators criticised

[96] Panel Report, *EC – Hormones (US)*, [8.72], [8.73].

[97] Appellate Body Report, *EC – Hormones*, [163]–[166].

[98] Ibid. [165] (original emphasis).

[99] Ibid. n. 154 (quoting Robert Jennings and Arthur Watts (eds.), *Oppenheim's International Law* (9th edn, 1992) vol. I, 1278).

[100] See, e.g., *Nuclear Tests (Australia* v. *France) (Merits)* [1974] ICJ Rep 253, 267.

the Appellate Body's use of the principle of *in dubio mitius* in this dispute, partly because of the implications of the principle itself, and partly because of its unstable foundation in international law, at least in the context the Appellate Body was using it (namely to interpret a multilateral treaty).[101]

Interpreting ambiguous WTO provisions in the least onerous manner risks unravelling the obligations agreed by the parties and hence the benefits accruing to WTO Members from the agreements. The Appellate Body's experience with the exceedingly complex details of the agreements over the years therefore seems to have led it to an interpretative approach that is more closely based on the VCLT and less reliant on problematic principles such as this. In any case, the principle of *in dubio mitius* demonstrates the importance of using in WTO disputes only those principles that have a reliable origin either in WTO law, international law, or some other form of law that WTO Tribunals may properly consider. *In dubio mitius* also highlights the possibility of conflict between principles. To the extent that *in dubio mitius* could be described as an interpretative principle of customary international law, it may conflict with another such principle, namely the principle of effectiveness.[102]

The principle of effectiveness may be better viewed as part of the requirement in Article 31(1) of the VCLT that treaties be interpreted in good faith, as discussed in Chapter 3 and Chapter 4. It is nevertheless worth considering its potential as an independent principle, given that disputing Members[103] and WTO Tribunals[104] rely on it relatively frequently. The Appellate Body has stated that 'the internationally recognized interpretive principle of effectiveness should guide the interpretation of the *WTO Agreement*', meaning that 'provisions of the *WTO Agreement* should not be interpreted in such a manner that whole clauses or paragraphs of a treaty would be reduced to redundancy or inutility'.[105]

[101] See, e.g., Michael Lennard, 'Navigating by the Stars: Interpreting the WTO Agreements' (2002) 5 *Journal of International Economic Law* 17, 63–6.

[102] Ibid. 65. *In dubio mitius* and the principle of effectiveness have also been described as general principles of law: Wolfgang Weiss, 'Security and Predictability under WTO Law' (2003) 2 *World Trade Review* 183, 186–7.

[103] See, e.g., Appellate Body Report, *EC – Export Subsidies on Sugar*, [59].

[104] See, e.g., Appellate Body Report, *Korea – Dairy*, [80]–[81].

[105] Appellate Body Report, *US – Offset Act (Byrd Amendment)*, [271].

Like the principle of *in dubio mitius*, the principle of effectiveness has certain shortcomings in interpreting WTO provisions. As Lennard explains:

> the often frenetic late drafting of treaties as complex as the WTO Agreements will often mean that caution should closely attend reliance on this maxim. It has been noted that the absence of a full measure of effectiveness may be the direct result of the inability of the parties to reach agreement on fully effective provisions, and the treaty should not be in effect revised to make good the parties' omissions.[106]

Moreover, the principle of effectiveness may be too readily asserted as a basis for a particular interpretation without considering how to apply it correctly or whether it is even helpful in a given case. In *Argentina – Footwear (EC)*, the Panel was faced with an apparent discrepancy between Article XIX of GATT 1994 (which provides certain general provisions on safeguards as previously contained in GATT 1947) and the Agreement on Safeguards (which was negotiated in the Uruguay Round and came into force in 1995). Specifically, GATT Article XIX indicates that the existence of 'unforeseen developments' is one criterion that must be satisfied for a Member to impose a safeguard, whereas the Agreement on Safeguards does not mention any such criterion, even though it sets out in much greater detail the requirements and procedures for Members to impose safeguards. The Panel read the Agreement on Safeguards as 'reflect[ing] the latest statement of WTO Members concerning their rights and obligations concerning safeguards'. It concluded that Members need not identify unforeseen developments in a safeguards investigation,[107] stating:

> in the light of the principle of effective treaty interpretation, the *express omission* of the criterion of unforeseen developments in the new agreement (which otherwise transposes, reflects and refines in great detail the essential conditions for the imposition of safeguard measures provided for in Article XIX of GATT) must, in our view, have meaning.[108]

On appeal, the Appellate Body also used the principle of effectiveness, but it did so to support the opposite conclusion. The Appellate Body found that:

> the Panel failed to give meaning and legal effect to *all* the relevant terms of the *WTO Agreement*, contrary to the principle of effectiveness (*ut res magis valeat*

106 Lennard, 'Navigating by the Stars', 59.

107 Panel Report, *Argentina – Footwear (EC)*, [8.67].

108 Ibid. [8.58] (original emphasis).

quam pereat) in the interpretation of treaties . . . [I]f they had intended to *expressly omit* [the clause concerning unforeseen developments in Article XIX of GATT 1994], the Uruguay Round negotiators would and could have said so in the *Agreement on Safeguards*. They did not.[109]

The Appellate Body has faced severe criticism for holding that Members must establish the existence of unforeseen developments before imposing safeguards, given the absence of any such requirement in the Agreement on Safeguards.[110] More importantly, in relation to the use of principles, the dispute in *Argentina – Footwear (EC)* shows how two judicial tribunals can purport to use the same principle to come to different conclusions on the correct interpretation of a particular provision. Leaving to one side whether the Panel or Appellate Body used the principle of effectiveness correctly or came to the right result, this discrepancy indicates that WTO Tribunals should take care not to use principles in a haphazard fashion without paying due attention to the content and scope of the principle and its relevance and implications for the provision in question.

B. The precautionary principle

A third principle that could be said to exist in customary international law and to be relevant in the context of the WTO is the precautionary principle. The most important Appellate Body decision regarding this principle is *EC – Hormones*.[111] In that case, the European Communities argued that the precautionary principle had become a 'general customary rule of international law' or a 'general principle of law'.[112] According to the European Communities, applying this principle in the context of the SPS Agreement meant that a Member could properly impose an SPS measure even if not all scientists or Members agreed on the possibility or magnitude of the risk that the measure was intended to address.[113]

[109] Appellate Body Report, Argentina – Footwear (EC) [88] (original emphasis).

[110] See, e.g., Donald McRae, 'Reflections on the Appellate Body of the World Trade Organization (WTO): Comments on Dr. Claus-Dieter Ehlermann's Lecture' (2003) 97 *American Society of International Law Proceedings* 87, 89; Yong-Shik Lee, 'Destabilization of the Discipline on Safeguards? Inherent Problems with the Continuing Application of Article XIX After the Settlement of the Agreement on Safeguards' (2001) 35 *Journal of World Trade* 1235, 1236–42.

[111] See also Appellate Body Report, *Japan – Apples*, [233]–[234]; Appellate Body Report, *Japan – Agricultural Products II*, [81].

[112] Appellate Body Report, *EC – Hormones*, [121]. [113] Ibid.

In *EC – Hormones*, the United States and Canada disputed the characterisation of the precautionary principle as a principle of customary international law,[114] and the Appellate Body itself referred to several academic writings[115] and concluded that '[t]he status of the precautionary principle in international law continues to be the subject of debate among academics, law practitioners, regulators and judges'.[116] The Appellate Body did not take a position on whether the precautionary principle is a principle of customary international law in *EC – Hormones*;[117] nor has it done so since. Evidently, this approach could change over time with the development of international law.[118] The issue was more recently considered in *EC – Biotech*, where the Panel closely followed the earlier reasoning of the Appellate Body in *EC – Hormones*. The Panel found that 'the legal debate over whether the precautionary principle constitutes a recognized principle of general or customary international law is still ongoing',[119] and it refrained from offering a view on whether or not the precautionary principle was a principle of either customary international law or general law.[120] This is probably a good indication of WTO Tribunals' likely attitude towards principles that have not been clearly established within customary international law. As discussed in Chapter 3, these are not tribunals of general jurisdiction in international law. Accordingly, they are unlikely to take an active, conscious role in developing principles of customary international law, particularly in view of their awareness of the WTO as a 'Member-driven' organisation and the need to refrain from adding to or diminishing the rights or obligations contained in the WTO agreements.[121]

The Appellate Body in *EC – Hormones* stated that the precautionary principle is reflected in the Preamble and in Articles 3.3 and 5.7 of the SPS Agreement, which 'explicitly recognize the right of Members to establish their own appropriate level of sanitary protection, which level may be higher (i.e., more cautious) than that implied in existing international standards, guidelines and recommendations'.[122] However, the SPS Agreement does not indicate that the precautionary principle provides a justification for measures that would otherwise be

[114] Ibid. [122]. [115] Ibid. n. 92. [116] Ibid. [123]. [117] Ibid. [123].

[118] See Gabrielle Marceau, 'La jurisprudence sur le principe de précaution dans le droit de l'OMC' (Paper presented at the Inaugural Professorial Lecture, Faculty of Law, Geneva, 19 May 2005) 15–16.

[119] Panel Report, *EC – Biotech*, [7.88]. [120] Ibid. [7.87]–[7.89].

[121] DSU, arts. 3.2, 19.2 (discussed further in Chapter 3).

[122] Appellate Body Report, *EC – Hormones*, [124].

WTO-inconsistent. Accordingly, the Appellate Body found that this principle does not override Articles 5.1 and 5.2 of the SPS Agreement.[123] *EC – Hormones* thus suggests that a principle that has been incorporated in the WTO agreements will derive its meaning primarily from the relevant WTO provisions, as interpreted according to the usual VCLT rules, whether or not it is well-established in customary international law.

2.4 General principles of law

2.4.1 Introduction

A third source of international law identified in Article 38(1) of the ICJ Statute is, as set out in paragraph (c), 'the general principles of law recognized by civilized nations'. Unfortunately, like customary international law, the scope of general principles of law is contested. Cheng, in the introduction to his classic study of these principles, states:

> Some writers consider that the expression refers primarily to general principles of international law and only subsidiarily to principles obtaining in the municipal law of the various States. Others hold that it would have been redundant for the Statute to require the Court to apply general principles of international law, and that, therefore, this provision can refer only to principles obtaining in municipal law.[124]

Apart from the definition of general principles of law, the ways in which such principles can be used or applied is also uncertain. In Jennings' words, '"general principles" have no very clear meaning'[125] and are 'enigmatic'.[126] Similarly, Cheng states:

> While some writers regard them merely as a means for assisting the interpretation and application of international treaty and customary law, and others consider them as no more than a subsidiary source of international law, some modern authors look upon 'general principles' as the embodiment of the highest principles – the 'superconstitution' – of international law.[127]

Degan also notes the problems arising from general principles of law, suggesting that '[n]o other source of international law raises so many doctrinal controversies'.[128]

[123] Ibid.
[124] Bin Cheng, *General Principles of Law as Applied by International Courts and Tribunals* (1987) 2–3 (footnotes omitted).
[125] Jennings, 'What is International Law', 60–1. [126] Ibid. 71.
[127] Cheng, *General Principles of Law*, 4–5 (footnotes omitted).
[128] Degan, *Sources of International Law*, 14.

In the following sections, I first consider the origins of Article 38(1)(c) in order to understand its intended scope, and then I address its interpretation and use by the Permanent Court of International Justice (PCIJ) and ICJ. Taking note of the conceptual critiques of general principles of law, I go on to draw certain conclusions about the types of general principles of law that can be said to exist and may therefore be useful in the context of the WTO.

2.4.2 Significance of general principles of law

A. Theoretical approaches to identifying general principles of law

According to Cheng, general principles of law are 'general propositions' that 'express the essential qualities of juridical truth', as evidenced by their existence in 'the municipal law of civilized people'.[129] From this description, it is possible to discern three main theoretical approaches to identifying general principles of law: comparativism, categorism, and synthesis.[130] I consider these three approaches in turn.

Parties before the ICJ have on occasion used comparative studies of domestic law to support their arguments; for example, Portugal in the *Right of Passage Case*[131] and Malta in its application to intervene in the *Continental Shelf Case*.[132] Under the comparative approach, general principles of law are those shared by all, or at least most (or the most 'representative'),[133] systems of municipal law. This approach uses comparative law analysis to determine these shared principles.[134] Although the principles need not exist in identical form in each legal system, their application in each system must not do 'violence to the fundamental concepts of any of those systems'.[135] The process of

[129] Cheng, *General Principles of Law*, 24–5.

[130] See generally Christopher Ford, 'Judicial Discretion in International Jurisprudence: Article 38(1)(C) and "General Principles of Law"' (1994) 5 *Duke Journal of Comparative and International Law* 35, 65.

[131] *Right of Passage over Indian Territory (Portugal* v. *India) (Merits)* [1960] ICJ Rep 6, 11–12.

[132] *Continental Shelf (Tunisia* v. *Libyan Arab Jamahiriya) (Application by Malta for Permission to Intervene)* [1981] ICJ Rep 3.

[133] F. A. Mann, 'Reflections on a Commercial Law of Nations' (1957) 33 *British Yearbook of International Law* 20, 38–9.

[134] Ford, 'Judicial Discretion', 66; Wolfgang Friedmann, 'The Uses of "General Principles" in the Development of International Law' (1963) 57 *American Journal of International Law* 279, 284–5.

[135] H. C. Gutteridge, *Comparative Law* (2nd edn, 1949) 65; Friedmann, 'The Uses of "General Principles"', 285.

comparison can prevent the use in international law of 'concepts or rules which either belong exclusively to a single system or are only to be found in a few of such systems'.[136] It thus increases the legitimacy of decisions in international law: 'even the most jealously independent of national sovereigns might find it difficult to deny the legal authority of a rule accepted as fundamental by his own domestic legal system'.[137]

Comprehensive studies to identify general principles of law using the comparative approach have been enormously time-consuming and largely unsuccessful.[138] This may reflect the fact that the comparative approach leaves a number of important questions unanswered. For example, how similarly does a principle need to be applied by different legal systems to be accepted by them? Which version of a principle should be applied at the international level?[139] The comparative approach may also improperly suggest that the judge is not using discretion in identifying general principles of law, even though the judge is left to determine, for example, 'the most representative systems of municipal law'.[140] Finally, the comparative approach raises questions of legitimacy and the rule of law. In order for states to comply with international law, they must be able to identify in advance that part of international law contained in general principles of law, as well as the precise nature of those general principles that might be relevant to their proposed course of action. Yet, as Thirlway points out, the 'legal adviser of a foreign ministry is . . . unlikely to be a specialist in comparative law'.[141] Therefore, it may go too far to hold a state to a general principle of law purely because it is contained in most municipal legal systems, unless the state could be expected to have known that such a principle exists as a matter of law and reason.

Under the categorist approach, general principles of law are those that, by their inherent nature, are fundamental principles of every legal system and the basis for all law.[142] For categorists, general principles

[136] H. C. Gutteridge, 'Comparative Law and the Law of Nations' (1944) 21 *British Yearbook of International Law* 1, 10.

[137] Ford, 'Judicial Discretion', 80. [138] Ibid. 68. [139] Ibid. 72. [140] Ibid. 71.

[141] Hugh Thirlway, 'The Law and Procedure of the International Court of Justice 1960–1989: Part Two' (1990) 61 *British Yearbook of International Law* 1, 112–13.

[142] Antonio Cassese, 'The Contribution of the International Criminal Tribunal for the Former Yugoslavia to the Ascertainment of General Principles of Law Recognized by the Community of Nations' in Sienho Yee and Wang Tieya (eds.), *International Law in the Post-Cold War World: Essays in Memory of Li Haopei* (2001) 43, 52. The following extract from *Factory at Chorzów (Claim for Indemnity) (Merits)* (1928) PCIJ (ser A) No 17, 4, 29 could be seen as supporting this approach: 'it is a principle of international law,

'express the essential qualities of juridical truth itself, in short of Law'.[143] Therefore it is not necessary to undertake a comparative exercise in establishing the existence of such principles,[144] which 'bea[r] witness to the fundamental unity of law'.[145] While this approach has the advantage of apparent simplicity, it provides no guidance about what inherent features a principle must have to be recognised as a general principle of law. This is left solely to the discretion of the decision-maker.[146] It may also increase the likelihood of non-Western legal systems not being considered, because judges will rely on their own, usually Western backgrounds, when determining what is fundamental to all legal systems.[147]

Ford maintains that the preferable approach to identifying general principles of law is a combination of the comparative and categorist approaches. Under this approach of synthesis, the decision-maker identifies general principles in two steps:

- First, is the proposed principle accepted by a majority of domestic legal systems? If so, this 'gives the necessary confirmation and evidence of the juridical character of the principle concerned'.[148] This step corresponds with the comparative approach, but it does not require a vast comparative survey but evidence that the principle is widespread in municipal law.
- Second, is the principle suitable for adoption at the international level? This step, which corresponds more closely to the categorist approach, recognises that international tribunals must employ 'elements of legal reasoning and private law analogies in order to make the law of nations a viable system for application a judicial process'.[149]

and even a general conception of law, that any breach of an engagement involves an obligation to make reparation'.

143 Cheng, *General Principles of Law*, 24.

144 Frances Jalet, 'The Quest for the General Principles of Law Recognized by Civilized Nations – A Study' (1963) 10 *UCLA Law Review* 1041, 1086.

145 Cheng, *General Principles of Law*, 376, 390: 'Since the general principles of law form the basis of positive rules of law, in seeking these principles, there is no inherent reason why they cannot be found by a process of induction from the positive law of any single system, and indeed this always appears to be the inevitable starting point.'

146 Ford, 'Judicial Discretion', 74.

147 Karen Knop, 'Reflections on Thomas Franck, Race and Nationalism (1960): "General Principles of Law" and Situated Generality' (2003) 35 *New York University Journal of International Law and Politics* 437, 457.

148 Cheng, *General Principles of Law*, 25.

149 Brownlie, *Principles of Public International Law*, 16.

All three approaches to identifying general principles of law are vulnerable to the criticism that the principles identified are too general and are divorced from the qualifications and restrictions that give them real meaning. Jennings gives the example of attempts to use the principle of *pacta sunt servanda* to construct in international law an unqualified norm that contracts are always binding. Such a norm would ignore the numerous other rules that temper the principle of *pacta sunt servanda* in domestic law,[150] for example, the rule that the binding nature of a contract may be modified by certain changes in circumstances.

B. Identification and use of general principles of law in the ICJ and PCIJ

The PCIJ never based a decision directly on general principles of law; nor has the ICJ done so to date.[151] Rather, both courts have used these principles as part of their reasoning or as supporting a decision based on other grounds.[152] There are several possible reasons for this merely ancillary use of general principles of law. First, many general principles of law may be assimilated into customary international law or treaty law,[153] removing the need to refer separately to the former. Second, the development of customary international law and treaty law has shrunk the *lacunae* in international law and therefore the instances in which it might have been necessary to refer to general principles of law as a distinct source. The *lacunae* can be further shrunk through 'judicial reasoning' techniques.[154] Third, the principle that specific law prevails over general law means that customary international law and treaty law typically prevail over general principles of law.[155] Fourth, the courts may have felt that states would find their decisions more acceptable if they did not explicitly use general principles of law, which could have the potential to expand the scope of international law.[156] Fifth, the parties themselves rarely rely on general principles of law.[157]

150 Jennings, 'What is International Law', 73.
151 Degan, *Sources of International Law*, 53.
152 Ibid. 58; Mark Janis, *An Introduction to International Law* (4th edn, 2003) 58.
153 Degan, *Sources of International Law*, 8; Cheng, *General Principles of Law*, 23.
154 Maurice Mendelson, 'The International Court of Justice and the Sources of International Law' in Vaughan Lowe and Malgosia Fitzmaurice (eds.), *Fifty Years of the International Court of Justice* (1996) 63, 80–1.
155 Daniel O'Connell, *International Law* (2nd edn, 1970) vol. I, 10.
156 Friedmann, 'The Uses of "General Principles"', 280.
157 Thirlway, 'Law and Procedure', 11.

On the rare occasions when these courts have referred to general principles of law, they have often been reluctant to refer specifically to Article 38(1)(c). This may be because a reference to that provision could necessitate a comprehensive comparative analysis of municipal law.[158] Thus, the courts have used rather loose nomenclature in referring to general principles of law, for example: a 'principle and almost universal opinion and practice'; 'well-known rule'; 'a general rule'; 'an accepted principle of law'; 'a principle generally accepted in the jurisprudence of arbitration, as well as by municipal courts'; 'a principle of international law, and even a general conception of law';[159] 'the essential principle'; or a 'principle universally accepted by international tribunals'.[160]

Despite these limitations, the decisions of the ICJ and the PCIJ provide some guidance on the meaning of general principles of law. Some judges have criticised the words 'recognized by civilized nations' in Article 38 of the ICJ and PCIJ statutes as incompatible with the UN Charter and reflecting a legacy of colonialism.[161] However, ICJ jurisprudence suggests that these words mean recognised by nations with an advanced or well-developed legal system.[162] The qualification 'civilized' is largely redundant 'since any State which is a member of the international society must be considered as civilised'.[163] However, it may play a useful role in excluding nations that are under a totalitarian regime, for example Germany under the national-socialist regime.[164]

[158] Cassese states of the PCIJ: 'the principles themselves were not identified through a detailed investigation of the legal systems of the various members of the international community. This, in itself, corroborates the view that they were not applied *qua* general principles obtaining *in foro domestico*, but as general tenets capable of being induced from the rules of international law or deduced from legal logic.': Cassese, 'Contribution of the International Criminal Tribunal', 45; Degan, *Sources of International Law*, 58, 67.

[159] '[I]t is a general principle of international law, and even a general conception of law that any breach of an engagement involves an obligation to make reparation.' *Factory at Chorzów (Claim for Indemnity) (Merits)* [1928] PCIJ (ser A) No 17, 4, 29.

[160] Degan, *Sources of International Law*, 58.

[161] See, e.g., Judge Ammoun: *North Sea Continental Shelf (Federal Republic of Germany* v. *Denmark; Federal Republic of Germany* v. *Netherlands)* [1969] ICJ Rep 3, 132–3; *Barcelona Traction, Light and Power Company Ltd (Belgium* v. *Spain) (Merits)* [1970] ICJ Rep 3, 309.

[162] Thirlway, 'Law and Procedure', 124.

[163] Cheng, *General Principles of Law*, 25. See also Humphrey Waldock, 'General Course on Public International Law' (1962-II) 106 *Recueil des Cours* 1, 65.

[164] Degan, *Sources of International Law*, 69.

Although the courts have not clearly endorsed a comparative, categorist or synthesis approach, they can be seen as having recognised general principles of law in the following categories:

1. standards common to all or a majority of the various systems of municipal law (for example the procedural principle of equality of the parties);[165]
2. standards applicable to international legal relations (for example, principles concerning the sovereign immunity of states);[166]
3. standards applicable to legal relations (domestic and international) generally (for example, good faith).

Few would dispute that the first category falls within the notion of general principles of law in Article 38(1)(c) of the ICJ Statute, particularly as it corresponds to the precise wording of that provision: 'the general principles of law recognized by civilized nations'. The principles in this category are identified through inductive (descriptive) analysis, in that the judge examines municipal legal systems to extract the applicable principle. It also involves comparative analysis and reasoning in that the judge makes an analogy between the international situation at issue and the domestic situation envisaged by the municipal law. This category seems most clearly aligned with the comparative approach to identifying general principles of law.[167]

The second category is more controversial because, by definition, principles within this category cannot be found in municipal legal systems. Nevertheless, they can still be 'general principles of law recognized by civilized nations' in the sense that they are required by the international legal system in which all civilized nations participate, and

[165] Christian Dominicé, 'Methodology of International Law' in Rudolf Bernhardt (ed.), *Encyclopaedia of Public International Law* (2003) vol. III, 354, 358.

[166] See the ICJ's references to clearly 'international' principles of non-intervention and the use of force *(Military and Paramilitary Activities in and against Nicaragua (Nicaragua* v. *United States of America) (Merits)* [1986] ICJ Rep 14, 99–100, 106–7) and the principle that delimitations of the continental shelf should occur by agreement where possible *(Case Concern Delimitation of the Maritime Boundary in the Gulf of Maine Area (Canada* v. *United States of America) (Merits)* [1984] ICJ Rep 246, 292–3). See Mendelson, 'International Court of Justice', 63, 80; 'It is not clear whether general principles refers to those of the international legal system or those of municipal legal systems. Such ambiguity is advantageous, as it imposes no restraint on the principles which may be applied.': Rebecca M. M. Wallace, *International Law* (4th edn, 2002) 22; 'It is now widely accepted that article 38(1)(c) applies to principles of both international and domestic law.': Hilary Charlesworth and Christine Chinkin, *The Boundaries of International Law: A Feminist Analysis* (2000) 64; O'Connell, *International Law*, 9.

[167] Dominicé, 'Methodology of International Law', 358.

all nations have accepted them for the purpose of resolving international legal issues.[168] Like the first category, principles in the second category can be identified through inductive (descriptive) analysis, but the judge examines the international legal system rather than municipal legal systems to extract the applicable principle.

Principles under the third category can be found through inductive (descriptive) reasoning because they are present in all legal systems. However, they are 'inherent', 'unalterable and cannot change'.[169] Therefore, they can also be identified through deductive (normative) reasoning, 'a process of reflection upon the nature of law'.[170] The second and third categories correspond more closely with a categorist than a comparative approach. Finally, it is interesting to note that Cheng did not distinguish between these three categories, because he regarded general principles of law as belonging not to one particular legal system but to all such systems.[171]

2.4.3 Possible examples of relevant general principles of law

General principles of law may be one of the most difficult types of principles to identify. The broad and undefined scope of this category of principles means it may have wide-ranging implications for WTO disputes. Below, I describe some of the general principles of law that might be relevant to WTO disputes, as an illustration of the potential significance of this category.

On 13 December 1920, the First Assembly of the League of Nations unanimously adopted Article 38 of the Statute of the PCIJ, which referred in paragraph (I)(c) to 'the general principles of law recognized by civilized nations', just as Article 38(1)(c) of the ICJ Statute does today. The history of Article 38(I)(c) of the PCIJ Statute provides some examples of the principles the drafters had in mind. One Member of the Committee, the Englishman Lord Phillimore, explained that general principles of law are those 'accepted by all nations – *in foro domestico* – such as certain principles of procedure, the principle of good faith and the principle of *res judicata*, etc.'[172] He also understood maxims of law to fall

[168] Cheng suggests that general principles of law may be inferred not only from domestic practice but also from the practice of international tribunals: see Cheng, *General Principles of Law*, 309.

[169] Dominicé, 'Methodology of International Law', 358. [170] Ibid.

[171] Cheng, *General Principles of Law*, 390.

[172] PCIJ: *Advisory Committee of Jurists, Procès-verbaux of the Proceedings of the Committee, June 16th–July 24th, 1920, with Annexes*, 1920, 335. Quoted in Degan, *Sources of International Law*, 49.

under this category. According to Cheng, the *travaux préparatoires* also indicate that 'the principle that what is not forbidden is allowed, the principle proscribing the abuse of rights, the principle according to which, under special circumstances, the stronger takes rightful precedence over the weaker, and the principle *lex specialis generalibus derogate*' were also envisaged as general principles of law.[173]

The ICJ and PCIJ have recognised the following as general principles of law: a party cannot take advantage of its own wrong,[174] violation of an engagement involves an obligation to make reparation,[175] good faith,[176] estoppel,[177] *nemo judex in re sua*,[178] *restitutio in integrum*,[179] abuse of rights, *lex specialis derogate legi generali*,[180] *res judicata*,[181] *compétence de la compétence*,[182] implied powers,[183] judicial procedure,[184] and equality of the parties.[185] Thus, many general principles relate to procedural issues:

> Many questions of procedure and evidence . . . which necessarily arise in treaty and non-treaty cases alike, are not regulated by specific provisions of treaty or charter; in filling the gap, an international court will expressly or silently resort to procedural and evidentiary principles which are felt to be inherent in all civilized legal systems.[186]

[173] Cheng, *General Principles of Law*, 25–6.

[174] *Factory at Chorzów (Claim for Indemnity) (Jurisdiction)* [1927] PCIJ (ser A) No 9, 4, 31.

[175] *Factory at Chorzów (Claim for Indemnity) (Merits)* [1928] PCIJ (ser A) No 17, 4, 29.

[176] *Nuclear Tests (Australia* v. *France) (Merits)* [1974] ICJ Rep 253, 268.

[177] *Legal Status of Eastern Greenland (Denmark* v. *Norway)* [1933] PCIJ Series A/B, No 53, 22, 69; *Temple of Preah Vihear (Cambodia* v. *Thailand) (Merits)* [1962] ICJ Rep 6, 31–2.

[178] (A State cannot be a judge in its own case.) *Article 3, Paragraph 2, of the Treaty of Lausanne (Frontier between Turkey and Iraq) (Advisory)* [1925] PCIJ Series B, No 12, 6, 32.

[179] Restoration to the original position or the status quo.

[180] *Right of Passage over Indian Territory (Portugal* v. *India) (Merits)* [1960] ICJ Rep 6, 43–4.

[181] The rule that if a dispute is judged by a tribunal of competent jurisdiction, the decision of the tribunal is final and conclusive as to the rights and obligations of the parties involved. *Effect of Awards of Compensation Made by the United Nations Administrative Tribunal (Advisory Opinion)* [1954] ICJ Rep 47, 53. See Panel Report, *India – Autos*, [7.42]–[7.104].

[182] The principle that any body with jurisdictional power has the authority to determine the extent of its jurisdiction. *Interpretation of the Greco-Turkish Agreement of December 1st, 1926 (Advisory Opinion)* [1928] PCIJ (ser B) No 31, 5, 20.

[183] *Reparation for Injuries (Advisory Opinion)* [1949] ICJ Rep 174, 182–3.

[184] *Application for Review of Judgment No 158 of the United Nations Administrative Tribunal (Advisory Opinion)* [1973] ICJ Rep 166, 209, [92].

[185] *Judgments of the Administrative Tribunal of the ILO upon Complaints Made Against the UNESCO (Advisory Opinion)* [1956] ICJ Rep 77, 85.

[186] Rudolf Schlesinger, 'Research on General Principles of Law Recognized by Civilized Nations' (1957) 51 *American Journal of International Law* 734, 736. See also Panel Report, *Guatemala – Cement II*, [8.21]–[8.22].

Because of their procedural focus, general principles of law may be of particular relevance in the exercise of inherent jurisdiction by WTO Tribunals, as discussed in Chapter 3. Many of the principles outlined above could also be said to fall within or relate to the notions of good faith and due process, as addressed in Part II of this book.

2.5 Conclusion

This chapter has described and analysed the three categories of principles that form the focus of this book: principles of WTO law, principles of customary international law, and general principles of law. Like all principles, those falling within one or more of these categories may be uncertain. Some of these uncertainties are common to all three categories, such as the distinction between principles and rules, and the use of normative and descriptive theories to explain their relevance and use as discussed in Chapter 1. Others are particular to individual categories of principles, such as determining what state practice counts in customary international law. Despite the vagueness of principles in general, this chapter has provided examples of the wide array of principles that may be relevant to WTO disputes.

This chapter has also demonstrated that the mere description of something as a principle does not necessarily validate it. Individual principles must be inspected and balanced against other values and principles to determine their worth in the WTO. Many principles will be subject to exceptions and will be applicable only in certain circumstances. A WTO Tribunal using a principle to resolve a dispute must therefore have a thorough understanding of the position of the principle in WTO law or international law, as well as the legal basis for using it. In the next chapter, I consider the extent to which WTO law allows WTO Tribunals to use these three categories of principles in dispute settlement, either to interpret WTO provisions or as an independent source of obligations or rights.

3 Legal basis for using principles in WTO disputes

3.1 Introduction

In this chapter, I consider the legal basis for WTO Tribunals to use the three types of principles identified in the previous chapter in WTO disputes, taking into account the limited jurisdiction of WTO Tribunals and the DSU provisions restricting their powers and functions. Broadly, WTO Tribunals could use these principles in one of two ways: either in an interpretative manner, to understand the meaning of a particular WTO rule; or in a non-interpretative manner, as an independent substantive rule or a rule of procedure or evidence. These two ways of using principles overlap to some extent, and WTO Tribunals do not always make clear whether or how they are using such principles. This lack of clarity makes it difficult to assess the legality of WTO Tribunals' use of principles. It is also exacerbated by the fact that a principle may sometimes be used in either an interpretative or a non-interpretative manner to achieve the same result. For example, in *Turkey – Textiles*, the Panel had to decide whether certain challenged measures were attributable to Turkey or the European Communities–Turkey customs union. The Panel resolved this question by applying customary international law rules regarding state responsibility.[1] However, Bartels argues that the Panel could have used these rules in interpreting the word 'Member' in GATT 1994 to achieve the same result.[2]

Below, I first address the use of principles by WTO Tribunals to interpret WTO provisions, before turning to the relevance of such principles beyond interpretation, in both cases taking into account the relationship between WTO law and international law more generally.

[1] Panel Report, *Turkey – Textiles*, [9.33]–[9.43].

[2] Lorand Bartels, 'Applicable Law in WTO Dispute Settlement Proceedings' (2001) 35 *Journal of World Trade* 499, 512.

The chapter suggests that WTO Tribunals can and should use principles in WTO dispute settlement in an interpretative manner. In a narrower set of circumstances, it may be appropriate for Panels and the Appellate Body to use certain principles in a non-interpretative manner. These conclusions are set out in Table A at the end of this chapter and relied on in examining the use of specific principles in Part II of this book.

3.2 Using principles to interpret WTO provisions

3.2.1 Introduction

In this section, I examine how WTO Tribunals could use principles in an interpretative manner, to understand the meaning of a particular WTO rule in a dispute. I begin by explaining that interpretation is not a mechanical exercise. Three broad theories of treaty interpretation exist, and principles may play a more or less significant role according to which theory applies. In particular, the teleological approach to interpretation (focusing on the object and purpose of the treaty) provides the strongest support for using principles in an interpretative manner. It is therefore important to understand these theories before considering the specific directions on treaty interpretation laid down in the WTO agreements. As I explain below, these directions require that the WTO agreements be interpreted in accordance with 'customary rules of interpretation of public international law'.[3] An examination of these rules suggests that WTO Tribunals pay insufficient attention to the aspects of the rules that reflect teleological considerations and support the use of principles. The nature of the WTO agreements also justifies a teleological approach to interpretation and more extensive use of principles.

3.2.2 Theories of interpretation and their relationship to principles

The three main theoretical approaches to treaty interpretation[4] are subjective interpretation, textual interpretation, and teleological interpretation. According to Sinclair, these approaches reflect differing conceptions of the purpose of treaty interpretation.[5] They clearly differ

[3] DSU, art. 3.2.

[4] Francis Jacobs, 'Varieties of Approach to Treaty Interpretation: With Special Reference to the Draft Convention on the Law of Treaties Before the Vienna Diplomatic Conference' (1969) 18 *International and Comparative Law Quarterly* 318, 318.

[5] Ian Sinclair, *The Vienna Convention on the Law of Treaties* (2nd edn, 1984) 114–15.

in their answers to fundamental questions such as: Is the meaning of the text fixed when the law is enacted or does it evolve? Is the meaning of the text determined by the interpreter's understanding of what was written or by the intent behind what was written? What is the role of principles, objectives and goals? However, all three approaches have the same purpose in that they seek to determine the meaning of the legal text and give effect to the intentions of the parties. None of these three approaches to interpretation provides a guide that can be mechanically followed. Moreover, they are not mutually exclusive, so a supporter of one approach may draw on others in some circumstances.[6] I discuss these three approaches in turn.

The *subjective* approach involves interpreting a treaty according to the actual intention of the parties when they adopted the text.[7] This approach is consistent with the theory that international law is based upon the will of states. It is also consistent with the theory of originalism, which posits that the meaning of a law is fixed (except where the law uses phrases that undeniably contemplate an evolutionary meaning). Principles may be relevant in subjective interpretation where, at the time of adopting the text, the parties intended it to correlate with certain broader beliefs, or to achieve particular goals.

One difficulty with the subjective approach is that it assumes that, upon adoption, the parties actually had a particular intention about the treaty term in dispute. Sir Hersch Lauterpacht, a strong advocate of the subjective approach, identifies five situations in which this assumption would not hold: (i) two or more parties, acting in good faith, give the term different meanings from each other; (ii) one of the parties, lacking good faith, gives the term a different meaning from the other party or parties; (iii) the term is intended to conceal a lack of consensus; (iv) the parties never contemplated the subject-matter relevant to the term; or (v) terms conflict with each other.[8] Another difficulty with the subjective approach is that, even assuming that the parties did originally have a 'common intentio[n]',[9] it may be extremely difficult to establish that intention at a later stage. This is especially so given that, in a dispute, the parties are likely to make conflicting assertions as to their

[6] Ibid. 115.

[7] Hersch Lauterpacht, 'De l'interprétation des traités' (1950) 43 *Annuaire de l'Institut de Droit International* 366.

[8] Julius Stone, 'Fictional Elements in Treaty Interpretation – A Study in the International Judicial Process' (1953–55) 1 *Sydney Law Review* 344, 347–8.

[9] Appellate Body Report, *EC – Chicken Cuts*, [250].

intent.[10] Finally, the subjective approach risks confusing the treaty that the parties actually made with a treaty that the parties might have made or intended to make.

The *textual*, *objective*, or *plain meaning* approach takes the text of the treaty as the basis of interpretation.[11] The textual approach may be justified as giving effect to the intent of the parties, in that the meaning the tribunal attributes to the text reflects that intent to the extent that it is contained in the text. This involves an acknowledgement that:

> [i]t is not, in actual fact, on the intentions of the contracting parties that agreement is reached, but only on the written formulas of the treaties and only on that. It is by no means certain that agreement on a text in any way implies agreement as to intentions. On the contrary, divergent, even conflicting, intentions may perfectly well underlie a given text.[12]

In a multilateral treaty context such as the WTO, the textual approach recognises that not all parties to a treaty were necessarily involved in its negotiation. Instead, some parties may have subsequently acceded to the treaty in reliance on the apparent meaning of the text.[13] On the other hand, the textual approach can be criticised as confining the interpreter to the text of the treaty, without permitting sufficient flexibility to take account of changed circumstances.

The textual approach is often said to involve interpreting text according to its plain and ordinary meaning. However, this description requires some clarification, because the words of a treaty only have significance in their context. The meaning of a term may be informed by the entire treaty containing that provision, including the text and structure of the treaty, and principles reflected in it. This context may indicate that the parties intended a particular treaty term to have a special meaning, or which of several possible meanings they intended.[14] Therefore, even a textual interpreter may not give a treaty term its plain meaning if that meaning would clearly violate the

[10] Jeff Waincymer, *WTO Litigation: Procedural Aspects of Formal Dispute Settlement* (2002) 397.

[11] Gerald Fitzmaurice, 'The Law and Procedure of the International Court of Justice 1951–4: Treaty Interpretation and Other Treaty Points' (1957) 33 *British Yearbook of International Law* 203, 204.

[12] Professor Pescatore cited in L Neville Brown and Francis Jacobs, *The Court of Justice of the European Communities* (2nd edn, 1983) 245.

[13] Fitzmaurice, 'Law and Procedure', 205.

[14] Harvard Research in International Law, 'Draft Convention on the Law of Treaties' (1935) 29 *American Journal of International Law* (Supp) 697, 947.

principles underlying the treaty and if the text supports another meaning that does not violate those principles.

The *teleological* or *object and purpose* approach involves interpreting treaty text in light of the object and purpose of the treaty.[15] This approach maintains that the treaty 'has a certain object or purpose, and the task of the tribunal is to ascertain and establish this object or purpose, and then to interpret the treaty so as to give effect to it'.[16] Under this approach, the significance of terms in a treaty must be determined taking into account the treaty's object and purpose.[17] The words should be in harmony with, and assist in accomplishing, this object and purpose. According to some versions of the teleological approach, 'it is not only legitimate but necessary – if it will promote the presumed objects of the convention – that the tribunal should fill in gaps, correct errors, and even, in effect, amend the text in order to remove undesirable ambiguities or obscurities'.[18] However, this is inappropriate. Treaties are the result of compromise, and a provision that only supports one reading must be respected even if it appears to conflict with the treaty's objects and purposes.[19]

A treaty like the WTO agreements may have 'a variety of different, and potentially conflicting, objects and purposes.'[20] The object and purpose of a treaty may be analogous to or incorporated in principles reflected in the treaty. Thus, pursuant to a teleological approach, a text supporting two readings should be interpreted in a manner consonant with the treaty's underlying principles. For example, principles of WTO law might incorporate the object and purpose of the WTO agreements at a particular level of abstraction. The principle of special and differential treatment might be considered one of the key objects and purposes of the WTO agreements as a whole. Other principles such as proportionality and due process may be considered as subsidiary objects and purposes or more specific to particular parts of the WTO agreements.

[15] Jacobs, 'Varieties of Approach', 319. [16] Fitzmaurice, 'Law and Procedure', 208.

[17] Harvard Research in International Law, 'Draft Convention on the Law of Treaties', 947.

[18] Fitzmaurice, 'Law and Procedure', 208.

[19] Kent Greenawalt, 'Constitutional and Statutory Interpretation' in Jules Coleman and Scott Shapiro (eds.), *The Oxford Handbook of Jurisprudence and Philosophy of Law* (2002) 268, 288; Hersch Lauterpacht, 'Restrictive Interpretation and the Principle of Effectiveness in the Interpretation of Treaties' (1949) 26 *British Yearbook of International Law* 48, 83–4.

[20] Appellate Body Report, *US – Shrimp*, [17].

The teleological approach is generally considered the most normative of these three approaches to interpretation. Although teleologists are constrained by the text, they may be more creative and more ready to adopt a meaning other than the ordinary meaning and other than the meaning the parties may have originally intended. However, the teleological approach may contain elements of the other two approaches. It has a textual element to the extent that it draws the treaty's object and purpose from its text, and a subjective element to the extent that it draws the object and purpose from the intent of the original parties.[21] Moreover, all three approaches leave significant room for judicial discretion and normative judgment. Thus the textual approach often draws on policy considerations when choosing between different possible meanings.[22] The subjective approach, when it must impute intention (because the parties did not have a particular intention about the treaty term in dispute), uses factors such as 'considerations of justice, canons of fairness and good faith, and, in proper cases, an equitable reconciliation of the interests of state'.[23] In this way, the three approaches provide scope for the use of principles in interpretation.

3.2.3 *Relevance of principles in interpreting the WTO agreements*

A. Article 3.2 of the DSU

Article 3.2 is the key DSU provision that guides Panels and the Appellate Body in their interpretation of WTO agreements, and it may reflect the three theoretical approaches to interpretation to a greater or lesser degree. Article 3.2 provides:

> The dispute settlement system of the WTO is a central element in providing security and predictability to the multilateral trading system. The Members recognize that it serves to preserve the rights and obligations of Members under the covered agreements, and to clarify the existing provisions of those agreements in accordance with customary rules of interpretation of public international law. Recommendations and rulings of the DSB cannot add to or diminish the rights and obligations provided in the covered agreements.

I now consider various elements of Article 3.2 that could be seen as guidelines for the proper interpretation of all WTO provisions, and how these elements relate to principles.

[21] Fitzmaurice, 'Law and Procedure', 208–9; Jacobs, 'Varieties of Approach', 319.
[22] Ian Brownlie, *Principles of Public International Law* (5th edn, 1998) 637.
[23] Stone, 'Fictional Elements', 349.

The main interpretative direction provided by Article 3.2 of the DSU is that WTO provisions are to be clarified 'in accordance with customary rules of interpretation of public international law'. Similarly, in the context of the Anti-Dumping Agreement, Panels are to 'interpret the relevant provisions . . . in accordance with customary rules of interpretation of public international law'.[24] According to the Appellate Body, Article 3.2 'reflects a measure of recognition that the [GATT 1994] is not to be read in clinical isolation from public international law'.[25] Customary international law rules of treaty interpretation are essentially default rules that apply to treaties in the absence of states contracting out of them. They assist to 'complete' international contracts, i.e. treaties, by filling in the gaps. Therefore, even in the absence of DSU Article 3.2, the WTO agreements would fail to be interpreted using these customary rules unless they expressly provided otherwise.[26]

Panels and the Appellate Body have explicitly recognised the role of Articles 31 and 32 of the VCLT in providing 'customary rules of interpretation of public international law' pursuant to DSU Article 3.2.[27] Therefore, even though not all WTO Members are party to the VCLT, to the extent that these provisions reflect customary international law, they are binding on all WTO Members (and, indeed, all states). I discuss the relevant provisions of the VCLT in detail below.[28] For present purposes, it is simply worth noting the primary rule of interpretation in Article 31(1) of the VCLT, which is to interpret a treaty 'in good faith in accordance with the ordinary meaning to be given to the terms of the treaty in their context and in the light of its object and purpose'.

DSU Article 3.2 lists several objectives of WTO dispute settlement, including to 'clarify the existing provisions' of the WTO agreements. In addressing the need for future clarification, the drafters recognised that the WTO provisions may be uncertain or difficult to interpret in relation to particular factual circumstances. In fact, many if not all disputes will raise tough interpretational questions regarding particular WTO provisions, with opposing Members arguing in favour of different interpretations. This provides an obvious role for principles in clarifying the meaning of WTO provisions in a transparent manner,

[24] Anti-Dumping Agreement, art. 17.6(ii). [25] Appellate Body Report, *US – Gasoline*, 17.
[26] Panel Report, *Korea – Procurement*, [7.96].
[27] Appellate Body Report, *US – Gasoline*, 17; Appellate Body Report, *Japan – Alcoholic Beverages II*, 10; Appellate Body Report, *US – Shrimp*, [114], n. 152; Appellate Body Report, *Carbon Steel*, [61]; Panel Reports, *EC – Chicken Cuts*, [7.88].
[28] See below, section 3.2.3(B).

consistent with international law. For example, a principle could aid interpretation by explaining how a series of WTO provisions fit together and their underlying rationale.

Another objective described in Article 3.2 is to provide 'security and predictability to the multilateral trading system'. In *Japan – Alcoholic Beverages II*, the Appellate Body stated that this objective was to be served by acknowledging the flexibility in the WTO rules 'for reasoned judgements in confronting the endless and ever-changing ebb and flow of real facts in real cases in the real world' and that 'WTO rules are reliable, comprehensible and enforceable'.[29] This suggests that WTO Tribunals should strive to reach consistent decisions, as does the Appellate Body's recognition that adopted reports create 'legitimate expectations' among Members and should therefore be taken into account in deciding subsequent disputes.[30] Countries and private actors alike tend to structure their international affairs on the basis of their perceived rights and obligations under relevant treaties. In this way, Article 3.2 supports the use of principles, which could provide a coherent framework for interpreting rules, particularly in the face of ambiguity.[31] The more well-defined and established the principle is, the more likely it is to enhance rather than detract from security and predictability.

The requirement in DSU Article 3.2 that recommendations and rulings of the DSB not add to or diminish the rights and obligations under the WTO agreements is reiterated in DSU Article 19.2, which states:

> In accordance with paragraph 2 of Article 3, in their findings and recommendations, the panel and Appellate Body cannot add to or diminish the rights and obligations provided in the covered agreements.

It could be argued that the effect of Articles 3.2 and 19.2 is that WTO Tribunals must simply declare the law as it already exists in the covered agreements and that this will ensure that WTO Tribunals do not usurp the will of Members as expressed in the text of those agreements. This would be a literalist approach, suggesting that the WTO agreements have only one obvious interpretation and that it is the responsibility of WTO Tribunals to 'find' this interpretation. The ICJ seems to have

[29] Appellate Body Report, *Japan – Alcoholic Beverages II*, [31]. [30] Ibid. [14].

[31] William Edmundson, 'The Antinomy of Coherence and Determinacy' (1996) 82 *Iowa Law Review* 1, 2; Rolf Sartorius, 'The Justification of the Judicial Decision' (1968) 78 *Ethics* 184.

adopted this view in certain cases, arguing that it cannot create law[32] or 'legislate'.[33] Unfortunately, for reasons discussed in Chapter 1, interpretation is rarely a mechanical exercise. Although an interpreter is constrained by the text, in many circumstances different interpretations will be possible, and the interpreter will need to choose between these options. Constructing a fiction of mechanical interpretation denies these choices and hence prevents them from being subject to scrutiny and constructive criticism.

If this requirement does not mean WTO Tribunals should simply declare WTO law or read it in favour of the responding Member, what does it mean? As the Appellate Body stated in *Chile – Alcoholic Beverages*, it is difficult to 'envisag[e] circumstances in which a panel could add to the rights and obligations of a Member of the WTO if its conclusions reflected a correct interpretation and application of provisions of the covered agreements'.[34] In other words, a proper interpretation of the covered agreements will by definition not add to or diminish the rights or obligations contained in those agreements.[35] This suggests that the direction to the DSB and WTO Tribunals not to add to or diminish rights and obligations does not alter the customary rules of treaty interpretation.[36] Instead, it is but a reminder that the function of an interpreter is to determine the meaning of the text as it is rather than as it could or should be. Accordingly, this aspect of Article 3.2 does not weaken my conclusion that several other aspects of that provision support the use of principles in interpreting WTO provisions in disputes.

B. VCLT Articles 31 and 32

(i) Introduction

As already stated, the WTO agreements are to be interpreted in accordance with the rules of treaty interpretation under customary international law (DSU Article 3.2), and these rules are widely regarded

[32] *United Kingdom* v. *Iceland (Merits)* [1974] ICJ Rep 3, 19.

[33] *Legality of the Threat or Use of Nuclear Weapons* [1996] ICJ Rep 226, 237.

[34] Appellate Body Report, *Chile – Alcoholic Beverages*, [79].

[35] Robert Howse, 'The Most Dangerous Branch? WTO Appellate Body Jurisprudence on the Nature and Limits of the Judicial Power' in Thomas Cottier and Petros C. Mavroidis (eds.), *The Role of the Judge in International Trade Regulation: Experience and Lessons for the WTO* (2003) vol. IV, 11, 15.

[36] Joost Pauwelyn, *Conflict of Norms in Public International Law: How WTO Law Relates to Other Rules of International Law* (2003) 353. See Appellate Body Report, *India – Patents (US)*, [46].

as being codified in Articles 31 and 32 of the VCLT.[37] These provisions appear to rule out the subjective approach to interpretation, but leave considerable scope for discretion by adjudicators. Sinclair states that these rules 'are expressed at a level of generality sufficient to ensure that questions of interpretation will still give rise to serious divisions of opinion as among the members of international tribunals and indeed among international jurists in general'.[38] In this section, I elaborate on various aspects of these two VCLT provisions and their implications for using principles to interpret the WTO agreements.

Article 31 of the VCLT is entitled 'General rule of interpretation', and it provides:

> 1. A treaty shall be interpreted in good faith in accordance with the ordinary meaning to be given to the terms of the treaty in their context and in the light of its object and purpose.
> 2. The context for the purpose of the interpretation of a treaty shall comprise, in addition to the text, including its preamble and annexes:
>   (a) any agreement relating to the treaty which was made between all the parties in connection with the conclusion of the treaty;
>   (b) any instrument which was made by one or more parties in connection with the conclusion of the treaty and accepted by the other parties as an instrument related to the treaty.
> 3. There shall be taken into account, together with the context:
>   (a) any subsequent agreement between the parties regarding the interpretation of the treaty or the application of its provisions;
>   (b) any subsequent practice in the application of the treaty which establishes the agreement of the parties regarding its interpretation;
>   (c) any relevant rules of international law applicable in the relations between the parties.
> 4. A special meaning shall be given to a term if it is established that the parties so intended.

If the primary rules in Article 31 fail to settle an issue involved in interpreting a particular treaty or provision, secondary or

[37] See, e.g., Appellate Body Report, *US – Gasoline*, 10; *Territorial Dispute Case (Libyan Arab Jamahiriya v. Chad)* [1994] 60 ICJ Rep 6, [41]. Articles 31 and 32 do not necessarily exhaust the rules of treaty interpretation under customary international law: Campbell McLachlan, 'The Principle of Systemic Integration and Article 31(3)(c) of the Vienna Convention' (2005) 54 *International and Comparative Law Quarterly* 279, 291.

[38] Sinclair, *Vienna Convention*, 154.

supplementary techniques of interpretation can be used in accordance with Article 32 of the VCLT, which states:

Recourse may be had to supplementary means of interpretation, including the preparatory work of the treaty and the circumstances of its conclusion, in order to confirm the meaning resulting from the application of article 31, or to determine the meaning when the interpretation according to article 31:

(a) leaves the meaning ambiguous or obscure; or
(b) leads to a result which is manifestly absurd or unreasonable.

(ii) Good faith and ordinary or special meaning: Article 31(1), (4)

Article 31(1) begins by stating that 'a treaty shall be interpreted in good faith'. This flows from the fundamental requirement of treaty law that parties perform their treaty obligations in good faith.[39] In the *Aerial Incident Case*, some ICJ judges stated: 'It is consistent with enlightened practice to apply the test of reasonableness to the interpretation of international instruments – a test which follows from the ever present duty of States to act in good faith.'[40] A number of other commentators consider that good faith requires interpreters to read treaty rules reasonably, honestly, and fairly.[41] It follows from the requirement of reasonable, honest and fair interpretation that an interpretation should not lead to an outcome that is obviously absurd or unreasonable.[42] This is part of the notion of effective interpretation. As the International Law Commission (ILC) has stated:

When a treaty is open to two interpretations one of which does and the other does not enable the treaty to have appropriate effects, good faith and the objects and purpose of the treaty demand that the former interpretation should be adopted.[43]

The inclusion of the good faith requirement in Article 31(1) of the VCLT thus confirms the indeterminate nature of treaty texts, as discussed earlier in this chapter. However, it does not provide a basis for using principles in interpreting the WTO agreements, apart from the

39 This requirement is found in VCLT, art. 26 and is part of the rule *pacta sunt servanda* (agreements must be kept). Arnold McNair, *Law of Treaties* (1961), 465.

40 *Aerial Incident of July 27, 1955 (Preliminary Objections) (Israel* v. *Bulgaria)* [1959] ICJ Rep 127, 188 (Judges Sir Hersch Lauterpacht, Wellington Koo and Sir Percy Spender).

41 See, e.g., J. O'Connor, *Good Faith in International Law* (1991) 110; Sinclair, *Vienna Convention*, 120; Jacobs, 'Varieties of Approach', 333–4.

42 Sinclair, *Vienna Convention*, 120; Jacobs, 'Varieties of Approach', 333–4.

43 *Yearbook of the International Law Commission* (1966) vol. II, 219.

principle of good faith. This principle has considerable substantive content beyond that expressed in Article 31(1), and I discuss it in detail in Chapter 4.

Usually, treaty terms are given their 'ordinary meaning' in accordance with VCLT Article 31(1), meaning the normal or common meaning of the terms 'taking into account all the consequences which normally and reasonably flow from the text'.[44] This provision of the VCLT reflects a textual approach to treaty interpretation. However, in some cases, the parties may not have intended that a term have its ordinary meaning. Therefore, Article 31(4) of the VCLT states that 'a special meaning shall be given to a term if it is established that the parties so intended'. Thus, in *Mexico – Telecoms*, the Panel found that the phrase 'cost-orientated rates' was a technical term with a special meaning.[45]

Ordinary meaning can be established in a number of ways, but WTO Tribunals have been particularly keen to establish it by reference to dictionary definitions.[46] While dictionaries appear neutral and can perhaps add authenticity to a particular interpretation, their use can hide prior interpretative choices such as which dictionary to use, and which definition to use from that dictionary. Further, when a dictionary gives more than one meaning for a particular term (as is common), ordinary meaning cannot be determined without reference to context to decide which meaning was intended. Therefore, although the Panel in *US – Gambling* referred to a significant number of dictionary definitions, it noted[47] the Appellate Body's observations that 'dictionaries are important guides to, not dispositive statements of, definitions of words appearing in agreements and legal documents'[48] and 'leave many interpretive questions open'.[49] The Appellate Body in *US – Gambling* reinforced its previous cautionary statements, maintaining that 'dictionaries, alone, are not necessarily capable of resolving complex questions of interpretation, as they typically aim to catalogue all

[44] Sinclair, *Vienna Convention*, 121.

[45] Panel Report, *Mexico – Telecoms*, [7.175], [7.177].

[46] For some of the limitations of using dictionaries in interpretation, see Note, 'Looking It Up: Dictionaries and Statutory Interpretation' (1994) 107 *Harvard Law Review* 1437; *Cabell* v. *Markham*, 148 F.2d 737, 739 (2d Cir, 1945) (Judge Learned Hand).

[47] Panel Report, *US – Gambling*, [6.67].

[48] Appellate Body Report, *US – Offset Act (Byrd Amendment)*, [248].

[49] Appellate Body Report, *Canada – Aircraft*, [153].

meanings of words – be those meanings common or rare, universal or specialized'.[50]

In *EC – Biotech*, the Panel controversially stated that relevant rules of international law may assist in identifying the 'ordinary meaning' of a term under VCLT Article 31(1). The Panel said, '[s]uch rules would not be considered because they are legal rules, but rather because they may provide evidence of the ordinary meaning of terms in the same way that dictionaries do'.[51] Arguably, principles of customary international law and general principles of law, like relevant rules of international law, could be used to establish ordinary meaning.

By relying less heavily on dictionary definitions, WTO Tribunals would leave more scope for reference to principles in interpreting the ordinary meaning of particular terms. However, principles are unlikely to be helpful in determining the ordinary or special meaning of a term unless the term itself evokes a principle (for example, the principle of good faith is mentioned explicitly in DSU Article 10.3). In some instances, a term in a WTO agreement may relate to a principle that has emerged or developed in some way since the time when the agreement was adopted. This raises the question whether the term should be interpreted according to its ordinary or special meaning at the time of drafting or at the time of interpretation. This question is the subject of some debate,[52] but the correct answer in any given instance is likely to depend on the term at issue and the context, object, and purpose, as discussed in the following section. It may be easier to justify the use of current rather than outdated principles in WTO disputes, such that principles may play a greater role where an evolutionary approach to interpretation applies, which the Appellate Body has recognised as appropriate in at least some circumstances.[53]

(iii) Context, object and purpose: Article 31(1), (2)

Article 31(1) of the VCLT requires the treaty interpreter to examine the terms of the treaty 'in their context', that is, 'the place which that [term]

[50] Appellate Body Report, *US – Gambling*, [164]. See generally Federico Ortino, 'Treaty Interpretation and the WTO Appellate Body Report in US – Gambling: A Critique' (2006) 9 *Journal of International Economic Law* 117.

[51] Panel Report, *EC – Biotech*, [7.92].

[52] See, e.g., Sinclair, *Vienna Convention*, 212; Pauwelyn, *Conflict of Norms*, 268; Michael Lennard, 'Navigating by the Stars: Interpreting the WTO Agreements' (2002) 5 *Journal of International Economic Law* 17, 21–2; McLachlan, 'Principle of Systemic Integration', 292–3, 316–18.

[53] See, e.g., Appellate Body Report, *US – Shrimp*, [130].

occupies in the text to be interpreted'.[54] Article 31(2) elaborates on the meaning of context, explaining that the context comprises the text of the treaty, including its preamble and annexes, as well as agreements and instruments made in connection with the conclusion of the treaty, subject to certain conditions. As the context of a treaty term is limited to the text of the treaty and a restricted category of related agreements, it is unlikely to reveal general principles of law or customary international law principles. However, the context of a term may well incorporate principles contained in the structure of the treaty or reflected in a series of provisions. Hence, examining the context of a term in a WTO provision may provide a basis for taking into account principles of WTO law.

Article 31(1) of the VCLT also requires a treaty to be interpreted 'in the light of its object and purpose'. This suggests a teleological approach to interpretation, although the three interpretative methods described earlier all use object and purpose to some extent.[55] The Doha Declaration on TRIPS and Public Health recognises the role of object and purpose pursuant to Article 3.2 of the DSU, stating:

> In applying the customary rules of interpretation of public international law, each provision of the TRIPS Agreement shall be read in the light of the object and purpose of the Agreement as expressed, in particular, in its objectives and principles.[56]

One question that arises in relation to the object and purpose of the WTO agreements is whether the object and purpose that is relevant is that of the WTO agreements as a whole (given that they comprise one treaty) or of individual WTO agreements. Article 31(1) may leave some scope for consideration of both kinds of object and purpose. The Appellate Body recently concluded that the reference to 'its' object and purpose in Article 31(1) suggests that it is referring to the object and purpose of 'the treaty itself, in its entirety'.[57] However, the Appellate Body also stated that Article 31(1) does not exclude consideration of 'the object and purpose of particular treaty terms, if doing so assists the interpreter in determining the treaty's object and purpose on the whole'.[58]

The identification of the object and purpose of a treaty is rarely easy, as 'most treaties have no single, undiluted object and purpose but a

[54] Sinclair, *Vienna Convention*, 121. [55] Jacobs, 'Varieties of Approach', 336.
[56] Doha Declaration on TRIPS and Public Health, [5(a)].
[57] Appellate Body Report, *EC – Chicken Cuts*, [238]. [58] Ibid. [238].

variety of differing and possibly conflicting objects and purposes'.[59] The preambles to treaties often assist in understanding the problem the treaty is directed towards and explain its reason, purpose, object, or scope.[60] Preambles may thus comprise both context, and object and purpose. The WTO Tribunals frequently refer to preambles in the various WTO agreements in the course of their interpretation.[61] In particular, the Appellate Body in *US – Shrimp* indicated that the 'preamble of the WTO Agreement ... informs [all] ... the other covered agreements'.[62]

A principle of WTO law reflected in a preamble to a WTO agreement could therefore influence the interpretation of a WTO provision either as context, or as object and purpose. Principles of customary international law and general principles of law could be relevant as context or object and purpose only to the extent that they are reflected in provisions of the WTO agreements.

(iv) Relevant rules of international law: Article 31(3)(c)

Article 31(3)(c) of the VCLT ensures that 'any relevant rules of international law applicable in the relations between the parties' are also taken into account in interpreting a treaty. Therefore, in its advisory opinion on the *Legal Consequences for States of the Continued Presence of South Africa in Namibia*, the International Court of Justice stated that: 'an international instrument has to be interpreted and applied within the framework of the entire legal system prevailing at the time of the interpretation'.[63] According to Howse, this requirement enhances coherence of the international legal system by reducing conflict and inconsistency between different areas of international law.[64] Howse and Nicolaïdis suggest that this may be particularly important for

59 Sinclair, *Vienna Convention*, 130.

60 Anne Winckel, 'The Contextual Role of a Preamble in Statutory Interpretation' (1999) 23 *Melbourne University Law Review* 184.

61 See, e.g., Appellate Body Report, *Chile – Price Band System*, [196]–[197]; Appellate Body Report, *EC – Hormones*, [124], [165]; Appellate Body Report, *EC – Bananas III*, [155], [197]; Appellate Body Report, *Brazil – Desiccated Coconut*, [18].

62 Appellate Body Report, *US – Shrimp*, [129]. See also Appellate Body Report, *EC – Tariff Preferences*, [161].

63 *Legal Consequences for States of the Continued Presence of South Africa in Namibia (South West Africa) Notwithstanding Security Council Resolution 276 (1970) (Advisory Opinion)* [1971] ICJ Rep 16, 31.

64 Robert Howse, 'Adjudicative Legitimacy and Treaty Interpretation in International Trade Law: The Early Years of WTO Jurisprudence' in Joseph Weiler (ed.), *The EU, the WTO and the NAFTA: Toward a Common Law of International Law* (2000) 35, 58.

legitimacy in the context of the WTO dispute settlement system: 'Instead of presupposing that the treaty text is animated by a constitutional telos of freer trade or looking primarily within the WTO for the relevant structural principles, we emphasize the importance of non-WTO institutions and norms in treaty interpretation that represent values other than free or freer trade.'[65] The Panel in *EC – Biotech* noted that Article 31(3)(c) mandates a treaty interpreter to take into account other rules of international law. It stated that, although this provision does not prescribe a 'particular outcome . . . where consideration of all other interpretative elements set out in Article 31 results in more than one permissible interpretation, a treaty interpreter . . . would . . . need to settle for that interpretation which is more in accord with other applicable rules of international law'.[66]

A fine line distinguishes interpretation from application, and a principle may sometimes be used in either an interpretative or a non-interpretative manner to achieve the same result. For example, in *Turkey – Textiles*, the Panel had to decide whether certain challenged measures were attributable to Turkey or to the customs union between Turkey and the European Communities. The Panel resolved this question by applying customary international law rules regarding state responsibility.[67] However, Bartels argues that the Panel could have used these rules in interpreting the word 'Member' in GATT 1994 to achieve the same result.[68] The distinction between interpretation and application was similarly blurred in a number of the ICJ opinions in *Oil Platforms*.[69]

In the context of a WTO dispute, it could be that the rules of international law applicable 'between the parties' encompass only those rules that apply to all WTO Members,[70] or that they extend to rules applicable between the disputing parties even if not to all Members.[71]

[65] Robert Howse and Kalypso Nicolaïdis, 'Enhancing WTO Legitimacy: Constitutionalization or Global Subsidiarity?' (2003) 16 *Governance* 73, 75.

[66] Panel Report, *EC – Biotech*, [7.69].

[67] Panel Report, *Turkey – Textiles*, [9.33]–[9.43].

[68] Bartels, 'Applicable Law', 512.

[69] *Oil Platforms (Islamic Republic of Iran* v. *United States of America) (Merits)*, [2003] ICJ Rep 161. Duncan French, 'Treaty Interpretation and the Incorporation of Extraneous Legal Rules' (2006) 55 *International and Comparative Law Quarterly* 281, 287–91.

[70] See, e.g., Pauwelyn, *Conflict of Norms*, 261; Panel Report, *EC – Biotech*, [7.68].

[71] See, e.g., Gabrielle Marceau, 'Conflicts of Norms and Conflicts of Jurisdictions: The Relationship between the WTO Agreement and MEAs and Other Treaties' (2001) 35 *Journal of World Trade* 1081, 1087; Wolfgang Weiss, 'Security and Predictability under WTO Law' (2003) 2 *World Trade Review* 183, 196.

The former view was supported by the Panel in *EC – Biotech*, which held that the reference to 'parties' in Article 31(3)(c) of the VCLT must be interpreted in accordance with that treaty. Article 2.1(g) of the VCLT states that a party (for the purposes of the VCLT) is 'a State which has consented to be bound by the treaty and for which the treaty is in force'. The Panel maintained that this definition includes all WTO Members.[72] However, in either case, Article 31(3)(c) would include principles of customary international law because customary international law binds all WTO Members. Similarly, general principles of law are not linked to specific conventions and therefore can be seen as applying more generally to all WTO Members.

McLachlan suggests that Article 31(3)(c) of the VCLT refers to 'rules of law, and not to broader principles or considerations which may not be firmly established as rules'.[73] Thus, it could be argued that Article 31(3)(c) does not include any principles of customary international law or general principles of law because these are 'principles' rather than 'rules'. Adopting such an approach would suggest that customary international law is only included in Article 31(3)(c) to the extent that it comprises 'rules' rather than 'principles'. This places too much emphasis on the distinction between principles and rules, which, as discussed in Chapter 2, is far from clear cut. Moreover, as McLachlan states, the reference in Article 31(3)(c) to 'rules of international law' extends to 'the international legal system as a whole, many of whose rules are necessarily expressed at a high level of generality'.[74] On the other hand, it may be going too far to include all general principles of law and principles of customary international law as 'rules of international law' under Article 31(3)(c), ignoring the distinction between principles and rules altogether.[75]

WTO Tribunals have considered this issue, holding that all customary international law falls within the 'rules of international law' and that although it is less self-evident from the text of Article 31(3)(c), general principles of law must also be considered when interpreting a provision in accordance with the VCLT.[76] In *US – Shrimp*, the Appellate Body provided little justification for its claim that Article 31(3)(c) of the VCLT required it to interpret the chapeau of Article XX of the GATT 'seeking

[72] Panel Report, *EC – Biotech*, [7.68].

[73] McLachlan, 'Principle of Systemic Integration', 290. [74] Ibid. 313.

[75] See Marceau, 'Conflicts of Norms', 1087. See also *Golder v. United Kingdom* (1975) 18 Eur Court HR (ser A), [35].

[76] Panel Report, *EC – Biotech*, [7.67]; Appellate Body Report, *US –Shrimp*, [158].

additional interpretative guidance, as appropriate, from the general principles of international law'.[77] The later Panel Report in *EC – Biotech* followed this statement by the Appellate Body, but the Panel also provided an additional justification for its position, stating that 'rules of international law' must include all sources of international law, 'that is to say, (i) international conventions (treaties), (ii) international custom (customary international law), and (iii) the recognized general principles of law'.[78] It appears in these decisions that WTO Tribunals have ignored the distinction between rules and principles altogether.

The answer probably lies somewhere between these two extremes. In my view, Article 31(3)(c) of the VCLT provides a legal basis for WTO Tribunals to interpret WTO provisions in light of both principles of customary international law and general principles of law, to the extent that such principles are reflected or incorporated in particular 'rules' of international law. Indeed, this provision indicates that WTO Tribunals are obliged to take principles falling within this description into account, to the extent that they are relevant and sufficiently well-defined. Thus, the meaning of WTO provisions may be influenced by principles of customary international law and general principles of law, and the text of a WTO provision when read in light of such principles could conceivably have quite a different meaning. Indeed, a principle that constituted a *jus cogens* norm of customary international law could dramatically alter the meaning of WTO law. As will be seen below, this does not necessarily mean that WTO Tribunals may 'apply' *jus cogens* norms or any other principle of customary international law, as some suggest.[79]

(v) Supplementary means of interpretation: Article 32

Article 32 of the VCLT allows a treaty interpreter to use 'supplementary means of interpretation' either to confirm the meaning suggested by the application of Article 31, or to determine the meaning when Article 31 'leaves the meaning ambiguous or obscure' or 'leads to a result which is manifestly absurd or unreasonable'. These supplementary means 'includ[e] the preparatory work of the treaty and the circumstances of its conclusion'. In the context of the WTO, it is difficult for WTO Tribunals

[77] Appellate Body Report, *US – Shrimp*, [158]. [78] Panel Report, *EC – Biotech*, [7.67].

[79] Weiss, 'Security and Predictability', 199; Georges Abi-Saab, 'The WTO Dispute Settlement and General International Law' in Rufus Yerxa and Bruce Wilson (eds.), *Key Issues in WTO Dispute Settlement: The First Ten Years* (2005) 4, 6.

to refer to the preparatory work because no official GATT or WTO negotiating history exists. Nevertheless, Panels and the Appellate Body have used documents from various negotiating rounds in a number of cases to confirm the meaning resulting from the application of Article 31,[80] while recognising the need for caution in doing so.[81]

Although the preparatory work and circumstances of conclusion of the WTO agreements are unlikely to involve customary international law principles or general principles of law, they may reinforce or clarify principles of WTO law as defined in Chapter 2. Thus, reference to supplementary means of interpretation pursuant to Article 32 of the VCLT may provide a basis for using principles of WTO law to interpret WTO provisions in appropriate circumstances.

C. WTO agreements as a constituent instrument or a constitution

In domestic law it is sometimes suggested that an adjudicator should select an interpretative approach according to the nature of the law under consideration, such as a contract or a constitution. Similarly, in international law, some commentators have suggested that different interpretative approaches are appropriate to treaties depending on their nature.[82] In particular, it is widely accepted that the constituent instruments of international organisations, for example the UN Charter, should be interpreted differently from other multilateral treaties,[83] focusing on the text but also emphasising the object and purpose of the organisation, as well as the need for efficiency and effectiveness in its operations over time.[84]

The WTO agreements comprise a 'single undertaking',[85] meaning that they apply to all WTO Members as a whole.[86] Included in this single

[80] See, e.g., Appellate Body Report, *Japan – Alcoholic Beverages II*, n. 39; Appellate Body Report, *EC – Poultry*, [83], [100]; Appellate Body Report, *US – Gambling*, [236]–[237].

[81] See, e.g., Appellate Body Report, *EC – Export Subsidies on Sugar*, [180]; Appellate Body Report, *US – Upland Cotton*, [623]–[625], [636]–[638].

[82] See, e.g., Robert Jennings and Arthur Watts, *Oppenheim's International Law* (9th edn, 1992) vol. I, 1268; Arnold McNair, 'Functions and Differing Legal Character of Treaties' (1930) 11 *British Yearbook of International Law* 100.

[83] Tetsuo Sato, *Evolving Constitutions of International Organizations* (1996) 8.

[84] Ibid. 12; Frederic Kirgis, 'Evolving Constitutions of International Organizations by Tetsuo Sato' (1998) 92 *American Journal of International Law* 153, 154; *Reparation for Injuries (Advisory Opinion)* [1949] ICJ Rep 174.

[85] See, e.g., Appellate Body Report, *Brazil – Desiccated Coconut*, [12–13].

[86] An exception is Annex 4 to the WTO Agreement, which contains four plurilateral agreements (of which two have expired) applying to only certain WTO Members.

undertaking is the Marrakesh Agreement, which establishes the WTO as an institution and explains its functions, structure, decision-making, and Membership. Accordingly, the WTO agreements as a whole could be seen as a constituent instrument creating an international organisation. This would have two consequences for the correct approach to interpreting WTO provisions. First, it would validate references to principles that relate to the objects and purposes of the WTO agreements. Second, it would justify a greater role for principles in interpretation to the extent that this may help achieve the objectives of WTO dispute settlement.

One problem with this argument is that the special interpretative approach for constituent instruments is typically reserved to organisational provisions that 'essentially relate ... to the structure and operation of the institution'[87] and not to substantive provisions that 'are independent, in the sense that they would have a legal content even if the organization did not exist (albeit that the organization may have an important role to play in securing their observance)'.[88] The implications of expansively reading provisions so that an international organisation can operate effectively are quite different from those of expansively reading obligations on members even if they are administered by an international organisation. Accordingly, it may be inappropriate to regard all the WTO agreements as a constituent instrument, regardless of their structure as a single undertaking.

However, the Marrakesh Agreement (to the extent that it relates to the structure and operation of the WTO as an institution) and the DSU (to the extent that it relates to the structure and operation of the WTO Tribunals) may properly be treated as constituent instruments. It is true that the international jurisprudence in favour of a special interpretative approach for constituent instruments predominantly concerns constituent instruments of international organisations rather than of international tribunals. But, as Orakhelashvili notes, the ICJ's 'application of the VCLT to its Statute [in the *LaGrand Case*] reveals a tendency to extend to constituent instruments of tribunals the methods of interpretation applicable to the constituent instruments of

[87] Maurice Mendelson, 'Reservations to the Constitutions of International Organizations' (1971) 45 *British Yearbook of International Law* 137, 146.

[88] Ibid. See Sato, *Evolving Constitutions*, 229.

international organisations'.[89] Given this convergence, the objects and purposes of the WTO Agreement and the DSU (and thereby certain principles) may be particularly important in interpreting them.

A related suggestion in interpreting the WTO agreements is that these are constitutional documents, in the sense of depicting 'an attitude and a framework capable of reasonably balancing and weighing different, equally legitimate and democratically defined basic values and policy goals of a polity dedicated to promote liberty and welfare in a broad sense',[90] or generating 'a set of constitutional-type norms and structures by judicial decision-making'.[91] This could provide an additional basis for suggesting that WTO Tribunals should take into account principles in interpreting the WTO agreements.

Howse argues against such an approach. He explains that, in *India – Patents (US)*,[92] the Appellate Body reversed the Panel's invocation of 'a principle of legitimate expectations',[93] thereby rejecting the use of 'general principles underlying the treaty regime' in interpreting the WTO agreements.[94] Howse sees this as a correct rejection of the proposition that the WTO agreements have 'an *internal* normativity or an internal *telos*, in the light of which the written positive law is to be interpreted and evolved'.[95] In his view, no global community (*demos*) holding shared values exists to lend legitimacy to 'unwritten structural or "constitutional" principles of trade law' in resolving interpretative controversies in the WTO.[96] This contrasts with human rights treaties, which, 'although they remain formally in the mode of classic interstate

[89] Alexander Orakhelashvili, 'Questions of International Judicial Jurisdiction in the LaGrand Case' (2002) 15 *Leiden Journal of International Law* 105, 118.

[90] Thomas Cottier, Matthias Oesch and Thomas Fischer, *International Trade Regulation: Law and Policy in the WTO, the EU and Switzerland* (2005) 534.

[91] Deborah Z. Cass, 'The "Constitutionalization" of International Trade Law: Judicial Norm-Generation as the Engine of Constitutional Development in International Trade' (2001) 12 *European Journal of International Law* 39, 39, 41–2. See generally Deborah Z. Cass, *The Constitutionalization of the World Trade Organization: Legitimacy, Democracy, and Community in the International Trading System* (2005).

[92] Appellate Body Report, *India – Patents (US)*, [33]–[48]. See also Appellate Body Report, *EC – Computer Equipment*, [83]–[88].

[93] This view can be compared to the concept of 'legitimate expectations' being imported into the test for establishing a non-violation complaint under Article XXIII:1(b) of GATT 1994. See Ernst-Ulrich Petersmann, *The GATT/WTO Dispute Settlement System: International Law, International Organizations and Dispute Settlement* (1997) 170–5; Panel Report, *Japan – Film*; [1050]; Appellate Body Report, *EC – Asbestos*, [182], [185]–[186].

[94] Robert Howse, 'The Jurisprudential Achievement of the WTO Appellate Body: A Preliminary Appreciation' (Working Paper, University of Michigan, 2004) 9.

[95] Ibid. [96] Ibid. 8–9.

obligation, *directly* engage citizens as bearers of rights, and the rights protected arguably themselves point to a universal community of humankind'.[97] Moreover, according to Howse, different considerations apply to the use of public international law norms in interpreting the WTO agreements, since such norms reflect 'global public opinion and values'.[98]

Applying the framework for principles established in Chapter 2 of this book to Howse's arguments, he appears to deny the legitimacy of using 'principles of WTO law' in interpreting the WTO agreements, while endorsing the use of principles of customary international law in interpreting those agreements. However, commentators such as Petersmann query the basis for this distinction, arguing that the WTO can also been seen as protecting values[99] such as economic freedom, which can be viewed as a form of human right.[100] Moreover, the multilateral trading system is 'composed not only of States but also, indeed mostly, of individual economic operators'.[101] Like human rights treaties, WTO agreements directly engage individuals, in that government barriers to free trade can affect individuals' abilities to run businesses, make consumer choices, and decide how to apply their talents and skills.

In any case, regardless of whether the WTO agreements incorporate values shared by some global community, principles drawn from the structure or underlying rationale of these agreements will frequently be relevant considerations pursuant to the customary international law rules on treaty interpretation, as discussed earlier. In particular, principles of WTO law may be reflected in the text, context, and object and purpose of a given provision.

3.3 Using principles to resolve WTO disputes: beyond interpretation

3.3.1 *Introduction*

The previous section concerned the use by WTO Tribunals of principles in interpreting the WTO agreements. In this section, I consider the

[97] Ibid. 10. [98] Ibid. 15.

[99] See Joost Pauwelyn, 'The Nature of WTO Obligations' (Working Paper No 1/02, Jean Monnet Centre for International and Regional Economic Law & Justice, 2002) 16.

[100] Ernst-Ulrich Petersmann, 'Trade Policy as a Constitutional Problem: On the Domestic Policy Functions of International Rules' (1996) 41 *Aussenwirtschaft* 405.

[101] Panel Report, *US – Section 301 Trade Act*, [7.76].

possibilities for WTO Tribunals, within their jurisdiction, to use principles in a non-interpretative manner in WTO disputes. Jurisdiction refers to the scope of a court or tribunal's power to hear claims and proceedings, examine and determine the facts, interpret and apply the law, make orders, and declare judgment.[102] Three relevant elements of jurisdiction can be identified: subject-matter jurisdiction (the particular types of claims and proceedings that may be brought before a court or tribunal); applicable law (the law that a court or tribunal may interpret and apply); and inherent jurisdiction (the court or tribunal's intrinsic powers, derived from its nature as a judicial body). Some treaties clearly distinguish between these three jurisdictional elements. For example, the *United Nations Convention on the Law of the Sea* clearly distinguishes between subject-matter jurisdiction of the International Tribunal for the Law of the Sea and the law that the tribunal is to apply.[103]

The DSU draws no explicit distinction between these jurisdictional elements of WTO Tribunals. Below, I consider these elements in turn in order to determine whether WTO Tribunals could address claims regarding principles as part of their subject-matter jurisdiction, apply principles (as defences or otherwise) in resolving claims, or use principles in the exercise of inherent jurisdiction.

3.3.2 *Subject-matter jurisdiction of WTO Tribunals: principles as claims?*

The subject-matter jurisdiction of WTO Tribunals limits the types of claims that a Member may bring before them. The first question that arises in connection with the non-interpretative use of principles is therefore whether principles could form the basis of a claim brought to a WTO Tribunal.

DSU Article 3.2 suggests that the subject-matter jurisdiction of WTO Tribunals is limited to matters concerning WTO agreements when it states that the WTO dispute settlement system 'serves to preserve the rights and obligations of Members under the covered agreements'. More specifically, DSU Article 1.1 limits the operation of the DSU to 'disputes brought pursuant to the consultation and dispute settlement provisions of the agreements listed in Appendix 1' of the DSU and disputes regarding rights and obligations under the Marrakesh Agreement

[102] Peter Nygh and Peter Butt (eds.), *Australian Legal Dictionary* (1997) 651.

[103] *United Nations Convention on the Law of the Sea*, opened for signature 10 December 1982, 1833 UNTS 3 (entered into force 16 November 1994) art. 288(1), (2).

or the DSU. The relevant provisions of these covered agreements vary, but in general Members may bring two main types of complaint: violation complaints (alleging the failure of another Member to carry out its obligations under a covered agreement)[104] and non-violation complaints (alleging that a Member has applied a measure that does not necessarily conflict with a WTO provision but that nullifies or impairs a benefit accruing directly or indirectly under a covered agreement or that impedes the attainment of an objective of a covered agreement).[105]

A principle of WTO law could form the basis for a violation complaint or a non-violation complaint. As discussed in Chapter 2, in order to be a part of WTO law, a principle must have a basis in the WTO agreements, although this does not require a specific reference to the principle in any provision. The more closely anchored the principle to the text of the WTO agreements, the more likely the complaint would be within jurisdiction. In order for a violation complaint to be based upon a principle the WTO agreements would need to refer directly to that principle. For example, good faith appears in Articles 3.10 and 4.3 of the DSU (see Chapter 4). In contrast, non-violation complaints do not require a direct breach of a WTO provision. Rather, these complaints by their very nature are 'based on broader legal principles' that underpin the WTO system, including the 'effectiveness of treaty obligations . . . reciprocity and *bona fide* protection of "reasonable expectations"'.[106]

Certain additional DSU provisions further delineate the subject-matter jurisdiction of particular WTO Tribunals. Beginning with Panels, Article 7.1 of the DSU sets out the standard terms of reference as follows:

> To examine, in the light of the relevant provisions in (name of the *covered agreement(s)* cited by the parties to the dispute), the matter referred to the DSB by (name of party) in document . . . and to make such findings as will assist the DSB in making the recommendations or in giving the rulings provided for in that/those agreement(s).[107]

This provision appears to restrict the subject-matter jurisdiction of Panels to claims based on the covered agreements, whether through

[104] GATT 1994, art. XXIII:1(a); GATS, art. XXIII:1. If made out, such a violation is presumed to nullify or impair benefits accruing under WTO agreements: DSU, art. 3.8.

[105] GATT 1994, art. XXIII:1(b); GATS, art. XXIII:3; DSU, art. 26.1.

[106] Petersmann, *GATT/WTO Dispute Settlement System*, 172. [107] Emphasis added.

violation or non-violation complaints.[108] Only if non-standard terms of reference[109] were adopted for a particular Panel might a Panel consider other claims.[110] This means that a Panel could not normally treat principles of customary international law or general principles of law, of themselves, as the basis for a WTO claim. A claim could only be based on such principles to the extent that they were incorporated in the WTO agreements.[111] For example, as described in Chapter 2, the Appellate Body has suggested that the 'precautionary principle' is reflected in the preamble and in Articles 3.3 and 5.7 of the SPS Agreement.[112] This conclusion is supported by Articles 3.7, 3.8, and 19.1 of the DSU, which all focus on the consistency of measures with the covered agreements.[113]

Turning to the provisions regarding the Appellate Body specifically, Article 17.6 of the DSU limits appeals to 'issues of law covered in the panel report and legal interpretations developed by the panel'. This means that the Appellate Body's subject-matter jurisdiction is a subset of Panels' subject-matter jurisdiction. Moreover, the Appellate Body may refuse to consider a claim or argument that a Member could have made but did not make at the Panel stage, on the grounds that this would fall outside the scope of Article 17.6.[114] The Appellate Body also sometimes declines to address claims that a Member made before the Panel if the Panel exercised judicial economy in relation to those claims or did not fully address them.[115] Accordingly, the possibility of the Appellate Body using principles as the basis for claims would be largely the same as for Panels.

The only claim that a Member could make before the Appellate Body that it could not make at the Panel stage would be a challenge to the Panel's fulfilment of its functions.[116] To this extent only, the Appellate Body might have subject-matter jurisdiction to consider a new claim on the basis of a principle, namely the principle of due process, as discussed further in Chapter 5. In these circumstances, the principle

108 Marceau, 'Conflicts of Norms', 1107; Pauwelyn, *Conflict of Norms*, 444. See Joel Trachtman, 'Book Review of Joost Pauwelyn, Conflict of Norms in Public International Law' (2004) 98 *American Journal of International Law* 855, 857.

109 DSU, art. 7.3. 110 Pauwelyn, *Conflict of Norms*, 444. 111 Ibid. 445.

112 Appellate Body Report, *EC – Hormones*, [124].

113 See Joel Trachtman, 'The Jurisdiction of the World Trade Organization' (2004) 98 *American Society of International Law Proceedings* 139, 140 (referring to these provisions in connection with applicable law).

114 See, e.g., Appellate Body Report, *Canada – Aircraft*, [211].

115 See, e.g., Appellate Body Report, *EC – Poultry*, [107].

116 See Appellate Body Report, *US – Countervailing Measures on Certain EC Products*, [74].

would most likely be linked to the DSU as a whole or to specific provisions of the DSU such as Article 11 or 12.7.

Apart from regular Panel and Appellate Body proceedings, WTO Tribunals may conduct three types of WTO dispute settlement proceedings that are connected to the implementation of recommendations or rulings that the DSB has made in adopting previous Panel or Appellate Body reports involving successful challenges to a Member's measure. The three types of proceedings may all arise in a given dispute, depending on how quickly and fully the Member concerned implements any adverse DSB rulings.

First, Article 21.3(c), provides for arbitration on the period of time provided for a Member to comply with recommendations and rulings of the DSB. The Article 21.3(c) arbitrator's subject-matter jurisdiction is limited to identifying a reasonable period of time for compliance,[117] and it could not address any other claim pursuant to a principle.

The second type of implementation proceedings under the DSU arises pursuant to Article 21.5. Where there 'is disagreement as to the existence or consistency with a covered agreement of measures taken to comply with the recommendations and rulings', the matter can be considered by what is often termed a 'compliance Panel' (which is often the original Panel); this decision may also be appealed to the Appellate Body. In Article 21.5 proceedings, a Member may claim that the measure taken by a Member to comply with DSB recommendations and rulings does not comply with those rulings or is otherwise inconsistent with the WTO agreements.[118] The scope for basing claims on principles is therefore the same as for regular Panel and Appellate Body proceedings. A Member could not bring an Article 21.5 claim on the basis of inconsistency with a principle of customary international law or a general principle of law not incorporated in any WTO provision.

The third type of implementation proceeding is in DSU Article 22.6, which provides for arbitration on the allowed level or type of suspension of concessions or other obligations in response to a Member's failure to implement recommendations and rulings of the DSB within a reasonable period of time. The Article 22.6 arbitrator (often the original Panel) also has a narrow subject-matter jurisdiction, which may include identifying a level of suspension of concessions that is equivalent to the

[117] See, e.g., Award of the Arbitrator, *US – Gambling*, [28], [33].

[118] See, e.g., Appellate Body Report, *Brazil – Aircraft (Article 21.5 – Canada)*, [35]–[36], [40]; Appellate Body Report, *EC – Bed Linen (Article 21.5 – India)*, [79].

level of the nullification or impairment resulting from the failure to implement[119] and determining whether the concessions to be suspended accord with the principles and procedures set out in Article 22.3 of the DSU (for example, preferably in the same sector as the nullification or impairment or otherwise under the same agreement).[120] This leaves little room for claims based on principles as defined in this book.

3.3.3 Principles as applicable law in WTO disputes

Whereas a broad consensus exists on the limitation of WTO Tribunals' subject-matter jurisdiction to claims pursuant to the WTO agreements,[121] the law that WTO Tribunals may apply in deciding a claim that is properly before them (the applicable law) is contested. This is primarily because the DSU does not address this question explicitly, in contrast to Article 38(1) of the ICJ Statute and Article 293(1) of the *United Nations Convention on the Law of the Sea*. However, it seems clear that, just as WTO Tribunals may hear claims based on principles of WTO law, so too may they apply principles of WTO law in resolving disputes. Obviously, the justification for doing so will be greater where the principles are emphasised in WTO provisions. For the purposes of this chapter, the problem lies in determining whether WTO Tribunals may apply other sources of international law (in particular, principles of customary international law and general principles of law) in resolving WTO disputes, where these sources are not incorporated into WTO provisions. Below, I first set out the main positions on this question before drawing my own conclusion.

According to Pauwelyn, the absence in the DSU of an express prohibition on WTO Tribunals applying non-WTO sources of international law leads to the conclusion that WTO Tribunals can and should apply non-WTO law in resolving WTO disputes.[122] He quotes the ICJ's 1971 *South West Africa Advisory Opinion*: the 'silence of a treaty as to the existence of . . . a right cannot be interpreted as implying the exclusion

119 DSU, art. 22.4.

120 Some arbitrators have also assessed the consistency of compliance measures, in the absence of prior Article 21.5 proceedings (see Decision by the Arbitrators, *EC – Bananas III (US) (Article 22.6 – EC)*, [4.1]–[4.15]). This is now rare due to the common practice of the parties to reach an agreement on sequencing of proceedings under Articles 21.5 and 22.6, pending resolution of this sequencing issue in the Doha negotiations.

121 See above, section 3.3.2, n. 108.

122 Joost Pauwelyn, 'The Role of Public International Law in the WTO: How Far Can We Go?' (2001) 95 *American Journal of International Law* 535, 561.

of a right which has a source outside of the treaty, in general international law'.[123] This would mean that a principle of customary international law or a general principle of law could provide a defence to a WTO violation, even if the relevant international law principle was not reflected in any WTO provision.[124] Bartels takes a similar view to Pauwelyn, in that he considers that WTO Tribunals may apply various sources of international law given the absence of an express prohibition.[125] However, he reads DSU Articles 3.2 and 19.2 as establishing a conflicts rule that prevents WTO Tribunals from applying international law that is incompatible with WTO law.[126] Hilf and Goettsche go so far as to say that Articles 3.2 and 7 of the DSU have the effect of 'bringing into the WTO system all sources of law stated in Article 38(1) of the Statute of the ICJ' as applicable law in WTO disputes, as long as those disputes arise within the limited jurisdiction of WTO Tribunals (who are limited by the DSU to hear claims that arise under WTO covered agreements).[127]

The Panel in *Korea – Procurement* also concluded that international law applies in the WTO to the extent that the Members have not contracted out of it, stating:

> Customary international law applies generally to the economic relations between the WTO Members. Such international law applies to the extent that the WTO treaty agreements do not 'contract out' from it. To put it another way, to the extent there is no conflict or inconsistency, or an expression in a covered WTO agreement that implies differently, we are of the view that the customary rules of international law apply to the WTO treaties and to the process of treaty formation under the WTO.[128]

The Appellate Body has not yet pronounced on this view, but it could be argued that international arbitrations support it. For example, in *Rann of Kutch*[129] and *Taba*,[130] no reference was made to the applicable law.

123 *Legal Consequences for States of the Continued Presence of South Africa in Namibia (South West Africa) notwithstanding Security Council Resolution* 276 (1970) *(Advisory Opinion)* [1970] ICJ Rep 16, [96].

124 See, e.g., Bartels, 'Applicable Law', 503. 125 Ibid. 126 Ibid. 506–9.

127 Meinhard Hilf and Goetz J. Goettsche, 'The Relation of Economic and Non-Economic Principles in International Law' in Stefan Griller (ed.), *International Economic Governance and Non-Economic Concerns: New Challenges for the International Legal Order* (2003) 12–14.

128 Panel Report, *Korea – Procurement*, [7.96] (footnotes omitted).

129 *Indo-Pakistan Western Boundary (Rann of Kutch) Case (India* v. *Pakistan)* (1968) 50 ILR 2.

130 *Agreement to Arbitrate the Boundary Dispute concerning the Taba Beachfront, Egypt-Israel (1986)* text in (1987) 26 ILR 1; *Boundary Dispute Concerning the Taba Area, Arbitration Award, (1988)*, text in (1988) 27 ILM 1421.

The arbitral courts in both cases followed the usual practice and 'assumed that what the parties wanted was a decision based on international law and gave their judgments accordingly'.[131] However, as discussed further below, the DSU does appear to make reference to the applicable law, so these authorities may not be very influential. The Appellate Body's refusal to apply the bilateral Oilseeds Agreement in *EC - Poultry* could also indicate that it regards only the covered agreements as applicable law.[132]

In my view, the presumption that WTO Tribunals may apply all sources of international law except to the extent that their use is expressly prohibited seems inappropriate, as would be a presumption that WTO Tribunals may apply only laws that are expressly allowed or mandated. The answer to whether the applicable law in WTO disputes includes principles of customary international law or general principles of law requires an interpretation of the relevant DSU provisions in accordance with the usual rules for interpreting treaties as discussed earlier. If there is a presumption in the process of interpreting DSU provisions regarding the applicable law, it is that the dispute settlement process must be effective, not that international law may or may not be applied in resolving WTO disputes.

Some of the DSU provisions addressed earlier in identifying the subject-matter jurisdiction of WTO Tribunals and the role of principles in interpreting WTO provisions could also shed light on the applicable law in WTO disputes. For example, the standard Panel terms of reference in Article 7.1 suggest that the applicable law is that contained in the covered agreements,[133] which would therefore exclude customary international law principles and general principles of law not reflected in those agreements. This is supported by the requirement in Article 7.2 that Panels 'address the relevant provisions in any covered agreement or agreements cited by the parties to the dispute'.[134] Article 11 also suggests that the law Panels are to apply is WTO law:[135]

> The function of panels is to assist the DSB in discharging its responsibilities under this Understanding and the covered agreements. Accordingly, a panel

[131] J. Merrills, *International Dispute Settlement* (3rd edn, 1998) 100.

[132] Joel Trachtman, 'Jurisdiction in WTO Disputes' in Rufus Yerxa and Bruce Wilson (eds.), *Key Issues in WTO Dispute Settlement* (2005) 132, 140.

[133] Joel Trachtman, 'The Domain of WTO Dispute Resolution' (1999) 40 *Harvard International Law Journal* 333, 342; Marceau, 'Conflicts of Norms', 1102.

[134] Marceau, 'Conflicts of Norms', 1102. [135] Weiss, 'Security and Predictability', 193.

should make an objective assessment of the matter before it, including an objective assessment of the facts of the case and *the applicability of and conformity with the relevant covered agreements*, and make such other findings as will assist the DSB in making the recommendations or in giving the rulings provided for in the covered agreements.[136]

Based on these provisions, the applicable law of WTO Tribunals appears limited to the law reflected in the WTO agreements, and it is only to that extent that WTO Tribunals may apply principles of customary international law or general principles of law in resolving disputes.

Other DSU provisions are less relevant to defining the applicable law in WTO disputes. Articles 3.2 and 19.2 of the DSU are sometimes said to limit the applicable law to WTO law because applying non-WTO law would involve adding to or diminishing the rights and obligations in the covered agreements.[137] Yet, as explained earlier, I regard these provisions as adding little to the correct interpretation of the WTO agreements. If the correct interpretation were that WTO Tribunals may apply non-WTO international law in resolving disputes, to do so would not add to or diminish Members' rights and obligations. And if international law beyond WTO law is not independently applicable in WTO disputes, then these provisions have no operation as a conflicts rule.[138] Finally, some contend that the reference in Article 3.2 of the DSU to 'customary rules of interpretation of public international law' demonstrates that WTO Tribunals may apply customary international law.[139] However, the better view is that this reference simply supports the use of Articles 31 and 32 of the VCLT in interpreting WTO provisions.[140]

To the extent that the applicable law of WTO Tribunals is WTO law, WTO law necessarily prevails over conflicting principles of customary international law or general principles of law. However, this conclusion relates solely to the question of applicable law and does not affect my earlier discussion of how to interpret WTO provisions. In the process of interpretation, WTO law cannot be said to prevail over principles of

[136] Emphasis added.

[137] See, e.g., Marceau, 'Conflicts of Norms', 1102; Trachtman, 'Domain of WTO Dispute Resolution', 342; 144; Debra Steger, 'Jurisdiction of the WTO' (2004) 98 *American Society of International Law Proceedings* 142, 144.

[138] Weiss, 'Security and Predictability', 193.

[139] Mitsuo Matsushita, Thomas Schoenbaum and Petros Mavroidis, *The World Trade Organization – Law and Practice* (2003) 55; David Palmeter and Petros Mavroidis, 'The WTO Legal System: Sources of Law' (1998) 92 *American Journal of International Law* 398, 399.

[140] Trachtman, 'Jurisdiction of the World Trade Organization', 139–40.

customary international law or general principles of law. Rather, the meaning of a given WTO provision must simply be determined in accordance with the customary rules of interpretation in public international law, including relevant rules of international law under Article 31(3)(c) of the VCLT. Nevertheless, the distinction between application and interpretation is not concrete, and it may in some cases be difficult to determine whether a WTO Tribunal is applying international law or simply using international law to interpret a WTO provision.

3.3.4 Principles within the inherent jurisdiction of WTO Tribunals

If WTO Tribunals possess inherent jurisdiction, this may allow them to use principles in a non-interpretative manner in WTO disputes, even though the DSU does not expressly confer such a power on them. This use of principles would represent a limited exception to the general rule, discussed above, that the applicable law of WTO Tribunals is limited to the law reflected in the WTO agreements. Domestic common law systems often employ the notion of inherent jurisdiction, typically to explain the authority of certain courts to regulate aspects of their own procedure to ensure the proper administration of justice.[141] However, international tribunals have also recognised inherent jurisdiction. This section begins by explaining that WTO Tribunals have inherent jurisdiction because they are international judicial tribunals. It then considers the scope of the Appellate Body's inherent jurisdiction in order to determine whether this may allow it to make non-interpretative use of principles.

A. WTO Tribunals have inherent jurisdiction

WTO Tribunals are judicial tribunals that follow a judicial process. In determining claims, WTO Tribunals act independently, much like international courts. They fix the boundaries of the dispute before them, marshal the evidence, determine the appropriate law, apply that law to the facts, and reach a decision. Some features of WTO dispute settlement are not typical of international judicial bodies. First, Panels are established on an ad hoc basis by the DSB, which is a political body comprising representatives of all WTO Members. Second, Panels and the Appellate Body merely issue recommendations, which the DSB must adopt if they are to have any legal effect. However, neither of these features significantly weakens the characterisation of WTO

[141] Nygh and Butt, *Australian Legal Dictionary*, 599.

adjudicating bodies as judicial. Primarily, this is because the exceptional rule of decision-making through negative consensus in Articles 6.1, 16.4 and 17.14 of the DSU renders the establishment of Panels and the adoption of reports essentially automatic.[142] This explains why Weiler has stated that 'the Appellate Body is a court in all but name'.[143] Similarly, McRae states that, 'although the euphemism "quasi-judicial" is sometimes used to describe the WTO dispute settlement process, in practice and in substance, it is a judicial process'.[144]

If WTO Tribunals are judicial, this means that they have inherent jurisdiction, like all other international judicial tribunals. This inherent jurisdiction (also termed incidental or implied jurisdiction) flows from the nature of the judicial function and does not depend on specific provisions in the instrument establishing the court or tribunal for its existence (although it does for its limits).[145] As the ICJ stated in the *Nuclear Tests Cases*:

> inherent jurisdiction ... derives from the mere existence of the Court as a judicial organ established by the consent of States, and is conferred upon it in order that its basic judicial functions may be safeguarded.[146]

Similarly, according to Orakhelashvili, 'the judicial nature of international tribunals and inherent powers following therefrom may produce a jurisdiction "supplement" not directly foreseen under a given jurisdictional clause'.[147] Inherent jurisdiction is the source of the incidental powers that an international court or tribunal needs to maintain and exercise its subject-matter jurisdiction and judicial function.[148] In some ways, inherent jurisdiction is analogous to the implied powers of international organisations, both resulting in the granting of powers to the body that are essential to the performance of its duties. The ICJ has held that, under international law, an organisation such as the United Nations is 'deemed to have those powers which, though not expressly provided in the Charter, are conferred upon it by necessary implication

142 See generally Pauwelyn, 'Role of Public International Law', 553.

143 Joseph Weiler, 'The Rule of Lawyers and the Ethos of Diplomats – Reflections on the Internal and External Legitimacy of WTO Dispute Settlement' (2001) 35 *Journal of World Trade* 191, 201.

144 Donald McRae, 'What is the Future of WTO Dispute Settlement?' (2004) 7 *Journal of International Economic Law* 3, 8.

145 H. Briggs, 'The Incidental Jurisdiction of the International Court of Justice as Compulsory Jurisdiction' in F. A. Frhr vd Heydte et al. (ed.), *Völkerrecht und Rechtliches Weltbild. Festschrift für Alfred Verdross* (1960).

146 *Nuclear Tests (Australia v. France) (Merits)* [1974] ICJ Rep 253, 259–60.

147 Orakhelashvili, 'Questions of International Judicial Jurisdiction', 115. 148 Ibid. 107.

as being essential for the performance of its duties'.[149] Even if WTO Tribunals were considered mere 'quasi-judicial' bodies (which I contend they should not), this does not prevent them from having inherent jurisdiction in relation to their judicial functions. WTO Tribunals must, under their standard terms of reference as specified in Article 7.1 of the DSU, make such findings under the relevant covered agreements 'as will assist the DSB in making the recommendations or in giving the rulings provided for in that/those agreement(s)'. This requires WTO Tribunals to gather evidence, make factual determinations, interpret covered agreements, and apply those interpretations to the facts of the dispute in order to make rulings or recommendations (even if those rulings or recommendations are not enforceable until adopted by negative consensus by the DSB). Thus incidental powers required for a WTO Tribunal to fulfil these functions are a part of their inherent jurisdiction, even if these powers have no basis in the text of the DSU.

B. Scope of the inherent jurisdiction of WTO Tribunals

Before turning to inherent jurisdiction in WTO Tribunals in particular, it is worth examining the content of inherent jurisdiction in international law more generally. The Trial Chamber of the International Criminal Tribunal for the former Yugoslavia has indicated that its inherent jurisdiction provides all the powers essential to fulfilling its mission in a just and efficient manner.[150] More specifically, the ICJ has described its inherent jurisdiction as providing it with the power to take such action as might be required to ensure that the exercise of its subject-matter jurisdiction is not frustrated, 'to provide for the orderly settlement of all matters in dispute', 'to ensure the observance of the "inherent limitations on the exercise of the judicial function" of the Court, and to "maintain its judicial character"'.[151] Pauwelyn[152] would add to these elements of inherent jurisdiction the ability of a court or tribunal to: (i) 'interpret the submissions of the parties' to 'isolate the real issue in the case and to identify the object of the claim';[153]

[149] *Reparation for Injuries (Advisory Opinion)* [1949] ICJ Rep 174.

[150] *Kupreskic et al. Case* (IT-95-16), International Criminal Tribunal for the former Yugoslavia, Judgment of 14 January 2000, [739].

[151] *Nuclear Tests (Australia* v. *France) (Merits)* [1974] ICJ Rep 253, 259 quoting in parts *Northern Cameroons (Cameroons* v. *United Kingdom)* [1963] ICJ Rep 15, 29. See also *Bremer Vulkan* v. *South India Shipping* [1981] AC 909, 971.

[152] Pauwelyn, *Conflict of Norms*, 447–8.

[153] *Nuclear Tests (Australia* v. *France) (Merits)* [1974] ICJ Rep 253, 262.

(ii) determine whether it is competent to hear a particular matter;[154] (iii) determine whether it should refrain from exercising jurisdiction that has been established;[155] and (iv) decide all issues concerning the exercise of its substantive jurisdiction, including 'claims under rules on burden of proof, due process, and other general international rules on the judicial settlement of disputes or state responsibility'.[156]

From these descriptions, it is evident that an international judicial tribunal's inherent jurisdiction cannot be precisely delineated. However, a key feature of inherent jurisdiction is that it concerns procedural as opposed to substantive matters. This feature is also reflected in the limited WTO jurisprudence on inherent jurisdiction, as shown in the following paragraphs.

Like other international judicial tribunals, the Appellate Body has recognised that WTO Tribunals have certain inherent powers that are necessary to carry out their tasks under the DSU, even though that agreement does not specifically mention such powers. For example, WTO Tribunals have inherent jurisdiction to determine jurisdictional questions. The Appellate Body held in *US – 1916 Act* that a Panel has the power to examine a jurisdictional objection even if not raised in a timely manner, because the 'vesting of jurisdiction in a panel is a fundamental prerequisite for lawful panel proceedings'.[157] Moreover, a Panel may be required to address jurisdictional issues even if no party raises them.[158] The Appellate Body itself has the power to consider a claim that a Panel exceeded its jurisdiction, even if the appellant failed to include this claim in the Notice of Appeal.[159] This is similar to the inherent jurisdiction of arbitral tribunals to determine their own jurisdiction.[160]

The inherent jurisdiction of WTO Tribunals goes beyond the power to determine questions of jurisdiction. As Steger writes, '[i]n some cases involving questions of practice and procedure not expressly provided

[154] The principle of *compétence de la compétence*. See Pauwelyn, *Conflict of Norms*, 448; H Thirlway, 'The Law and Procedure of the International Court of Justice' (1998) 69 *British Yearbook of International Law* 1, 21; Appellate Body Report, *US – 1916 Act*, n. 30.

[155] Appellate Body Report, *US – Wool Shirts and Blouses*, [19].

[156] Pauwelyn, 'Role of Public International Law', 555.

[157] Appellate Body Report, *US – 1916 Act*, [54].

[158] Appellate Body Report, *Mexico – Corn Syrup (Article 21.5 – US)*, [36].

[159] Appellate Body Report, *US – Offset Act (Byrd Amendment)*, [208].

[160] Andrew Mitchell and Gavan Griffith, 'Contractual Dispute Resolution in International Trade: The UNCITRAL Arbitration Rules (1976) and the UNCITRAL Conciliation Rules (1980)' (2002) 3 *Melbourne Journal of International Law* 184.

for in the WTO DSU, the Appellate Body has sought guidance from the practice of other international legal systems and tribunals'.[161] This guidance is essentially drawn from general principles of law and principles of customary international law, as the following examples demonstrate.

In *US – Shirts and Blouses*, the Appellate Body found no rules on burden of proof in the DSU, so it used general principles of law under its inherent jurisdiction to supply them. The Appellate Body adopted the rule that 'the party who asserts a fact, whether claimant or the respondent, is responsible for providing proof thereof', stating that 'various international tribunals, including the International Court of Justice, have generally and consistently accepted and applied the rule'. It also found that the 'burden of proof rests upon the party, whether complaining or defending, who asserts the affirmative of a particular claim or defence'. The Appellate Body added that, if a complainant 'adduces evidence sufficient to raise a presumption that what is claimed is true, the burden then shifts to the other party, who will fail unless it adduces sufficient evidence to rebut the presumption', describing this as 'a generally-accepted canon of evidence in civil law, common law and, in fact, most jurisdictions'.[162]

In *India – Patents (US)*, the Appellate Body drew on principles to resolve an evidentiary issue. It stated that, '[i]n public international law, an international tribunal may treat municipal law in several ways. Municipal law may serve as evidence of facts and may provide evidence of state practice. However, municipal law may also constitute evidence of compliance or non-compliance with international obligations'.[163] It therefore held that the Panel could examine Indian law for the purposes of determining whether India had met its obligations under the TRIPS Agreement.

In *Canada – Aircraft*, the Appellate Body drew on 'the general practice and usage of international tribunals' to find that Panels examining claims of prohibited export subsidies could draw adverse inferences from a Member's refusal to provide information. It considered this authority 'an ordinary aspect of the task of all panels to determine the relevant facts of any dispute involving any covered agreement'.[164]

161 Steger, 'Jurisdiction of the WTO', 146.
162 Appellate Body Report, *US – Wool Shirts and Blouses*, 14.
163 Appellate Body Report, *India – Patents (US)*, [65].
164 Appellate Body Report, *Canada – Aircraft*, [202].

C. Using principles through inherent jurisdiction

The above analysis demonstrates that it is legitimate for WTO Tribunals to use principles in the exercise of inherent jurisdiction in WTO disputes, subject to two conditions. When these two conditions are met, the use of principles in the exercise of inherent jurisdiction does not run into the difficulties that arise in the application of non-WTO law in WTO disputes more generally. The first condition is that the use of the principle must be necessary to the maintenance and exercise of the tribunal's subject-matter jurisdiction and judicial function. It is not possible to define in the abstract the circumstances in which this condition would be satisfied. However, in the context of the WTO, a key purpose of dispute settlement is to achieve 'a satisfactory settlement of the matter' or 'a positive solution to a dispute'.[165] Where WTO Tribunals find it necessary to use a principle in order to ensure such a result, this would appear to meet the first condition.

The second condition is that the principle must be used to resolve procedural matters and not as a source of substantive rights or obligations. Thus, one Appellate Body member contends that, as a judicial body, it must determine appropriate rules of evidence based on 'general principles of international procedural law'.[166]

Evidently, some principles are likely to be better suited to resolving procedural matters than others. Turning to the four principles addressed in Part II of this book, due process is by definition concerned with procedural matters, to the extent that it governs WTO dispute settlement rather than imposing substantive obligations on WTO Members to ensure fair procedure. Good faith may also be used in connection with procedural matters because, for example, Members must engage in the WTO dispute settlement procedures in good faith.[167] WTO Tribunals could therefore use these two principles in the exercise of inherent jurisdiction in a WTO dispute, as elaborated in Chapters 5 and 4 respectively. The principle of special and differential treatment (primarily a principle of WTO law) also has procedural aspects. Several special and differential treatment provisions in the DSU mandate the consideration of participants' developing country status in dispute settlement proceedings. For example, Article 24 of the DSU provides 'Special Procedures Involving Least-Developed Country

[165] DSU, arts. 3.4, 3.7. [166] Abi-Saab, 'WTO Dispute Settlement', 6.
[167] DSU, art. 3.10.

Members'. The principle of proportionality, examined in Chapter 6, is less relevant to procedural matters and therefore a less appropriate candidate for application in a WTO dispute pursuant to inherent jurisdiction.

3.4 Conclusion

This chapter set out the various ways in which WTO Tribunals could use the three types of principles outlined in Chapter 2 in interpreting WTO provisions in WTO disputes, and the more limited circumstances in which WTO Tribunals could use such principles in a non-interpretative manner. The need for interpretation drawing on principles of customary international law and general principles of law, as well as principles of WTO law, stems from the inherent uncertainty in the WTO texts, as in any legal text. Principles are particularly important if a teleological approach to interpretation is adopted, but they may also play a role in subjective or textual approaches to interpretation. More significantly, Article 3.2 of the DSU and, in turn, Articles 31 and 32 of the VCLT provide a clear legal basis for using principles in the process of interpreting the WTO agreements. Principles may also play a non-interpretative role, particularly in relation to procedural matters.

The specific criteria for legitimately using principles depends on the type of principle in question, its specific content and status, and the particular use being made of it. In Table A below, I summarise the legal basis for WTO Tribunals to use the three types of principle in an interpretative or non-interpretative manner in resolving WTO disputes. Relying on these conclusions, Part II of this book examines in more detail four specific candidates for 'principles' that could be used in WTO dispute settlement, beginning in the next chapter with the principle of good faith.

Table A: *Legal basis for using different types of principle in an interpretative or non-interpretative manner*

Manner of using principles		Principles of WTO law	Principles of customary international law	General principles of law
Interpretative use	To clarify existing provisions and provide security and predictability (DSU Art. 3.2)	✓	✓	✓
	Ordinary or special meaning (VCLT Art. 31(1), (4))	✓	To the extent reflected in a relevant WTO provision.	
	Context, object and purpose (VCLT Art. 31(1), (2))	✓		
	Relevant rules of international law (VCLT Art. 31(3)(c))	✗	To the extent reflected in relevant rules of international law.	
	Preparatory work (VCLT Art. 32)	✓	✗	✗
Non-interpretative use	As claims (subject-matter jurisdiction)	✓	To the extent reflected in a relevant WTO provision. In particular, Appellate Body may assess whether Panel complied with principle of due process.	
	As applicable law	✓	To the extent reflected in a relevant WTO provision.	
	In the exercise of inherent jurisdiction	To resolve a procedural matter, where necessary to maintain and exercise subject-matter jurisdiction and judicial function (for example, due process, good faith, and special and differential treatment).		

PART II · SELECTED PRINCIPLES EXAMINED

4 Good faith

> Men must be able to assume that those with whom they deal in the general intercourse of society will act in good faith.[1]

4.1 Introduction

The principle of good faith has a great deal of normative appeal, and most commentators would acknowledge that it plays a role in all legal systems. The ordinary meaning of 'good faith' is 'honesty of purpose or sincerity of declaration' or the 'expectation of such qualities in others'.[2] Good faith is often used interchangeably with *bona fides*, which is defined as 'freedom from intent to deceive'.[3] The touchstone of good faith is therefore honesty, a subjective state of mind, but the principle can also incorporate notions of fairness and reasonableness, both of which concern an objective state of affairs. Unfortunately, terms like honesty, fairness and reasonableness are almost as vague as good faith. This leads Rosenne to ask of good faith: 'Is it a principle and a rule of law, having an identifiable and where necessary enforceable legal content, or is it nothing more than a throw-back to outmoded natural law concepts?'[4] If good faith has no independent legal content, it may be of little use to WTO Tribunals in resolving disputes: 'one may acknowledge the power and attraction of a general idea but the idea may be so general that it is of no practical utility to the merchant'.[5]

1 Roscoe Pound, *An Introduction to the Philosophy of Law* (1922) 188.
2 Arthur Delbridge et al. (eds.), *The Macquarie Dictionary* (2nd edn, 1991) 754.
3 John Simpson and Edmund Weiner (eds.), *The Oxford English Dictionary* (2nd edn, 1989) vol. II, 379.
4 Shabtai Rosenne, *Developments in the Law of Treaties 1945–1986* (1989) 135.
5 Royston Goode, 'The Concept of Good Faith in English Law' (Paper presented at the Centro di Studi e Ricerche di Diritto Comparato e Straniero, Rome, Italy, March 1992).

In this chapter, I attempt to clarify the meaning of good faith to the extent relevant to the WTO, by examining good faith as a general principle of law, a principle of customary international law, and a principle of WTO law. Below, I start by considering the existence and meaning of the principle of good faith in international law outside the WTO. Although I do not aim to establish definitively whether good faith is a general principle of law or a principle of customary international law, it is undoubtedly a well-accepted fundamental norm in many domestic and international contexts. It takes several more specific forms in relation to the interpretation and performance of treaties, as well as in the doctrines of abuse of rights and estoppel. Having considered good faith outside the WTO, I turn to the use of this principle in WTO disputes. I first determine the scope of good faith as a principle of WTO law, before assessing the procedural and substantive implications of good faith for WTO dispute settlement. I pay particular attention to the ways in which WTO Tribunals have used the principle of good faith so far.

4.2 Good faith in international law outside the WTO

4.2.1 A general principle of law

Unquestionably, the obligation to act in accordance with good faith, being a general principle of law, is also part of international law.[6]

Good faith was recognised as a general principle of law during the drafting of the PCIJ Statute.[7] This principle is described as 'the foundation of all law, or a fundamental principle of law'.[8] O'Connor suggests that good faith derived from 'the necessity for a minimum of human co-operation and tolerance if group living is to emerge and survive'.[9] Although good faith has origins in the earliest human societies, O'Connor suggests that the Roman concept of *bona fides* (associated with trustworthiness, conscientiousness and honourable conduct) represents its most direct ancestor.[10] By about 1450 it was applied in both civil and common law systems, and was 'reflected in specific rules

[6] Certain Norwegian Loans *(France* v. *Norway) (Jurisdiction)* [1957] ICJ Rep 9, 53 (Judge Hersch Lauterpacht).

[7] See comments of Lord Phillimore in PCIJ: *Advisory Committee of Jurists, Procès-verbaux of the Proceedings of the Committee, June 16th–July 24th*, 1920, with Annexes (1920) 335.

[8] John O'Connor, *Good Faith in International Law* (1991) 2.

[9] Ibid. 6. See also Robert Kolb, 'Principles as Sources of International Law (with Special Reference to Good Faith)' (2006) 53 *Netherlands International Law Review* 1, 17–20.

[10] O'Connor, *Good Faith*, 18–19.

incorporating or referring to good conscience, fairness, equitable dealing and reasonableness'.[11]

Today, the principle of good faith is recognised in most civil codes, in essence being 'a principle of fair and open dealing'.[12] Most importantly, civil law regimes tend to require that contracts be formed and performed in good faith.[13] One explanation for this may be economic. If parties act in bad faith, this leads to mistrust, making contracting more complex and expensive. A rule of good faith increases contracting parties' confidence that contractual obligations will be performed.[14]

The principle of good faith is less established and less uniform in common law systems. At one extreme is the United Kingdom, which has no general doctrine of good faith.[15] However, equity developed many doctrines to promote specific notions of good faith, including the concepts of undue influence and promissory estoppel.[16] Good faith is also recognised in relation to particular classes of contracts - for example, contracts of insurance. At the other extreme is the United States, where 'every contract imposes upon each party a duty of good faith and fair dealing in its performance and its enforcement'.[17] Farnsworth notes that United States courts have used good faith in at least three different ways: to imply terms to fill gaps; to prevent a party from reclaiming opportunities it agreed to forgo when entering a

[11] Ibid. 30.

[12] *Interfoto Picture Library Ltd* v. *Stiletto Visual Programmes Ltd* [1988] 1 All ER 348, 352 (Bingham LJ). See, e.g., *Code Civil du Québec* c. 64; Charles Gonthier, 'Liberty, Equality, Fraternity: The Forgotten Leg of the Trilogy, or Fraternity: The Unspoken Third Pillar of Democracy' (2000) 45 *McGill Law Journal* 567, 584.

[13] William Tetley, 'Good Faith in Contract: Particularly in the Contracts of Arbitration and Chartering' (2004) 35 *Journal of Maritime Law and Commerce* 561, 567; Disa Sim, 'The Scope and Application of Good Faith in the Vienna Convention on Contracts for the International Sale of Goods' in Pace International Law Review (ed.), *Review of the Convention on Contracts for the International Sale of Goods* (CISG) 2002–2003 (2004) 19, 31; *Bürgerliches Gesetzbuch* § 242; *Code Civil Suisse* art. 3; *Code Civil de la France* arts. 550, 1134.

[14] Paul Powers, 'Defining the Undefinable: Good Faith and the United Nations Convention on the Contracts for the International Sale of Goods' (1998–99) 18 *Journal of Law and Commerce* 333, 351.

[15] Roy Goode, *Commercial Law* (2nd edn, 1995) 117; *Allen* v. *Flood* [1898] AC 1, 46 (Wills J).

[16] Rosenne, *Developments in the Law of Treaties*, 164. See also Mary Hiscock, 'The Keeper of the Flame: Good Faith and Fair Dealing in International Trade' (1996) 29 *Loyola of Los Angeles Law Review* 1059, 1061.

[17] American Law Institute, *Restatement of the Law Second, Contracts* § 205 (1981). See also *Uniform Commercial Code* §§ 1-304.

contract; and to exclude bad faith.[18] One disadvantage of using 'bad faith' to define or justify the principle of good faith

> is that it seems tantamount to saying that the good faith duty is breached whenever a judge decides that it has been breached . . . [which] hardly advances the cause of intellectual inquiry and . . . provides absolutely no guide to the disposition of future cases, except to the extent that they may be on all fours with a decided case.[19]

Rosenne argues that while examples of good faith from domestic laws are of limited relevance for international law, they nevertheless 'illustrate vividly that "good faith" *is* a recognized legal notion, and one that can be creative of significant legal institutions'.[20]

4.2.2 A principle of customary international law

The principle of good faith in customary international law has a long history. Grotius recognised that 'good faith should be preserved, not only for other reasons but also in order that the hope of peace may not be done away with'.[21] Schwarzenberger and Brown list good faith as one of the seven fundamental principles of international law.[22]

Good faith is 'included in a long series of law-declaring instruments of major significance',[23] some or all of which may be collectively regarded as codifying customary international law.[24] Many of these

18 E. Allan Farnsworth, 'Duties of Good Faith and Fair Dealing under the UNIDROIT Principles, Relevant International Conventions, and National Laws' (1995) 3 *Tulane Journal of International and Comparative Law* 47, 59–60. See also David Stack, 'The Two Standards of Good Faith in Canadian Contract Law' (1999) 62 *Saskatchewan Law Review* 201.

19 M. G. Bridge, 'Does Anglo-Canadian Contract Law Need a Doctrine of Good Faith?' (1984) 9 *Canadian Business Law Journal* 385, 398.

20 Rosenne, *Developments in the Law of Treaties*, 165 (original emphasis).

21 Hugo Grotius, *De Jure Belli ac Pacis Libri Tres* (1625), as quoted in O'Connor, *Good Faith*, 56.

22 Georg Schwarzenberger and Edward D. Brown, *A Manual of International Law* (6th edn, 1976) 7.

23 Rosenne, *Developments in the Law of Treaties*, 135.

24 See, e.g., *Charter of the Organization of American States*, art. 3(c); *United Nations Convention on the Law of the Sea*, opened for signature 10 December 1982, 1833 UNTS 3, arts. 105, 157, 300 (entered into force 16 November 1994); *Peaceful Settlement of Disputes between States*, GA Res 37/10, UN GAOR, 37th sess, 68th plen mtg, Annex, UN Doc A/RES/37/10 (15 November 1982) I(1), II(2); *Report of the Secretary-General on the Work of the Organization*, GA Res 37/67, UN GAOR, 37th sess, 91st plen mtg, UN Doc A/RES/37/67 (3 December 1982) [2]; *Charter of Economic Rights and Duties of States*, GA Res 3281 (XXIX), UN GAOR, 29th sess, 2315th plen mtg, UN Doc A/RES/29/3281 (12 December 1974) ch 1 (j); *Permanent Sovereignty over Natural Resources*, GA Res 1803 (XVII), UN GAOR, 17th

references to good faith are broadly analogous to domestic obligations to perform contracts in good faith. For example, Article 2(2) of the UN Charter states that '[a]ll Members . . . shall fulfil in good faith the obligations assumed by them in accordance with the present Charter'.[25] This represents the first modern and universalised statement of the principle of good faith in treaty law,[26] and it 'constitutes . . . an undertaking to comply with the whole of public international law, in so far as it is not amended by the UN Charter'.[27] Müller and Kolb explain in relation to this provision:

> a set of treaties with such comprehensive objectives as those of the UN does not survive merely on the strength of the terms used and on its individual provisions, but only achieves its reality via the communal will of its members, for which there is ultimately no guarantee.[28]

The *Declaration on Principles of International Law concerning Friendly Relations and Cooperation among States* contains several references to good faith, including the following:

> Every State has the duty to fulfil in good faith its obligations under the generally recognized principles and rules of international law.
>
> Every State has the duty to fulfil in good faith its obligations under international agreements valid under the generally recognized principles and rules of international law.[29]

A number of international tribunals have recognised the principle of good faith. According to the ICJ, although good faith is '[o]ne of the basic principles governing the creation and performance of legal obligations',[30] it is 'not in itself a source of obligation where none would otherwise exist'.[31] This could suggest that, in a treaty context, a violation

sess, UN Doc A/RES/17/1803 (14 December 1962) [8]; *UNIDROIT Principles of International Commercial Contracts* 2004, art. 1.7.

25 See further Jörg Müller and Robert Kolb, 'Article 2(2)' in Bruno Simma (ed.), *The Charter of the United Nations: A Commentary* (2nd edn, 2002) vol. I, 91, n. 3.

26 Rosenne, *Developments in the Law of Treaties*, 156. But see Elisabeth Zoller, *La Bonne Foi en Droit International Public* (1977) 5.

27 Albrecht Randelzhofer, 'Article 2' in Bruno Simma (ed.), *The Charter of the United Nations: A Commentary* (2nd edn, 2002) vol. I, 63, 65.

28 Müller and Kolb, 'Article 2(2)', 96.

29 *Declaration on Principles of International Law concerning Friendly Relations and Cooperation among States in accordance with the Charter of the United Nations*, GA Res 2625 (XXV), UN GAOR, 25th sess, 1883rd plen mtg, UN Doc A/RES/2625 (24 October 1970) 124.

30 Nuclear Tests *(Australia* v. *France) (Merits)* [1974] ICJ Rep 253, 268.

31 Border and Transborder Armed Actions *(Nicaragua* v. *Honduras) (Jurisdiction and Admissibility)* [1988] ICJ Rep 69, 105.

of good faith cannot arise in the absence of a violation of a treaty provision (a possibility to which I return below).[32] Conversely, the ICJ has rejected the contention that a violation of a treaty provision cannot arise in the absence of a violation of good faith.[33] This distinction may reflect the gravity of a good faith violation, which also explains why international tribunals often presume that states act in good faith and why they do not lightly find bad faith.[34]

In the *Nuclear Tests Case*, the ICJ used the principle of good faith to find that unilateral statements by the French Government indicating its intention to cease atmospheric nuclear testing in the South Pacific were legally binding.[35] In the *WHO/Egypt Agreement Case*, the ICJ recognised 'the mutual obligations incumbent upon Egypt and the [World Health] Organization to cooperate in good faith with respect to the implications and effects of the transfer of the Regional Office from Egypt'.[36] These included a duty upon the parties to 'consult together in good faith'[37] and to continue to fulfil in good faith their obligations during any transition between the decision to move the office and the completion of the move.[38] In the *North Sea Continental Shelf Case*, the ICJ relied on good faith to explain why certain states were required to enter into meaningful negotiations with the objective of reaching an agreement, 'which will not be the case when either of them insists upon its own position without contemplating any modification of it'.[39]

4.2.3 *Towards a definition of good faith*

Unfortunately, of all the principles of international law, the principle of good faith is perhaps the hardest to define. Cheng considered the principle capable of illustration but not of definition, like other 'rudimentary terms applicable to human conduct' such as 'honesty' or

32 See below, section 4.3.3(A).

33 See, e.g., *Legal Consequences for States of the Continued Presence of South Africa in Namibia (South West Africa) notwithstanding Security Council Resolution 276* (1970) (Advisory Opinion) [1971] ICJ Rep 16, 56–7; Gillian White, 'The Principle of Good Faith' in Vaughan Lowe and Colin Warbrick (eds.), *The United Nations and the Principles of International Law: Essays in Memory of Michael Akehurst* (1994) 230, 241.

34 See, e.g., Tacna-Arica *(Chile* v. *Peru)* (1925) 2 RIAA 921, 930; Affaire du Lac Lanoux *(France* v. *Espagne)* (1957) 12 RIAA 281, 313.

35 Nuclear Tests *(Australia* v. *France) (Merits)* [1974] ICJ Rep 253, 268–9.

36 Interpretation of the Agreement of 25 March 1951 between the WHO and Egypt (Advisory Opinion) [1980] ICJ Rep 73, 95.

37 Ibid. 38 Ibid. 96–7.

39 North Sea Continental Shelf *(Federal Republic of Germany* v. *Denmark; Federal Republic of Germany* v. *Netherlands)* [1969] ICJ Rep 3, 47.

'malice'.[40] O'Connor, in his study on the principle, considered that good faith includes the general elements of 'honesty, fairness and reasonableness',[41] but then went on to propose the following more specific definition:

> The principle of good faith in international law is a fundamental principle from which the rule *pacta sunt servanda* and other legal rules distinctively and directly related to honesty, fairness and reasonableness are derived, and the application of these rules is determined at any particular time by the compelling standards of honesty, fairness and reasonableness prevailing in the international community at that time.[42]

This definition makes it clear that good faith is a general principle of law or a principle of customary international law that manifests itself in various other obligations, such as the following obligations on states:

> (1) to settle disputes in good faith; (2) to negotiate in good faith; (3) having signed a treaty, not to frustrate the achievement of its object and purpose prior to ratification; (4) having ratified a treaty, to apply and perform it in good faith and not to frustrate the achievement of its object and purpose; (5) to interpret treaties in good faith, in accordance with their ordinary meaning considered in context and in the light of their object and purpose; (6) to fulfil in good faith any obligations arising from other sources of international law; and (7) to exercise rights in good faith.[43]

Obligations such as these may be more precise than the broader principle of good faith, and eventually they may develop sufficiently to be used without reference to the principle. Therefore, as legal systems develop and mature, resort to the principle of good faith may be less frequent.[44] In this sense, the principle of good faith 'is both a first principle and one of last resort, finding practical relevance chiefly when a more definable rule cannot be found, when there is a collision of rights, or when seemingly contradictory concepts are at play'.[45]

[40] Bin Cheng, *General Principles of Law as Applied by International Courts and Tribunals* (1987) 105 (footnotes omitted).
[41] O'Connor, *Good Faith*, 118–19.
[42] Ibid. 124. See also Anthony D'Amato, 'Good Faith' in Rudolf Bernhardt (ed.), *Encyclopaedia of Public International Law* (2003) vol. II, 599, 599.
[43] Guy Goodwin-Gill, 'State Responsibility and the "Good Faith" Obligation in International Law' in Malgosia Fitzmaurice and Dan Sarooshi (eds.), *Issues of State Responsibility before International Judicial Institutions* (2004) 75, 88 (footnotes omitted).
[44] O'Connor, *Good Faith*, 123.
[45] Detlev Vagts and Gabe Varges, 'Book Review: Good Faith in International Law' (1992) 86 *American Journal of International Law* 841, 843.

As regards the relationship between the general and particular notions of good faith, Sim writes:

> [T]here is nothing wrong with subscribing to the very general notion that 'good faith' is synonymous with anything that requires contracting parties to behave in a manner that ensures justice and fairness. The merit of this approach is that we do not omit anything that can assist us in circumscribing unethical behaviour. This idea, however, is not concrete enough to form the basis of a workable legal doctrine.[46]

In the following section, I consider some expressions or particularisations of the principle of good faith in international law, namely: (i) good faith performance of treaties; (ii) good faith interpretation of treaties; (iii) estoppel; and (iv) abuse of rights. These expressions could themselves be regarded as rules, obligations, principles or doctrines. They may also exist in domestic law, treaty law, customary international law, and general principles of law. I am concerned here not with their precise categorisation, but with their meaning.[47]

4.2.4 Particularisations of good faith

A. Performance of treaties: pacta sunt servanda

Like good faith generally, *pacta sunt servanda* (agreements must be kept) originated in Roman law and was later incorporated into customary international law and treaty obligations.[48] In 1910, for example, the Permanent Court of Arbitration held that 'every State has to exercise the obligation incurred by treaty bona fide and is urged thereto by the ordinary sanctions of international law'.[49] Also as regards treaties, Article 26 of the VCLT is entitled '*[p]acta sunt servanda*' and provides that '[e]very treaty in force is binding upon the parties to it and must be performed by them in good faith'.

The ICJ has read the good faith requirement in Article 26 as meaning that 'the purpose of the Treaty, and the intentions of the Parties in concluding it ... should prevail over its literal application. The principle of good faith obliges the Parties to apply it in a reasonable way

[46] Sim, 'Scope and Application of Good Faith', 31.

[47] See also Kolb, 'Principles as Sources of International Law', 19–20, who characterises such particularisations as 'concretizations' of the legal content of the principle of good faith.

[48] O'Connor, *Good Faith*, 37.

[49] North Atlantic Coast Fisheries Arbitration *(United States* v. *Great Britain)* (1910) 11 RIAA 167, 186.

and in such a manner that its purpose can be realized'.[50] Similarly, in drafting the VCLT, the Special Rapporteur stated in relation to this provision:

> [T]he intended meaning was that a treaty must be applied and observed not merely according to its letter, but in good faith. It was the duty of the parties to the treaty not only to observe the letter of the law, but also to abstain from acts which would inevitably affect their ability to perform the treaty.[51]

This suggests that a state may violate the obligation to perform treaties in good faith even if it does not violate the treaty itself (that is, the 'letter' of the treaty). For example, this could arise where the state 'seeks to avoid or to "divert" the obligation which it has accepted, or to do indirectly what it is not permitted to do directly'.[52] Thus, McNair states:

> A State may take certain action or be responsible for certain inaction, which, though not in form a breach of a treaty, is such that its effect will be equivalent to a breach of treaty; in such cases a tribunal demands good faith and seeks for the reality rather than the appearance.[53]

Accordingly, *pacta sunt servanda* may overlap with the doctrine of abuse of rights, as discussed below.[54]

Article 26 of the VCLT applies to treaties 'in force'. However, Article 18 of the VCLT, which concerns treaties before they enter into force, may inform the meaning of good faith in Article 26. Article 18 states:

> Obligation not to defeat the object and purpose of a treaty prior to its entry into force
>
> A State is obliged to refrain from acts which would defeat the object and purpose of a treaty when:
>
> (a) it has signed the treaty or has exchanged instruments constituting the treaty subject to ratification, acceptance or approval, until it shall have made its intention clear not to become a party to the treaty; or
>
> (b) it has expressed its consent to be bound by the treaty, pending the entry into force of the treaty and provided that such entry into force is not unduly delayed.

50 Gabcíkovo-Nagymaros Project *(Hungary* v. *Slovakia) (Merits)* [1997] ICJ Rep 7, 79.

51 International Law Commission, 'Report of the International Law Commission Covering its 16th Session, 727th Meeting, 20 May 1964' [1964] 1 *Yearbook of the International Law Commission* [70].

52 Goodwin-Gill, 'State Responsibility', 93.

53 Arnold McNair, The Law of Treaties (1961) 540.

54 See below, section 4.2.4(D).

In relation to these 'pre-conventional' obligations to refrain from acts that would defeat the object and purpose of a treaty, the Special Rapporteur stated, '*[a] fortiori*, when the treaty is in force the parties are under an obligation of good faith to refrain from such acts'.[55] Thus, the obligation on states to perform in good faith treaties to which they are a party may include an obligation not to defeat the object and purpose of such treaties.

B. Interpretation of treaties: VCLT Article 31(1)

As discussed in Chapter 3, Article 31(1) of the VCLT states that a 'treaty shall be interpreted in good faith in accordance with the ordinary meaning to be given to the terms of the treaty in their context and in light of its object and purpose'. According to O'Connor, the requirement that the interpreter have regard to 'the ordinary meaning to be given to the terms of the treaty' may itself reflect the principle of *pacta sunt servanda*, in that it focuses on what the parties actually agreed.[56] Rosenne explains the relationship between good faith interpretation and good faith performance of treaties as follows:

> whenever the expression 'good faith' is used, it is a pointer to the close link that exists between the obligation itself and its performance - for even interpretation as presented is not an exercise in abstraction but has an essential functional role in the decision-making process of a party or of a court or tribunal as regards the performance of the obligation.[57]

Rosenne contends that the essential function of good faith in this context is 'to give a broad interpretation of the scope of equitable principles, provided that in so doing the treaty is not revised; and in turn to emphasize the flexibility by appropriate language in the treaty'.[58] Accordingly, although the requirement of good faith in interpreting treaties may be related to the requirement of good faith in performing treaties, it appears to add little to the correct understanding of good faith as a substantive principle in international law.

55 International Law Commission, 'Third Report on the Law of Treaties, by Sir Humphrey Waldock, Special Rapporteur' [1964] 2 *Yearbook of the International Law Commission* 8.

56 O'Connor, *Good Faith*, 109. For a discussion of the significance of good faith interpretation and good faith performance of treaties in the context of the United States, see Michael P. Van Alstine, 'The Death of Good Faith in Treaty Jurisprudence and a Call for Resurrection' (2005) 93 *Georgetown Law Journal* 1885.

57 Rosenne, *Developments in the Law of Treaties*, 175. 58 Ibid. 178–9.

C. Estoppel

Estoppel might be regarded as a principle of customary international law as well as a general principle of law:

> a man shall not be allowed to blow hot and cold – to affirm at one time and deny at another ... Such a principle has its basis in common sense and common justice, and whether it is called 'estoppel,' or by any other name, it is one which courts of law have in modern times most usefully adopted.[59]

Estoppel operates in different ways depending on the context of a given case,[60] but its common elements are to preclude Party X from denying a particular state of things against Party Y if:

- X clearly and unambiguously represented to Y the existence of such a state;
- Y altered its position in reliance on that representation in good faith; and
- Y would suffer injury if the representation was groundless.[61]

Estoppel is also related to the principle of 'acquiescence', which involves silence or inaction by X instead of a specific representation.[62] I leave this slightly different principle to one side.

In the *Land and Maritime Boundary Case*, the ICJ stated:

> An estoppel would only arise if by its acts or declarations Cameroon had consistently made it fully clear that it had agreed to settle the boundary dispute submitted to the Court by bilateral avenues alone. It would further be necessary that, by relying on such an attitude, Nigeria had changed position to its own detriment or had suffered some prejudice.[63]

[59] *Cave* v. *Mills* (1862) 7 *Hurlstone & Norman* 913, 927 (quoted in Bin Cheng, *General Principles of Law*, 141–2). But see O'Connor, *Good Faith*, 122–3.

[60] Jörg Müller and Thomas Cottier, 'Estoppel' in Rudolf Bernhardt (ed.), *Encyclopaedia of Public International Law* (2003) vol. II, 116, 117.

[61] Ibid. 116; Cheng, *General Principles of Law*, 143. See also Ian Brownlie, *Principles of Public International Law* (6th edn, 2003) 616; Derek Bowett, 'Estoppel Before International Tribunals and Its Relation to Acquiescence' (1957) 33 *British Yearbook of International Law* 176, 202.

[62] Bowett, 'Estoppel Before International Tribunals', 200.

[63] *Land and Maritime Boundary between Cameroon and Nigeria* (*Cameroon* v. *Nigeria*) (*Preliminary Objections*) [1998] ICJ Rep 275, 303. See also Aerial Incident of 10 August 1999 (*Pakistan* v. *India*) (Jurisdiction) [2000] ICJ Rep 12, 31–2.

The ICJ also discussed the principle of estoppel in the *North Sea Continental Shelf Case*, where it found that a 'very definite, very consistent course of conduct'[64] would have to be established for a state to be bound by a treaty to which it had not formally acceded. The Court went on to declare that

> only the existence of a situation of estoppel could suffice to lend substance to [the contention that the Federal Republic of Germany was bound by the Geneva Convention on the Continental Shelf] . . . that is to say if the Federal Republic were now precluded from denying the applicability of the conventional régime, by reason of past conduct, declarations, etc., which not only clearly and consistently evinced acceptance of that régime, but also had caused Denmark or the Netherlands, in reliance on such conduct, detrimentally to change position or suffer some prejudice.[65]

In some descriptions of estoppel, the requirement of injury to Party Y is expanded to cover a benefit to Party X. In *Temple of Preah Vihear*, the ICJ rejected an attempt by Thailand to resile from a clear and unequivocal representation it had made to Cambodia concerning the boundary between them.[66] In this case, Judge Spender in his dissenting opinion gave the following description of the principle of estoppel:

> the principle operates to prevent a State contesting before the Court a situation contrary to a clear and unequivocal representation previously made by it to another State, either expressly or impliedly, on which representation the other State was, in the circumstances, entitled to rely and in fact did rely, and as a result that other State has been prejudiced or the State making it has secured some benefit or advantage for itself.[67]

Similarly, in *Land, Island and Maritime Frontier Dispute (El Salvador* v. *Honduras) (Application by Nicaragua for Permission to Intervene)*, the ICJ described the conditions for estoppel as 'a statement or representation made by one party to another and reliance upon it by that other party to his detriment or to the advantage of the party making it'.[68]

[64] *North Sea Continental Shelf (Federal Republic of Germany* v. *Denmark; Federal Republic of Germany* v. *Netherlands)* [1969] ICJ Rep 3, 25.
[65] Ibid. 26.
[66] *Temple of Preah Vihear (Cambodia* v. *Thailand) (Merits)* [1962] ICJ Rep 6, 32–3.
[67] Ibid. 143–4.
[68] *Land, Island and Maritime Frontier Dispute (El Salvador* v. *Honduras) (Application by Nicaragua for Permission to Intervene)* [1990] ICJ Rep 92, [188]–[189].

D. Abuse of rights

In international law, the doctrine of abuse of rights (*abus de droit*) forbids a state from 'exercising a right either in a way which impedes the enjoyment by other States of their own rights or for an end different from that for which the right was created, to the injury of another State'.[69] Abuse of rights is also reflected in civil law systems.[70] In common law systems, although the phrase 'abuse of rights' is not commonly used, '[t]he law of torts as crystallized in various systems of law in judicial decisions or legislative enactment is to a large extent a list of wrongs arising out of what society considers to be an abuse of rights'.[71]

Cheng conceives abuse of rights as an application of the principle of good faith.[72] Byers contends that this does not render abuse of rights redundant; rather, abuse of rights should be viewed as 'supplemental to the principle of good faith: [providing] the threshold at which a lack of good faith gives rise to a violation of international law, with all the attendant consequences'.[73]

International law can be seen as recognising three broad categories of abuse of rights.[74] The first contemplates a state exercising a right in a manner other than the manner in which it was intended to be exercised (for example, against the spirit of the law conferring the right), including: (a) solely for a malicious purpose;[75] or (b) as a guise to evade the law.[76] An example of such an abuse would be a state using a right to establish a police cordon at a political border as a guise for a customs barrier in breach of a treaty obligation to maintain certain zones free from customs barriers.[77]

[69] Alexandre Kiss, 'Abuse of Rights' in Rudolf Bernhardt (ed.), *Encyclopaedia of Public International Law* (2003) vol. I, 4, 4. See also O'Connor, *Good Faith*, 38; G. D. S. Taylor, 'The Content of the Rule against Abuse of Rights in International Law' (1972–73) 46 *British Yearbook of International Law* 323, 333.

[70] Peter Nygh and Peter Butt (eds.), *Butterworths Australian Legal Dictionary* (1997) 10; Irina Petrova, '"Stepping on the Shoulders of a Drowning Man": The Doctrine of Abuse of Right as a Tool for Reducing Damages for Lost Profits: Troubling Lessons from the Patuha and Himpurna Arbitrations' (2004) 35 *Georgetown Journal of International Law* 455, 464–6.

[71] Sir Hersch Lauterpacht, *The Function of Law in the International Community* (1966) 297.

[72] Cheng, *General Principles of Law*, 121.

[73] Michael Byers, 'Abuse of Rights: An Old Principle, A New Age' (2002) 47 *McGill Law Journal* 389, 411.

[74] Kiss, 'Abuse of Rights', 5. [75] Cheng, *General Principles of Law*, 122. [76] Ibid. 122–3.

[77] *Free Zones of Upper Savoy and the District of Gex (France* v. *Switzerland) (Merits)* [1932] PCIJ (ser A/B) No 46.

The second category involves a state exercising a right in a way that impinges on another state's enjoyment of its rights when, 'weighing the conflicting interests', the exercise of the right is not fair and equitable between the parties.[78] An example of such an abuse would be a state exercising its right to regulate activities in its territorial waters in a way that unnecessarily interferes with a right granted under a treaty permitting the residents of another state to fish in those waters.[79]

Third, a state could exercise a discretionary right unreasonably, dishonestly, or without due regard for the interests of others. An example of such an abuse is the arbitrary expulsion of an alien.[80] Cheng cautions that, as 'discretion implies subjective judgment, it is often difficult to determine categorically that the discretion has been abused'.[81] He refers to the ICJ's advisory opinion in *Conditions of Admission of a State to the United Nations (Advisory Opinion)*,[82] where the minority noted that, although the discretion of members to admit states to the UN is limited, it would be almost impossible to prove that the discretionary right had been exercised wrongly.[83]

In all three categories, the party alleging an abuse of rights must establish,[84] through 'clear and convincing evidence',[85] that the abuse has caused injury 'of serious consequence'.[86]

The potential breadth of abuse of rights is quite large, leading some to caution against its overuse. In Lauterpacht's words:

> There is no legal right, however well established, which could not, in some circumstances, be refused recognition on the ground that it has been abused. The doctrine of abuse of rights is therefore an instrument which . . . must be wielded with studied restraint.[87]

[78] Cheng, *General Principles of Law*, 125.
[79] *North Atlantic Coast Fisheries Arbitration* (*United States* v. *Great Britain*) (1910) 11 RIAA 167.
[80] Cheng, *General Principles of Law*, 133. [81] Ibid. 134.
[82] Conditions of Admission of a State to the United Nations (Advisory Opinion) [1948] ICJ Rep 57, 93 (Dissenting Opinion of Judges Basdevant, Winiarski, Sir Arnold McNair and Read).
[83] See Cheng, *General Principles of Law*, 134.
[84] *Certain German Interests in Polish Upper Silesia* (*Germany* v. *Polish Republic*) (*Merits*) [1926] PCIJ (ser A) No 7, 30; *Free Zones of Upper Savoy and the District of Gex* (*France* v. *Switzerland*) (*Merits*) [1932] PCIJ (ser A/B) No 46, 167.
[85] Trail Smelter Arbitration (*United States* v. *Canada*) (1938 and 1941) 3 RIAA 1905, 1965.
[86] Ibid.
[87] Sir Hersch Lauterpacht, *The Development of International Law by the International Court* (1958) 164. See also Petrova, '"Stepping on the Shoulders of a Drowning Man"', 464–5.

The breadth of the doctrine of abuse of rights depends largely on the answers to two questions. First, what factors are relevant in determining whether a right has been abused? These may range from an injurious or deceitful motive to an unbalanced outcome. The doctrine broadens as one moves from subjective factors (such as the intention and purpose of the party exercising the right) to objective factors (such as the consequences of the exercise of the right).[88] On one view, objective factors are key,[89] particularly given the 'natural reluctance to ascribe bad faith to States, in the sense of a deliberate intention knowingly to circumvent an international obligation'.[90] The second question that must be answered in delineating the scope of abuse of rights is: to whom must the injury be caused? The answer could be the narrow class of those with whom the exerciser of the right has a specific contractual or treaty obligation, or the broader class of those with whom it has an obligation 'arising from the general rules and principles of the legal order' or from some more generalised notion of fairness or equity.[91]

4.3 Using good faith in WTO disputes

4.3.1 Good faith as a principle of WTO law

According to McRae, the 'WTO agreements are themselves creatures of international law; they are treaties binding only because of the underlying norm of international law *pacta sunt servanda*'.[92] This suggests that good faith may underlie the WTO agreements as a whole. Perhaps this is what the Appellate Body had in mind when it referred to

[88] Joseph Voyame, Bertil Cottier and Bolívar Rocha, 'Abuse of Rights in Comparative Law' in Council of Europe (ed.), *Abuse of Rights and Equivalent Concepts: The Principle and Its Present Day Application* (1990) 23, 28–39; Georges Margue, 'Abuse of Rights and Luxembourg Law' in Council of Europe (ed.), *Abuse of Rights and Equivalent Concepts: The Principle and Its Present Day Application* (1990) 56, 58; Petrova, '"Stepping on the Shoulders of a Drowning Man"', 470.

[89] *Conditions of Admission of a State to Membership in the United Nations (Article 4 of the Charter) (Advisory Opinion)* [1948] ICJ Rep 57, 80 (Azevedo J, dissenting).

[90] Gerald Fitzmaurice, 'The Law and Procedure of the International Court of Justice, 1954–9: General Principles and Sources of Law' (1959) 35 *British Yearbook of International Law* 183, 209.

[91] Cheng, *General Principles of Law*, 130, as cited in Petrova, '"Stepping on the Shoulders of a Drowning Man"', 471.

[92] Donald McRae, 'Comments on Dr Claus-Dieter Ehlermann's Lecture' (2003) 97 *American Society of International Law Proceedings* 87, 89.

the 'general principle of *good faith* that underlies all treaties'.[93] In addition, the requirement in Article 31(1) of the VCLT to interpret treaties in good faith – as incorporated in Article 3.2 of the DSU – influences the interpretation of every WTO provision. Good faith might be described as a principle of WTO law on either of these bases. Finally, several WTO provisions refer specifically to 'good faith', without elaborating on its meaning. The absence of any definition of good faith in the WTO agreements supports the view that good faith is not a specific rule but a broader principle of WTO law, perhaps informed by good faith notions in international law.

The WTO provisions that refer to good faith include, most significantly for WTO disputes, Articles 3.10 and 4.3 of the DSU. In Article 3.10, the Members set out their understanding that, 'if a dispute arises, all Members will engage in these procedures in good faith in an effort to resolve the dispute'. Article 4.3 creates a more specific good faith obligation in relation to the consultation stage of disputes. The first sentence of this provision reads:

> If a request for consultations is made pursuant to a covered agreement, the Member to which the request is made shall, unless otherwise mutually agreed, reply to the request within 10 days after the date of its receipt and shall enter into consultations in good faith within a period of no more than 30 days after the date of receipt of the request, with a view to reaching a mutually satisfactory solution.

Articles 3.10 and 4.3 of the DSU provide examples of how principles of good faith may underlie claims in WTO disputes. For instance, a complaining Member could claim in the course of a dispute that the respondent had failed to comply with the good faith requirement in Article 4.3 by attending consultations without being willing to attempt to find a mutually satisfactory solution. A responding Member could claim that the complainant was using the dispute settlement mechanism as a mere strategy or tactic to achieve some unrelated result instead of in an effort to resolve the dispute as required by Article 3.10.

Another reference to good faith is found in the *Understanding on the Interpretation of Article XXIV of the General Agreement on Tariffs and Trade 1994*,[94] which relates in part to the requirement to provide for compensatory adjustment when increasing bound tariffs in the process of

[93] Appellate Body Report, *US – Cotton Yarn*, [81] (original emphasis).
[94] GATT Doc LT/UR/A-1A/1/GATT/U/4 (15 April 1994).

forming a customs union or free trade area. Members are to enter negotiations 'in good faith with a view to achieving mutually satisfactory compensatory adjustment'.[95] Thus, this good faith obligation is similar to the DSU requirement to engage in consultations and dispute settlement procedures in good faith.

Good faith is also mentioned in several provisions of the TRIPS Agreement. Article 24, which relates to negotiations to increase the protection of individual geographical indications,[96] contains three references to good faith. These references relate to the 'good faith' of the nationals or domiciliaries of WTO Members in applying for or registering trademarks, and in using trademarks or geographical indications.[97] Articles 48.2 and 58(c) of the TRIPS Agreement refer to the 'good faith' of public authorities or officials in administering laws for the protection or enforcement of intellectual property rights. The references to good faith in the TRIPS Agreement are therefore less relevant to the principle of good faith examined in this chapter, because they concern the good faith of persons within WTO Members rather than the good faith of WTO Members themselves.

In the following sections, I consider some of the ways in which good faith as a principle of the WTO, a principle of customary international law, or a general principle of law could be used in WTO disputes. For the sake of clarity, I first consider certain aspects of good faith that might be regarded as procedural, in that they relate to the conduct of WTO disputes. I then turn to more substantive implications of good faith, which relate to obligations of WTO Members more generally.

4.3.2 Procedural implications of good faith

A. Engaging in dispute settlement procedures (DSU Article 3.10)

One of the most significant reflections of good faith in the WTO agreements is in the general statement in Article 3.10 of the DSU that Members will engage in the WTO dispute settlement procedures in good faith. The meaning of 'good faith' in this provision, whether regarded as an ordinary or special meaning, is clearly informed by good faith as a general principle of law and a principle of customary international law. Indeed, the Appellate Body has described Article 3.10 as a 'specific manifestation of the principle of good faith which . . . is at once

[95] Ibid. [5]. [96] TRIPS Agreement, art. 24.1. [97] TRIPS Agreement, arts. 24.4, 24.5.

a general principle of law and a principle of general international law'.[98] But it is necessary to examine WTO Tribunals' pronouncements on good faith in relation to Article 3.10 more closely in order to determine whether they have properly interpreted this provision, taking into account this broader good faith principle.

The principle of due process (discussed in the following chapter) obviously concerns issues of honesty, fairness and reasonableness, as does the principle of good faith. But the fact that these principles are related does not mean that they are interchangeable. Accordingly, the obligation in Article 3.10 of the DSU to 'engage in these procedures in good faith in an effort to resolve the dispute' should be read as obliging Members to remain open to resolution of their dispute, whether through a mutually satisfactory solution or pursuant to recommendations of the DSB. These obligations cannot be breached by due process failures of the parties such as the late filing of a defence. Rather, they might be breached by actions such as refusing to meet with a Member that has requested consultations or refusing to participate in proceedings.

In some submissions to and reports of WTO Tribunals, the principle of good faith or one of its specific rules has been muddled with the principle of due process.[99] For example, the Appellate Body appears to have confused the due process obligations imposed on Members in relation to the conduct of anti-dumping investigations with the principle of good faith.[100] In addition, WTO Tribunals have repeatedly but incorrectly read the reference to good faith in DSU Article 3.10 as referring to due process.[101] For example, in its report in *US – Gambling*, the Appellate Body noted that 'the DSU is silent about a deadline or a method by which a responding party must state the legal basis for its defence'.[102] Rather than simply relying on the principle of due process to resolve this issue, it pointed to DSU Article 3.10 and suggested that

98 Appellate Body Report, *US – FSC*, [166].

99 See, e.g., Panel Report, *US – Steel Safeguards*, [7.1987]; Panel Report, *US – Hot-Rolled Steel*, [A-76]; Appellate Body Report, *Mexico – Corn Syrup* (Article 21.5 – US), [47].

100 See Appellate Body Report, *US – Hot-Rolled Steel*, [101], [193].

101 See, e.g., Appellate Body Report, *Canada – Aircraft*, [190]; Appellate Body Report, *EC – Sardines*, [139]–[141] (discussed in Arthur Appleton and Veijo Heiskanen, 'The Sardines Decision: Fish Without Chips?' in Andrew Mitchell (ed.), *Challenges and Prospects for the WTO* (2005) 165, 169–70); Panel Report, *EC – Asbestos*, n. 3; Appellate Body Report, *US – Lamb*, [115].

102 Appellate Body Report, *US – Gambling*, [269].

this provision 'implies' that the respondent must state the legal basis for its defence 'at the earliest opportunity'.[103]

Similarly, in *US – FSC*, the Appellate Body stated that Article 3.10 contains a reference to the principle of good faith, requiring Members' 'good faith compliance' with DSU requirements.[104] The Appellate Body read 'good faith compliance' as requiring that 'complaining Members accord to the responding Members the full measure of protection and opportunity to defend, contemplated by the letter and spirit of the procedural rules' and that 'responding Members seasonably and promptly bring claimed procedural deficiencies to the attention of the complaining Member'.[105] In other words, the Appellate Body considered that 'good faith compliance' requires parties to act consistently with the objective of protecting due process in WTO proceedings. It is not clear why the Appellate Body felt compelled to refer to good faith in Article 3.10 rather than some of the WTO provisions that do relate specifically to due process. For example, in relation to the due process interest of providing respondents with sufficient notice of the case they have to answer, these provisions include those concerning the request for consultations (DSU Article 4.4), the request for the establishment of a Panel (Article 6.2), and written submissions to the Panel (Articles 12.6, 15.1).

In other international tribunals, due process is not generally invoked in connection with good faith. The WTO Tribunals' unusual approach to Article 3.10 of the DSU may have arisen from a desire to point to specific WTO provisions to support particular propositions or interpretations, even if this involves straining the meaning of the provision in question. This may reflect a genuine concern not to impinge on the sovereignty of Members nor to add to or diminish the rights and obligations under the covered agreements contrary to Articles 3.2 and 19.2 of the DSU. However, as explained in Chapter 3, WTO Tribunals need not feel constrained by this part of Articles 3.2 and 19.2, provided that they carefully follow the rules of treaty interpretation as they are mandated to do. It would be far better for WTO Tribunals to rely on the principle of due process as discussed in the next chapter (including in the exercise of inherent jurisdiction) than to read due process into the notion of good faith in Article 3.10 without legal basis. Keeping good faith and due process distinct will promote legal certainty and predictability.

[103] Ibid. [269]. [104] Appellate Body Report, *US – FSC*, [166]. [105] Ibid. [166].

B. Resorting to dispute settlement (DSU Articles 3.7, 23)

WTO Tribunals have also referred to good faith in interpreting certain provisions of the DSU that do not include the words 'good faith'. These provisions relate to a Member's decision to resort to the WTO dispute settlement procedures.

DSU Article 3.7 states that, '[b]efore bringing a case, a Member shall exercise its judgement as to whether action under these procedures would be fruitful'. The Appellate Body stated in *Mexico – Corn Syrup (Article 21.5 – US)* that 'this sentence reflects a basic principle that Members should have recourse to WTO dispute settlement in good faith, and not frivolously set in motion the procedures contemplated in the DSU'.[106] However, this requirement is 'largely self-regulating' and, accordingly, WTO Tribunals 'must presume, whenever a Member submits a request for establishment of a panel, that such a Member does so in good faith, having duly exercised its judgement as to whether recourse to that panel would be "fruitful"'.[107] In that case, the Appellate Body held that the Panel was not obliged to consider, of its own initiative, whether the complainant had exercised its judgement as required by Article 3.7.[108] Thus, the Appellate Body appeared to leave open the possibility that a Panel might find, upon request, that a Member had not exercised its judgement in accordance with Article 3.7.[109] Bartels suggests that a WTO Member might not be acting in good faith if it requested the establishment of a Panel 'for the *purpose* of nullifying the substantive rights of another WTO Member'.[110]

Given that Article 3.7 does not refer expressly to WTO Members' obligations to engage in dispute settlement in good faith, what basis did the Appellate Body have to infer a requirement of good faith in interpreting that provision? The most obvious answer is Article 3.10 of the DSU, which provides relevant context for the interpretation of Article 3.7 and can be read as encapsulating the 'basic principle'[111] that Members must engage in dispute settlement in good faith. Against this

106 Appellate Body Report, *Mexico – Corn Syrup (Article 21.5 – US)*, [73].

107 Ibid. [74] (quoting Appellate Body Report, *EC – Bananas III*, [135]. 108 Ibid. [74].

109 Were it otherwise, one might wonder whether the Appellate Body's interpretation renders the first sentence of art. 3.7 meaningless.

110 Lorand Bartels, 'The Separation of Powers in the WTO: How to Avoid Judicial Activism' (2004) 53 *International and Comparative Law Quarterly* 861, 890 (original emphasis).

111 Appellate Body Report, *Mexico – Corn Syrup (Article 21.5 – US)*, [73].

background, it seems unnecessary to refer to good faith as a general principle of law or a principle of customary international law to justify the Appellate Body's interpretation of Article 3.10 of the DSU.

Another DSU provision in relation to which WTO Tribunals have referred to good faith is Article 23, which one Panel described as 'embed[ding]' the 'fundamental principle' that 'the dispute settlement system of the WTO [provides] . . . the exclusive means to redress any violations of any provisions of the WTO Agreement'.[112] In *US – Section 301 Trade Act*, the Panel suggested that a 'good faith' interpretation of Article 23 of the DSU, within the meaning of Article 31(1) of the VCLT, suggests that Members should 'refrain from adopting national laws which threaten prohibited conduct', namely resolving disputes through unilateral action rather than in accordance with the DSU.[113] However, the Panel was reluctant to impute 'bad faith' to either party in relation to its interpretation of this provision, preferring to seek the 'better faith' interpretation.[114] This reasoning reflects the overlap between good faith interpretation and performance of treaties, as mentioned earlier.[115] It also raises the question (which I address further below) of the circumstances in which a WTO Tribunal might find that a Member had acted in bad faith (or had failed to act in good faith), in the absence of a specific provision imposing an obligation of good faith.[116]

C. Good faith and inherent jurisdiction: estoppel

Although several Members have pleaded estoppel before GATT Panels[117] and WTO Tribunals, none has succeeded in such a claim. This series of cases provides one of the most illuminating illustrations of WTO Tribunals' understanding of the principle of good faith. It is not surprising that claims of estoppel are difficult to make out, but WTO Tribunals have responded to such claims with mixed degrees of legal accuracy. Some of the decisions reveal unnecessary hostility to this important expression of the principle of good faith, as well as a misunderstanding of the role of principles in WTO disputes.

[112] Panel Report, *US – Certain EC Products*, [6.13].

[113] Panel Report, *US – Section 301 Trade Act*, [7.68]. [114] Ibid. [7.64].

[115] See above, section 4.2.4(B). [116] See below, section 4.3.3(A).

[117] See James Cameron and Kevin Gray, 'Principles of International Law in the WTO Dispute Settlement Body' (2001) 50 *International and Comparative Law Quarterly* 248, 294; Pieter Kuyper, 'The Law of GATT as a Special Field of International Law: Ignorance, Further Refinement or Self-Contained System of International Law?' (1994) 25 *Netherlands International Law Review* 227, 231.

In *US – FSC*, the Appellate Body prevented the United States from objecting to an alleged failure by the European Communities to include a 'statement of available evidence' with its request for consultations as required by SCM Agreement Article 4.2, on the basis that the United States had forgone several earlier opportunities to raise this objection.[118] Trachtman suggests that the Appellate Body applied a form of estoppel in this instance, even though estoppel was neither pleaded nor expressly mentioned.[119] However, as the Appellate Body made no mention of the European Communities relying to its detriment on the silence or inaction of the United States in this regard, this dispute does not present a true example of estoppel.[120]

Two WTO Panels appear to have understood the notion of estoppel and dealt with Members' claims of estoppel accordingly. In *Guatemala – Cement II*, Guatemala argued that Mexico was estopped from alleging certain violations of the Anti-Dumping Agreement because Mexico had not made these allegations at the earliest opportunity.[121] In defining estoppel, the Panel stated that 'where one party has been induced to act in reliance on the assurances of another party, in such a way that it would be prejudiced were the other party later to change its position, such a change in position is "estopped", that is precluded'.[122]

The Panel rejected Guatemala's claim of estoppel because 'Mexico was under no obligation to object immediately to the violations' and raised the allegations 'at an appropriate moment under the dispute settlement procedure'.[123] Accordingly, the Panel did not consider that Guatemala could reasonably have relied on Mexico's delay in making these allegations, and it was also not persuaded that Guatemala would have acted any differently had Mexico made the allegations earlier.[124] This reasoning is in line with the principle of estoppel in international law as described earlier in this chapter.[125] Although the Panel did not explicitly consider the basis for making a claim of estoppel in a WTO dispute or the applicable law in dealing with such a claim, it can be regarded as having addressed this claim in the proper exercise of its

[118] Appellate Body Report, *US – FSC*, [165].
[119] Joel Trachtman, 'United States: Tax Treatment for "Foreign Sales Corporations" ', *European Journal of International Law:* Survey of Decisions of the Appellate Body of the World Trade Organization, available at www.ejil.org/journal/curdevs/sr8.html.
[120] See Michael Lennard, 'Navigating by the Stars: Interpreting the WTO Agreements' (2002) 5 *Journal of International Economic Law* 17, 78.
[121] Panel Report, *Guatemala – Cement II*, [8.23]. [122] Ibid. [123] Ibid. [8.24]. [124] Ibid.
[125] See above, section 4.2.4(C).

inherent jurisdiction to resolve procedural matters, as discussed in Chapter 3. This dispute was not appealed.

In *Argentina – Poultry Anti-Dumping Duties*, Argentina argued that Brazil was estopped from pursuing its WTO claim because Brazil had already brought proceedings against the same measure before an Ad Hoc Arbitral Tribunal of MERCOSUR. The Panel rejected Argentina's claim of estoppel. Mexico had made no clear and unambiguous statement that, 'having brought a case under the MERCOSUR dispute settlement framework, it would not subsequently resort to WTO dispute settlement proceedings'.[126] In addition, the Panel found no evidence that Argentina had 'actively relied in good faith on any statement made by Brazil, either to the advantage of Brazil or to the disadvantage of Argentina'.[127] Like the earlier Panel in *Guatemala – Cement II*, this Panel's approach to estoppel accords generally with the requirements of estoppel in international law outside the WTO. Again, the Panel here did not explain its rationale for addressing the claim on its terms, but this can be seen as a valid exercise of the Panel's inherent jurisdiction. Neither party appealed the Panel report.

In two other WTO disputes, the Panels were far less adept at handling claims of estoppel. In *EC – Bed Linen (Article 21.5 – India)*, India claimed that the European Communities was estopped 'from advocating before us an interpretation of a provision of the AD Agreement which is different from the interpretation by the European Court of First Instance of a provision in the EC's municipal anti-dumping law which is identical to the AD Agreement provision'.[128] Curiously, India attempted to buttress its estoppel argument by positing that 'the principle of good faith, as enshrined in the Vienna Convention, ensures that such case law can serve as relevant context'.[129] This argument regarding good faith interpretation under Article 31(1) of the VCLT has very little to do with estoppel.[130] Unfortunately, the Panel also provided a curious response to India's claim. Perhaps baffled by India's reference to good faith interpretation, the Panel stated that '"estoppel" based on national court decisions interpreting municipal law does not limit the decisions of WTO panels interpreting a covered agreement'.[131] The Panel

[126] Panel Report, *Argentina – Poultry Anti-Dumping Duties*, [7.38]. [127] Ibid. [7.39].

[128] Panel Report, *EC – Bed Linen (Article 21.5 – India)*, [6.89]. [129] Ibid.

[130] This argument failed even as an interpretive context. The Panel held that the court decision 'does not constitute "context", as that term is used in Article 31 of the Vienna Convention': ibid. [6.90].

[131] Ibid. [6.91].

concluded that WTO Tribunals may not find that a Member has violated a WTO provision on the basis that the Member is applying the provision in bad faith,[132] adding:

> We know of no basis in international law, and India has not cited any, that would require us to conclude that a measure which is consistent with a Member's obligations under a provision of a covered agreement that we have interpreted in accordance with customary rules of interpretation of public international law could nonetheless be found to be in violation of that provision on the basis of alleged 'bad faith'.[133]

All in all, the Panel appears to have been thoroughly confused and anxious about India's claim of estoppel. It may have wanted to assuage Members' fears that Panels could find that a Member has acted in bad faith (an issue discussed further below). But India was not asking the Panel to find that the European Communities had acted in bad faith. It was simply arguing that the European Communities was precluded from submitting an interpretation of a WTO provision that was inconsistent with one of its court's interpretations of the municipal law equivalent.

The Panel could have dismissed this claim quite easily in the exercise of its inherent jurisdiction, relying on the doctrine of estoppel as part of the principle of good faith in international law. The European Communities made no representation to India that could form the basis of an estoppel. The European Court of First Instance is a separate institution from the European Communities as a WTO Member. Statements by that court should not be regarded as being authorised by the European Communities, addressed to India, or likely to affect India's conduct. Accordingly, such statements cannot found an estoppel.[134] Finally, the decision of the European Court of First Instance seems to be an interpretation of a particular legal rule, rather than a representation of fact, which is required to make out an estoppel.[135]

In *EC – Export Subsidies on Sugar* the European Communities argued, '[o]n the basis of . . . its good faith expectations', that the complainants (Australia, Brazil and Thailand) were estopped from bringing certain claims[136] because the violations alleged in those claims 'would have been flagrant and immediately manifest upon the conclusion of the *WTO Agreement*'.[137] Yet the complainants had only raised these

[132] Ibid. [133] Ibid. [134] Bowett, 'Estoppel Before International Tribunals', 185–6, 192. [135] Ibid. 196. [136] Panel Reports, *EC – Export Subsidies on Sugar*, [7.55]. [137] Ibid. [7.55].

violations in bringing this dispute several years later.[138] The Panel considered the meaning of estoppel in law generally as well as its meaning as a 'principle' in public international law.[139] It suggested that estoppel might be a 'general principle of law',[140] a 'customary rule of interpretation',[141] or part of the 'good faith principle reflected in Article 3.10 of the *DSU*'.[142] However, the Panel declared:

> it is far from clear whether the principle of estoppel is applicable to disputes between WTO Members in relation to their WTO rights and obligations. The principle of estoppel has never been applied by any panel or the Appellate Body. Estoppel is not mentioned in the DSU or anywhere in the WTO Agreement.[143]

Once it is accepted that the WTO agreements (like all legal texts) cannot possibly cover every conceivable issue that could arise in the WTO and do not purport to do so, the fact that the WTO agreements do not refer explicitly to estoppel means very little. More specifically, the WTO agreements leave many procedural issues up to the WTO Tribunals. Why, then, was the Panel so intent on rejecting the role of estoppel in WTO disputes? Looking more closely at the Panel's reasoning, it becomes clear that the Panel had several unspoken concerns about the European Communities' reference to good faith in conjunction with estoppel, as well as fundamental fears about the incorporation of international law in WTO law.

The Panel stressed that 'both the European Communities and the Complainants have acted in good faith in the initiation and conduct of the present dispute proceedings',[144] indicating its perception that accepting the European Communities' estoppel argument might suggest that the complainants had acted in bad faith. The Panel also revealed its concern not to infringe the sovereignty of WTO Members by emphasising again the 'largely self-regulating' nature of Article 3.7 of the DSU,[145] even though the European Communities' claim of estoppel was not grounded in that provision. The Panel also referred to the Appellate Body's treatment of the precautionary principle in *EC – Hormones*, indicating a desire to avoid the suggestion that a principle of non-WTO law might impose an independent obligation on WTO

[138] Ibid. [7.54]. [139] Ibid. [7.61]–[7.62] (footnotes omitted). [140] Ibid. [7.64].
[141] Ibid. [7.65]. [142] Ibid. [143] Ibid. [7.63] (original emphasis). [144] Ibid. [7.74].
[145] Ibid. [7.66] –[7.67] (quoting Appellate Body Report, *Mexico – Corn Syrup (Article 21.5 – US)*, [73]).

Members or even override an explicit WTO provision.[146] It stated that, if estoppel 'were applicable' in WTO disputes, Members 'would . . . have to find a way to comply in good faith with both the provisions of the DSU and those of estoppel'.[147] Yet estoppel imposes no requirements on WTO Members, and it need not constitute applicable law in WTO disputes to be relevant. WTO Tribunals have inherent jurisdiction to resolve procedural matters and can rule on claims of estoppel on that basis.

Finally, the Panel stated that, even assuming that estoppel could be 'invoked' in WTO disputes, the elements of estoppel were not made out.[148] The complainants' silence did not create 'a clear and unambiguous representation upon which the European Communities could rely', especially given that the complainants had no legal duty to notify the European Communities of its alleged violations.[149] The Panel added that accepting the European Communities' estoppel argument would be contrary to the prohibition in Articles 3.2 and 19.2 of the DSU on adding to or diminishing the rights and obligations in the covered agreements.[150] In my view, recognising a well-established general principle of law and principle of customary international law in the exercise of inherent jurisdiction would involve no infringement of Article 3.2 or 19.2. If anything, the Panel abdicated its judicial function in failing to do so.

On appeal, the Appellate Body rejected the European Communities' claim of estoppel.[151] It agreed with the Panel that 'it is far from clear that the estoppel principle applies in the context of WTO dispute settlement',[152] and went on to state:

> The principle of estoppel has never been applied by the Appellate Body. Moreover, the notion of estoppel, as advanced by the European Communities, would appear to inhibit the ability of WTO Members to initiate a WTO dispute settlement proceeding. We see little in the DSU that explicitly limits the rights of WTO Members to bring an action; WTO Members must exercise their 'judgement as to whether action under these procedures would be fruitful', by virtue of Article 3.7 of the DSU, and they must engage in dispute settlement procedures in good faith, by virtue of Article 3.10 of the DSU. This latter obligation covers, in our view, the entire spectrum of dispute settlement, from the point of initiation of a case through implementation. Thus, even assuming

[146] Panel Reports, *EC – Export Subsidies on Sugar*, [7.64]. [147] Ibid. [148] Ibid. [7.70].
[149] Ibid. [7.73]. [150] Ibid. [7.75].
[151] Appellate Body Report, *EC – Export Subsidies on Sugar*, [317]. [152] Ibid. [310].

arguendo that the principle of estoppel could apply in the WTO, its application would fall within these narrow parameters set out in the DSU.[153]

This passage may reflect some of the Panel's concerns regarding estoppel, including a desire to focus on the text of the DSU and thus avoid criticism by Members for adding to or diminishing their rights and obligations. However, even if the Appellate Body did not wish to exercise its inherent jurisdiction to address the claim of estoppel, it could and should have acknowledged that the requirement of 'good faith' in Article 3.10 of the DSU (which, incidentally, the European Communities had relied on as an adjunct to its estoppel claim)[154] must be interpreted by reference to the principle of good faith in international law and, in turn, the doctrine of estoppel in international law. Properly understood, Article 3.10 of the DSU does not narrow the concept of good faith or estoppel. It is the principle of good faith that informs and elaborates Article 3.10 of the DSU.

Ultimately, the Appellate Body adopted the same strategy as the Panel, finding that estoppel was not made out even assuming that it applied.[155] First, the complainants made no representations regarding the WTO-consistency of the European Communities measure.[156] Second, there was no 'shared understanding' between the parties as alleged by the European Communities.[157] It is not clear how the alleged 'shared understanding' was supposed to fit into the elements of estoppel. Had the Appellate Body shown more confidence in addressing this claim, it might have more carefully evaluated its meaning in international law, thereby providing clearer and better reasoning for its conclusion.

4.3.3 *Substantive implications of good faith*

A. Performance of WTO obligations: pacta sunt servanda

The Appellate Body has stated that WTO Tribunals should not presume that Members have acted in bad faith[158] and, conversely, that WTO Tribunals should presume that Members have acted in good faith in carrying out their WTO obligations 'as required by the principle of *pacta sunt servanda* articulated in Article 26 of the Vienna Convention'.[159]

153 Ibid. [312]. 154 Ibid. [307]. 155 Ibid. [313]. 156 Ibid. [315]. 157 Ibid. [316].

158 Appellate Body Report, *Chile – Alcoholic Beverages*, [74].

159 Appellate Body Report, *EC – Sardines*, [278]. See also Appellate Body Report, *US – Oil Country Tubular Goods Sunset Reviews*, [173]; Panel Report, *US – Shrimp (Article 21.5 – Malaysia)*, [5.19].

These statements suggest that Members are obliged to carry out their treaty obligations in good faith and that, in appropriate circumstances, the presumption that they have done so might be successfully rebutted. Nevertheless, WTO Tribunals typically refrain from calling Members to account or from questioning the accuracy of the presumption in light of the circumstances before them. To do so would involve acknowledging the principle of good faith as applicable law or as the basis for a valid claim in WTO disputes.

The significant exception was in *US – Offset Act (Byrd Amendment)*. That case concerned the Continued Dumping and Subsidy Offset Act of 2000 (CDSOA), which provides for the distribution of anti-dumping or countervailing duties to affected domestic producers who supported the application for the initiation of the investigation that led to the imposition of those duties. The complainants (Australia, Brazil, Canada, Chile, the European Communities, India, Indonesia, Japan, Korea, Mexico and Thailand) challenged the CDSOA under Article 5.4 of the Anti-Dumping Agreement and Article 11.4 of the SCM Agreement, among other provisions. These provisions relate to the initiation of investigations to determine whether to impose anti-dumping or countervailing duties respectively. Essentially, they preclude domestic authorities from initiating investigations on the application of the domestic industry unless the application is supported by a sufficient proportion of domestic producers, determined according to certain statistical thresholds. The complainants argued:

> [W]hen a treaty provision specifies that actions of private parties are necessary to establish a Member's right to take action, government provision of a financial incentive for those private parties to act one way rather than another is inconsistent with the requirement that Members perform their treaty obligations in good faith.[160]

The Panel read the text of the relevant provisions as merely imposing 'statistical thresholds' rather than a 'requirement that the investigating authorities inquire into the motives or intent of a domestic producer in electing to support a petition'.[161] However, it went on to agree with the complainants, stating that the CDSOA

> recreates the spectre of an investigation being pursued where only a few domestic producers have been affected by the alleged dumping, but industry support is forthcoming because of the prospect of offset payments being

[160] Panel Report, *US – Offset Act (Byrd Amendment)*, [7.54]. [161] Ibid. [7.63].

distributed if dumping is found in consequence of the investigation and antidumping duties imposed. In consequence the CDSOA may be regarded as having undermined the value of AD Article 5.4/SCM Article 11.4 to the countries with whom the United States trades, and the United States may be regarded as not having acted in good faith in promoting this outcome.[162]

The Panel supported this conclusion by reference to 'the principle of good faith as a general rule of conduct in international relations', which 'requires a party to a treaty to refrain from acting in a manner which would defeat the object and purpose of the treaty as a whole or the treaty provision in question'.[163] The Panel characterised the object and purpose of Article 5.4 of the Anti-Dumping Agreement and Article 11.4 of the SCM Agreement as follows: 'to require the authority to examine the degree of support which exists for an application and to determine whether the application was thus filed by or on behalf of the domestic industry'.[164] The Panel concluded that the CDSOA is inconsistent with those provisions because it effectively 'mandates domestic producers to support the application and renders the threshold test . . . completely meaningless'.[165]

The Appellate Body reversed the Panel's finding that the CDSOA is inconsistent with Article 5.4 of the Anti-Dumping Agreement and Article 11.4 of the SCM Agreement.[166] The Appellate Body considered that the Panel failed to apply correctly the 'principles of interpretation codified in the *Vienna Convention*'.[167] In particular, the Appellate Body queried the Panel's reference to the 'object and purpose' of the relevant provisions. The Appellate Body stated:

> Clearly, the matter at issue before the Panel included whether the CDSOA is inconsistent with the *Anti-Dumping Agreement* and the *SCM Agreement* in the light of their object and purpose, since interpreting Articles 5.4 and 11.4 involves an inquiry into the object and purpose of those Agreements. In our view, however, the Panel dismissed all too quickly the textual analysis of those provisions as irrelevant.[168]

Whether deliberately or not, the Appellate Body appears to have missed the point of the Panel's analysis of object and purpose in this instance. The Panel was not relying on object and purpose in the course of interpreting the relevant provisions under Article 31(1) of the VCLT. The Panel was relying on the substantive principle reflected in Article

[162] Ibid. [163] Ibid. [7.64] (footnotes omitted). [164] Ibid. [165] Ibid. [7.66].
[166] Appellate Body Report, *US – Offset Act (Byrd Amendment)*, [294]. [167] Ibid. [281].
[168] Ibid. [285].

18 of the VCLT[169] (and, presumably, Article 26 of the VCLT), which requires states to perform their treaty obligations in good faith. Thus, the Panel was using the principle of good faith (whether a general principle of law or as a principle of customary international law) as applicable law or the basis for a claim in a WTO dispute.

Strangely, although the Appellate Body appeared to misunderstand the Panel's use of the substantive principle of good faith, it went on to accept the independent applicability of such a principle. The United States argued that there 'is no basis or justification in the WTO Agreement for a WTO dispute settlement panel to conclude that a Member has not acted in good faith, or to enforce a principle of good faith as a substantive obligation agreed to by WTO Members'.[170] In response, the Appellate Body referred to its previous recognition of 'the relevance of the principle of good faith'[171] and stated: 'Clearly, therefore, there is a basis for a dispute settlement panel to determine, in an appropriate case, whether a Member has not acted in good faith'.[172]

The previous pronouncements that the Appellate Body referred to involved misapplications of the principle of good faith[173] and, even if correct, would not demonstrate why WTO Tribunals may rule on whether a Member has acted in good faith, independent of any particular provision. Such a ruling would fall outside the procedural matters that WTO Tribunals may resolve in the exercise of inherent jurisdiction. It would also not be based on a valid claim or applicable law by virtue of the reflection of good faith in Article 5.4 of the Anti-Dumping Agreement or Article 11.4 of the SCM Agreement (in that these provisions do not specifically reflect the principle of good faith beyond the general requirement that they be interpreted in good faith). As suggested earlier,[174] good faith might be a principle of WTO law in the sense that it explains the binding nature of the WTO agreements, but this does not mean that WTO Tribunals may apply an independent, substantive principle of good faith in relation to every WTO provision.

[169] Panel Report, *US – Offset Act (Byrd Amendment)*, n. 314.

[170] Appellate Body Report, *US – Offset Act (Byrd Amendment)*, [296].

[171] Ibid. [297], citing Appellate Body Report, *US –Shrimp*, [158]; Appellate Body Report, *US – FSC*, [166]; Appellate Body Report, *US – Hot-Rolled Steel*, [101].

[172] Appellate Body Report, *US – Offset Act (Byrd Amendment)*, [297].

[173] See above section 4.3.2(A), and below, section 4.3.3(C).

[174] See above section 4.3.1.

In any case, the Appellate Body rejected the Panel's conclusion that the United States had not acted in good faith in enacting the CDSOA.[175] It added:

> Nothing . . . in the covered agreements supports the conclusion that simply because a WTO Member is found to have violated a substantive treaty provision, it has therefore not acted in good faith. In our view, it would be necessary to prove more than mere violation to support such a conclusion.[176]

Of course, the source of any independent, substantive obligation of good faith is not the covered agreements but international law more generally. The Appellate Body's conclusion implies that a violation is a necessary but not sufficient condition for a finding that a Member did not act in good faith. This is consistent with the ICJ's statement in *Border and Transborder Armed Actions (Nicaragua* v. *Honduras)* that good faith is 'not in itself a source of obligation where none would otherwise exist'.[177] However, had the Appellate Body engaged in a more open and rigorous analysis of good faith in international law, it might have noted the possibility that good faith could be violated even in the absence of a breach of a treaty provision.[178]

Upon adoption of the Panel and Appellate Body reports in *US – Offset Act (Byrd Amendment)*, the United States referred to the Appellate Body's 'troubling' discussion of good faith,[179] and in particular its conclusion that WTO Tribunals could find that a Member had not acted in good faith:

> The US concern did not relate to whether Members were to implement their obligations in 'good faith' under international law. The United States agreed that they were. However, the WTO dispute settlement system had a limited mandate, which was to determine conformity with the 'covered agreements,' and not international law more generally . . . A finding that a Member had not acted in 'good faith' would clearly and unambiguously exceed the mandate of dispute settlement panels and the Appellate Body.[180]

Members' statements to the DSB are generally self-serving, and this is no exception, but in this case the United States was correct.

[175] Appellate Body Report, *US – Offset Act (Byrd Amendment)*, [299]. [176] Ibid. [298].

[177] *Border and Transborder Armed Actions* (*Nicaragua* v. *Honduras*) (Jurisdiction and Admissibility) [1988] ICJ Rep 69, 105.

[178] See above section 4.2.4(A).

[179] DSB, *Minutes of Meeting Held on 27 January 2003*, WT/DSB/M/142 (6 March 2003) [57].

[180] Ibid.

B. Non-violation complaints

In the previous section, I queried the Appellate Body's suggestion that WTO Tribunals may apply the principle of good faith to find that a Member has not acted in good faith independently of any WTO provision. At least one aspect of WTO law does seem to reflect the principle of good faith: the possibility of bringing 'non-violation' complaints. The main non-violation provisions are in Article XXIII:1(b) of GATT 1994, Article XXIII:3 of GATS, and Article 26.1 of the DSU. Essentially, a Member may claim that another Member has 'nullified or impaired' benefits accruing to the complainant under the WTO agreements by applying a measure even if the measure does not violate those agreements.[181]

In *Korea – Procurement*, the Panel stated that 'the non-violation remedy as it has developed in GATT/WTO jurisprudence should not be viewed in isolation from general principles of customary international law',[182] apparently merging the categories of 'general principles of law' and 'customary international law' as reflected in Articles 38(1)(c) and 38(1)(b) of the ICJ Statute respectively. The Panel explained this 'non-violation remedy' as follows:

> [T]he basic premise is that Members should not take actions, even those consistent with the letter of the treaty, which might serve to undermine the reasonable expectations of negotiating partners. This has traditionally arisen in the context of actions which might undermine the value of negotiated tariff concessions. In our view, this is a further development of the principle of *pacta sunt servanda* . . . [which] is expressed in Article 26 of the *Vienna Convention*.[183]

The Panel was correct that the non-violation complaint seems analogous to the requirement in international law that states perform their treaty obligations in good faith, at least according to the view that a state may breach this requirement without necessarily breaching the treaty obligations themselves. However, this alone seems insufficient to conclude that WTO Tribunals, in addressing non-violation complaints, may determine more generally whether a Member has acted in good

[181] See generally Frieder Roessler and Petina Gappah, 'A Re-Appraisal of Non-Violation Complaints under the WTO Dispute Settlement Procedures' in Patrick Macrory et al. (eds.), *The World Trade Organization: Legal, Economic and Political Analysis* (2005) vol. I, 1371; Thomas Cottier and Krista Schefer, 'Non-Violation Complaints in WTO/GATT Dispute Settlement: Past, Present and Future' in Ernst-Ulrich Petersmann (ed.), *International Trade Law and the GATT/WTO Dispute Settlement System* (1997) 145.

[182] Panel Report, *Korea – Procurement*, [7.93]. [183] Ibid.

faith. The question of whether a state has violated a treaty obligation is separate from the question of whether the state has acted in good faith (thus, a treaty violation does not necessarily mean an absence of good faith). Similarly, asking whether a non-violation complaint is made out is not the same as asking whether a Member has acted in good faith. The fact that a Member may have nullified or impaired benefits of another Member (whether or not it has also violated a WTO provision) does not necessarily mean that it has not acted in good faith.

The Panel seemed to recognise this. It went on to explain its view, as mentioned in Chapter 1,[184] that 'the customary rules of international law apply to the WTO treaties'[185] and, implicitly, that WTO Tribunals may apply those rules in WTO disputes and determine whether they have been breached. In Chapter 3, I took a narrower view of the extent to which principles of customary international law and general principles of law can underlie claims or constitute applicable law in WTO disputes. The Panel added:

> [W]hile the overall burden of proof is on the complainant, we do not mean to introduce here a new requirement that a complainant affirmatively prove actual bad faith on the part of another Member ... Rather, the affirmative proof should be that measures have been taken that frustrate the object and purpose of the treaty and the reasonably expected benefits that flow therefrom.[186]

The Panel took the relationship between WTO law and international law even further, using its conclusion that non-violation complaints are an extension of *pacta sunt servanda* to justify the application of the VCLT rules on errors in treaty formation.[187] Ultimately, the Panel found that the United States had not made out its non-violation claim.[188]

This dispute did not proceed to the Appellate Body. Had it been appealed, there is little doubt that the Appellate Body would have chastised the Panel for failing to interpret the relevant non-violation provisions in the WTO agreements in accordance with Articles 31 and 32 of the VCLT. The Panel did fail in this regard. Although the principle of good faith in international law may have been relevant in interpreting the non-violation provisions, the Panel skipped the usual steps of text, context, and object and purpose in interpreting these

[184] See above, section 1.3.2, para. beginning 'In 2000, the Panel in *Korea – Procurement* ...', entire para.

[185] Panel Report, *Korea – Procurement*, [7.96]. [186] Ibid. [7.99].

[187] Ibid. [7.100]–[7.102], [7.123]. [188] Panel Report, *Korea – Procurement*, [7.126].

provisions, instead overlaying the non-violation remedy with its understanding of *pacta sunt servanda* in international law. Not surprisingly, upon the DSB's adoption of the Panel report, several Members (including Korea) expressed concern regarding the Panel's handling of the non-violation claim.[189]

C. General exceptions and abuse of rights

In several cases, WTO Tribunals have relied on the principle of good faith in interpreting the general exceptions in GATT 1994 (Article XX) and GATS (Article XIV). These cases can be traced to *US – Shrimp*, where the Appellate Body made a fairly lengthy statement regarding good faith, particularly in relation to the chapeau (first paragraph) of GATT Article XX, which states that the general exceptions in that provision are '[s]ubject to the requirement that such measures are not applied in a manner which would constitute a means of arbitrary or unjustifiable discrimination between countries where the same conditions prevail, or a disguised restriction on international trade'. The Appellate Body stated:

> The chapeau of Article XX is, in fact, but one expression of the principle of good faith. This principle, at once a general principle of law and a general principle of international law, controls the exercise of rights by states. One application of this general principle, the application widely known as the doctrine of *abus de droit*, prohibits the abusive exercise of a state's rights and enjoins that whenever the assertion of a right 'impinges on the field covered by [a] treaty obligation, it must be exercised bona fide, that is to say reasonably.' An abusive exercise by a Member of its own treaty right thus results in a breach of the treaty rights of the other Members and, as well, a violation of the treaty obligation of the Member so acting. Having said this, our task here is to interpret the language of the chapeau, seeking additional interpretative guidance, as appropriate, from the general principles of international law.[190]

Several questions arise from this paragraph. The Appellate Body's characterisation of good faith as 'a general principle of law and a general principle of international law' is not entirely clear. Perhaps it can be regarded as viewing good faith as a general principle of law and a principle of customary international law, as I do. I also agree with the Appellate Body that *abus de droit* could be described as an application of

[189] DSB, *Minutes of Meeting Held on 19 June 2000*, WT/DSB/M/84 (24 July 2000) [57]–[59], [64], [69].

[190] Ibid. [158], citing Cheng, *General Principles of Law*, ch. 4 (see especially 125); VCLT, art. 31(3)(c).

the principle of good faith. In the last sentence of this paragraph, the Appellate Body makes clear that it is not applying *abus de droit* independently; rather, it is interpreting Article XX of GATT 1994 taking into account this application of the principle of good faith. In adopting this approach, the Appellate Body relies on Article 31(3)(c) of the VCLT, without explaining its apparent assumption that general principles of law and principles of customary international law are the same as rules of international law under Article 31(3)(c). As explained in Chapter 3, I consider that such principles may fall within Article 31(3)(c) only to the extent that they are encompassed in relevant rules of international law.

The Appellate Body appeared to rely on the doctrine of *abus de droit* to support its earlier conclusion that

> a balance must be struck between the *right* of a Member to invoke an exception under Article XX and the *duty* of that same Member to respect the treaty rights of the other Members. To permit one Member to abuse or misuse its right to invoke an exception would be effectively to allow that Member to degrade its own treaty obligations as well as to devalue the treaty rights of other Members.[191]

This description may correspond with the second category of abuse of rights listed earlier in this chapter, but it also appears to flow simply from the Appellate Body's interpretation of Article XX of GATT 1994 in accordance with Article 31(1) of the VCLT.

The Appellate Body applied this balancing requirement to the case at hand in determining whether the challenged United States measure conformed to the requirements of the chapeau of Article XX. This measure was a prohibition on the import of shrimp caught using technology that might adversely affect sea turtles unless the imports came from countries that were certified by the United States as having (i) a fishing environment that did not pose a threat of incidental turtle capture; or (ii) a regulatory programme for the prevention of such capture comparable to that of the United States and with an average rate of such capture comparable to that of United States vessels.[192] The Appellate Body found that the import ban was not justified under Article XX, in part because the United States failed

> to engage the appellees, as well as other Members exporting shrimp to the United States, in serious, across-the-board negotiations with the objective of

[191] Appellate Body Report, *US – Shrimp*, [156] (original emphasis). See also [159].
[192] Ibid. [3]–[4].

> concluding bilateral or multilateral agreements for the protection and conservation of sea turtles, before enforcing the import prohibition against the shrimp exports of those other Members.[193]

In a subsequent case under Article 21.5 of the DSU regarding the consistency of measures that the United States took to comply with the ruling in *US – Shrimp*, the Panel appeared to read the Appellate Body's discussion of the absence of negotiations as arising from its recognition in the same case of the principle of good faith and *abus de droit*. Relying on that discussion,[194] the Panel concluded that the United States was obliged to make 'serious good faith efforts'[195] to negotiate an 'international agreement'[196] relating to the protection of sea turtles 'before resorting to the type of unilateral measure currently in place'.[197] The Panel found that the revised United States measure was justified by Article XX as long as the United States continued to make 'serious good faith efforts to reach a multilateral agreement'.[198] The Appellate Body upheld the Panel's finding that the revised United States measure complied with the chapeau of Article XX 'in view of the serious, good faith efforts made by the United States to negotiate an international agreement'.[199]

Although 'good faith' efforts to negotiate may be required to satisfy the chapeau of Article XX in some circumstances, this should not be confused with the broader principle of good faith or the doctrine of *abus de droit*. The Appellate Body decisions in *US – Shrimp* and *US – Shrimp (Article 21.5 – Malaysia)* are better understood as imposing this requirement regarding negotiations as a result of their interpretation of Article XX. Giving the Appellate Body the benefit of the doubt, its reasoning rested neither on the application of a substantive principle of good faith in international law or the doctrine of *abus de droit*, nor on the influence of such notions pursuant to Article 31(3)(c) of the VCLT.

Similar issues arose more recently in *US – Gambling* in connection with the general exception provision in GATS Article XIV. Like the Panel in *US – Shrimp (Article 21.5 – Malaysia)*, the Panel in *US – Gambling* read the Appellate Body's reference to the principle of good faith and *abus de droit* in *US – Shrimp* as leading to the conclusion that the United States

[193] Ibid. [166]. [194] Panel Report, *US – Shrimp (Article 21.5 – Malaysia)*, [5.60].
[195] Ibid. [5.67].
[196] See, e.g., Panel Report, *US – Shrimp (Article 21.5 – Malaysia)*, [5.73], [5.75].
[197] Ibid. [5.67]. [198] Ibid. [6.1(b)].
[199] Appellate Body Report, *US – Shrimp (Article 21.5 – Malaysia)*, [134].

had not met the requirements of the chapeau of GATT Article XX because it had negotiated with only some Members.[200] The Panel found that the United States restrictions on internet gambling that Antigua and Barbuda had challenged were not provisionally justified under GATS Article XIV(a),[201] in part because, 'in rejecting Antigua's invitation to engage in bilateral or multilateral consultations and/or negotiations, the United States failed to pursue in good faith a course of action that could have been used by it to explore the possibility of finding a reasonably available WTO-consistent alternative'.[202] The Appellate Body reversed this finding,[203] stating:

> Engaging in consultations with Antigua, with a view to arriving at a negotiated settlement that achieves the same objectives as the challenged United States' measures, was not an appropriate alternative for the Panel to consider because consultations are by definition a process, the results of which are uncertain and therefore not capable of comparison with the measures at issue in this case.[204]

Leaving to one side the correctness of the Appellate Body's decision in this dispute, its response to the Panel's discussion of the importance of negotiations confirms that any requirement to negotiate in these circumstances must arise from the relevant provision itself (GATS Article XIV(a)), and not from the incorporation of any broader principle of good faith or *abus de droit* under international law.

4.4 Conclusion

The nebulous nature of good faith as a principle in international law outside the WTO intensifies the difficulties associated with relying on any principle, which is by definition unlikely to be spelled out in any complete, precise manner. Thus, Virally concludes that, 'in practice, this general principle of law has only marginal value as an autonomous source of rights and duties'.[205] That is not to say that good faith is meaningless or that it has no role in WTO disputes. Good faith can properly be regarded as a principle of WTO law, in particular through its reflection in several DSU provisions and its inclusion in the inherent jurisdiction of WTO Tribunals, in the form of estoppel. However, WTO

[200] Panel Report, *US – Gambling*, [6.576]. [201] Ibid. [6.535]. [202] Ibid. [6.531].
[203] Appellate Body Report, *US – Gambling*, [321]. [204] Ibid. [317].
[205] Michael Virally, 'Review Essay: Good Faith in Public International Law' (1983) 77 *American Journal of International Law* 130, 133.

Tribunals should exercise caution in using this principle as if it carried more weight than specific WTO provisions that might be based on similar rationales, such as those governing non-violation complaints, general exceptions, or Members' resort to the dispute settlement system. Whenever WTO Tribunals rely on good faith, whether to interpret WTO provisions or as an independent substantive principle, they should ensure they have a valid legal basis for doing so, in the terms described in Chapter 3, and should identify and explain this basis in their reports. They should also take care to use the principle precisely, consistent with its meaning in international law. In particular, good faith should not be confused with due process, which is discussed in the following chapter.

WTO Tribunals have shown some reluctance to find that a Member has failed to act in good faith. At the same time, WTO Tribunals have sometimes been keen to leave open the possibility that they could make such a finding in an appropriate case. If a WTO Tribunal were ever to find a Member had failed to act in good faith independent of any WTO provision, it would need a solid legal basis for doing so within its mandate as a judicial body and taking into account the relevant provisions of the DSU. I see none.

5 Due process

5.1 Introduction

The principle of 'due process' (also called 'fundamental fairness', 'procedural fairness', or 'natural justice') broadly requires administrative and judicial proceedings to be fair. Administrative and judicial systems attempt to achieve due process by exercising their discretion in a fair manner and by developing procedural or evidentiary rules explaining how rights, duties, powers, and liabilities are administered.[1] As will be seen in this chapter, the principle of due process is difficult to define precisely, because the demands of fairness depend on the circumstances.[2] For example, it may be necessary to balance an individual's interest in additional procedures with the value and cost of such procedures.[3] Thus, in particular circumstances, due process might require a full trial, whereas in other circumstances, basic notice and the right to speak might be sufficient.[4] Considerations of due process might also conflict. For instance, parties' rights to be heard and give evidence might weigh in favour of the last-minute introduction of evidence. On the other hand, the need for equality between the parties and their right to have sufficient time to respond and challenge evidence might weigh against its introduction.[5] Discretion is required to resolve such conflicts.

1 Peter Nygh and Peter Butt (eds.), *Australian Legal Dictionary* (1997) 929, 1129.

2 See, e.g., *Schweiker* v. *McClure*, 456 US 188, 200 (1982): 'due process is flexible and calls for such procedural protections as the particular situation demands'.

3 See, e.g., *Matthews* v. *Eldridge*, 424 US 319 (1976), where it was held that an evidentiary hearing held after termination of a disability benefit was sufficient due process.

4 Kermit Hall (ed.), *Oxford Companion to the Supreme Court of the United States* (1992) 237.

5 Jeff Waincymer, *WTO Litigation: Procedural Aspects of Formal Dispute Settlement* (2002) 72.

Due process is a necessary component of any legal system seeking legitimacy and effectiveness.[6] The dispute settlement system of the WTO is no exception. Howse suggests that 'the further removed the decision-maker is from responsibility to a particular electorate, the greater the extent to which legitimacy depends on procedural fairness itself'.[7] This suggests an increased need for due process in the WTO. Indeed, the potentially vast political and economic effects of trade liberalisation and protectionism, the opportunity for Members to challenge domestic regulations of sovereign governments using WTO rules, and the power differences between WTO Members all heighten the need for fair rule enforcement in the WTO.

This chapter begins by examining the content of the principle of due process and its justification, placing the specific meaning of the principle in the WTO within its wider context in domestic law and international law generally. It then addresses the two main ways in which due process may be used in WTO disputes: first, as a procedural guide to the conduct of proceedings; second, as background for the interpretation of WTO provisions that impose due process requirements on Members in their conduct of judicial or administrative proceedings.

5.2 Due process as a principle

5.2.1 *A general principle of law*

The principle of due process has its origins in domestic law. Due process was embedded in English common law and was expressed in Article 39 of the Magna Carta, whereby the King promised that '[n]o freemen shall be taken or imprisoned or disseised or exiled or in any way destroyed . . . except by the legal judgment of his peers or by the law of the land'. The concept of 'the law of the land' as used in this provision incorporated the notion of due process.[8] In the context of English criminal law,

[6] 'To be effective, the system must be *seen* to be effective. To be seen as effective, its decisions must be arrived at discursively in accordance with what is accepted by the parties as *right process*. In procedural terms: humanity wants reassurance that the emerging legal system is capable of ensuring both stability and progressive change.': Thomas M. Franck, *Fairness in International Law and Institutions* (1995) 7.

[7] Robert Howse, 'Adjudicative Legitimacy and Treaty Interpretation in International Trade Law: The Early Years of WTO Jurisprudence' in Joseph Weiler (ed.), *The EU, the WTO and the NAFTA: Toward a Common Law of International Law* (2000) 35, 43.

[8] *Murray's Lessee* v. *Hoboken Land & Improvement Co*, 59 US (18 How) 272, 276 (1856).

Walker defines due process as '[t]he conduct of legal proceedings according to established principles and rules which safeguard the position of the individual charged'.[9]

The common law scope of due process has expanded well beyond criminal law, to other court proceedings (such as civil proceedings), as well as to proceedings of other tribunals, and administrative and arbitral bodies.[10] A broader Australian definition reflecting the potential scope of due process is '[p]rinciples developed at common law to ensure the fairness of the decision-making procedure of courts and administrators'.[11] In the United States, due process is similarly broadly defined as the 'conduct of legal proceedings according to established rules and principles for the protection and enforcement of private rights'.[12] Due process is often protected in particular tribunals by written rules of procedure, which the decision-maker typically interprets in light of the objective of fairness. Where the rules are silent on a particular procedural issue, the decision-maker must decide it in light of that same objective.

The objective of the principle of due process in the domestic context has been described in the United States as follows: 'to prevent arbitrary government, avoid mistaken deprivations, allow persons to know about and respond to charges against them, and promote a sense of the legitimacy of official behaviour'.[13] The Fifth and Fourteenth Amendments of the United States Constitution incorporate the principle of due process. The jurisprudence on those amendments draws a distinction between procedural due process (which concerns the rights to notice, a hearing, counsel, appeal, and a fair and objective trial) and substantive due process (which requires 'legislation to be fair and reasonable in content and further a legitimate governmental objective').[14]

Commonwealth legal systems often consider that due process involves at least two basic rules: the 'bias rule' and the 'hearing rule'. These rules concern procedural due process, according to the United States framework. That is, they are concerned with how the decision is

[9] David M. Walker, *The Oxford Companion to Law* (1980) 381.

[10] See, e.g., *Arbitration Act 1996* (UK) c 23, s. 33. In relation to due process in arbitration at the international level, see Alan Redfern et al., *Law and Practice of International Commercial Arbitration* (4th edn, 2004) 245; UNICTRAL Arbitration Rules, art. 15.

[11] Nygh and Butt (eds.), *Australian Legal Dictionary*, 928.

[12] Bryan A. Garner (ed.), *Black's Law Dictionary* (7th edn, 1999) 516–17.

[13] Hall, *Oxford Companion to the Supreme Court of the United States*, 236.

[14] Garner, *Black's Law Dictionary*, 516–17.

made rather than its substance.[15] The bias rule precludes a decision-maker from acting in circumstances in which a fair-minded observer would have a reasonable apprehension of bias, arising for example from the decision-maker's interest in the outcome.[16] This rule is based on the maxim *nemo debet esse judex in propria sua causa* (no one can be a judge in his own cause). The hearing rule requires a decision-maker to provide to persons whose interests may be adversely affected by a decision an opportunity to present their case. This rule encompasses requirements such as: providing reasonable notice of the decision; informing affected persons of the case to be met; disclosing adverse material so that it may be challenged; and permitting representation at hearings.[17] In relation to the bias rule, Cheng states that the existence of the bias rule as a general principle of law 'is hardly . . . open to question and its application extends beyond purely judicial procedures'.[18]

The hearing rule is based on the maxim *audi alteram partem* (to hear the other side). Providing prior notice that a decision adversely affecting interests is going to be made promotes equality between the parties. This prior notice must contain 'sufficient particulars of the allegation and the grounds upon which it is based' to permit an understanding of 'the nature and ambit of the allegation' and therefore a response.[19] This particularisation also assists the decision-maker by defining the issues on which to focus.[20] Obviously, to be meaningful, the notice must also give the recipient sufficient time to prepare a response.[21] The requirement to disclose adverse material is also a fundamental aspect of due process. The disclosure of this material can help prevent inaccurate or untested material being used. In some circumstances, the non-disclosure of adverse material could constitute both a breach of the hearing rule and the bias rule. Apart from promoting equality between the parties, the hearing rule also ensures that there are sufficient facts on the record for the decision-maker to arrive at a proper conclusion.[22] The concept of 'equality of arms', which requires 'a fair balance between the

[15] *Chief Constable of North Wales Police* v. *Evans* [1982] 3 All ER 141.
[16] Nygh and Butt, *Australian Legal Dictionary*, 126. [17] Ibid., 546.
[18] Bin Cheng, *General Principles of Law as Applied by International Courts and Tribunals* (1987) 279.
[19] Margaret Allars, *Introduction to Australian Administrative Law* (1990) 263.
[20] *Arafura Seafood Products Pty Ltd* v. *Landos* (1988) 16 ALD 519, 520.
[21] *Claro* v. *Minister for Immigration, Local Government & Ethnic Affairs* (1993) 46 FCR 494, 505–6 (Burchett J).
[22] Cheng, *General Principles of Law*, 298.

opportunities afforded the parties involved in litigation',[23] can be considered part of the hearing rule.

A third rule has been suggested as a basic component of due process. Under this 'no evidence' rule, decision-makers must base their decisions on 'logically probative evidence'.[24] Therefore, decision-makers must provide reasons that are adequate, intelligible and that deal with the substantial points raised by the parties.[25] In addition, decision-makers must base their findings on material that shows the existence or non-existence of facts consistent with the findings, and decision-makers' reasons must not be internally contradictory.[26] This rule is more clearly directed towards the fairness of the decision itself (in other words, substantive due process) than the hearing and bias rules. However, it is arguably a logical consequence or extension of the other two rules: 'If the decision were determined by the toss of a coin or some other arbitrary procedure, the "right" to a hearing would be illusory. If the decision could be based on unreasoned prejudice, the *audi alteram partem* rule would be pointless.'[27]

The circumstances in which due process must be accorded and the specific requirements of due process vary considerably between different municipal legal systems. Even within a given municipal legal system, the need for and content of due process depend on the context, and may vary, for example, between judicial, quasi-judicial, and administrative decision-makers, and between criminal and other cases. The inherent flexibility of due process and its 'undefined boundaries . . . make it a legal chameleon. It straddles the divide between legislative and judicial power, between executive discretion and judicial values'.[28]

5.2.2 *A principle of customary international law*

International courts and tribunals have long recognised that they must ensure due process in their proceedings. For example, the ICTY Appeals Chamber has explained that 'each party must be afforded a reasonable

[23] Elizabeth Martin, *A Dictionary of Law* (5th edn, 2002) 176.

[24] Nygh and Butt, *Australian Legal Dictionary*, 788.

[25] *Re Poyser and Mills' Arbitration* [1964] 2 QB 467, 478 (Megaw J); *Earl of Iveagh* v. *Minister of Housing and Local Government* [1962] 2 QB 147, 160 (Megaw J); *Westminster City Council* v. *Great Portland Street Estates plc* [1985] AC 661, 673 (Lord Scarman).

[26] *Mahon* v. *Air New Zealand Ltd* [1984] AC 808, 821 (Lord Diplock); *Minister for Immigration & Ethnic Affairs* v. *Pochi* (1980) 44 FLR 41, 67–8 (Deane J).

[27] *Australian Broadcasting Tribunal* v. *Bond* (1990) 170 CLR 321, 366 (Deane J, dissenting).

[28] Tony Blackshield, Michael Coper and George Williams (eds.), *Oxford Companion to the High Court of Australia* (2001) 498.

opportunity to present his case – including his evidence – under conditions that do not place him at a substantial disadvantage vis-à-vis his opponent'.[29] In addition, due process has emerged as a principle according to which states must meet certain standards of fairness and reasonableness in administering or enforcing their laws.

Under customary international law, the doctrine of denial of justice requires states to administer justice relating to aliens according to a minimum standard. Denial of justice incorporates the principle of due process to some extent, including procedural and substantive aspects of due process.[30] Procedurally, denial of justice can take a number of forms and arise at any stage of the legal process. Put simply:

> If the courts or other appropriate tribunals of a state refuse to entertain proceedings for the redress of injury suffered by an alien, or if the proceedings are subject to undue delay, or if there are serious inadequacies in the administration of justice . . . there will be a 'denial of justice' for which the state is responsible.[31]

Substantively, the state will be held responsible if an alien is injured by 'gross defects in the substance of the judgment itself'[32] or by a 'manifestly unjust judgment'.[33] However, an error that does not rise to the level of manifest injustice is not a denial of justice.[34] Generally, a denial

[29] ICTY Decision, Decision of the Prosecutor's Appeal on Admissibility of Evidence, *Prosecutor* v. *Aleksovski*, Case No I-95-14/1-A, Appeals Chamber International Tribunal for the Former Yugoslavia, 16 February 1999, 24.

[30] See *Mondev International Ltd* v. *United States of America*, Notice of Arbitration, 1 September 1999, 80–7; A. O. Adede, 'A Fresh Look at the Meaning of Denial of Justice under International Law' (1976) 14 *Canadian Yearbook of International Law* 73, 91.

[31] Robert Jennings and Arthur Watts (eds.), *Oppenheim's International Law* (9th edn, 1992) vol. I, 543–4. See also Ian Brownlie, *Principles of Public International Law* (6th edn, 2003) 507, which quotes the Hague Codification Conference: 'A State is responsible as a result of the fact that, in a manner incompatible with the international obligations of the State, the foreigner has been hindered by the judicial authorities in the exercise of his right to appear in Court, or has encountered in his proceedings unjustifiable obstacles or delays implying a refusal to do justice.'

[32] Alwyn V. Freeman, *The International Responsibility of States for Denial of Justice* (1938, reprinted 1970) 309.

[33] Harvard Research in International Law, 'The Law of Responsibility of States for Damage Done in Their Territory to the Person or Property of Foreigners' (1929) 23 *American Journal of International Law (Supp)* 131, 173 (art. 9). See also *Articles on Responsibility of States for Internationally Wrongful Acts*, in *Report of the International Law Commission on the Work of Its Fifty-third Session*, UN GAOR, 56th sess, Supp No 10, UN Doc A/56/10 (2001) art. 4; James Crawford, *The International Law Commission's Articles on State Responsibility: Introduction, Text, and Commentaries* (2002) 96.

[34] Harvard Research in International Law, 'The Law of Responsibility of States', 173 (art. 9).

of justice will require a 'serious and intentional perversion of justice' as a result of bad faith.[35] Discrimination against the alien or obvious maliciousness will be particularly probative of this bad faith.[36]

Several human rights treaties impose due process obligations on states, including the Geneva Convention relative to the Treatment of Prisoners of War,[37] the International Covenant on Civil and Political Rights,[38] the European Convention for the Protection of Human Rights and Fundamental Freedoms[39] and the American Convention on Human Rights.[40] These might reflect or codify principles of customary international law. These due process protections vary, even when they concern a particular type of trial (such as a criminal trial). The ICTY has noted that variations in the understanding of concepts such as due process and fair trial mean they must be understood in the 'context of the legal system in which the concepts are being applied'.[41] The Statute of the International Criminal Court refers to both 'the principles of due process recognized by international law'[42] and 'the norms of due process recognized by international law'.[43]

In addition, a number of bilateral trade or investment treaties contain standards regarding the treatment of aliens,[44] and these often include due process requirements. One of the most common standards included

[35] See *Azinian, Davitian and Baca* v. *United Mexican States*, Award, 1 November 1999, 5 *ICSID Reports* 269, [103].

[36] Stephan Verosta, 'Denial of Justice' in Rudolf Bernhardt (ed.), *Encyclopedia of Public International Law* (2003) vol. I, 1007, 1008. See also A. O. Adede, 'A Fresh Look at the Meaning of Denial of Justice under International Law' (1976) 14 *Canadian Yearbook of International Law* 73, 93.

[37] Signed 12 August 1949, 75 UNTS 135 (entered into force 21 October 1950), arts. 104, 99, 105.

[38] Opened for signature 19 December 1966, 999 UNTS 171 (entered into force 23 March 1976) arts. 14–15.

[39] Signed 4 November 1950, 213 UNTS 221, art. 6 (entered into force 3 September 1953): 'In the determination of his civil rights and obligations or of any criminal charge against him, everyone is entitled to a fair and public hearing within a reasonable time by an independent and impartial tribunal established by law.'

[40] Signed 22 November 1969, OASTS 36 (entered into force 18 July 1978) art. 8.1: 'Every person has the right to a hearing, with due guarantees and within a reasonable time, by a competent, independent, and impartial tribunal, previously established by law, in the substantiation of any accusation of a criminal nature made against him or for the determination of his rights and obligations of a civil, labor, fiscal, or any other nature.'

[41] *Prosecutor* v. *Tadic*, Case No IT-94-I-T, [30] (Trial Chamber, ICTY, 10 August 1995).

[42] Article 17(2). [43] Article 30(3)(b).

[44] Giorgio Sacerdoti, 'Bilateral Treaties and Multilateral Instruments on Investment Protection' (1997) 269 *Recueil des Cours* 251, 345.

in such treaties is 'fair and equitable treatment'.[45] According to Sacerdoti, this requires a state 'to attain a certain result by whatever appropriate means: it requires that the State acts in such a way in all circumstances and instances so that the foreigner be always treated in a fair and equitable manner'.[46] Commentators disagree as to whether this standard provides protection beyond that imposed under customary international law.[47] Article 5(2)(a) of the United States Model Bilateral Investment Treaty of 2004 states:

> 'fair and equitable treatment' includes the obligation not to deny justice in criminal, civil, or administrative adjudicatory proceedings in accordance with the principle of due process embodied in the principal legal systems of the world.[48]

Article 1105(1) of NAFTA requires a NAFTA state to accord 'investments of investors of another Party treatment in accordance with international law, including fair and equitable treatment and full protection and security'.[49] Several claims have been made under this provision. In *Mondev*, the investor claimed that 'flagrant procedural deficiencies' in proceedings before the Massachusetts Supreme Judicial Court and 'gross defects in the substance of the judgment itself' constituted a denial of justice.[50] The NAFTA tribunal set out the following standard for assessing whether a particular decision regarding a NAFTA investment involves a denial of justice:

> [T]he question is whether, at an international level and having regard to generally accepted standards of the administration of justice, a tribunal can conclude in the light of all the available facts that the impugned decision was clearly improper and discreditable, with the result that the investment has been subjected to unfair and inequitable treatment.[51]

[45] Christoph Schreuer, 'Fair and Equitable Treatment in Arbitral Practice' (2005) 6 *Journal of World Investment and Trade* 357, 357.

[46] Sacerdoti, 'Bilateral Treaties', 341.

[47] For the negative see ibid., 341, n. 143. For the affirmative see F. A. Mann, 'British Treaties for the Promotion and Protection of Investments' (1982) 52 *British Yearbook of International Law* 241, 243–4; Kenneth Vandevelde, *United States Investment Treaties: Policy and Practice* (1992) 76; Schreuer, 'Fair and Equitable Treatment', 364.

[48] Article 5(2)(a), available at www.ustr.gov/assets/Trade_Sectors/Investment/Model_BIT/asset_upload_file847_ 6897.pdf.

[49] See also NAFTA Free Trade Commission, *Notes of Interpretation of Certain Chapter 11 Provisions* (31 July 2001).

[50] *Mondev International Ltd* v. *United States of America*, ICSID Case No ARB(AF)/99/2 (Notice of Arbitration dated 1 September 1999) [135].

[51] *Mondev International Ltd* v. *United States of America*, ICSID Case No ARB(AF)/99/2 (Award dated 11 October, 2002) [127] (some footnotes omitted).

In *Loewen*, the NAFTA tribunal found that the conduct of a Mississippi trial 'was so flawed that it constituted a miscarriage of justice amounting to a manifest injustice as that expression is understood in international law'.[52] It considered that the NAFTA and general international law standards are breached where there is a '[m]anifest injustice in the sense of a lack of due process leading to an outcome which offends a sense of judicial propriety'.[53] The tribunal pointed to the inappropriate 'manner in which the large and excessive verdict was constructed by the judge and the jury'.[54] The tribunal also considered that the judge had failed to protect the foreign litigant from clear discrimination and prejudice, as a result of: repeated references to the investor's foreign nationality; suggestions that the investor only did business with whites; and appeals to class-based prejudice.[55] The tribunal held that 'the whole trial and its resultant verdict were clearly improper and discreditable and cannot be squared with minimum standards of international law and fair and equitable treatment'.[56]

5.2.3 *A principle of WTO law*

In assessing due process as a principle of WTO law, it is necessary to distinguish between two distinct but related expressions of due process in the WTO agreements. I consider these two in turn: first, the requirements of due process in dispute settlement proceedings before WTO Tribunals; second, the obligations of due process imposed on Members in the conduct of judicial or administrative proceedings at the domestic level.

A. Due process before WTO Tribunals

[P]rocedural rules of WTO dispute settlement are designed to promote . . . the fair, prompt and effective resolution of trade disputes.[57]

This section considers how certain provisions in the DSU and related instruments incorporate a principle of due process, using the framework commonly employed in Commonwealth domestic legal systems: the bias, hearing, and no evidence rules. These rules are intended to promote the fair resolution of trade disputes, primarily by protecting the procedural interests of the disputing parties. In most instances,

[52] *Loewen Group, Inc and Raymond L. Loewen* v. *United States of America*, ICSID Case No ARB (AF)/98/3 (Award dated 26 June 2003) [54].
[53] Ibid. [132]. [54] Ibid. [122]. [55] Ibid. [56]–[70]. [56] Ibid. [137].
[57] Appellate Body Report, *US – FSC*, [166].

these interests take precedence over the interests of other stakeholders, such as WTO Members that are not party to the dispute, states that are not WTO Members, NGOs, and corporations. This explains certain aspects of WTO disputes that may not be strictly required in achieving due process, such as the secrecy of Panel and Appellate Body proceedings (DSU Articles 14.1 and 17.10) and the confidentiality of submissions (DSU Article 18.2).

Several provisions in the DSU incorporate due process by imposing some form of the bias rule, which precludes decision-makers from acting where there is a reasonable apprehension that they may be biased, for example, because they have an interest in the outcome.[58] In particular, the DSU makes clear that panelists should be free of any actual or perceived bias. Article 8.2 of the DSU states that panelists should be selected with a view to ensuring their independence, and Article 8.3 states that citizens of Members involved in the dispute (as parties or third parties) should not serve as panelists unless the parties agree otherwise. Article 9 states that panelists serve in their individual capacity and that Members shall 'not give them instructions nor seek to influence them as individuals with regard to matters before a panel'. However, it is interesting to note that persons who are currently servants of their governments may nevertheless be panelists (Article 8.8). Prevention of bias may be achieved, in practice, through the opportunity afforded to disputing parties to object to proposed panelists for compelling reasons (Article 8.6).

At the appellate level, a similar but not identical version of the bias rule applies. Article 17.3 of the DSU states that members of the Appellate Body 'shall be unaffiliated with any government' and that they 'shall not participate in the consideration of any disputes that would create a direct or indirect conflict of interest'. However, unlike at the Panel stage, a member of the Appellate Body that is a citizen of a disputing party is not prevented from serving on the division hearing the appeal.[59] Nevertheless, the apprehension of bias may be diminished through the appointment of Appellate Body members for terms of four years (Article 17.2) and through the requirement that the Appellate Body membership be broadly representative of WTO membership (Article 17.3).[60]

58 Nygh and Butt, *Australian Legal Dictionary*, 126.

59 Working Procedures for Appellate Review, Rule 6(2).

60 See also Cheng, *General Principles of Law*, 284, 288.

Communications between a decision-maker and a party or witness without the knowledge or consent of other parties may create a reasonable apprehension of bias (and may also breach the decision-maker's duty to afford a fair hearing). Accordingly, Article 18.1 of the DSU prohibits *ex parte* communications with WTO Tribunals concerning matters under consideration by them.[61] In addition, paragraph 10 of the Panel working procedures in Appendix 3 of the DSU requires presentations, rebuttals, and statements in the first and second substantive meetings to be made in the presence of the parties.

Additionally, the DSB adopted Rules of Conduct to maintain the integrity and impartiality of dispute settlement proceedings in the WTO. These rules also reflect the bias rule. They apply to panelists, Appellate Body members, arbitrators, experts, members of the Secretariat assisting panels or arbitrations, and members of the Appellate Body Secretariat.[62] The governing principle of these rules is that these persons should be 'independent and impartial, [and] shall avoid direct or indirect conflicts of interest'.[63] Accordingly, they should 'disclose the existence or development of any interest, relationship or matter that that person could reasonably be expected to know and that is likely to affect, or give rise to justifiable doubts as to, that person's independence or impartiality'.[64] An illustrative list of the information to be disclosed is contained in Annex 2 of the rules and includes financial, professional, and other active interests. Any material violation may be challenged and may result in disqualification of the person from the proceedings, or other appropriate action. This provides a way of enforcing the bias rule.

The Working Procedures for Appellate Review, which are issued by the Appellate Body pursuant to DSU Article 17.9, reiterate some of these aspects of the bias rule. In particular, Appellate Body members are prohibited from: accepting employment or pursuing activities inconsistent with their duties and responsibilities (Rule 2(2)); accepting or seeking instructions from any organisation or private source (Rule 2(3)); and participating in decision-making or exchange of views when a material violation of an obligation of independence or impartiality has occurred (Rule 11).

[61] This rule is reinforced for the Appellate Body by Rule 19 of the Working Procedures for Appellate Review. See also Appellate Body Report, *US – Wheat Gluten*, [168].

[62] Rules of Conduct, Rule IV. [63] Rules of Conduct, Rule II.

[64] Rules of Conduct, Rule III.1.

The hearing rule requires the decision-maker to give to those people who may be directly affected by a decision prior notice of the case they have to answer, and the time and place of the hearing. The DSU contains a number of provisions reflecting this requirement. For example, the complainant must give sufficient notice to the respondent of the basis of its claim, the key facts it alleges, and the legal principles on which it relies. This is achieved through the request for consultations (DSU Article 4.4),[65] the request for the establishment of a Panel (often known as the 'Panel request') (Article 6.2), and written submissions to the Panel (Articles 12.6, 15.1). The Appellate Body has held that, pursuant to Article 6.2, a Panel request must specifically identify the relevant WTO provisions and, in some cases, the relevant sub-provisions.[66] The Panel request must also clearly 'identify the specific measures at issue'. As the Panel's terms of reference typically incorporate the Panel request (Article 7), the terms of reference also 'fulfil an important due process objective – they give the parties and third parties sufficient information concerning the claims at issue in the dispute in order to allow them an opportunity to respond to the complainant's case'.[67] Similarly, at the appellate level, the appellant must make clear the alleged errors of the Panel in the Notice of Appeal (Working Procedures for Appellate Review, Rule 20(2)(d)), and support its position through arguments contained in a written submission (Working Procedures for Appellate Review, Rule 21). Again, the Appellate Body has made clear that it will dismiss claims that are not properly set out in the Notice of Appeal, on the basis that the respondent did not receive sufficient notice of the case it had to meet.[68]

The hearing rule also encompasses, unsurprisingly, a requirement that the decision-maker give interested parties an opportunity to be heard, including an opportunity to respond to adverse evidence. In the WTO dispute settlement system, parties are given an extensive opportunity to be heard. Particularly at the Panel level, the opportunities provided appear greater than in many other domestic or international

[65] See Panel Report, *Korea – Alcoholic Beverages*, [10.23]; Appellate Body Report, *Mexico – Corn Syrup (Article 21.5 – US)*, [54].

[66] Appellate Body Report, *India – Patents (US)*, [93]; Appellate Body Report, *Korea – Dairy*, [124].

[67] Appellate Body Report, *Brazil – Desiccated Coconut*, 22.

[68] See, e.g., Appellate Body Report, *US – Upland Cotton*, [495]; Appellate Body Report, *EC – Bananas III*, [152]; Appellate Body Report, *US – Countervailing Measures on Certain EC Products*, [62], [74].

tribunals. The standard working procedures set out in Appendix 3 of the DSU[69] provide for Panels to conduct two substantive meetings with the parties, who are asked to provide written submissions and also to present their case orally.[70] Panels also frequently provide questions to the parties (which may offer parties a chance to respond to adverse material), and parties typically provide written replies after due deliberation. More unusually, Panels submit to the parties in advance not only the descriptive parts of their reports but also their entire reasoning and conclusions. Parties then have an opportunity to comment on the report before it is finalised and circulated to Members (DSU Article 15).[71] On appeal, the parties make written submissions and also represent their views at an oral hearing.[72]

Finally, a number of DSU provisions can be seen to reflect the requirement under the no evidence rule that a decision-maker deal with the substantial points raised by the parties. In particular, DSU Article 7.2 states: 'Panels shall address the relevant provisions in any covered agreement or agreements cited by the parties to the dispute.' In addition, DSU Article 12.7 requires each Panel to 'set out the findings of fact, the applicability of relevant provisions and the basic rationale behind any findings and recommendations that it makes'. Finally, DSU Article 17.12 provides that the 'Appellate Body shall address each of the issues raised in accordance with [Article 17.6] during the appellate proceeding', that is 'issues of law covered in the panel report and legal interpretations developed by the panel' raised by the parties.

B. Members' obligations to accord due process

An extensive range of WTO provisions may be seen as imposing due process requirements on Members in the conduct of domestic proceedings, which are broadly analogous to the due process requirements imposed on WTO Tribunals in the conduct of WTO disputes. Here I will provide an outline of just some of these provisions.

69 Panels must follow these procedures unless they decide otherwise after consultation with the parties: DSU, art. 12.1.

70 See Cheng, *General Principles of Law*, 293.

71 The US and Chile have suggested making provision for interim reports at the Appellate Body stage in the Special Session of the DSB: Dispute Settlement Body, Special Session, 'Negotiations on Improvements and Clarifications of the Dispute Settlement Understanding on Improving Flexibility and Member Control in WTO Dispute Settlement', TN/DS/W/52 (14 March 2003).

72 Working Procedures for Appellate Review, Rules 21, 22, 27.

Many WTO provisions require Members to administer their laws, regulations, and procedures in a fair and uniform manner. For example, GATS Article VI:1 – which is similar to GATT Article X:3(a), discussed further below – requires Members to ensure that 'all measures of general application affecting trade in services are administered in a reasonable, objective and impartial manner'. Where a person must apply for authorisation to supply a service, Article VI:3 requires a Member's authorities to 'inform the applicant of the decision concerning the application' 'within a reasonable period of time' after the submission of a complete application. Upon request, Members must also 'provide, without undue delay, information concerning the status of the application'. Article VI:4 requires the Council for Trade in Services to establish disciplines to ensure that 'technical standards and licensing requirements do not constitute unnecessary barriers to trade in services'. These disciplines should ensure that requirements are 'based on objective and transparent criteria, such as competence and the ability to supply the service'.

The TRIPS Agreement also contains important due process requirements in relation to the administration of laws and regulations for the enforcement of intellectual property rights. Article 41.2 requires Members' procedures for such enforcement to be 'fair and equitable. They shall not be unnecessarily complicated or costly, or entail unreasonable time-limits or unwarranted delays'. Under Article 41.3, decisions 'shall preferably be in writing and reasoned', made available to the parties 'without undue delay', and 'based only on evidence in respect of which parties were offered the opportunity to be heard'. In addition, Article 42 requires 'civil judicial procedures' to be made available concerning the enforcement of intellectual property rights, and specifies that in such procedures:

> Defendants shall have the right to written notice which is timely and contains sufficient detail, including the basis of the claims. Parties shall be allowed to be represented by independent legal counsel, and procedures shall not impose overly burdensome requirements concerning mandatory personal appearances. All parties to such procedures shall be duly entitled to substantiate their claims and to present all relevant evidence.

Many other WTO agreements impose due process requirements in connection with the administration of laws and other requirements. For instance, Article 1:3 of the Agreement on Import Licensing Procedures requires the 'rules for import licensing procedures [to] be neutral in application and administered in a fair and equitable manner'. The Anti-Dumping Agreement, SCM Agreement, and Agreement on Safeguards all impose detailed, far-reaching due process requirements on Members in relation to the conduct of investigations to determine whether to impose anti-dumping measures, countervailing measures, or safeguard measures, respectively. As an example, Article 6 of the Anti-Dumping Agreement provides for investigating authorities to give all interested parties an opportunity to present evidence and arguments to defend their interests, and Article 12 requires the authorities to give public notice at certain stages of the investigation and to explain their determinations.

A number of the WTO agreements also contain due process requirements in the form of obligations to provide appeal and review mechanisms. GATT Article X:3(b) requires Members to maintain 'judicial, arbitral or administrative tribunals or procedures for the purpose, *inter alia*, of the prompt review and correction of administrative action relating to customs matters'.[73] TRIPS Article 41.4 provides a right for review by a judicial authority of final administrative decisions regarding enforcement of intellectual property rights, and Article 62.5 mandates review rights for certain final administrative decisions concerning the acquisition or maintenance of intellectual property rights. Article 23 of the SCM Agreement requires WTO Members to maintain judicial, arbitral, or administrative tribunals or procedures for the prompt review of administrative actions relating to final subsidies and countervailing determinations and reviews of these determinations.

The right to take private actions goes beyond appeal and review procedures and can be considered an important aspect of due process. When this right exists, an affected private party can bring an action to protect their expectations of due process even when a government authority is unwilling or unable to act. In this regard, it is significant that Article 42 of the TRIPS Agreement states that Members are required to make available to 'rights holders' civil judicial procedures concerning the enforcement of intellectual property rights covered by the agreement. Article XX of the Agreement on Government Procurement also creates a right of private action. Article XX:2 requires parties to that agreement to create procedures 'enabling suppliers to challenge alleged breaches of the Agreement arising in the context of procurements in which they have, or have had, an interest'. These

[73] See also GATS, art. VI:2.

challenges are to be heard by a court or an impartial and independent review body.[74]

5.3 Using due process in WTO disputes

The following sections first examine the implications of the principle of due process for the conduct of WTO dispute settlement proceedings, and then its implications for the conduct of domestic proceedings by WTO Members. The second of these issues may be more analogous to good faith as a general principle of law and a principle of customary international law as discussed in Chapter 4, but these principles also obviously inform the conduct of WTO disputes just as they do those before other international courts and tribunals.

5.3.1 Ensuring due process before WTO Tribunals

A. Panel compliance with due process (DSU Articles 11, 12.7)

(i) Introduction

In Chapter 3, I mentioned that one example of a general principle of law or a principle of customary international law forming the basis of a claim in a WTO dispute would be when parties claim that Panels have failed to accord due process.[75] The Appellate Body might be able to hear such claims in the exercise of its inherent jurisdiction. In any case, Articles 11 and 12.7 of the DSU impose certain due process obligations on Panels, providing a concrete basis for the Appellate Body to review Panels' conduct in this regard.

Article 11 of the DSU provides in part:

> [A] panel should make an objective assessment of the matter before it, including an objective assessment of the facts of the case and the applicability of and conformity with the relevant covered agreements, and make such other findings as will assist the DSB in making the recommendations or in giving the rulings provided for in the covered agreements.

This provision is the subject of a growing number of complaints at the appellate stage, and the Appellate Body has found that a Panel failed to comply with Article 11 on several occasions. In the following section, I concentrate on the primary due process aspects of Article 11, leaving

[74] Agreement on Government Procurement, art. XX:6.

[75] See above, section 3.3.2 para. beginning 'The only claim that a member could make'.

to one side related issues such as whether the Panel applied the correct standard of review, which the Appellate Body also regards as falling within Article 11.[76]

Article 12.7 of the DSU states that, unless parties reach a 'mutually satisfactory solution', a Panel is to 'submit its findings in the form of a written report to the DSB', which 'shall set out the findings of fact, the applicability of relevant provisions and the basic rationale behind any findings and recommendations that it makes'. The Appellate Body has never found that a Panel violated the requirement to provide a basic rationale under Article 12.7, which may explain why far fewer appellants raise this provision in challenging a Panel's decision.

In considering the due process implications of these provisions below, I first consider the requirement that the Panel address the matter before it, which is reflected in both Article 11 and Article 12.7. I then turn to the requirement in Article 11 that the Panel conduct an 'objective assessment'.

(ii) The matter before the panel (hearing rule)

Articles 11 and 12.7 of the DSU reflect different aspects of the hearing rule in relation to the Panel's obligation to address the matter before it. On the one hand, pursuant to Article 11, a Panel must assess the 'matter before it', meaning that it cannot address issues that are not before it. On the other hand, pursuant to Articles 11 and 12.7, a Panel may be precluded from ignoring issues that are before it. I consider these two aspects of the matter before the Panel in turn.

In *Chile - Price Band System*, the Appellate Body agreed with Chile's claim that the Panel violated Article 11 of the DSU in ruling on claims that were not made or argued by Argentina.[77] The Appellate Body based this finding on two main grounds. The first was that Article 11 requires a Panel to assess 'the matter before it', which excludes claims that are not before it.[78] The second was 'the requirement of due process', according to which the Panel had to give Chile a right of response to any claims on which the Panel ruled.[79] The Appellate Body explained the relationship between due process and Article 11 as follows:

> [I]n making 'an objective assessment of the matter before it', a panel is . . . duty bound to ensure that due process is respected. Due process is an obligation

[76] See, e.g., Appellate Body Report, *US - Cotton Yarn*, [74].

[77] Appellate Body Report, *Chile - Price Band System*, [176] -[177]. [78] Ibid. [173].

[79] Ibid. [174].

inherent in the WTO dispute settlement system. A panel will fail in the duty to respect due process if it makes a finding on a matter that is not before it, because it will thereby fail to accord to a party a fair right of response.[80]

The reference to due process as an 'inherent' obligation in WTO dispute settlement suggests, contrary to the Appellate Body's explicit reasoning, that Panels must accord due process and the Appellate Body may review the Panel's conduct in this regard independent of Article 11 of the DSU. In *US – Gambling*, the Appellate Body had to determine whether the Panel's consideration of a defence submitted by the United States in its second written submission violated Article 11 by depriving Antigua and Barbuda of a full and fair opportunity to respond. The Appellate Body held that the principle of due process 'obliges a responding party to articulate its defence promptly and clearly' and may oblige a Panel either to refuse to consider a defence to which 'the complaining party had no meaningful opportunity to respond',[81] or to adjust its timetables to allow additional time to respond.[82] That due process arises through the inherent obligations and jurisdiction of WTO Tribunals as judicial bodies is demonstrated by other cases regarding the right to respond.[83] In these circumstances, it is not possible to fall back on the words 'the matter before it' in Article 11 to explain why Panels must ensure due process. The challenged arguments were clearly before the Panel, so the connection to Article 11 is tenuous. However, the Appellate Body found no breach of Article 11 in this case given that Antigua was aware of the possibility that the US would make such a defence, raised no objection when it was made, and acknowledged that it did have an opportunity to respond.[84]

The other side of the coin, in relation to the 'matter before' the Panel, is whether the Panel may decline to address in its report certain aspects of the dispute such as claims or arguments. This issue also relates to Article 12.7 of the DSU. In *Mexico – Corn Syrup (Article 21.5 – US)*, the Appellate Body stated that the duty to provide a 'basic rationale' in Article 12.7 of the DSU

reflects and conforms with the principles of fundamental fairness and due process that underlie and inform the provisions of the DSU. In particular, in cases where a Member has been found to have acted inconsistently with its

[80] Ibid. [176]. [81] Appellate Body Report, *US – Gambling*, [273]. [82] Ibid. [272].

[83] See, e.g., Panel Report, *Canada – Aircraft*, [9.77]; Decision by the Arbitrator, *Canada – Aircraft Credits and Guarantees (Article 22.6 – Canada)* [2.16].

[84] Appellate Body Report, *US – Gambling*, [276].

obligations under the covered agreements, that Member is entitled to know the reasons for such finding as a matter of due process.[85]

The Appellate Body suggested that a Panel's obligation to address issues raised by the parties could derive from Article 7.2 of the DSU and 'the requirements of due process',[86] in addition to Article 12.7. Indeed, the hearing rule, as part of the principle of due process, requires decision-makers to provide reasons for their decisions and to take into account the submissions of interested parties.

Even though a Panel must provide a basic rationale for its findings in accordance with Article 12.7 and must assess the matter before it under Article 11, the Appellate Body has recognised Panels' discretion to leave unanswered certain claims. In other words, the Appellate Body has endorsed Panels' use of judicial economy in appropriate circumstances. In *US – Wool Shirts and Blouses*, the Appellate Body made clear that Article 11 does not oblige a Panel to address every claim before it:[87] 'A panel need only address those claims which must be addressed in order to resolve the matter in issue in the dispute.'[88]

Where does this leave due process? In some cases, it seems that due process requirements will preclude the exercise of judicial economy. In the appeal in *EC – Export Subsidies on Sugar*, the Appellate Body referred to the requirement in Article 11 of the DSU that Panels 'make such other findings as will assist the DSB in making the recommendations or in giving the rulings provided for in the covered agreements'.[89] The Appellate Body found that the Panel failed to comply with this requirement and exercised 'false judicial economy' because, in not ruling on certain claims under Article 3 of the SCM Agreement, the Panel 'precluded the possibility' of the complainants obtaining the special remedy under Article 4.7 of the SCM Agreement available for successful claims under Article 3.[90] Again, the link to Article 11 of the DSU is rather tenuous. The Panel's due process obligations and the Appellate Body's right to review them in the exercise of its inherent jurisdiction might have provided a more logical basis for this decision.

[85] Appellate Body Report, *Mexico – Corn Syrup (Article 21.5 – US)*, [107] (footnote omitted).

[86] Ibid. [49]. [87] Appellate Body Report, *US – Wool Shirts and Blouses*, 18. [88] Ibid. 19.

[89] Appellate Body Report, *EC – Export Subsidies on Sugar*, [330], [331]. [90] Ibid. [335].

(iii) Objective assessment (bias and no evidence rules)

Certain aspects of the no evidence rule also appear to be reflected in Article 11 of the DSU, as interpreted by the Appellate Body. In the appeal in *EC – Hormones*, the European Communities claimed that the Panel 'disregarded or distorted' evidence it had submitted, as well as that of scientific experts, and therefore did not make an objective assessment as required by Article 11.[91] For example, the European Communities claimed that, in its report, the Panel did not refer to the opinion of particular experts, misquoted some statements, and mischaracterised others. The Appellate Body found that an Article 11 violation involves more than 'simply an error of judgment'. Rather, it involves 'an egregious error that calls into question the good faith of the panel'.[92] The requirement under Article 11 that Panels make an objective assessment of the facts of the case includes 'an obligation to consider the evidence presented to a panel and to make factual findings on the basis of that evidence'.[93] A Panel that deliberately disregards or wilfully distorts or misrepresents evidence will therefore fail to make an objective assessment, causing a denial of 'fundamental fairness . . . due process of law or natural justice'.[94] In the case at hand, the Appellate Body found that the Panel had misinterpreted some evidence, but that this did not rise to the level of arbitrarily ignoring or manifesting distorting evidence in violation of Article 11.[95]

The Appellate Body's interpretation of Article 11 in *EC – Hormones* accords with the ordinary meaning of 'objective'[96] and suggests a high threshold for appellate review of Panels' factual findings, similar to the standard required to demonstrate a denial of justice in international law.[97] Although the Appellate Body did not say so explicitly, its concern related primarily to the fairness of the Panel's decision itself (substantive due process as in the no evidence rule), rather than the fairness of

[91] Appellate Body Report, *EC – Hormones*, [131]. [92] Ibid. [133]. [93] Ibid. [94] Ibid.

[95] Ibid. [253(e)].

[96] The *Oxford English Dictionary* defines one of the meanings of 'objective' as 'presenting facts uncoloured by feelings, opinions, or personal bias; disinterested': William Trumble and Angus Stevenson (eds.), *Shorter Oxford English Dictionary on Historical Principles* (5th edn, 2002) vol. II, 1965.

[97] See also Appellate Body Report, *EC – Poultry*, [133], where the Appellate Body stated that an allegation that a Panel has failed to conduct an objective assessment is 'very serious' and goes to 'the very core of the integrity of the WTO dispute settlement process itself'. A similarly high standard was employed in Appellate Body Report, *Australia – Salmon*, [262]–[266]; Appellate Body Report, *Korea – Alcoholic Beverages*, [164]; Appellate Body Report, *Canada – Wheat Exports and Grain Imports*, [195].

the Panel proceedings (procedural due process as in the bias and hearing rules). This is reflected in the fact that the Appellate Body examined whether errors in the Panel Report amounted to an Article 11 violation. The Appellate Body has adopted a similar approach in several subsequent reports.[98]

In *US – Wheat Gluten*, the European Communities claimed that, contrary to Article 11, the Panel 'did not have sufficient facts before it to justify its conclusion' that a report by the United States International Trade Commission (ITC) provided 'an adequate, reasoned and reasonable explanation with respect to "profits and losses" '.[99] In this regard, the European Communities challenged the Panel's 'appreciation of the evidence' rather than the legal standard it applied.[100] The Appellate Body found that the Panel's requests for clarification of the report, and its reliance on these clarifications in making its decision, were 'at odds' with its conclusion that the ITC report itself adequately explained its assessment of profits and losses.[101] Accordingly, the Appellate Body found that the Panel acted inconsistently with its obligations under Article 11. Therefore, it reversed the Panel's finding that the ITC report provided an adequate explanation with respect to profits and losses.[102]

Unfortunately, the Appellate Body failed to explain its conclusion in *US – Wheat Gluten* in terms of its earlier discussion in *EC – Hormones* about the nature of Article 11 violations. Did the Panel deliberately disregard, refuse to consider, wilfully distort or misrepresent the evidence before it? Did it commit an egregious error calling into question its good faith? It is far from evident that the Panel's error reached this level. Therefore, perhaps the Appellate Body read *EC – Hormones* as providing an example of what kind of conduct might constitute an Article 11 violation, rather than setting a minimum threshold for Article 11 violations.[103] In *US – Wheat Gluten*, the Panel's error seems to have been that its reasons were internally contradictory, which is closer to the no evidence rule recognised in some domestic common law jurisdictions than to the higher

[98] See Appellate Body Report, *EC – Poultry*, [133]; Appellate Body Report, *Australia – Salmon*, [262]–[266]; Appellate Body Report, *Korea – Alcoholic Beverages*, [164]; Appellate Body Report, *Canada – Wheat Exports and Grain Imports*, [195]; Appellate Body Report, *EC – Chicken Cuts*, [186].

[99] Appellate Body Report, *US – Wheat Gluten*, [158], [159]. [100] Ibid. [149].

[101] Ibid. [158], [161]. [102] Ibid. [163].

[103] Claus-Dieter Ehlermann, 'Six Years on the Bench of the "World Trade Court": Some Personal Experiences as Member of the Appellate Body of the World Trade Organization' (2002) 36 *Journal of World Trade* 605, 622.

denial of justice standard under international law. The Appellate Body appeared to adopt a similarly low standard in finding a violation of Article 11 by the Panel in *US – Oil Country Tubular Goods Sunset Reviews*.[104]

As mentioned earlier, the Appellate Body has read into Article 11 of the DSU certain obligations regarding the standard of review adopted by a Panel (an issue not addressed here). In particular, Panels are not to conduct a *de novo* review of the evidence before domestic authorities in making determinations regarding the imposition of unilateral trade remedies.[105] However, although *US – Wheat Gluten* and *US – Oil Country Tubular Goods Sunset Reviews* involved Panels reviewing determinations made by domestic authorities in relation to trade remedies, the Appellate Body did not fault the standard of review that these Panels applied. Accordingly, it is difficult to understand the apparent discrepancy between these disputes and the Appellate Body's statements regarding the purportedly high threshold for finding that a Panel has failed to make an 'objective assessment' under Article 11.

B. Due process and inherent jurisdiction

In several early appeals, the Appellate Body lamented the lack of detailed working procedures for Panels to resolve procedural issues.[106] However, the relevant provisions of the DSU and related instruments, in conjunction with the inherent jurisdiction of WTO Tribunals, have proved adequate to resolve most procedural matters arising to date.

WTO Tribunals have the ability to establish additional procedural rules where none are provided. In the case of Panels, this ability is created by Article 12.1 of the DSU, which provides for the Panel to follow the working procedures in Appendix 3 of the DSU unless it 'decides otherwise after consulting the parties to the dispute', and by paragraph 11 of Appendix 3, which allows Panels to follow '[a]ny additional procedures specific to the panel'. The Appellate Body has read the DSU, and Appendix 3 in particular, as granting to 'panels a margin of discretion to deal, always in accordance with due process, with specific situations that may arise in a particular case and that are not explicitly regulated'.[107] The Appellate Body's emphasis on due process highlights that, in an appropriate case, the Appellate Body might

[104] Appellate Body Report, *US – Oil Country Tubular Goods Sunset Reviews*, [215].
[105] See, e.g., Appellate Body Report, *US – Countervailing Duty Investigation on DRAMS*, [190].
[106] Appellate Body Report, *EC – Bananas III*, [144]; Appellate Body Report, *India – Patents (US)*, [95]; Appellate Body Report, *Argentina – Textiles and Apparel*, n. 68.
[107] Appellate Body Report, *EC – Hormones*, n. 138.

conclude that the Panel failed to accord due process in establishing an additional procedural rule.[108]

In the case of the Appellate Body, Rule 16(1) of the Working Procedures for Appellate Review is even more explicit in according additional discretion linked to the requirements of due process. That rule states:

> In the interests of fairness and orderly procedure in the conduct of an appeal, where a procedural question arises that is not covered by these Rules, a division may adopt an appropriate procedure for the purposes of that appeal only, provided that it is not inconsistent with the DSU, the other covered agreements and these Rules.

In addition, Rule 16(2) of the Working Procedures for Appellate Review grants the Appellate Body the specific ability to modify time periods upon request 'where strict adherence . . . would result in a manifest unfairness'.

As an example of Rule 16(1) in operation, the Appellate Body in one appeal held two oral hearings instead of one because one member of the Division hearing the appeal passed away after the first oral hearing. The Appellate Body decided to hold the second hearing 'in the interests of fairness and orderly procedure in the conduct of this appeal'.[109] In another instance, the Appellate Body used Rule 16(1) to adopt detailed additional procedures for the receipt and consideration of *amicus curiae* briefs.[110] The Appellate Body has also used Rule 16(2), for example, to grant additional time for the filing of a third participant's submission due to the time needed to translate the appellant's submission from Spanish to English.[111]

Some commentators have suggested that international tribunals may be required to exercise their inherent jurisdiction, to apply general principles of law that protect fundamental procedural norms.[112] Carlston states:

> Express provisions are usually made in rules of procedure with a view to safeguarding fundamental procedural rights . . . While observing the provisions of the instrument – which is the basic law for the tribunal – the

[108] Appellate Body Report, *Australia – Salmon*, [278].

[109] Appellate Body Report, *US – Lead and Bismuth II*, [8].

[110] Appellate Body Report, *EC – Asbestos*, [50]–[56].

[111] Appellate Body Report, *Guatemala – Cement I*, [4].

[112] Cheng, *General Principles of Law*, 291. See Duward Sandifer, *Evidence Before International Tribunals* (rev. edn, 1975) 44: 'It might be going too far to say that a tribunal is bound, in the absence of provisions in the arbitral agreement, to follow these rules.'

tribunal is also expected to conform its operations to the basic procedural norms. Accordingly, the fundamental procedural norms, whether or not expressly provided for, comprise (1) 'certain fundamental rules of procedure' (2) which are 'inherent in the judicial process,' and (3) generally recognized in all procedure.[113]

The Appellate Body has also suggested that panels may be required to exercise their inherent jurisdiction in a manner consistent with procedural norms. For example, in *Mexico – Corn Syrup (Article 21.5 – US)*, the Appellate Body stated that, 'as a matter of due process, and the proper exercise of judicial function, panels are required to address issues that are put before them by the parties to a dispute'.[114] Thus, even in the absence of the specific WTO provisions allowing WTO Tribunals to determine procedural matters to ensure due process, WTO Tribunals would have this function.[115] This explains WTO Tribunals' approach to certain procedural issues that might not be regarded as falling specifically within Article 12.1 of the DSU or Rules 16(1) and 16(2) of the Working Procedures for Appellate Review.

One aspect of providing interested parties an adequate opportunity to be heard, as part of the hearing rule, is the right to representation at hearings. Neither the DSU nor the related WTO dispute settlement instruments set forth expressly the right to representation by private counsel as opposed to solely government officials. In *EC – Bananas III*, the Panel refused to admit private lawyers to a Panel meeting, on grounds including that: their presence could give rise to confidentiality concerns; some parties objected to their presence; and the Panel had already indicated that it expected only members of government to attend.[116] This decision was not appealed. However, at the appellate stage of the same dispute, taking into account 'customary international law [and] the prevailing practice of international tribunals', the Appellate Body ruled that WTO Members may choose the members of their delegation appearing in oral hearings on appeal.[117] The Appellate Body also stated that the right to representation by counsel 'may well be a matter of particular significance – especially for developing-country

[113] Kenneth Carlston, *The Process of International Arbitration* (1946) 34, quoted in Natasha Affolder, 'Tadic, the Anonymous Witness and the Sources of International Procedural Law' (1998) 19 *Michigan Journal of International Law* 445, 490.

[114] Appellate Body Report, *Mexico – Corn Syrup (Article 21.5 – US)*, [36].

[115] See Panel Report, *EC – Tariff Preferences*, [7.8], relying on certain DSU provisions to explain this 'inherent authority'.

[116] Panel Report, *EC – Bananas III*, [7.11]. [117] Appellate Body Report, *EC – Bananas III*, [10].

Members – to enable them to participate fully in dispute settlement proceedings'.[118] Private counsel have since become commonplace in WTO disputes. In two subsequent proceedings, panels have allowed private counsel to attend Panel meetings as representatives of parties, while emphasising that all parties' representatives are subject to the provisions of the DSU, including those regarding confidentiality.[119] Permission has been granted in order to ensure that each party 'has every opportunity to fully defend its interests'.[120]

A final example of WTO Tribunals properly exercising their inherent jurisdiction taking into account considerations of due process relates to the Appellate Body's approach to 'completing the analysis'. When the Appellate Body reverses a Panel's finding on an issue, it may need to consider whether to complete the analysis of that issue itself. Sometimes the Appellate Body has declined to complete the analysis on the basis that it lacks a sufficient factual basis, keeping in mind the restriction of appeals under Article 17.6 of the DSU to issues of law.[121] However, a factual basis is not the only condition for the Appellate Body to complete the analysis. Sometimes the Appellate Body has regarded the outstanding issue as insufficiently related to the issues that the Panel addressed,[122] perhaps due to a concern that the parties would not have a sufficient chance to present arguments on the issue, contrary to the requirements of due process. In *EC – Export Subsidies on Sugar*, the Appellate Body declined to complete the analysis, in part based on its view that, 'in the absence of a full exploration' of the relevant issues in the participants' submissions, 'completing the analysis might affect the due process rights of the participants'.[123]

5.3.2 *Understanding Members' obligations to accord due process*

A. Fair administration (GATT Article X:3(a))

(i) Introduction

A number of WTO provisions incorporate due process by requiring Members to administer laws in a uniform, impartial and reasonable manner. Perhaps most importantly, GATT Article X:3(a) states:

[118] Ibid. [12].
[119] Panel Report, *Indonesia – Autos*, [14.1]; Panel Report, *Korea – Alcoholic Beverages*, [10.31]–[10.32].
[120] Panel Report, *Korea – Alcoholic Beverages*, [10.31].
[121] See, e.g., Appellate Body Report, *Australia – Salmon*, [117], [213].
[122] See, e.g., Appellate Body Report, *Canada – Periodicals*, 24.
[123] Appellate Body Report, *EC – Export Subsidies on Sugar*, [339].

Each Member shall administer in a uniform, impartial and reasonable manner all its laws, regulations, decisions and rulings of the kind described in [Article X:1].

Article X:1 refers to:

Laws, regulations, judicial decisions and administrative rulings of general application . . . pertaining to the classification or the valuation of products for customs purposes, or to rates of duty, taxes or other charges, or to requirements, restrictions or prohibitions on imports or exports or on the transfer of payments therefor, or affecting their sale, distribution, transportation, insurance, warehousing inspection, exhibition, processing, mixing or other use.

In this section, I am interested in the due process implications of Article X:3(a). Accordingly, I do not address the various decisions by WTO Tribunals regarding the broader scope of Article X:3(a) (in particular, WTO Tribunals' emphasis in interpreting this provision on the 'administration'[124] of laws, regulations, judicial decisions and administrative rulings 'of general application').[125] This discussion focuses on Panel decisions, since Article X:3(a) claims have only infrequently reached the stage of appeal.

(ii) Uniformity, impartiality, and reasonableness

Although Article X:3(a) does not explicitly refer to due process, WTO Tribunals and commentators have recognised its due process aspects. For example, the Appellate Body has stated that Article X:3(a) establishes 'certain minimum standards for transparency and procedural fairness' in the administration of trade laws.[126] Bhala suggests that the 'central thrust of Article X . . . is to inject procedural fairness and due process into the mechanism for establishing laws, regulations, and rules governing international trade'.[127] The requirements of uniformity, impartiality, and reasonableness may be seen as incorporating aspects of the hearing and bias rules (uniformity and impartiality) as well as the no evidence rule (reasonableness). I consider these three requirements in turn.

[124] See, e.g., Appellate Body Report, *EC – Bananas III*, [200].
[125] See, e.g., Appellate Body Report, *EC – Poultry*, [113].
[126] Appellate Body Report, *US – Shrimp*, [183].
[127] Raj Bhala, *Modern GATT Law: A Treatise on the General Agreement on Tariffs and Trade* (2005) 452–3, n. 4.

The Panel in *Argentina – Hides and Leather* stated that '[u]niform administration requires that Members ensure that their laws are applied consistently and predictably'.[128] However, this requirement has important limitations and does not require Members to treat all products identically.[129] The Panel in *US – Stainless Steel* made clear that different circumstances might justify different approaches: 'the requirement of uniform administration of laws and regulations must be understood to mean uniformity of treatment in respect of persons similarly situated; it cannot be understood to require identical results where relevant facts differ'.[130] The Panel found that the challenged trade remedy investigation did not involve an 'unprecedented departure' from 'established policy' and was therefore neither non-uniform nor unreasonable.[131] If persons subject to administrative decisions are treated differently, this may mean the result or basis for the decision is unexpected and the persons had no opportunity to defend their case, contrary to the hearing rule. A lack of uniformity in similar circumstances might also raise the suspicion that the decision-maker was biased.

Turning to the requirement of impartiality, the Panel in *Argentina – Hides and Leather* indicated that a decision could be rendered partial by the presence at the time of making the decision of a person with an inherent or potential conflict of interest. The Panel explained:

> Whenever a party with a contrary commercial interest, but no relevant legal interest, is allowed to participate in an export transaction such as this, there is an inherent danger that the Customs laws, regulations and rules will be applied in a partial manner so as to permit persons with adverse commercial interests to obtain confidential information to which they have no right.[132]

The Panel concluded that, in the circumstances before it, the decision-makers adopted insufficient safeguards to protect against the risk of misuse of confidential information by the party in question, and the proceedings were therefore not impartial, contrary to Article X:3(a).[133] This decision is harder to square with the principle of due process, unless the presence of the party with a contrary commercial interest can be seen as reflecting bias on the part of the decision-maker. In any case, the Panel's reference to confidential information as a basis for finding impartiality under Article X:3(a) is quite odd, particularly since Article X:1 of GATT 1994 relates specifically to confidential

[128] Panel Report, *Argentina – Hides and Leather*, [11.83]. [129] Ibid. [11.84].
[130] Panel Report, *US – Stainless Steel*, [6.51]. [131] Ibid. [6.51].
[132] Panel Report, *Argentina – Hides and Leather*, [11.100]. [133] Ibid. [11.101].

information. The Panel also pointed to the 'the possibility of revealing confidential business information' to justify its finding of inconsistency with Article X:3(a) on the basis of unreasonableness, again straining the due process meaning of Article X:3(a) and ignoring the specific confidentiality requirements in Article X:1.

In *Dominican Republic – Import and Sale of Cigarettes*, the Panel considered the 'reasonableness' requirement of Article X:3(a). The Panel described the ordinary meaning of the word 'reasonable' as referring to 'notions such as "in accordance with reason", "not irrational or absurd", "proportionate", "having sound judgement", "sensible", "not asking for too much", "within the limits of reason, not greatly less or more than might be thought likely or appropriate", "articulate" '.[134] It found that the Dominican Republic had not met this standard of reasonableness in administering certain tax laws, because the 'authorities did not support its decisions regarding the determination of the tax base for imported cigarettes by resorting to the rules in force at the time'.[135] This demonstrates how the reasonableness requirement may reflect not merely the no evidence rule (in relation to whether a reasonable person could have come to the conclusion reached) but also the hearing rule (in that a failure to rely on existing laws could deprive interested parties of the chance to respond to the methodology to be used).

(iii) Consistency with WTO law and domestic law

Several Panel reports reveal a reluctance to find a violation of Article X:3(a) of GATT 1994, particularly in the absence of a violation of another WTO provision. In *US – Hot-Rolled Steel*, the Panel stated:

> Where we have found that a particular action or category of action is not inconsistent with a specific provision of the AD Agreement, we are faced with the question whether a Member can be found to have violated Article X:3(a) of GATT 1994 by an action which is not inconsistent with the specific WTO obligations governing such actions. We have serious doubts as to whether such a finding would be appropriate.[136]

More often, Panels have expressed the concern that finding an Article X:3(a) violation might involve inquiring into the consistency of WTO Members' administration of their laws and regulations with those very

[134] Panel Report, *Dominican Republic – Import and Sale of Cigarettes*, [7.385].
[135] Ibid. [7.388]. [136] Panel Report, *US – Hot-Rolled Steel*, [7.267].

laws and regulations. In other words, Panels seem to worry that finding that a Members' authorities administer its laws and regulations in a non-uniform, impartial, or unreasonable manner might suggest those authorities are acting inconsistently with their domestic obligations. Several Panels have insisted that '[i]t is not . . . properly a panel's task to consider whether a Member has acted consistently with its own domestic legislation'.[137] This insistence may stem from a reluctance to interfere in Members' domestic affairs. Thus, one Panel states that Article X:3(a)

> was not in our view intended to function as a mechanism to test the consistency of a Member's particular decisions or rulings with the Member's own domestic law and practice; that is a function reserved for each Member's domestic judicial system, and a function WTO Panels would be particularly ill-suited to perform.[138]

It is not surprising that WTO Tribunals should wish to avoid becoming courts of last resort, reviewing the consistency of administrative conduct and perhaps indirectly contradicting domestic judicial decisions in this regard. However, this should not be of major concern to WTO Tribunals; nor should it in any way affect their interpretation of Article X:3(a). Although interpreting and applying that provision may involve a consideration of some of the same questions that would arise in assessing the consistency of Members' administrative practice and procedures with their own domestic laws, the purpose and scope of this inquiry is obviously quite different. WTO Tribunals are interested only in whether Members have administered certain laws in a uniform, impartial, and reasonable manner. This may be influenced by the content and meaning of the relevant laws, but not by a direct consideration of whether the administration is valid under domestic law.

B. General exceptions (GATT Article XX)

Article XX of GATT 1994 provides general exceptions from the usual WTO disciplines for certain measures, provided that they are not applied 'in a manner which would constitute a means of arbitrary or unjustifiable discrimination between countries where the same conditions prevail, or a disguised restriction on trade'. The Appellate Body held in *US – Shrimp* that the chapeau of GATT Article XX incorporates not only substantive norms but also 'procedural requirements' in the

[137] Ibid. [7.267]. [138] Panel Report, *US – Stainless Steel*, [6.50] (footnotes omitted).

sense that arbitrary or unjustifiable discrimination may arise 'where a measure, otherwise fair and just on its face, is actually applied in an arbitrary or unjustifiable manner'.[139]

The Appellate Body found that the challenged United States measure (an import ban as mentioned in Chapter 4) did not comply with the chapeau because it involved arbitrary and unjustifiable discrimination between countries where the same conditions prevail.[140] The key due process difficulty with the chapeau was that imports from countries that were 'certified' were not subject to the ban, and the certification process involved arbitrary and unjustifiable discrimination. To be certified, countries had to show that they had either (i) a fishing environment that did not pose a threat of incidental turtle capture in shrimp trawling, or (ii) a regulatory programme for the prevention of such capture comparable to that of the United States and with an average rate of such capture comparable to that of United States vessels.[141] The Appellate Body did not define the criteria for establishing the existence of such discrimination. Nevertheless, some of the factors that the Appellate Body relied on in reaching this conclusion appear to reflect due process considerations.

One of these factors was that the United States measure established:

> a rigid and unbending standard by which United States officials determine whether or not countries will be certified, thus granting or refusing other countries the right to export shrimp to the United States. Other specific policies and measures that an exporting country may have adopted for the protection and conservation of sea turtles are not taken into account, in practice, by the administrators making the comparability determination.[142]

This passage reveals concerns relevant to the no evidence rule (that is, decision-makers must base decisions on logically probative evidence) and the bias rule (that is, decision-makers must impartially consider the merits of each case). The Appellate Body also considered the lack of 'formal opportunity for an applicant country to be heard, or to respond to any arguments that may be made against it, in the course of the certification process before a decision to grant or to deny certification is made', and the absence of 'formal written, reasoned decision[s]', notice of denial or procedures for review and appeal to be relevant factors.[143] This calls to mind certain aspects of the hearing rule.

[139] Appellate Body Report, *US – Shrimp*, [160]. [140] Ibid. [176], [184].
[141] Ibid. [3] –[4]. [142] Ibid. [163]. [143] Ibid. [180].

Although Article X:3 of GATT 1994 was not at issue, the Appellate Body stated that several aspects of the certification process were also 'contrary to the spirit, if not the letter, of Article X:3'.[144] It added:

> Inasmuch as there are due process requirements generally for measures that are otherwise imposed in compliance with WTO obligations, it is only reasonable that rigorous compliance with the fundamental requirements of due process should be required in the application and administration of a measure which purports to be an exception to the treaty obligations of the Member imposing the measure and which effectively results in a suspension *pro hac vice* of the treaty rights of other Members.[145]

US – Shrimp provides an unusual example of the Appellate Body using the principle of due process to explain its decision. On their face, the words 'arbitrary or unjustifiable discrimination' in the chapeau of Article XX do not necessarily imply discrimination in procedural matters. In addition, Article XX does not appear to contemplate the need for any judicial or administrative decision-making in the context of the chapeau. Finally, the Appellate Body had no obvious reason to consider GATT Article X:3 in interpreting or justifying its decision regarding GATT Article XX. In sum, this seems like another illustration of the Appellate Body grasping at international law principles to buttress its reasoning without sufficient explanation of the legal basis or rationale for doing so.

5.4 Conclusion

It has been claimed that due process 'is probably the greatest contribution ever made to modern civilization by lawyers or perhaps any other professional group'.[146] Certainly due process plays a vital role in the WTO and makes an important contribution to the legitimacy of WTO dispute settlement. The concept of due process is necessarily broad but unnecessarily vague in current WTO jurisprudence.

WTO Tribunals seem confident exercising inherent jurisdiction to resolve procedural matters in accordance with due process, perhaps because of the comfort provided by Article 12.1 of the DSU and Rules 16(1) and 16(2) of the Working Procedures for Appellate Review. However, the Appellate Body has been less self-assured in reviewing Panel proceedings to ensure that due process requirements were met. It

[144] Ibid. [183]. [145] Ibid. [182]. [146] P. S. Atiyah, *Law and Modern Society* (1983) 42.

places a great deal of faith in Article 11 of the DSU, including in circumstances where that provision, properly interpreted, has nothing to say about the due process question at issue. The Appellate Body should instead rely on its inherent jurisdiction to review Panels' compliance with due process. At the same time, the Appellate Body's overuse of Article 11 of the DSU has led it to find that Panels have failed to fulfil their function under Article 11 of the DSU where they have violated no due process requirement. In a few disputes, the Appellate Body has inexplicably lowered the threshold for finding that a Panel failed to make an objective assessment, effectively meaning that the Panel acted inconsistently with the bias rule or the no evidence rule, which would normally be a very serious charge in international law.

When it comes to imposing due process requirements on Members, WTO Tribunals have also had mixed success. The principle of due process may inform the meaning of uniformity, impartiality, and reasonableness in Article X:3(a) of GATT 1994, and it may also explain the rationale behind these requirements. WTO Tribunals' decisions in this regard have been largely consistent with the underlying due process concerns. However, on occasion, Panels have moved away from the due process elements of Article X:3(a) and come to unusual conclusions regarding impartiality and reasonableness based on the need to protect confidential information. The Appellate Body's reasons and legal basis for relying on due process in interpreting Article XX of GATT 1994 are equally mysterious. A more solid legal framework for these decisions would assist in ensuring that the principle of due process is used in a legitimate and consistent manner in WTO disputes.

6 Proportionality

> It goes without saying that a breach of a commercial treaty may not justify the taking of hostages in response.[1]

6.1 Introduction

The ordinary meaning of 'proportionality' is the 'quality, character, or fact of being proportional', which in turn is defined as 'corresponding in degree, size, amount, etc.'.[2] In law, the notion of proportionality has several meanings, of varying breadth, depending on the context. At its broadest, proportionality in legal terms refers to the requirement for a 'proper or balanced relationship between competing considerations',[3] a definition that is only marginally more specific than the meaning of the word in ordinary English and that seems to lack normative direction. More particularly, proportionality 'is said to involve the idea that there should be a reasonable relationship or balance between an end and the means used to achieve this end'.[4] Table B provides a sample of the many WTO provisions that could be said to involve some sort of proportionality.

In this chapter, I try to narrow the meaning of proportionality to the extent relevant to the WTO, by examining the existence and content of proportionality as a general principle of law, a principle of customary international law, and a principle of WTO law, as summarised in Table C.

[1] Enzo Cannizzaro, 'The Role of Proportionality in the Law of International Countermeasures' (2001) 12 *European Journal of International Law* 889, 906.

[2] William Trumble and Angus Stevenson (eds.), *Shorter Oxford English Dictionary on Historical Principles* (5th edn, 2002) vol. II, 2371.

[3] Peter Nygh and Peter Butt (eds.), *Australian Legal Dictionary* (1997) 941.

[4] Jeremy Kirk, 'Constitutional Guarantees, Characterisation and the Concept of Proportionality' (1997) 21 *Melbourne University Law Review* 1, 2.

Table B: *Some WTO provisions that may incorporate proportionality*

		Words or concepts used			
Agreement	Provision	Necessary	Proportionate	Less/least trade restrictive	Commensurate
Language incorporating GATT 1994 into the WTO Agreement	3(d)		✓		
GATT 1994	VIII:3	✓			
	IX:2	✓			
	XI:2(b), (c)	✓			
	XII:2(a), 3(c)(i)	✓			
	XVIII:2, 9, 10, 14, 15, 16, 18, 22	✓			
	XIX:1(a), (b), 3(b)	✓			
	XX(a), (b), (d), (i)	✓			
	XXI:(b)	✓			
	XXIV:5, 8(a)(i), 8(b)	✓			
Understanding on the Balance of Payments Provisions of GATT 1994	4	✓			
GATS	VI:4, 4(b)	✓			
	XII:2(c), 2(d)	✓			
	XIV(a), (b), (c)	✓			
	XIVbis:1(b)	✓			
	XXI:2(a)	✓			
	Annex on Movement of Natural Persons, para. 4				
	Annex on Telecommunications, paras. 5(d), 5(e), 5(g)	✓			

Decision on Professional Services	2(a)	✓			
Anti-Dumping Agreement	7.1(iii)	✓			
	8.1	✓			
	11.1, 11.2	✓			
SCM Agreement	2.1(c)		✓		
	4.10 and footnote 9, 4.11 and footnote 10		✓		
	7.9, 7.10				✓
	8.2(b)(ii) and footnote 32 (expired)		✓		
	9.4				✓
	17.1(c)	✓			
	18.1(b)	✓			
	21.1, 21.2	✓			
	27.4	✓			
	29.1, 29.4	✓			
Agreement on Safeguards	5.1	✓			
	7.1, 7.2	✓			
SPS Agreement	Preamble	✓			
	2.1, 2.2	✓			
	3.2	✓			
	5.6 and footnote 3			✓	
	9.1	✓			
	Annex B, para. 6	✓			
	Annex C, para. 1(a)	✓			

TBT Agreement	Preamble	✓			
	2.2, 2.3, 2.5	✓		✓	
	5.1.2	✓			
	12.3, 12.7	✓			
	Annex 3, paras. E, N	✓			
TRIPS Agreement	3.2	✓			
	8.1	✓			
	27.2	✓			
	39.3	✓			
	46		✓		
	73(b)	✓			
Agreement on Agriculture	20(d)	✓			
ATC	5.3, 5.4	✓			
TRIMS Agreement	5.5	✓			
	Annex, paras. 1, 2	✓			
Preshipment Inspection	Preamble	✓			
	2.12(b), (e)	✓			
Rules of Origin	Preamble	✓			
Import Licensing	Preamble	✓			
	1.5, 1.7	✓			
	3.2	✓			
Civil Aircraft (plurilateral)	VI:1	✓			
	XV:1(c), 1(f)	✓			
	XXIII:1, 2	✓			
Government Procurement (plurilateral)	XXIII:2	✓			

Table C: *Comparison of proportionality in relation to penalties*

Type of Principle and Context			Unfair or Unlawful Conduct	Form of Penalty	Maximum penalty must be proportionate (or not disproportionate) . . .	Additional comments/suggestions
General principle of law			Criminal offence	Fine, imprisonment etc	To *harm* caused and *culpability* (seriousness of offence)	
Principle of customary international law			Internationally wrongful act	Countermeasures in the form of non-performance of international obligations	To *harm* caused, taking into account *culpability* (gravity of internationally wrongful act and rights in question)	
Principle of WTO law	Multilateral remedies	DSU	General WTO violation	Suspension of concessions or other obligations under the WTO	To *harm* caused (level of nullification or impairment)	*Culpability* (the violation itself) could give rise to nullification or impairment
		SCM Agreement, Part III	Actionable subsidy	Countermeasures	To *harm* caused (degree and nature of adverse effects)	*Culpability* is present (granting of actionable subsidy)
		SCM Agreement, Part II	Prohibited subsidy	Appropriate countermeasures	In light of *culpability* (granting of prohibited subsidy)	*Harm* need not be shown to establish culpability (granting of prohibited subsidy), but it is still relevant
	Unilateral remedies	SCM Agreement, Part V	Subsidy causing injury	Countervailing duties	To *culpability* (amount of subsidy)	*Harm* is caused (injury to domestic industry); desirable that penalty not exceed that harm
		Anti-Dumping Agreement	Dumping causing injury	Anti-dumping duties	To *culpability* (dumping margin)	*Harm* is caused (injury to domestic industry); desirable that penalty not exceed that harm

I do not propose to conduct an exhaustive investigation of the many different circumstances in which the notion of proportionality arises in law. Nor is my goal to establish definitively whether proportionality is a general principle of law[5] or a principle of customary international law.[6] Rather, in the following sections I examine some of the evidence that could support a suggestion that proportionality has achieved such a status (which would add legitimacy to any use of the principle in the WTO), while attempting to understand the meaning of and rationale for proportionality. I then consider how such a principle might be used in WTO disputes, either to interpret WTO provisions or as the basis of a claim.

At the outset, it is necessary to distinguish two main forms in which proportionality could be said to exist as a general principle of law: a principle of customary international law, and a principle of WTO law. The first, more general, form of the proportionality principle provides a guide to balancing competing rights, values, or other objectives.[7] In this form, for example, proportionality may impose limits on the restriction of human rights and individual freedoms in domestic constitutions[8] or in international law.[9] Similarly, in the WTO, some commentators have used the notion of 'proportionality' to explain how to evaluate infringements of or exceptions to stated WTO objectives,

[5] For different views on this question, see the sources cited in Judith Gardam, 'Proportionality as a Restraint on the Use of Force' (1999) 20 *Australian Yearbook of International Law* 161, 161. On one view, the principle 'has found almost universal acceptance in some way or another in domestic legal orders': Jost Delbrück, 'Proportionality' in Rudolf Bernhardt (ed.), *Encyclopaedia of Public International Law* (2003) vol. III, 1140, 1141.

[6] On this question, see D. W. Grieg, 'Reciprocity, Proportionality, and the Law of Treaties' (1994) 34 *Virginia Journal of International Law* 295, 322–4. Again, on one view, 'the widespread acceptance of the principle in various areas of international law and its fundamental importance for the international law-applying process suggests that proportionality can already be characterized as a general principle of international law': Delbrück, 'Proportionality', 1140, 1144.

[7] See, e.g., Gráinne de Búrca, 'Subsidiarity and Proportionality as General Principles of Law' in Joakim Nergelius and Ulf Bernitz (eds.), *General Principles of European Community Law: Reports from a Conference in Malmö, 27–28 August 1999* (2000) 97; George Bermann, 'The Principle of Proportionality' (1977–78) 26 *American Journal of Comparative Law Supplement* 415.

[8] See, e.g., Kyung Park, 'Korean Principle of Proportionality, American Multi-Leveled Scrutiny, and Empiricist Elements in US-Korean Constitutional Jurisprudence' (2001) 1 *Journal of Korean Law* 105, 109–10; Kirk, 'Constitutional Guarantees', 5–9.

[9] See, e.g., *Universal Declaration of Human Rights*, GA Res 217A(III) (10 December 1948) art. 29(2); *International Covenant on Civil and Political Rights*, opened for signature 19 December 1966, 999 UNTS 171 (adopted 16 December 1966) arts. 21, 22(1).

rules, or disciplines.[10] Hilf can be seen as recognising this form of proportionality as a principle of WTO law, in the following terms:

> [T]he principle of proportionality is one of the more basic principles underlying the multilateral trading system, although there is no explicit reference to it in WTO law. However, the basic idea of proportionality, i.e. the due balancing of competing rights, is reflected several times in WTO agreements.[11]

WTO provisions that may be seen as reflecting a principle of proportionality often include words such as 'necessary', 'proportionate', 'less trade restrictive',[12] and 'commensurate'. Table B summarises certain provisions in the WTO agreements that use such words and could be seen as reflecting some notion of proportionality.

The second form of proportionality is narrower. It is addressed to the requisite relationship between the penalty imposed for a given offence. Broadly speaking, proportionality may be required between punishment and crime (at the domestic level), countermeasure and internationally wrongful act (at the international level), and retaliation and violation or other undesirable conduct (in the WTO).

These two forms of proportionality are related and not necessarily mutually exclusive. The second form could be described as a subset of the first, for instance, in the sense that it may involve balancing the rights of an individual who has committed a crime against the various goals of punishment and the rights of the community. However, for the sake of clarity, I will look at each of these two forms of proportionality separately. I will begin by examining proportionality as a principle used to balance competing interests and values, with particular reference to the ability of Members to enact domestic measures to promote non-trade interests, such as health, safety and environmental protections. I then turn to the second form of proportionality, examining how it may be used in the WTO in the context of remedies and retaliation,

[10] See, e.g., TBT Agreement, arts. 2.4, 5.4; SPS Agreement, art. 2.4; GATT 1994, art. XX; Alan Sykes, 'The Least Restrictive Means' (2003) 70 *University of Chicago Law Review* 403; Jan Neumann and Elisabeth Türk, 'Necessity Revisited: Proportionality in World Trade Organization Law After *Korea – Beef, EC – Asbestos* and *EC – Sardines*' (2003) 37 *Journal of World Trade* 199.

[11] Meinhard Hilf, 'Power, Rules and Principles – Which Orientation for WTO/GATT Law?' (2001) 4 *Journal of International Economic Law* 111, 120–1 (footnote omitted).

[12] Axel Desmedt, 'Proportionality in WTO Law' (2001) 4 *Journal of International Economic Law* 441, 442–3.

which bears particular examination because it has been little considered in the context of the WTO.[13]

6.2 Proportionality as a principle for balancing competing interests

In this section, I examine the principle of proportionality as a tool to weigh competing values and interests in legal systems. In this respect, proportionality is closely linked to the ideas of necessity and balancing.[14] Proportionality and related tests based upon 'balancing' competing interests are found in a vast range of legal systems. As such, it is difficult to discern one universal principle of proportionality. Rather, this chapter will attempt to establish the common features of proportionality as it is applied in different legal contexts. It will then consider proportionality in the context of the WTO, analysing proportionality as a principle of WTO law and examining its relevance and limits as a balancing tool where conflicting (or potentially conflicting) interests, such as trade liberalisation and environmental protection, are at issue.

6.2.1 A general principle of law

The principle of proportionality is 'a prominent legal principle in many legal orders, and all legal systems have to undertake different forms of balancing, both in determining the content of rules and in their application'.[15] When courts and tribunals review the actions of other bodies, they must make a range of value choices. This applies in a domestic context, through the review of legislative and administrative action, as well as at an international level, through the review of states' compliance with their international obligations.[16] Proportionality is one of the most frequently used principles to assist in making these value judgements. Common uses of this principle are as a test to control the exercise of discretion by public authorities, to assess limitations or restrictions placed on human rights,[17] and to determine the extension of rights.[18]

[13] However this issue is receiving increasing attention. See, e.g., Thomas Sebastian, 'World Trade Organization Remedies and the Assessment of Proportionality: Equivalence and Appropriateness' (2007) 48 *Harvard International Law Journal* 337.

[14] Mads Andenas and Stefan Zleptnig, 'Proportionality: WTO Law: In Comparative Perspective' (2007) 42 *Texas International Law Journal* 371, 372.

[15] Ibid. 373. [16] Ibid.

[17] See generally Evelyn Ellis (ed.), *The Principle of Proportionality in the Laws of Europe* (1999).

[18] Mads Andenas and Stefan Zleptnig, 'Proportionality and Balancing in the WTO: A Comparative Perspective' (2007) 20 *Cambridge Review of International Affairs* 71, 73–4.

It is impossible in this book to examine all of the areas in which proportionality is used as a legal principle. In order to establish the content of this principle, this section will examine the principle of proportionality in domestic legal systems, through an analysis of United States administrative law and United Kingdom human rights law, and in international legal systems, through an analysis of European Communities law. It will be shown that the principle of proportionality is applied in a variety of different ways in different contexts, but that it has common elements. At its broadest, proportionality involves comparing costs and benefits in order to determine the legitimacy or justifiability of an action. However, in many legal systems the principle of proportionality has also developed to include more specific requirements, including that laws be 'suitable' and 'necessary' for achieving their objectives.

A. Proportionality in domestic legal systems

The principle of proportionality has been used since the nineteenth century in German administrative law as a simple requirement that 'the government ... take no action the overall costs of which are excessive in relation to its overall benefits'.[19] By contrast, Bermann argues that it is no 'easy matter' to determine if proportionality is a requirement of US administrative law.[20] The difficulty in viewing proportionality as a principle of US administrative law is that the underlying terms are not well defined. The term 'excessive' could simply mean that the costs outweigh the benefits, or it could require that they outweigh them by a 'considerable margin'.[21] If the former of these two definitions of excessive is accepted, then the courts are left with substantial leeway to replace the actions of the legislature or executive with their own 'policy preferences'.[22] This is why there is no simple 'proportionality' requirement in US administrative law.

However, Bermann concludes that the principle of proportionality is reflected in US administrative law through three different tests. The first of these is a 'reasonableness test', where government action is assessed on the basis of its rationality. Actions that are too harsh or restrictive may be struck down on the basis that they are 'unreasonable', 'arbitrary, capricious [or] abuse[s] of discretion'.[23] Under this test, the courts assess the rationality of administrative action without

[19] Bermann, 'Principle of Proportionality', 415. [20] Ibid. 418. [21] Ibid. [22] Ibid.
[23] Ibid. 418–26.

having the broad power to '[tell] public officials what to do'.[24] Second, there is a 'balancing test', where an authority is required to balance certain considerations when taking action, for example creating an environmental impact statement, and where failure to adequately engage in the relevant balancing exercise would lead to the invalidation of the authority's action.[25] Third, there is a 'least drastic means test', which requires government authorities to act in a manner that 'interferes least with other values'.[26] While none of these tests impose an absolute requirement on all administrative action in the United States, they are common to many statutes that mandate or limit government action and are often applied (and blurred) in judicial review. For example, the United States Supreme Court held that in evaluating the reasonableness of a local ordinance for the purposes of judicial review:

> we . . . need to know such things as the nature of the menace against which it will protect, the availability and effectiveness of other less drastic protective steps and the loss which appellants will suffer from the imposition of the ordinance.[27]

These comments of the United States Supreme Court demonstrate that while there may not be a specific requirement called 'proportionality' in US administrative law, the principle of balancing competing interests is embodied in the reasonableness, balancing, and least drastic means requirements.

The principle of proportionality is applied through a similar series of tests in the United Kingdom in the interpretation of the *Human Rights Act 1998* (UK) c. 42.[28] Although this Act does not contain a general provision stating that limitations on human rights must be proportionate, courts have used proportionality as a 'tool' or 'metwand' for assessing the validity of a curtailment of rights.[29] United Kingdom courts apply a three-step test to determine if a limitation on rights is 'proportionate'. The test, which is derived from a decision of the

[24] Ibid. 418. [25] Ibid. 426–9. [26] Ibid. 430–2.

[27] *Goldblatt* v. *Town of Hempstead*, 369 US 590, 594–5 (1962).

[28] Proportionality is also used as a tool for evaluating limitations upon rights in many jurisdictions, such as South Africa, Canada, and New Zealand. See Andrew Butler and Petra Butler, *The New Zealand Bill of Rights Act: A Commentary* (2005) 117–18, 142–9; Peter W. Hogg, *Constitutional Law of Canada* (2002) 764–6, 801–2; Stu Woolman and Henk Botha, 'Limitations' in *Constitutional Law of South Africa* (2nd edn, Original Service 07-06) [34-12]–[34-16].

[29] *London Regional Transport* v. *Mayor of London* [2001] EWCA Civ 1491, [57] (Sedley LJ).

Privy Council in *de Freitas* (an appeal from Antigua and Barbuda), asks whether:

> (i) the legislative objective is sufficiently important to justify limiting a fundamental right; (ii) the measures designed to meet the legislative objective are rationally connected to it; and (iii) the means used to impair the right or freedom are no more than is necessary to accomplish the objective.[30]

One important characteristic of proportionality in relation to human rights law in the United Kingdom,[31] which is less apparent in United States administrative law, is that a measure may be necessary and rationally connected to achieving a legislative objective and yet still be invalid. This would occur when the infringement of rights is disproportionate to the benefits of achieving the objective (in other words, the legislative objective is not sufficiently important to justify limiting the fundamental right). Furthermore, the UK courts emphasise the 'severity and consequences of the interference' with rights[32] and adjust the intensity of review according to the importance of the subject-matter under consideration.[33] This reflects the broad principle of proportionality, as it exists in German administrative law as mentioned above, where the societal costs and benefits of laws or measures are weighed in order to assess their justifiability. This approach gives courts a great degree of power to determine how to balance competing interests in society, which is a function that is typically seen as legislative and outside the courts' 'proper sphere of activity'.[34] While judges in the United Kingdom courts have been careful to state that proportionality does not allow 'a shift towards merits review', there is also an acknowledgement that '[this] proportionality test may go further than the traditional grounds of review inasmuch as it may require attention to be directed to the relative weight accorded to interests and considerations'.[35]

[30] *de Freitas* v. *Permanent Secretary of Ministry of Agriculture, Fisheries, Lands and Housing* [1999] 1 AC 69, 80, quoting *Nyambirai* v. *National Social Security Authority* [1996] 1 LRC 64, 75. This test was first applied to the *Human Rights Act 1998* (UK) c. 42 in *R (Daly)* v. *Secretary of State for the Home Department* [2001] 2 AC 532, [27] (Lord Steyn) and has been reaffirmed in *Huang* v. *Secretary of State for the Home Department; Kashmiri* v. *Same* [2007] 2 AC 167, [19].

[31] Outside of human rights law there is a general resistance to proportionality in United Kingdom law. See de Búrca, 'Subsidiarity and Proportionality', 99.

[32] *Huang* v. *Secretary of State for the Home Department; Kashmiri* v. *Same* [2007] UKHL 11; [2007] 2 AC 167, [19].

[33] *R (Daly)* v. *Secretary of State for the Home Department* [2001] 2 AC 532, [28] (Lord Steyn).

[34] Bermann, 'Principle of Proportionality', 418.

[35] *R (Daly)* v. *Secretary of State for the Home Department* [2001] 2 AC 532, [28] (Lord Steyn).

B. Proportionality in international legal systems

The principle of proportionality was 'one of the earliest legal principles articulated by the European Court of Justice (ECJ) as a general principle of European Communities law', in spite of the fact that it has no textual basis in the Communities' treaties.[36] One of the reasons that the principle was so easily incorporated into the law of the European Communities was that it was already well established in the jurisprudence of the European Court of Human Rights[37] and in the domestic laws of many of its Member States.[38] The basic question that is being asked when proportionality is used in European Communities law as a 'balancing principle' is 'whether some legally protected interest or right was being excessively restricted'.[39] As with proportionality in United Kingdom human rights law, the intensity of the scrutiny that the ECJ will apply depends on the importance or nature of the right or interest being infringed.[40]

When the ECJ has applied proportionality it has used a three-step test.[41] The first element of this test requires that the measure adopted be suitable to achieve its objective. This requirement does not examine the results of the measure; rather, it is used to prevent measures that were never going to be suited to pursuing the stated objective.[42] Second, in order to be proportionate, a measure must be necessary. Necessity is determined by examining whether or not less restrictive alternatives could be equally effective in achieving the measure's stated aim. In the context of trade, this has been read as a requirement to adopt the least trade restrictive measure when a state is pursuing non-trade related policies.[43] The third requirement is known as proportionality *stricto sensu*, which means the benefits of the measure must not be disproportionate to the interests or rights that the measure curtails.[44] The three elements of this test are cumulative, and if either the first or second is not fulfilled, it is impossible for the other elements to be fulfilled. For example, if a law is not suitable for its

[36] de Búrca, 'Proportionality and Subsidiarity', 95.
[37] See, e.g., *Handyside* v. *United Kingdom* (1979) 1 EHRR 737.
[38] de Búrca, 'Proportionality and Subsidiarity', 95. [39] Ibid. 97. [40] Ibid.
[41] See generally Frederico Ortino, *Basic Legal Instruments for the Liberalisation of Trade* (2004); Ellis, *Principle of Proportionality*; Andenas and Zleptnig, 'Proportionality and Balancing in the WTO', 71, 74–7.
[42] See, e.g., Case C-240/95 *Schmitt* [1996] ECR I-3179, [24]–[25].
[43] See, e.g., Case C-104/75 *de Peijper* [1976] ECR 613, [16]–[29].
[44] See, e.g., Case C-169/91 *Stoke-on-Trent* [1992] ECR I-6625, [15].

purpose it will automatically also not be necessary. The cumulative nature of these requirements is one of the reasons why the ECJ rarely discusses the third requirement, proportionality *stricto sensu.*

Ortino argues that proportionality *stricto sensu* is often subsumed into the second 'necessity' element of the test.[45] The reason for this is that proportionality under European Communities law does not take into consideration the right of Member States to determine the level of protection that they believe is adequate. For example, in the famous *Cassis de Dijon* case, the ECJ held that the measure that Germany imposed was disproportionate because it was not 'necessary', for the objective of the legislation could have been achieved through means that were less restrictive of trade.[46] According to Ortino, this ECJ decision failed to take into account the fact that the German measure was designed to create a zero-risk of consumer confusion, not just to reduce consumer confusion.[47] While some consumer protection could have been achieved through less trade restrictive means, the high level of consumer protection achieved through a zero-risk approach could not have been achieved through less restrictive means. Characterising the aim of the German measure as consumer protection, rather than creating a zero-risk of consumer confusion, the ECJ decided that the measure did not meet the necessity requirement of the proportionality test. In doing so, the ECJ effectively blurred the second and third elements of proportionality, because it held that the measure was not necessary because of the scope of its impact on intra-Community trade.

These three case studies of the use of the proportionality principle to balance competing interests in different legal contexts demonstrate that no universal rule or test embodies this principle. However, the three-stage structure used in European Communities law can be seen to incorporate the key elements of the tests used in the domestic laws of the United States and the United Kingdom. First, the suitability requirement requires a link to be shown between a measure and the objective it seeks to achieve. This is equivalent to the requirement that an infringement of human rights be 'rationally connected' to its legislative objective, and to the 'reasonableness test' of United States administrative law. If a law or government action fails the

[45] This also occurs in some cases under the *Human Rights Act 1998* (UK) c. 42. See, e.g., *R* v. *Shayler* [2003] 1 AC 247, discussed in Andenas and Zleptnig, 'Proportionality and Balancing in the WTO', 71, 75.

[46] Case C-120/78, *Cassis de Dijon* [1979] ECR 649.

[47] Ortino, *Basic Legal Instruments*, 471.

'reasonableness test' because it is unreasonable, arbitrary, or capricious, it will almost certainly also fail to be 'rationally connected' to or suitable for achieving its legislative objective. Second, the necessity requirement in European Communities law requires an absence of any less trade restrictive alternative measures available to the Member State to achieve its objective. The 'least restrictive means test' applied in the United States is clearly equivalent to this standard, as is the United Kingdom requirement that a limitation on rights be no more than necessary to achieve its objective. Third, the proportionality *stricto sensu* test under European Communities law requires an overall weighing or balancing of the costs and benefits of a measure. This final requirement is similar to the United States' 'balancing test' and to the United Kingdom requirement that a legislative objective be sufficient to justify infringing human rights; each of these tests requires a direct comparison between the value and importance of the competing interests.

While the exact standard used for each of these tests varies between the legal systems I have discussed, this analysis shows three common or overarching requirements incorporated within proportionality. These three requirements – suitability, necessity, and proportionality *stricto sensu* – thus reflect the content of proportionality as a general principle of law.

6.2.2 Principle of WTO law

In this section, I consider whether proportionality could be described as a principle of WTO law, based on the objectives of the WTO and the WTO agreements. Desmedt concludes from a detailed review of several WTO agreements that

> there is no uniform proportionality principle in WTO law . . . In order for such a principle to apply in the WTO, one should expect Members to negotiate a rule, rather than wait for such a principle to emerge from dispute settlement cases in the WTO.[48]

The contrasting viewpoint is supported by Hilf, who argues that 'the principle of proportionality is one of the more basic principles underlying the multilateral trading system'.[49] As will be seen from the

[48] Desmedt, 'Proportionality in WTO Law', 479–80.

[49] Hilf, 'Power, Rules and Principles', 120. See also Meinhard Hilf and Goetz J. Goettsche, 'The Relation of Economic and Non-Economic Principles in International Law' in Stefan Griller (ed.), *International Economic Governance and Non-Economic Concerns: New Challenges for the International Legal Order* (2003) 5, 12–14.

following discussion, in my view, proportionality is reflected in various aspects of the WTO agreements and is not simply something that is 'emerging' from the decisions of WTO Tribunals. It is true that proportionality has different meanings in the WTO according to the context. However, this does not mean that no overarching principle can be discerned, nor that the notion of proportionality outside the WTO is irrelevant to WTO disputes.

Using either the normative or descriptive theory for identifying principles, proportionality can be seen to have been incorporated in various provisions of the WTO agreements. In *US – Cotton Yarn*, the Appellate Body recognised for the first time a 'principle of proportionality', although this was in the context of remedies.[50] While the term proportionality features very rarely in the provisions of the WTO agreements, there are numerous references to measures that must be 'necessary' or 'least trade restrictive', as summarised in Table B.[51] The use of these terms is closely related to the general principle of proportionality, as outlined above. In this section I will consider the use of these terms in relation to exceptions to the general obligations of Members under Article XX of GATT 1994. I then consider how these terms are used in relation to positive obligations under the SPS and TBT Agreements.

A. Exceptions to general obligations – GATT 1994 Article XX

Article XX of GATT 1994 allows Members to derogate from their general obligations in relation to the liberalisation of trade in goods in order to enact and enforce measures that protect certain non-trade interests, such as public health, morals, and the conservation of exhaustible natural resources. Article XX opens with a general clause mandating that these exceptions cannot be used 'as a means of arbitrary or unjustifiable discrimination between countries where the same conditions prevail, or a disguised restriction on international trade'. This clause is known as the 'chapeau'. The remainder of Article XX comprises a series of paragraphs specifying the non-trade interests that Members are allowed to pursue under the Article. For example, Article XX(a) allows the protection of 'public morals'. The Appellate Body held

[50] See below, section 6.5.2(B).

[51] Hilf and Goettsche, 'Relation of Economic and Non-Economic Principles', 19; Desmedt, 'Proportionality in WTO Law', 442–3; Andenas and Zleptnig, 'Proportionality and Balancing in the WTO', 71, 77–8.

in *US – Gasoline* that the correct approach to interpreting Article XX is to consider, first, whether or not the measure falls within one of the legitimate non-trade interests outlined in paragraphs (a)–(j) and, then, whether the measure was applied in the facts of the dispute in a manner consistent with the chapeau.[52]

Each of paragraphs (a)–(j) contains a requirement that the measure at issue be connected to the non-trade interest. Most of these requirements require the measure to be 'necessary' for the protection of the non-trade interest (for example, Article XX(a), (b), (d) and (i)) or be 'related to' the non-trade interest (for example, Article XX(c), (g) and (e)). These paragraphs reflect a proportionality analysis, because they require an evaluation of the relationship between two competing interests – namely, the objective of trade liberalisation and the protection of non-trade interests. The language used in these paragraphs closely reflects elements of the general principle of proportionality, as discussed above. First, the suitability requirement of proportionality in the law of the European Communities, while not identical to the phrase 'related to' in Article XX(c), (g) and (e), involves a similar evaluation of the connection between a measure and its stated objective. The second element of proportionality in the law of the European Communities, the necessity test, is clearly analogous to the requirement that a measure be 'necessary'. Although Article XX of GATT 1994 does not refer directly to the principle of proportionality, it contains elements of this principle through the use of language such as 'necessary' and 'related to'. As will be discussed in further detail below, the use of the principle of proportionality in interpreting these provisions is closely linked to this language.

The chapeau of Article XX can also be seen as embodying elements of a proportionality analysis, although the language used is less clearly linked to the general principle of proportionality. In *US – Shrimp*, the Appellate Body held that 'the task of interpreting and applying the chapeau is ... one of locating and marking out a line of equilibrium between the right of a Member to invoke an exception under Article XX ... and the rights of the other Members under varying substantive provisions' of GATT 1994.[53] However, this balancing exercise centres on the language of the chapeau, which requires that the

[52] Appellate Body Report, *US – Gasoline*, section IV; Appellate Body Report, *US – Shrimp*, [115]–[116].

[53] Appellate Body Report, *US – Shrimp*, [159].

application of a measure not be used as 'a means of arbitrary or unjustifiable discrimination' or a 'disguised restriction on international trade'.[54] Andenas and Zleptnig argue that this means Members must employ the principle of proportionality in their domestic processes in order to ensure that their measures are not applied in an arbitrary or unjustifiable manner.[55] This is very closely analogous to the obligation of Members to observe due process (discussed above in Chapter 5) and the abuse of rights doctrine of the principle of good faith (discussed above in Chapter 4), and it is better viewed in that context than as a proportionality requirement.

B. Positive obligations on Members – the SPS and TBT Agreements

Both of these agreements establish standards that WTO Members must meet in their domestic regulations, including requirements that a measure be 'necessary' or 'least trade restrictive'.[56] Unlike Article XX of GATT 1994, the provisions of the SPS and TBT Agreements do not represent defences for prima facie violations of a Member's obligations; rather, they are a source of independent positive obligations that apply to all Members' domestic regulations.

Article 1.1 of the SPS Agreement states that it applies to all sanitary and phytosanitary measures that may directly or indirectly affect trade. These measures are closely linked to issues of health and safety, such as quarantine and customs laws. Accordingly, the Appellate Body held in *Australia – Salmon* that all Members have the 'prerogative' under the SPS Agreement to determine what is the appropriate level of protection for them.[57] However, the means or instrument through which a Member seeks to reach that level of protection will be scrutinised to see if it complies with the SPS Agreement.

Article 2.2 of the SPS Agreement sets out key requirements for domestic regulations. It requires that there be 'sufficient scientific evidence' to justify the measure. The Appellate Body in *Japan – Apples* interpreted this as requiring a 'rational and objective relationship' between the evidence and the measure, and in that case the measure was found to be in violation of the SPS Agreement because it was 'clearly

[54] GATT 1994, art. XX.
[55] Andenas and Zleptnig, 'Proportionality and Balancing in the WTO', 81–2.
[56] See, e.g., SPS Agreement, art. 2.2; TBT Agreement, art. 2.2.
[57] Appellate Body Report, *Australia – Salmon*, [199].

disproportionate to the risk identified on the basis of the scientific evidence available'.[58] The next requirement of Article 2.2 is that the measure be applied only to the 'extent necessary to protect human, animal or plant life or health'. This requirement is elaborated in Article 5.6, which states that sanitary and phytosanitary measures must not be 'more trade restrictive than required to achieve [the Member's] appropriate level of . . . protection, taking into account technical and economic feasibility'. This necessity test is then further elaborated in Footnote 3, which provides that a measure is not 'more trade restrictive than required unless there is another measure, reasonably available taking into account technical and economic feasibility, that achieves the appropriate level of . . . protection and is significantly less restrictive to trade'. In *Australia – Salmon*, the Appellate Body applied this necessity test, relying in particular on the requirements in Footnote 3, which it regarded as cumulative.[59] The SPS Agreement, while not specifically referring to the principle of proportionality, contains a necessity test that requires a consideration of any effective, less trade restrictive alternatives. This is very similar to the necessity test in the European Communities' principle of proportionality and the 'least restrictive means test' of United States administrative law. In this way, the SPS Agreement incorporates the principle of proportionality.

The TBT Agreement governs technical barriers to trade, which are described in the Preamble of the agreement as 'technical regulations and standards, including packaging, marking and labelling requirements'. Article 2.2 of the TBT Agreement states:

> Members shall ensure that technical regulations are not prepared, adopted or applied with a view to or with the effect of creating unnecessary obstacles to international trade. For this purpose, technical regulations shall not be more trade-restrictive than necessary to fulfil a legitimate objective, taking account of the risks non-fulfilment would create. Such legitimate objectives are, inter alia: national security requirements; the prevention of deceptive practices; protection of human health or safety, animal or plant life or health, or the environment. In assessing such risks, relevant elements of consideration are, inter alia: available scientific and technical information, related processing technology or intended end-uses of products.

The text of this provision employs the terms 'necessary' and not 'more trade restrictive', which reflects the way in which elements of the

[58] Appellate Body Report, *Japan – Apples*, [147].
[59] Appellate Body Report, *Australia – Salmon*, [194].

general principle of proportionality have been incorporated into the SPS Agreement and Article XX of GATT 1994. However, the TBT Agreement incorporates an even broader proportionality requirement than these other WTO agreements, due to the use of the term 'legitimate objective'. The Appellate Body has held that Article 2.2 provides a non-exhaustive list of legitimate objectives, and thus other objectives could also be considered 'legitimate'.[60] The TBT Agreement requires WTO Tribunals to assess the legitimacy of the objective that a Member pursues when they adopt a technical barrier, not just whether or not the measure is proportionate (in the sense of being necessary and/or least trade restrictive) to the objective. Even under Article XX of GATT 1994, which limits the categories of objectives for which there can be valid exceptions to Members' general obligations, once a Member can establish that their objective is within one of these categories (such as intending to protect public morals or prevent the exhaustion of natural resources), WTO Tribunals have no ability to question the legitimacy of that objective.

Like GATT 1994, the SPS Agreement and the TBT Agreement do not use the word proportionality. However, these three agreements have all incorporated different elements of proportionality into WTO law through their use of text such as 'necessary', 'least trade restrictive' and 'legitimate objectives', which reflect the elements of the general principle of proportionality. It is important to note that the idea of proportionality *stricto sensu*, which involves a genuine cost-benefit analysis of the measure at issue, is not reflected in GATT 1994 or in the SPS Agreement, although it may be embodied to a limited extent in the 'legitimate objective' criteria of the TBT Agreement. In the next section I will consider the use of proportionality in WTO disputes as a principle for interpreting these tests.

6.3 Using proportionality in WTO disputes to balance competing interests

The potential significance of this principle for WTO law is great, given that 'one of the most important challenges for WTO law is the balancing of competing rights, principles, values and interests'.[61] Andenas and Zleptnig believe that opposition to the use of proportionality as a

[60] Appellate Body Report, *EC – Sardines*, [286].

[61] Andenas and Zleptnig, 'Proportionality and Balancing in the WTO', 88.

principle in the WTO is due to a belief that it 'is institutionally not ready for such a fundamental balancing of values and interests', particularly as the clash is often between economic and non-economic interests (for example in relation to the exceptions enshrined in Article XX of GATT 1994).[62] In contrast, Hilf argues that 'the principle of proportionality should rule any process of interpretation and application of WTO law with a view to obtaining a due relation between the different interests at stake'.[63] As outlined in the previous section, the principle of proportionality is incorporated in WTO law through provisions imposing tests that are elements of proportionality as a general principle of law. The correct way to use proportionality as a principle for balancing competing interests in WTO disputes is not to import it as a substantive requirement of WTO law, but rather to apply it in interpreting particular language, such as 'necessary' or 'least trade restrictive', in the provisions of the WTO agreements. In the next section, I will outline how this principle may be used in relation to Article XX of GATT 1994, the SPS Agreement and the TBT Agreement.

6.3.1 GATT 1994 Article XX

The most important thing to keep in mind when applying the principle of proportionality to Article XX of GATT 1994 is that 'it is undisputed that WTO Members have the right to determine the level of protection' of a protected non-trade interest 'that they consider appropriate in a given situation'.[64] Similarly, in *US – Gasoline*, the Appellate Body said that WTO Members were free to set their own 'policies on the environment (including its relationship with trade), their environmental objectives and the environmental legislation they enact and implement'.[65] Desmedt argues that 'in no case will the proportionality requirements contained in Article XX of the GATT allow for a "balancing test" of advantages resulting from overall trade objectives underlying the WTO Agreements with the advantages resulting from national policy objectives as mentioned in the individual clauses of Article XX'.[66] Andenas and Zleptnig argue that it is indeed too simplistic to reduce 'this balancing solely to general trade versus non-trade concerns', but that at various stages of assessing the compliance of a

62 Andenas and Zleptnig, 'Proportionality: WTO Law: In Comparative Perspective', 371, 372.

63 Hilf, 'Power, Rules and Principles', 130.

64 Appellate Body Report, *EC – Asbestos*, [168].

65 Appellate Body Report, *US – Gasoline*, 29–30.

66 Desmedt, 'Proportionality in WTO Law', 476.

measure with Article XX its necessity, reasonableness, or proportionality must be determined.

A. Measures that are 'necessary'

The GATT Panel in *Thai – Cigarettes* held that 'necessity' required that there were 'no alternative measures consistent with the [GATT 1947] or less inconsistent with it which Thailand could reasonably be expected to employ to achieve its health policy objectives'.[67] This is clearly reminiscent of the 'necessity' and 'least trade restrictive' tests that are found in the general principle of proportionality. The consideration of whether or not a measure is necessary under European Communities law rests on two issues. First, are there alternative less restrictive measures available and, second, are those less restrictive means effective in achieving the objective of the measure at issue. In this respect, the general principle of proportionality could provide a useful interpretative tool to give structure to the analysis of whether a measure is necessary under Article XX of GATT 1994. The Appellate Body recently applied a very similar test in *Brazil – Retreaded Tyres*. The proposed alternatives in that dispute were remedial measures, while the actual measure at issue in the dispute was a preventative measure (an import ban). The remedial measures, which included landfilling and stockpiling, were clearly less trade restrictive than the import ban. However, the Appellate Body found that the remedial measures posed more significant risks to human health than the preventative measure and could not be considered an effective less trade restrictive alternative; thus, the import ban could be considered necessary.[68]

As I outlined above in relation to the law of the European Communities, the necessity test is the second element of the general principle of proportionality, and the elements of this principle are cumulative.[69] Thus, in order for a measure to be necessary, it must be suitable to achieve its objective. The Appellate Body considered this issue in *Brazil – Retreaded Tyres*, holding that an import ban must have a genuine 'relationship of ends and means' with the objective pursued, in the sense that it must make a 'material contribution' to the realisation of the ends.[70] In recognition of the difficulty of applying this standard, the

[67] Panel Report, *Thai – Cigarettes*, [75].
[68] Appellate Body Report, *Brazil – Retreaded Tyres*, [175].
[69] See above, section 6.2.1(B).
[70] Appellate Body Report, *Brazil – Retreaded Tyres*, [150].

Appellate Body held that Panels could make this factual determination through either quantitative or qualitative means.[71] Thus, as well as considering whether or not a measure is the least restrictive means, for a measure to be necessary under Article XX of GATT 1994, it must also be suitable, in the sense of making a material contribution towards its objective.

Since the *Thai – Cigarettes* GATT Panel decision, WTO Tribunals have examined the issue of necessity on several occasions. In *Korea – Beef*, the Appellate Body identified two factors to consider in adopting a 'weighing and balancing' approach to determine if a measure is 'necessary'. First, 'the extent to which the measure contributes to the realisation of the end pursued' and, second, 'the extent to which the compliance measure produces restrictive effects on international commerce'.[72] As a consequence of this test, according to Andenas and Zleptnig, 'measures with a lesser impact on international commerce "might more easily be considered 'necessary' than a measure with intensely restrictive effects"'.[73] In *EC – Asbestos*, the Appellate Body held that the factors to be taken into account in this balancing process included the extent to which an alternative measure would achieve the pursued end, and the importance of the interest and values the Member is pursuing.[74] The WTO Secretariat has interpreted these decisions as meaning that the necessity test has shifted from a 'least-trade restrictive' approach to a 'less-trade restrictive one, supplemented with a proportionality test',[75] in which Panels and the Appellate Body will be able to assess the 'relative importance of domestic interests or values pursued' and evaluate 'the legitimacy and necessity of domestic measures'.[76] On the other hand, Neumann and Türk believe that the shift to a proportionality based 'less-trade restrictive' approach has created a more 'relaxed' necessity test that provides a greater margin of appreciation to the Members.[77]

[71] Appellate Body Report, *Brazil – Retreaded Tyres*, [145]–[147].
[72] Appellate Body Report, *Korea – Beef*, [163]; reaffirmed in Appellate Body Report, *Brazil – Retreaded Tyres*, [139]–[143].
[73] Andenas and Zleptnig, 'Proportionality and Balancing in the WTO', 79.
[74] Appellate Body Report, *EC – Asbestos*, [172].
[75] 'Note by the Secretariat, "GATT/WTO Dispute Settlement Practice relating to GATT Article XX, Paragraphs (b), (d) and (g)"', WTO Doc WT/CTE/W/203, 8 March 2002, [42].
[76] Andenas and Zleptnig, 'Proportionality and Balancing in the WTO', 79.
[77] Neumann and Türk, 'Necessity Revisited', 211.

The Appellate Body in *EC – Asbestos* was careful to state that its approach does not call into question the objective pursued by the Member, and that this 'weighing and balancing' is confined to determining necessity. In *Brazil – Retreaded Tyres*, the Appellate Body evaluated the Panel's 'weighing and balancing' and found that it was properly a 'holistic operation' of 'putting all the variables of the equation together and evaluating them in relation to each other'.[78] However, by considering the importance of the interest that a Member is pursuing when determining necessity, WTO Tribunals are blurring the lines between necessity on the one hand and proportionality *stricto sensu* on the other.[79] Following *EC – Asbestos* and *Korea – Beef*, the test for 'least restrictive means' has effectively become a 'cost-benefit' analysis,[80] which does not accord with the necessity test that is part of proportionality as a general principle of law. As Article XX of GATT 1994 includes no reference to 'proportionality' as such, the use of this general principle when interpreting this provision should be limited to its textual basis, which, in this case, is the test of necessity. Thus, WTO Tribunals have erred in considering the significance of a Members' objectives when determining if a measure is necessary. This compromises the clear principle that it is the prerogative of Members to determine what interests they wish to protect (within the categories specified in the paragraphs of GATT 1994 Article XX) and to what extent. As Ortino argues, the correct approach to applying proportionality to necessity tests in WTO law is to consider whether less restrictive means are available to achieve the Member's objective, and not to evaluate the appropriateness of the Member's chosen level of protection.[81]

B. Measures that are 'related to'

The requirement that a measure be 'related to' a particular objective is more flexible than the requirement that a measure be 'necessary' to a particular objective.[82] It implies only a loose connection between the measure at issue under Article XX and the end the Member is pursuing.[83] In *US – Gasoline*, the Appellate Body held the term 'relating to' to require at least a 'substantial relationship' between the means and the

[78] Appellate Body Report, *Brazil – Retreaded Tyres*, [182].
[79] In much the same way that this distinction has been blurred in the law of the European Communities, see above, section 6.2.1(B).
[80] See Sykes, 'Least Restrictive Means'. [81] Ortino, *Basic Legal Instruments*, 471.
[82] Appellate Body Report, *Korea – Beef*, n. 104.
[83] See, e.g., Appellate Body Report, *US – Gasoline*, 19; Appellate Body Report, *US – Shrimp*, [141].

ends, and this in turn meant not being 'merely ancillary or inadvertently aimed' at the ends.[84] In *US – Shrimp*, the Appellate Body said that 'related to' requires a 'close and genuine relationship of end and means'.[85] In that report it found that the measure was related to the protection of natural resources (Article XX(g)) because it was 'not disproportionately wide in its scope and reach in relation to the policy objective of protection and conservation of sea turtle species'.[86] Thus, measures that only need to be 'related to' their legitimate aim under GATT Article XX(c), (e) and (g) should be easier to justify than measures that must be 'necessary'. This means that the principle of proportionality has less relevance to these paragraphs of Article XX, as only the suitability test, and not the necessity test, is relevant to their interpretation. Moreover, the suitability test, particularly the standard of 'material contribution' outlined by the Appellate Body in *Brazil – Retreaded Tyres*, may impose too high a standard for assessing if a measure is 'related to' an objective. Thus, the principle of proportionality should be used carefully in relation to these paragraphs of Article XX. It should be limited to the relationship of the measure to its intended purpose, rather than any consideration of less restrictive alternatives or overall cost-benefit analysis.

6.3.2 The SPS and TBT Agreements

As noted above, the SPS Agreement has incorporated the principle of proportionality in Article 2.2 through the requirement that measures be not 'more trade restrictive than required to achieve [the Member's] appropriate level of . . . protection, taking into account technical and economic feasibility'. The elaboration of this requirement in Footnote 3 closely mirrors the necessity test of United States administrative law and European Communities law, which requires that the least restrictive/drastic means be used. Footnote 3 provides that a measure is not 'more trade restrictive than required unless there is another measure, reasonably available taking into account technical and economic feasibility, that achieves the appropriate level of . . . protection and is significantly less restrictive to trade'.

WTO Tribunals have recognised these provisions as incorporating a necessity test. Implicit in this test is the requirement that the measures be suitable for the protection of human, animal or plant life, or health.

[84] Appellate Body Report, *US – Gasoline*, 19.
[85] Appellate Body Report, *US – Shrimp*, [136]. [86] Ibid. [141].

This suitability requirement reflects not only the standard used for proportionality in European Communities law, but also the idea that a rational relationship or connection must exist between the measure and the objective (which is similar to the requirement under United Kingdom human rights law). This 'rational connection' is based upon the requirements in Article 2.2 that there is 'sufficient scientific evidence' for the SPS measure and that it is 'based on risk assessment'.[87] The Appellate Body acknowledged the relevance of the principle of proportionality in interpreting these requirements in *Japan – Apples*, where a measure was found to be invalid because it was 'clearly disproportionate' to the risk identified on the evidence available.[88] The measure was disproportionate in that case because the risk was found to be 'negligible'.[89]

In *Australia – Salmon*, the Appellate Body applied this necessity test, and in doing so particularly relied on Footnote 3, which it held contained three cumulative requirements.[90] The three limbs of this test are that an alternative must be reasonably available taking into account technological and economic feasibility; that the alternative must achieve the Member's appropriate level of protection; and that the alternative is 'significantly less restrictive to trade'.[91] This necessity test is comparable to that used under Article XX of GATT 1994 and to the test as it exists as part of a general principle of proportionality, but the emphasis on 'significantly' represents a slight shift in the standard imposed under this test. This reinforces the importance of tailoring the use of the principle of proportionality as an interpretative tool to the text of the provisions that incorporate this principle, rather than trying to apply a universal formula. This is again reflected in the fact that the suitability requirements of Article 2.2 of the SPS Agreement have been interpreted to include procedural requirements (to do with the gathering and evaluation of evidence), and that measures may violate these suitability requirements while meeting the necessity requirement.[92] This is very different to the general operation of the principle of proportionality, as outlined above, where the elements of the test are cumulative.[93]

[87] Ortino, *Basic Legal Instruments*, 447.
[88] Appellate Body Report, *Japan – Apples*, [147]. [89] Ibid.
[90] Appellate Body Report, *Australia – Salmon*, [194]. [91] Ibid.
[92] See, e.g., Appellate Body Report, *Japan – Apples* discussed in Ortino, *Basic Legal Instruments*, 462.
[93] The difference in approach under the SPS Agreement is due to the procedural requirements that are linked to the suitability requirement. See Ortino, *Basic Legal Instruments*, 462.

Compared to Article XX of GATT 1994 and the SPS Agreement, the TBT Agreement gives WTO Tribunals the greatest scope to use the general principle of proportionality, as Article 2.2 requires them to scrutinise whether a Member's objective is 'legitimate', as well as whether its chosen measure is suitable and necessary to achieve that objective.[94] No WTO dispute has yet had to apply Article 2.2 of the TBT Agreement,[95] so the approach that WTO Tribunals will take to this provision is still unclear. However, one important thing to note is that the level of protection is still at the discretion of the Member; only the objective itself can be scrutinised.[96] One potential approach to the issue of 'legitimate objective' is to compare this to the interpretation of the phrase 'legitimate interest' in Article 30 of the TRIPS Agreement.[97] The Panel in *Canada – Pharmaceutical Patents* held that a legitimate interest was one that had a basis in social norms or public policies.[98] When combined with its obligation to take into account 'the risks non-fulfilment would create', Article 2.2 of the TBT Agreement may be considered to incorporate a proportionality *stricto sensu* test, which would be that a measure that was disproportionate could be found to be in violation of the TBT Agreement, even though it was the least restrictive means available.[99] In order for WTO Tribunals to apply such an analysis, they would need to provide a clear link to the text of Article 2.2 of the TBT Agreement.

6.4 Proportionality as a principle in assessing remedies

6.4.1 *A general principle of law: crime and punishment*

I begin my assessment of proportionality in relation to remedies by examining the relationship between crime and punishment as a general principle of law. A Trial Chamber of the International Criminal Tribunal for the former Yugoslavia has recognised the requirement that a punishment be proportionate to the crime for which it is imposed as a 'general principle of criminal law'.[100] This principle forms part of the

[94] See Appellate Body Report, *EC – Sardines*, [286].
[95] Although the Appellate Body has clearly ruled that it can and will assess the legitimacy of objectives: see ibid. [286].
[96] Andenas and Zleptnig, 'Proportionality and Balancing in the WTO', 86–7.
[97] Ibid. See Neumann and Türk, 'Necessity Revisited', 219.
[98] Panel Report, *Canada – Pharmaceutical Patents*, [7.69].
[99] Andenas and Zleptnig, 'Proportionality and Balancing in the WTO', 87.
[100] *Prosecutor* v. *Blaskic* (IT-95-14) (Trial Chamber, ICTY, 3 March 2000), [796].

law of several common law countries. Below, I use the United States and Australia as examples.

In the United States, proportionality is incorporated in the Eighth Amendment, which has been held to prohibit punishments that are disproportionate to the offence. This amendment states that '[e]xcessive bail shall not be required, nor excessive fines imposed, nor cruel and unusual punishments inflicted'. The most important of these prohibitions has been the prohibition of cruel and unusual punishment.[101] Many rights (such as freedom of speech or freedom of interstate trade) are stated in absolute terms, even though they may need to be balanced against other rights or objectives. However, the right not to suffer excessive punishment itself incorporates the notion of proportionality.

The text of the Eighth Amendment clearly requires proportionality between the punishment and the offence when the punishment involves bail or fines. On its terms, proportionality is not strictly required for other forms of punishment. However, the Supreme Court has read the reference to 'cruel and unusual punishment' to encompass the principle of proportionality. In 1983, the Court stated in a majority opinion in *Solem* v. *Helm*:

> The Eighth Amendment declares: 'Excessive bail shall not be required, nor excessive fines imposed, nor cruel and unusual punishments inflicted.' The final clause prohibits not only barbaric punishments, but also sentences that are disproportionate to the crime committed ... The principle that a punishment should be proportionate to the crime is deeply rooted and frequently repeated in common-law jurisprudence ... When the Framers of the Eighth Amendment adopted the language of the English Bill of Rights, they also adopted the English principle of proportionality ... The constitutional principle of proportionality has been recognized explicitly in this Court for almost a century.[102]

The inclusion of a principle of proportionality within the words 'cruel and unusual punishment' is supported by the suggestion that 'it would be anomalous indeed' if proportionality were required in connection with bail and fines but not other forms of punishment.[103] Nevertheless, for some Justices at least, the application of the principle depends on the type of punishment imposed. As regards capital punishment (the

[101] Kermit Hall (ed.), *Oxford Companion to the Supreme Court of the United States*, 247.

[102] *Solem* v. *Helm*, 454 US 277, 284–6 (1983) (majority: Powell J, joined by Brennan, Marshall, Blackmun, and Stevens JJ) (footnote omitted).

[103] *Ewing* v. *California*, 538 US 11, 33 (2003) (Stevens J, joined by Souter, Ginsburg, and Breyer JJ) (quoting *Solem* v. *Helm*, 454 US 277, 289 (1983)).

death penalty), it seems fairly well-established that the principle of proportionality applies.[104] When it comes to non-capital punishment, the jurisprudence is less clear, with some judges maintaining that no test of proportionality is necessary[105] and others maintaining that strict proportionality is required.[106] However, the prevailing majority view is that, '[t]hrough this thicket of Eighth Amendment jurisprudence, one governing legal principle emerges as "clearly established" . . . A gross disproportionality principle is applicable to sentences for terms of years'.[107] This means that such a sentence must not be grossly disproportionate to the offence committed. Although the parameters for determining whether a sentence violates this standard are not clearly defined, a violation will occur only in rare or extraordinary circumstances.[108] In *Ewing* v. *California*, a plurality of the Court endorsed this 'gross disproportionality' principle, but using instead (rather confusingly) the label 'narrow proportionality principle'.[109] The principle can be described as narrow in the sense that it will not be violated by the imposition of a punishment that is disproportionate to the offence as long it is not grossly disproportionate.

The reason that several Justices of the Supreme Court take the view that strict proportionality between an offence and punishment in the form of a sentence of some years is not required probably relates in part to their perception of the proper role of the judiciary: a reviewing

[104] See, e.g., *Coker* v. *Georgia*, 433 US 584, 592 (1977) (plurality: White J, joined by Stewart, Blackmun, and Stevens JJ); *Enmund* v. *Florida*, 458 US 782, 797–8 (1982) (majority: White J, joined by Brennan, Marshall, Blackmun, and Stevens JJ).

[105] See, e.g., *Harmelin* v. *Michigan*, 501 US 957, 994 (1991) (Scalia J, concurring in the judgment, joined by Rehnquist CJ); *Ewing* v. *California*, 538 US 11, 32 (2003) (Thomas J, concurring in the judgment).

[106] *Ewing* v. *California*, 538 US 11, 35 (2003) (Stevens J, joined by Souter, Ginsburg, and Breyer JJ) (stating that 'a broad and basic proportionality principle' applies, rather than a narrow proportionality principle as held by a plurality of the Court in that case).

[107] *Lockyer* v. *Andrade*, 538 US 63, 72 (2003) (majority: O'Connor J, joined by Rehnquist CJ, and Scalia, Kennedy, and Thomas JJ). See also *Harmelin* v. *Michigan*, 501 US 957, 1001 (1991) (Kennedy J, joined by O'Connor and Souter JJ); *Ewing* v. *California*, 538 US 11, 23–4 (2003) (plurality: O'Connor J, joined by Rehnquist CJ and Kennedy J); Joshua Pater, 'Struck out Looking: Continued Confusion in Eighth Amendment Proportionality Review after *Ewing* v. *California*, 123 S. Ct. 1179 (2003)' (2003–04) 27 *Harvard Journal of Law & Public Policy* 399.

[108] *Lockyer* v. *Andrade*, 538 US 63, 73 (2003) (majority: O'Connor J, joined by Rehnquist CJ, and Scalia, Kennedy, and Thomas JJ).

[109] *Ewing* v. *California*, 538 US 11, 20 (2003) (plurality: O'Connor J, joined by Rehnquist CJ and Kennedy J).

court must accord legislatures and sentencing courts 'substantial deference . . . in determining the types and limits of punishments for crimes, as well as . . . in sentencing convicted criminals'.[110] The gross disproportionality test therefore relies, to the extent possible, on 'objective factors'.[111] Thus, the Court considers not only the 'gravity of the offense and the harshness of the penalty' (which might depend on the Court's own policy assessments) but also 'the sentences imposed on other criminals in the same jurisdiction' and 'the sentences imposed for commission of the same crime in other jurisdictions' (which can be determined as a matter of fact).[112]

In Australia, as in the United States, the High Court has emphasised the need to take account of 'objective circumstances' in determining whether a particular sentence is disproportionate to the offence. Thus, the High Court has described the principle of proportionality as follows:

> [A] basic principle of sentencing law is that a sentence of imprisonment imposed by a court should never exceed that which can be justified as appropriate or proportionate to the gravity of the crime considered in the light of its objective circumstances.[113]

The High Court has used the principle of proportionality to determine the outer limits of sentencing discretion, only intervening where the exercise of that discretion 'reflects an error of principle or results in some manifest injustice'.[114] The notion of 'manifest injustice' may be comparable to the high threshold of 'gross disproportionality' applied by the Supreme Court of the United States.

The High Court has not yet provided clear guidance on how to apply this principle.[115] However, the Court's reasoning does point to certain considerations that may be relevant in sentence-setting, which may

110 *Solem* v. *Helm*, 454 US 277, 290 (1983) (majority: Powell J, joined by Brennan, Marshall, Blackmun, and Stevens JJ). See also *Harmelin* v. *Michigan*, 501 US 957, 1001 (1991) (Kennedy J, joined by O'Connor and Souter JJ) (referring to the 'primacy of the legislature').

111 *Harmelin* v. *Michigan*, 501 US 957, 1001 (1991) (Kennedy J, joined by O'Connor and Souter JJ).

112 *Solem* v. *Helm*, 454 US 277, 292 (1983) (majority: Powell J, joined by Brennan, Marshall, Blackmun, and Stevens JJ).

113 *Hoare* v. *The Queen* (1989) 167 CLR 348, [7] (see also [20]).

114 *Bugmy* v. *The Queen* (1990) 169 CLR 525, [24] (Mason CJ and McHugh J, dissenting); see also [7] (majority: Dawson, Toohey, and Gaudron JJ).

115 See generally Richard Fox, 'The Meaning of Proportionality in Sentencing' (1994) 19 *Melbourne University Law Review* 489.

shed light on the reasons underlying the proportionality principle. Although these considerations may differ in nature or weight in setting a minimum as opposed to a maximum sentence,[116] they may include the sentences previously imposed for the offence in question,[117] the possibility of rehabilitation,[118] 'the propensity of the offender to commit violent crimes, the likelihood of his re-offending and the need to protect the community'.[119] These considerations are linked to the objectives of punishment, which Scalia J of the United States Supreme Court of the United States addressed briefly in *Ewing* v. *California*. In his Honour's view, proportionality derives from the notion of punishment as retribution (meaning 'punishment imposed as repayment or revenge for the offense committed'),[120] but it has no place to the extent that the objective of a punishment is deterrence, incapacitation, or rehabilitation.[121]

The various theories of retribution 'justify punishment on the ground that persons who culpably commit or attempt acts and omissions that are morally wrong deserve punishment'.[122] Under these theories, the proportionality principle plays a dominant role.[123] Assuming that retribution provides one reason for punishment, the question arises whether the punishment that a culprit deserves should be determined absolutely (the non-comparative or cardinal approach) or according to the punishment received by other people committing the same or other offences (the comparative or ordinal approach).[124] The comparative approach attends to the concern expressed by several Justices of the United States Supreme Court and the High Court of Australia that higher courts should assess punishments objectively and without intervening unduly in the decision-making of the legislature or lower

[116] *Bugmy* v. *The Queen* (1990) 169 CLR 525, [13] (majority: Dawson, Toohey, and Gaudron JJ); [20] (Mason CJ and McHugh J, dissenting). See also *The Queen* v. *Shrestha* (1991) 173 CLR 48; 100 ALR 757, 768 (Brennan and McHugh JJ, dissenting).

[117] *Bugmy* v. *The Queen* (1990) 169 CLR 525, [12] (majority: Dawson, Toohey, and Gaudron JJ).

[118] *The Queen* v. *Shrestha* (1991) 173 CLR 48; 100 ALR 757, 772 (Deane, Dawson, and Toohey JJ).

[119] *Bugmy* v. *The Queen* (1990) 169 CLR 525, [23] (Mason CJ and McHugh J, dissenting); see also [9] (majority: Dawson, Toohey, and Gaudron JJ).

[120] Bryan Garner (ed.), *Black's Law Dictionary* (7th edn, 1999) 1318.

[121] *Ewing* v. *California*, 538 US 11, 31–2 (2003) (Scalia J, concurring in the judgment).

[122] Larry Alexander, 'The Philosophy of Criminal Law' in Jules Coleman and Scott Shapiro (eds.), *The Oxford Handbook of Jurisprudence & Philosophy of Law* (2002) 815, 816.

[123] Andrew von Hirsch, 'Proportionality in the Philosophy of Punishment' (1992) 16 *Crime & Justice* 55, 56.

[124] Ibid. 76–7; Alexander, 'Philosophy of Criminal Law', 818.

courts. Yet a purely comparative approach would leave the courts no room to assess the gravity of the offence (in terms of the harm caused and the fault or culpability of the person committing the offence).[125] This may explain why sentencing in both jurisdictions appears to require more than a simple inspection of sentences previously imposed for the offence committed.

If retribution demands proportionality, what scope is there for utilitarian concerns such as the need to protect the community?[126] Put differently, is Scalia J correct that the principle of proportionality cannot apply to the extent that a punishment aims to prevent the offender from re-offending? The answer seems to lie in the type and stringency of the proportionality principle applied. According to Cohen, 'everyone is to be punished alike in proportion to the gravity of his offense or to the extent to which he has made others suffer'.[127] Thus, simplifying for the sake of clarity, the current Australian and United States positions could be explained as follows. Non-comparative proportionality, derived from notions of fairness and retribution, sets an absolute ceiling on the severity of the punishment for a given offence, based on the seriousness of the offence in terms of the culpability of the offender and the harm caused. Below this ceiling, sentences should be uniform in a comparative sense unless some justification exists (utilitarian or otherwise) for departing from the usual degree of punishment.

6.4.2 *A principle of customary international law: countermeasures for wrongful acts*

The previous section addressed the principle of proportionality as it relates to infringement of individuals' rights, namely infringement taking the form of punishment for a recognised offence by an individual. However, the proportionality principle also operates in international law to limit infringement of the rights of states and, in particular, infringement taking the form of countermeasures for an internationally wrongful act committed by a state.

Article 51 of the ILC Articles provides that countermeasures 'must be commensurate with the injury suffered, taking into account the

125 von Hirsch, 'Proportionality in the Philosophy of Punishment', 81.

126 See generally ibid.; Nigel Walker, 'Legislating the Transcendental: Von Hirsch's Proportionality' (1992) 51 *Cambridge Law Journal* 530.

127 Morris Cohen, *Reason and Law* (1961) 53.

gravity of the internationally wrongful act and the rights in question'. Arguably, this provision reflects the proportionality principle that applies with respect to countermeasures under customary international law.[128] In his commentaries on the ILC Articles, Crawford states that '[p]roportionality is a well-established requirement for taking countermeasures, being widely recognized in State practice, doctrine and jurisprudence'.[129] This observation is borne out by several pronouncements of the ICJ[130] and in international arbitrations.[131] Indeed, in terms very similar to Article 51 as finally drafted, the ICJ held in *Gabcíkovo-Nagymaros Project* that 'the effects of a countermeasure must be commensurate with the injury suffered, taking account of the rights in question' – this is 'the proportionality which is required by international law'.[132]

Just as the objectives of punishment are relevant in assessing the role of proportionality in domestic sentencing, the objective of imposing countermeasures is crucial to their validity and may reflect on whether they meet the requirement of proportionality in international law. Under Article 49(1) of the ILC Articles, '[a]n injured State may only take countermeasures against a State which is responsible for an internationally wrongful act in order to induce that State to comply with its obligations under Part Two', which includes obligations to cease the unlawful act[133] and to provide reparation for the injury.[134] According to Crawford, 'a clearly disproportionate measure may well be judged not to have been necessary to induce the responsible State to comply with

[128] See, e.g., N. D. White and A. Abass, 'Countermeasures and Sanctions' in Malcolm Evans (ed.), *International Law* (2003) 505, 507 (referring to 'the codification of countermeasures by the International Law Commission').

[129] James Crawford, *The International Law Commission's Articles on State Responsibility: Introduction, Text and Commentaries* (2002) 294.

[130] See, e.g., Military and Paramilitary Activities in and against Nicaragua *(Nicaragua* v. *United States of America)* [1986] ICJ Rep 14, [249] (referring to 'proportionate countermeasures').

[131] See, e.g., "Naulilaa" (Responsibility of Germany for Damage Caused in the Portuguese Colonies in the South of Africa) (1928) II Reports of International Arbitral Awards 1013; Air Services Agreement of 27 March 1946 *(United States* v. *France)* (1978) XVIII Reports of International Arbitral Awards 417 (cited in Crawford, *International Law Commission's Articles on State Responsibility*, 294).

[132] Gabcíkovo-Nagymaros Project (Hungary/Slovakia) [1997] ICJ Rep 7, [85].

[133] ILC Articles, art. 30.

[134] Reparation may take the form of restitution, compensation, or satisfaction, which themselves incorporate a requirement of proportionality: ILC Articles, arts. 31, 34–7.

its obligations but to have had a punitive aim and to fall outside the purpose of countermeasures enunciated in article 49'.[135]

Proportionality under Article 51 primarily involves an assessment of the relationship between the countermeasure and the injury suffered as a result of the initial wrongful act, while 'taking into account' the gravity of the wrongful act and the rights in question. The gravity of the act is thus separated from the injury it causes, even though one might normally expect the injury caused to be a component in assessing the gravity of the act. The consideration of the gravity of the act and the rights infringed, separately from the injury suffered, suggests that countermeasures may serve some fairness or retributive purposes, contrary to the purely utilitarian or consequentialist approach suggested by Crawford and the text of Article 49. Cannizzaro explains this 'contradiction'[136] as indicating 'that the ILC conceives proportionality as a factor mitigating the instrumental nature of countermeasures'.[137] Another explanation could be that the drafters considered that determining the level of countermeasures necessary to induce compliance would be more subjective or difficult than determining (i) the injury suffered and (ii) the gravity of the wrongful act and the rights in question. Accordingly, these two factors are used as a proxy in identifying countermeasures necessary to induce compliance.

The need for proportionality to take into account non-utilitarian purposes arises in the context of international law on countermeasures in much the same way as it does in the context of domestic laws regarding punishment. If the goal is solely utilitarian, the response to an internationally wrongful act (or an individual's offence) risks being far worse than the original breach, if that is what is required to prevent future breaches.[138] Thus, as in the domestic criminal law systems

[135] Crawford, *International Law Commission's Articles on State Responsibility*, 296. Here, Crawford seems to assume that a countermeasure that is disproportionate to the injury suffered, within the meaning of Article 51, will also be disproportionate to the need to induce compliance, within the meaning of Article 49. See also at 284 ('Countermeasures are not intended as a form of punishment for wrongful conduct but as an instrument for achieving compliance with the obligations of the responsible State under Part Two').

[136] White and Abass, 'Countermeasures and Sanctions', 513 ('[T]here appears to be a contradiction in the approach of the ILC. The issue ought not to be one of proportionality to the injury caused, because this would suggest that countermeasures are taken to punish the responsible State').

[137] Cannizzaro, 'Role of Proportionality', 894.

[138] See ibid. 892, 905; von Hirsch, 'Proportionality in the Philosophy of Punishment', 63–4.

examined above, fairness and retribution require proportionality, which sets an absolute ceiling on the severity of countermeasures according to the 'the injury suffered'[139] (that is, the harm caused), 'taking into account the gravity of the internationally wrongful act and the rights in question'[140] (that is, the culpability of the actor).

Article 51 addresses countermeasures taking the form of 'non-performance for the time being of international obligations of the State taking the measures towards the responsible State'.[141] It does not allow countermeasures involving the use of force,[142] which appear to be prohibited by Article 2 of the UN Charter (except perhaps in the context of self-defence)[143] and which are less relevant in the context of the WTO. Nevertheless, it is worth noting that, even in the context of war, the principle of proportionality applies to the imposition of countermeasures (often called belligerent reprisals).[144]

6.4.3 *A principle of WTO law*

A. Introduction

Now I turn to considering whether proportionality is a principle of WTO law in relation to remedies, based on the WTO agreements and the organisation's objectives. Later in this chapter I will consider how proportionality could be used by Panels and the Appellate Body when applying and interpreting the WTO agreements. In the next two sections I assess the role of proportionality in limiting the extent of retaliatory actions that WTO Members may take against each other. Such measures take two broad forms, which I discuss in turn: first, the suspension of concessions (pursuant to the DSU) in response to a failure by a Member to bring its WTO-inconsistent measures into conformity with the WTO agreements as recommended in a Panel or Appellate Body report adopted by the DSB;[145] second, unilateral use of trade remedies in response to certain kinds of unfair conduct or other

[139] ILC Articles, art. 51. [140] ILC Articles, art. 51. [141] ILC Articles, art. 49(2).

[142] ILC Articles, arts. 22, 50(1)(a).

[143] Andrew Mitchell, 'Does One Illegality Merit Another? The Law of Belligerent Reprisals in International Law' (2001) 170 *Military Law Review* 155, 158.

[144] Ibid. 160–1. On proportionality in the laws of war, see also William Fenrick, 'The Rule of Proportionality and Protocol in Conventional Warfare' (1982) 98 *Military Law Review* 91; Gardam, 'Proportionality as a Restraint', 161.

[145] See generally Thomas Jürgensen, 'Crime and Punishment: Retaliation under the World Trade Organization Dispute Settlement System' (2005) 39 *Journal of World Trade* 327.

situations, pursuant to the Anti-Dumping Agreement, the SCM Agreement, or the Agreement on Safeguards.

B. Multilateral remedies for WTO violations

At the outset, it is worth noting that Article 60(2)(b) of the VCLT provides that, where a party to a multilateral treaty commits a material breach of the treaty, another party that is specially affected by the breach may suspend the operation of the treaty in connection with that party.[146] This provision would not normally apply to breaches of the WTO agreements, because these agreements contain special provisions on the impact of a breach, which override the relevant provisions of the VCLT.[147] Similarly, the WTO Members have agreed not to impose countermeasures on each other, even when this might otherwise have been an option under customary international law.[148] Instead, disputes are to be settled pursuant to the DSU and Members are not to cease performing their WTO obligations towards each other except in accordance with the DSU.[149]

Despite the special and overriding nature of the WTO rules regarding Members' rights in the event of a breach by another Member, these rules are remarkably similar to those under customary international law, and in particular the principle of proportionality as reflected in the international law on countermeasures. Thus, Palmeter and Mavroidis comment that the relevant DSU provisions 'conform to the principle of proportionality recognized by the World Court'.[150] Waincymer makes a similar suggestion,[151] while Renouf states that, '[a]s in general international law, countermeasures under the DSU have to be proportionate to the damage caused by non-compliance'.[152]

146 See generally Grieg, 'Reciprocity', 342–60.

147 VCLT, art. 60(4): 'The foregoing paragraphs are without prejudice to any provision in the treaty applicable in the event of a breach.'

148 See also ILC Articles, art. 55: 'These articles do not apply where and to the extent that the conditions for the existence of an internationally wrongful act or the content or implementation of the international responsibility of a States are governed by special rules of international law.' See also Crawford, *International Law Commission's Articles on State Responsibility*, 291.

149 DSU, arts. 23.1, 23.2(c).

150 David Palmeter and Petros Mavroidis, 'The WTO Legal System: Sources of Law' (1998) 92 *American Journal of International Law* 398, 408.

151 Jeff Waincymer, *WTO Litigation: Procedural Aspects of Formal Dispute Settlement* (2002) 681.

152 Yves Renouf, 'A Brief Introduction to Countermeasures in the WTO Dispute Settlement System' in Rufus Yerxa and Bruce Wilson (eds.), *Key Issues in WTO Dispute Settlement: The First Ten Years* (2005) 75, 77.

I reach much the same conclusion in the following paragraphs. That is not to say that proportionality as a principle of customary international law is identical to the proportionality principle in the WTO, or that the structure and rules on multilateral remedies for WTO violations align precisely with countermeasures under international law. To begin with, multilateral remedies, as this name suggests, are authorised by the DSB, whereas countermeasures for internationally wrongful acts are taken unilaterally by individual states without multilateral authorisation. Another key difference is that multilateral remedies in the WTO typically operate only prospectively from the expiry of the reasonable period of time for implementation.[153] Nevertheless, several key features of the principle of proportionality in the WTO accord with the principle in customary international law. This suggests that customary international law may prove useful in guiding or evaluating dispute settlement decisions on proportionality in the WTO.

The aim of the WTO dispute settlement system is 'to secure a positive solution to a dispute'.[154] Ideally, this is to be achieved through a mutually agreed solution between the parties, or withdrawal of any measures of Members that are inconsistent with the WTO agreements (as determined by Panels or the Appellate Body in reports that are adopted by the DSB). However, as a 'last resort', if the Member fails to bring the inconsistent measure into conformity within a reasonable period of time, the complainant has the possibility of 'suspending the application of concessions or other obligations under the covered agreements on a discriminatory basis vis-à-vis the other Member, subject to authorization by the DSB'.[155] Essentially, the DSB is required to grant such authorisation 'within 30 days of the expiry of the reasonable period of time unless the DSB decides by consensus to reject the request'.[156] Members must follow the relevant dispute settlement procedures before suspending concessions in response to a failure to bring an inconsistent measure into conformity within the required period.[157]

[153] Ibid. 76. But see Petros Mavroidis, 'Remedies in the WTO Legal System: Between a Rock and a Hard Place' (2000) 11 *European Journal of International Law* 763, 789–90.

[154] DSU, art. 3.7.

[155] DSU, art. 3.7. See also art. 22.1. Suspension of concessions was also provided as a last resort under GATT 1947 (art. XXIII:2).

[156] DSU, art. 22.6.

[157] DSU, art. 22.3(c). See also Panel Report, *US – Certain EC Products*, [6.87] (issue not appealed: Appellate Body Report, *US – Certain EC Products*, [117]).

Proportionality in retaliatory actions under the WTO dispute settlement system has qualitative and quantitative requirements. The qualitative requirement relates to the form of the retaliatory action. Significantly, the ultimate sanction by a complainant against a respondent's WTO violation is to cease performing some of its WTO obligations towards that Member. This 'suspension of concessions' is analogous to the form of countermeasures envisaged by Article 49(2) of the ILC Articles ('non-performance for the time being of international obligations') and the response provided for in Article 60(2)(b) of the VCLT for a material breach of a treaty ('suspending the operation of the treaty in whole or in part'). In addition, Article 22.3 of the DSU provides that the suspension of concessions should preferably be in the same sector and, if this is not practicable or effective, the suspension should be with respect to other sectors but under the same agreement. Only if this is not practicable or effective, and only if the circumstances are serious enough, may concessions be suspended under another WTO agreement. This qualitative requirement of proportionality may spring from the same rationale as *lex talionis* (infliction on the wrongdoer the injury the wrongdoer has caused – simply put, an eye for an eye).[158]

As to the level of suspension of concessions that the DSB authorises (the quantitative requirement of proportionality), Article 22.4 of the DSU provides that this must be 'equivalent to the level of nullification or impairment'. The reference to 'nullification or impairment' derives from Article XXIII of GATT 1994, which refers to the settlement of disputes where a Member considers 'that any benefit accruing to it directly or indirectly under this Agreement is being nullified or impaired' due to, for example, another Member's inconsistent measure. Thus, the level of nullification or impairment is, broadly speaking, the amount of injury that the Member has suffered due to the inconsistent measure. In that sense, the aim is to ensure that the penalty (suspension of concessions) is not disproportionate to the injury suffered (nullification or impairment).[159] Thus, as in the international law of

[158] Sebastian, 'World Trade Organization Remedies', 350–1; Fox, 'Meaning of Proportionality', 490; Garner, *Black's Law Dictionary*, 924.

[159] Two unusual features of the WTO dispute settlement system are that the injury is measured only from the expiry of the reasonable period of time and not retrospectively from the time when the inconsistency began, and that the penalty imposed on the Member acting inconsistently may also harm the complaining Member. For further discussion of these and related problems with the compliance mechanism, see generally Gary Horlick, 'Problems with the Compliance Structure of

countermeasures, the focus of the proportionality inquiry is on the harm caused rather than the culpability of the actor or the need to induce compliance (which could weigh in favour of a lower or higher penalty).

If the Member concerned objects to the level of suspension proposed by the complainant, or claims that the principles and procedures set forth in Article 22.3 of the DSU have not been followed, the matter is referred to arbitration under Article 22.6 of the DSU. It is up to the arbitrators (generally comprising the original Panel) to determine whether the level of suspension proposed is equivalent to the level of nullification or impairment and/or to confirm whether the principles of Article 22.3 have been followed.

Under the SCM Agreement, special dispute settlement procedures apply and take precedence over the usual DSU rules.[160] For actionable subsidies that are not brought into compliance within six months of adoption, in the absence of agreement on compensation, the DSB grants authorisation to the complaining Member, by reverse consensus, to 'take countermeasures, commensurate with the degree and nature of the adverse effects determined to exist', which may be determined by arbitrators under Article 22.6 of the DSU.[161] For prohibited subsidies that are not brought into compliance within the timeframe specified by the Panel, the DSB grants authorisation to the complaining Member, by reverse consensus, to 'take appropriate countermeasures'.[162] Footnotes 9 and 10 to the SCM Agreement make clear that the reference to 'appropriate' countermeasures 'is not meant to allow countermeasures that are disproportionate in light of the fact that the subsidies dealt with under these provisions are prohibited'. This is one of the few explicit references to proportionality in the WTO agreements. Again, Article 22.6 arbitrators may determine whether countermeasures proposed fulfil this requirement.[163] Later in this chapter, I consider the significance for the principle of proportionality of the differences between these provisions under the SCM Agreement and the corresponding provisions of the DSU.

the WTO Dispute Resolution Process' in Daniel Kennedy and James Southwick (eds.), *The Political Economy of International Trade Law: Essays in Honor of Robert E. Hudec* (2002) 636; Steve Charnovitz, 'Should the Teeth Be Pulled? An Analysis of WTO Sanctions' in Daniel Kennedy and James Southwick (eds.), *The Political Economy of International Trade Law: Essays in Honor of Robert E. Hudec* (2002) 602, 619–27; Kym Anderson, 'Peculiarities of Retaliation in WTO Dispute Settlement' (2002) 1 *World Trade Review* 123.

160 DSU, art. 1.2 and Appendix 2. 161 SCM Agreement, arts. 7.9–7.10.

162 SCM Agreement, art. 4.10. 163 SCM Agreement, art. 4.11.

C. Unilateral remedies for certain other conduct

An unusual form of retaliatory action available in the WTO is the trade remedy or unilateral remedy. These remedies, which generally take the form of increased tariffs (or, sometimes, import quotas), come in three guises: anti-dumping measures, safeguards, and countervailing measures. Each is imposed for a different reason.

Anti-dumping and countervailing measures are closest to penalties in domestic law or countermeasures in international law, because Members may impose them in response to conduct that is accepted as 'unfair' (dumping or certain forms of subsidy). Thus, the Members recognise that 'dumping, by which products of one country are introduced into the commerce of another country at less than the normal value of the products, is to be condemned if it causes or threatens material injury to an established industry in the territory of a Member'.[164] They also agree that '[n]o Member should cause, through the use of any [specific subsidy], adverse effects to the interests of other Members', including 'injury to the domestic industry of another Member'.[165] In response to one Member's dumping or subsidisation causing injury, another Member may therefore (subject to certain stringent conditions) impose anti-dumping[166] or countervailing measures[167] respectively.

Under Article 9.3 of the Anti-Dumping Agreement, a Member may not impose an anti-dumping duty in excess of the margin of dumping.[168] Similarly, under Article 19.4 of the SCM Agreement, Members must not impose countervailing duties in excess of the amount of the subsidy.[169] The ceiling on the amount of penalty (in the form of duties) is therefore set by the undesirable act (dumping or the imposition of certain kinds of subsidies), even if the injury caused by that act is higher. A Member could, of course, choose to impose no anti-dumping or countervailing duties, even if it had the right to do so. Moreover, '[i]t is desirable' that the amount of duties imposed should be less than the margin of

164 GATT 1994, art. VI. The normal value of a dumped product is 'the comparable price, in the ordinary course of trade, for the like product when destined for consumption in the exporting country': Anti-Dumping Agreement, art. 2.1.

165 SCM Agreement, art. 5. 166 Anti-Dumping Agreement, art. 9.

167 SCM Agreement, art. 19.

168 See also GATT 1994, art. VI:2. The margin of dumping is the difference between the normal value and the export price of the product.

169 See also GATT 1994, art. VI:3.

dumping or the amount the subsidy, 'if such lesser duty would be adequate to remove the injury to the domestic industry'.[170]

In the context of anti-dumping and countervailing measures, the difference between the undesirable act and the injury caused is clear, and even potentially quantifiable, although the WTO agreements do not currently require Members to calculate a margin of injury. This contrasts with the situation in domestic law or customary international law, where it may be extremely difficult in practice to distinguish between the seriousness of the act and the degree of harm caused. In addition, the degree of proportionality required for anti-dumping and countervailing measures is exact. The parties may have different views as to the margin of dumping or the amount of the subsidy, but once the Member's relevant authorities have determined that level in an investigation in accordance with the WTO requirements, the Member cannot impose a duty that exceeds it.[171]

Safeguards are a little different. Most importantly, safeguards are imposed in response to increased imports causing serious injury.[172] No unfairness is involved,[173] and all Members are subject to the safeguards.[174] Therefore, safeguards are less analogous to penalties imposed for unlawful actions. Safeguards do involve some sort of proportionality requirement, in the sense that a Member may apply safeguards 'only to the extent necessary to prevent or remedy serious injury and to facilitate adjustment'.[175] However, as safeguards are not

[170] Anti-Dumping Agreement, art. 9.1; SCM Agreement, art. 19.2.

[171] The precision of this exercise may be diminished in certain circumstances, for example where the investigation authorities limit their examination because the number of exporters, producers, importers or types of products is so large as to render impracticable a determination of individual dumping margins: Anti-Dumping Agreement, arts. 6.10, 9.4.

[172] Agreement on Safeguards, art. 2.1.

[173] The Appellate Body has recognised this distinction between safeguards, on the one hand, and anti-dumping or countervailing measures, on the other hand. See, e.g., Appellate Body Report, *Argentina – Footwear (EC)*, [94].

[174] Agreement on Safeguards, art. 2.2. Some uncertainty surrounds the application of safeguards to products from partners from a regional trade agreement falling within Article XXIV of GATT 1994. See generally Joost Pauwelyn, 'The Puzzle of WTO Safeguards and Regional Trade Agreements' (2004) 7 *Journal of International Economic Law* 109; Nicolas Lockhart and Andrew Mitchell, 'Regional Trade Agreements Under GATT 1994: An Exception and Its Limits' in Andrew Mitchell (ed.), *Challenges and Prospects for the WTO* (2005) 217.

[175] Agreement on Safeguards, art. 5.1. See also art. 7.1. In addition, Article 8.1 of the Agreement on Safeguards requires a Member proposing to apply a safeguard to 'endeavour to maintain a substantially equivalent level of concessions and other

imposed in response to an unlawful or undesirable act by any other Member, and as a Member may continue to impose safeguards to the extent necessary 'to facilitate adjustment' (which may bear no relationship to the conduct of other Members), these cannot be seen as retributive measures or measures imposed to induce compliance. Accordingly, I do not view the current WTO provisions on the imposition of safeguards as incorporating the principle of proportionality in the sense described earlier in this chapter in relation to criminal penalties and international countermeasures.[176] I return to this issue below in addressing certain Appellate Body pronouncements regarding the principle of proportionality.

6.4.4 *Conclusion*

Several WTO provisions, although not uniform, together make up a thread of proportionality running through the WTO agreements. Broadly, this thread shares characteristics with proportionality as a general principle of law and a principle of customary international law, as shown in Table C of this chapter. For many of the reasons explained in Chapter 3, this may be insufficient for proportionality to rise to the status of a principle applicable throughout the WTO agreements, independent of the text. Many Members would also object to Panels or the Appellate Body using such a principle to inform their interpretation of WTO provisions that seem to involve proportionality. Nevertheless, in my view valid arguments can be made for regarding proportionality as a general principle of law, a principle of customary international law, and a principle of WTO law. On this basis, I now proceed to examine

obligations to that existing under GATT 1994 between it and the exporting Members which would be affected by such a measure'.

[176] The Agreement on Safeguards provides for an additional unilateral remedy when the Member applying a safeguard is unable to agree with other Members on how to achieve a 'substantially equivalent level of concessions and other obligations' as specified in Article 8.1. Specifically, upon satisfaction of certain conditions, 'the affected exporting Members shall be free . . . to suspend . . . the application of substantially equivalent concessions or other obligations under GATT 1994, to the trade of the Member applying the safeguard measure' (Agreement on Safeguards, art. 8.2). Again, the requirement of equivalence introduces the notion of proportionality, but this kind of unilateral remedy does not involve a response to unlawful or undesirable conduct, assuming that the safeguard was imposed in a manner consistent with the Agreement on Safeguards. Accordingly, I do not regard Article 8 of the Agreement on Safeguards as incorporating the principle of proportionality in the sense described in this chapter.

how WTO Tribunals might use the principle of proportionality in WTO disputes, taking into account their use of this principle to date.

6.5 Using proportionality for assessing remedies in WTO disputes

I first consider the relevance of proportionality to the imposition of multilateral remedies – that is, the suspension of concessions authorised by the DSB in response to either a general WTO violation or an actionable or prohibited subsidy that has not been remedied in accordance with the recommendations and rulings of the DSB in a given dispute. I then turn to proportionality in connection with unilateral remedies, namely the imposition of anti-dumping or safeguard measures.

6.5.1 *Multilateral remedies*

A. General WTO violations

(i) Understanding the purpose of suspending concessions

As mentioned earlier, Article 22.4 of the DSU requires that the level of suspension of concessions for a particular WTO violation be equivalent to the level of nullification or impairment caused by that violation. In understanding the role of proportionality, it is useful to consider the purpose of this requirement. Most of the interpretation of the Article 22.4 requirement of equivalence has come from arbitrators pursuant to Article 22.6 of the DSU. Several arbitrators have suggested that the purpose of suspending concessions is to induce compliance but that:

> this purpose does not mean that the DSB should grant authorization to suspend concessions beyond what is *equivalent* to the level of nullification or impairment. In our view, there is nothing in Article 22.1 of the DSU, let alone in paragraphs 4 and 7 of Article 22, that could be read as a justification for counter-measures of a *punitive* nature.[177]

The Appellate Body has endorsed this view.[178]

[177] Decision by the Arbitrators, *EC – Bananas III (US) (Article 22.6 – EC)*, [6.3]. See also Decision by the Arbitrators, *Brazil – Aircraft (Article 22.6 – Brazil)*, [3.55]; Decision by the Arbitrators, *EC – Hormones (US) (Article 22.6 – EC)*, [40]; Decision by the Arbitrators, *US – 1916 Act (Article 22.6 – US)*, [5.5]–[5.8]; Decision by the Arbitrators, *EC – Bananas III (Ecuador) (Article 22.6 – EC)*, [76]. However, in Decision by the Arbitrators, *US – Offset Act (Byrd Amendment) (Brazil) (Article 22.6 – US)*, [3.73]–[3.74], [6.2]–[6.4], the arbitrators suggested that inducing compliance is simply one of several possible purposes.

[178] Appellate Body Report, *US – Cotton Yarn*, [120] and n. 92; Appellate Body Report, *US – Line Pipe*, n. 252. See also Joost Pauwelyn, 'Enforcement and Countermeasures in the

Palmeter and Alexandrov argue that the purpose of retaliatory measures 'is not to induce compliance, but to maintain the balance of reciprocal trade concessions negotiated in the WTO agreements'.[179] Likewise, Sebastian argues that 'equivalent' in this context can be reduced to a mathematical calculation that requires that the 'nullification and impairment caused by the underlying violation be equal to the nullification and impairment caused by the retaliatory response'.[180] In contrast, Charnovitz considers that suspension of concessions in the WTO 'is conceived primarily as a sanction, while the rebalancing idea retains vestigial influence'.[181] In my view, the suspension of concessions is intended to induce compliance. This is consistent with Article 22.8 of the DSU, which states that the suspension of concessions is a temporary measure available only until the inconsistent measure has been removed. It is also consistent with Article 3.2 of the DSU, which indicates that, '[i]n the absence of a mutually agreed solution, the first objective of the dispute settlement mechanism is usually to secure the withdrawal of the [inconsistent] measures'.[182] It is true that this purpose is somewhat at odds with the fact that, pursuant to Article 22.4 of the DSU, the DSB cannot authorise suspension of concessions beyond the level of nullification or impairment.[183] However, this reflects a strikingly similar approach to the ILC Articles.[184] In both cases, the purpose of the penalty is said to be to induce compliance, but the penalty itself must not be disproportionate to the harm caused, even if a greater penalty would be required to induce compliance. This contradiction seems no worse under WTO law than under international law, and it seems to flow from the WTO provisions themselves rather than any faulty interpretation in dispute settlement.

WTO: Rules are Rules - Toward a More Collective Approach' (2000) 94 *American Journal of International Law* 335, 343.

179 David Palmeter and Stanimir Alexandrov, '"Inducing Compliance" in WTO dispute settlement', in Daniel Kennedy and James Southwick (eds.), *The Political Economy of International Trade Law: Essays in Honor of Robert E. Hudec* (2002) 646, 647.

180 Sebastian, 'World Trade Organization Remedies', 350–1.

181 Charnovitz, 'Should the Teeth Be Pulled?', 611.

182 Contra: Palmeter and Alexandrov, ' "Inducing Compliance"', 650.

183 Charnovitz, 'Should the Teeth Be Pulled?', 614; Pauwelyn, 'Enforcement and Countermeasures', 343–4.

184 See above, section 6.4.2.

(ii) Claims based on disproportionality

As mentioned in Chapter 3, in some circumstances a WTO Member could base a claim on a principle. The principle of proportionality provides one example of how a principle could in this way fall within the subject-matter jurisdiction of WTO Tribunals. Under Article 22.6 of the DSU, a Member could claim before an arbitrator that the level of suspension proposed is disproportionate to the level of nullification or impairment or disproportionate in a qualitative sense because it does not comply with the principles in Article 22.3 of the DSU. The arbitrator's subject-matter jurisdiction can thus be seen as encompassing claims of disproportionality.

(iii) Interpreting 'nullification or impairment'

In the first Article 22.6 arbitration, the arbitrators explicitly recognised the 'general international law principle of proportionality'.[185] They relied on this principle in determining how to calculate the level of nullification or impairment where a given WTO violation nullifies or impairs benefits accruing to several Members at once.[186] Specifically, the arbitrators held that the need for proportionality precluded 'double-counting' of a given amount of nullification or impairment.[187] On this basis, the arbitrators refused to include, in the calculation of nullification or impairment suffered by the United States as a result of certain measures of the European Communities in relation to bananas, lost United States exports in the form of inputs (such as fertiliser) in the cultivation of Latin American bananas.[188] In the arbitrators' view, only the relevant Latin American countries could seek authorisation to suspend concessions for nullification or impairment suffered with respect to Latin American bananas.[189]

Reading the relevant WTO provisions in light of the principle of proportionality, it is clear that the maximum level of suspension of concessions by all WTO Members for a given violation cannot exceed the total level of nullification or impairment suffered by those Members. However, this does not mean that the amount of nullification or impairment suffered by one Member must be reduced according to the amount of nullification or impairment suffered by other Members. The arbitrators suggested that 'the *same* amount of nullification or

[185] Decision by the Arbitrators, *EC – Bananas III (US) (Article 22.6 – EC)*, [6.16].
[186] Ibid. [6.15]. [187] Ibid. [6.15]–[6.16] (emphasis omitted). [188] Ibid. [6.12].
[189] Ibid. [6.14].

impairment inflicted on *one* Member cannot simultaneously be inflicted on *another*'.[190] Yet this is far from self-evident. A WTO violation may nullify or impair benefits accruing to one Member while at the same time nullifying or impairing benefits accruing to another Member. In that instance, the nullification or impairment suffered by one Member is quite different from the nullification or impairment suffered by another Member, even though it results from the same act. Therefore, perhaps the arbitrators could have better explained their decision regarding exports of United States inputs into Latin American bananas by elaborating on why exports of this kind did not constitute a benefit accruing to the United States directly or indirectly under the WTO agreements, instead of by reference to the proportionality principle.

In assessing the level of nullification or impairment resulting from a WTO violation, Article 22.6 arbitrators have focused on the trade or economic effects of the violation.[191] Moreover, they have shied away from measuring factors that cannot be quantified based on 'credible, factual, and verifiable information'.[192] In *US – 1916 Act (Article 22.6 – US)*, the arbitrators rejected a request by the European Communities to include as nullification or impairment the 'alleged deterrent or "chilling effect" ' of the United States' 1916 Act, which a Panel and the Appellate Body had found inconsistent as such with WTO obligations, because this effect was not quantifiable.[193]

In *US – Offset Act (Byrd Amendment) (Brazil) (Article 22.6 – US)*, the arbitrators stated that a WTO violation is distinct from the nullification or impairment that may arise from that violation.[194] In support of this conclusion, the arbitrators referred to Article 3.8 of the DSU, which provides that a WTO violation is presumed to nullify or impair benefits of other Members. According to the arbitrators, the fact that the defending Member may rebut this presumption suggests that the violation does not of itself constitute nullification or impairment. Rather, 'the benefit nullified or impaired must necessarily be something else'.[195]

[190] Ibid. [6.16].

[191] See, e.g., Decision by the Arbitrators, *US – 1916 Act (Article 22.6 – US)*, [5.23]–[5.28]; Decision by the Arbitrators, *US – Offset Act (Byrd Amendment) (Brazil) (Article 22.6 – US)*, [3.35], [3.39].

[192] Decision by the Arbitrators, *US – 1916 Act (Article 22.6 – US)*, [5.54].

[193] Ibid. [5.64]–[5.72].

[194] See, e.g., Decision by the Arbitrators, *US – Offset Act (Byrd Amendment) (Brazil) (Article 22.6 – US)*, [3.20]–[3.23], [3.30], [3.32], [3.54].

[195] See, e.g., ibid. [3.21]–[3.23], [3.34], [3.55].

As a result, the arbitrators refused Brazil's suggestion that the minimum level of nullification or impairment caused by the Continued Dumping and Offset Act (which the Panel and Appellate Body had found inconsistent as such with the United States' WTO obligations)[196] corresponded to the amount of payments made under that Act.[197]

Applying this reasoning in a domestic context, one might contend that the offence of drunk driving is separate from the injury caused by drunk driving. Indeed, drunk driving could cause no injury or very significant injury, depending on the circumstances. At these two extremes, the offence would be the same, but the punishment might vary. On the other hand, determining the punishment solely on the basis of the degree of injury could lead to some situations being wrongly equated. For example, the death of a person could be caused by a deliberate, premeditated act (murder), negligence (manslaughter), or natural events (no offence). The appropriate punishment in these different circumstances would likely differ. This may explain why, pursuant to proportionality as a general principle of law and a principle of customary international law, the decision-maker should take into account not only the harm caused but also the culpability of the actor in ensuring the penalty is proportionate to the unlawful act.

Under the DSU, the concept of nullification or impairment is indeed separate from that of a WTO inconsistency or violation, and Article 22.4 of the DSU does prevent a Member from imposing a penalty (in the form of suspension of concessions) that exceeds the harm caused (in the form of nullification or impairment).[198] However, this does not necessarily preclude the possibility that the violation itself may constitute nullification or impairment in at least some circumstances.[199] This would show how culpability may be relevant to proportionality as a principle of WTO law, just as it is to proportionality as a general principle of law and as a principle of customary international law.

This suggestion is consistent with previous Panel and Appellate Body rulings regarding nullification or impairment. In *EC – Bananas III*, the European Communities tried to rebut the presumption in Article 3.8 of the DSU that a violation of a WTO provision nullifies or impairs benefits

[196] Panel Report, *US – Offset Act (Byrd Amendment)*, [8.1]; Appellate Body Report, *US – Offset Act (Byrd Amendment)*, [318(a), (b)].

[197] See, e.g., Decision by the Arbitrators, *US – Offset Act (Byrd Amendment) (Brazil) (Article 22.6 – US)*, [3.10], [3.16], [3.56].

[198] See Mavroidis, 'Remedies in the WTO Legal System', 773, 800–1, 807.

[199] See Pauwelyn, 'Enforcement and Countermeasures', n. 46.

of other Members. The Panel found, and the Appellate Body agreed, that the European Communities had failed to rebut the presumption simply by arguing that the United States had never exported bananas to the European Communities and therefore could not have suffered trade damage as a result of the European Communities' inconsistent measures with respect to bananas.[200] The Appellate Body appeared to base this conclusion, first, on certain evidence suggesting possible trade effects of the inconsistent measures on the United States,[201] and second, on the suggestion in GATT Panel report *US – Superfund* that a demonstration of an absence of trade effects is insufficient to establish an absence of nullification or impairment.[202] Similarly, in the context of non-violation complaints pursuant to Article XXIII:1(b) of GATT 1994, Panels have taken the view that a measure that has no adverse trade effects may still nullify or impair benefits of WTO Members. A measure will nullify or impair such benefits (including Members' legitimate expectations under the WTO agreements)[203] if it upsets the competitive relationship between the relevant domestic and foreign products.[204]

Where the degree of culpability is high but the trade effects are low, accepting that a WTO violation itself may be a form of nullification or impairment would promote the effectiveness of suspension of concessions in inducing compliance and would recognise the retributive element of such action. Conversely, where the degree of culpability is low but the trade effects are high, it could place a further limit on retaliatory action. Granted, Members may impose anti-dumping and countervailing measures beyond the level of harm caused, which seems to depart somewhat from the prevailing general and international law principle of proportionality. However, this follows from a clear decision, expressed in the text itself, about the relevance of harm to the penalty imposed.[205] The same cannot be said in relation to whether nullification or impairment is restricted to trade or economic effects independent of the violation. It is therefore preferable to read the requirement of equivalence between suspension of concessions and nullification or impairment in a manner consistent with proportionality as a general principle of law and a principle of customary

[200] Appellate Body Report, *EC – Bananas III*, [249]–[250]. [201] Ibid. [251].

[202] Ibid. [252]–[254] (referring to *US – Superfund*, [5.1.9]).

[203] Panel Report, *Japan – Film*, [10.61]; Panel Report, *EC – Asbestos*, [8.285].

[204] Panel Report, *Japan – Film*, [10.82]; Panel Report, *EC – Asbestos*, [8.288].

[205] Anti-Dumping Agreement, art. 9.1; SCM Agreement, art. 19.2.

international law, such that culpability (the violation itself) should be considered in assessing the level of nullification or impairment.

B. Actionable and prohibited subsidies

I now turn to how proportionality may be used in connection with retaliatory action for failure to bring actionable or prohibited subsidies into conformity with the WTO agreements as recommended in a Panel or Appellate Body report adopted by the DSB.

Beginning with actionable subsidies, the rule seems fairly similar to that for usual WTO violations. In both cases, the acceptable level of retaliation focuses on the harm caused – in the case of an actionable subsidy, the harm caused is 'the degree and nature of the adverse effects determined to exist'.[206] These are 'adverse effects to the interests of other Members', in the form of injury to the domestic industry of another Member, nullification or impairment of benefits accruing directly or indirectly to other Members, or serious prejudice to the interests of another Member.[207] However, the wording of the proportionality requirement ('countermeasures' are to be 'commensurate with the degree and nature of the adverse effects determined to exist')[208] seems to grant greater discretion to the arbitrator than in the usual case under the DSU (where the 'level of suspension of concessions . . . shall be equivalent to the level of nullification or impairment').[209]

No arbitrators have yet been called upon to determine whether proposed countermeasures are commensurate with the adverse effects.[210] However, as with general WTO violations, reading this requirement in light of the principle of proportionality suggests that culpability (and not just harm caused) should play some role. This is consistent with the fact that the unlawful conduct giving rise to culpability (that is, granting an actionable subsidy) is itself defined by reference to the harm caused (that is, adverse effects to the interests of other Members). Specifically, under Article 5 of the SCM Agreement, '[n]o Member should cause, through the use of any [specific subsidy], adverse effects to the interests of other Members'. Thus, in identifying countermeasures commensurate with the degree and nature of such adverse effects, the arbitrator or retaliating Member takes into account not only the harm caused but also the culpability of the subsidising Member. It could be said that the principle of proportionality not only informs the

[206] SCM Agreement, art. 7.9. [207] SCM Agreement, art. 5.
[208] SCM Agreement, art. 7.9. [209] DSU, art. 22.4. [210] SCM Agreement, art. 7.10.

interpretation of Article 7.9 of the SCM Agreement, but is incorporated in the use of the term 'countermeasures' (which is a term of art in customary international law) and is therefore part of the applicable law.

As for prohibited subsidies, under Article 4.10 of the SCM Agreement, countermeasures must be 'appropriate', and this 'expression is not meant to allow countermeasures that are disproportionate in light of the fact that the subsidies dealt with under these provisions are prohibited' (footnote 9). Proportionality, as a general principle of law or a principle of customary international law, could influence the ordinary meaning of the words 'countermeasures' and 'disproportionate'.

Three Article 22.6 arbitrations have examined the proscription of disproportionality in footnote 9 of the SCM Agreement. As the arbitrators in the first of these arbitrations (*Brazil – Aircraft*) (*Article 22.6 – Brazil*) pointed out:

> it seems difficult to clearly identify how the second part of the sentence ('in light of the fact that the subsidies dealt with under these provisions are prohibited') relates to the first part of the sentence ('This expression is not meant to allow countermeasures that are disproportionate'). This is probably due to the use of the words 'in light of the fact that'.[211]

Indeed, one might have expected the drafters to state that countermeasures must not be disproportionate 'to' the gravity of the offence or the harm caused. Instead, the use of the words 'in light of the fact that' the subsidies are prohibited leaves open the question of what it is that countermeasures must not be disproportionate to. The ordinary meaning of a 'countermeasure' does not resolve this question (as it may be directed towards the illegal subsidy or the harm caused by that subsidy).[212] However, reading footnote 9 of the SCM Agreement consistently with the principle of proportionality in general and international law suggests that both culpability and harm should be considered in assessing whether countermeasures are disproportionate. The reference to the fact that the subsidies are prohibited indicates that the degree of culpability is fairly high for this kind of WTO violation. In other words, the prohibited nature of the subsidies in question is an 'aggravating' rather than a 'mitigating' factor.[213] But that does not mean that culpability alone is determinative in assessing proportionality. Indeed, although a

[211] Decision by the Arbitrators, *Brazil – Aircraft (Article 22.6 – Brazil)*, [3.51].

[212] Decision by the Arbitrators, *US – FSC (Article 22.6 – US)*, [5.6].

[213] Decision by the Arbitrators, *Brazil – Aircraft (Article 22.6 – Brazil)*, [3.51]; Decision by the Arbitrators, *US – FSC (Article 22.6 – US)*, [5.23].

complaining Member need not demonstrate that a prohibited subsidy is causing harm in order to establish a violation, this may be because such subsidies are regarded as inherently or necessarily harmful rather than because harm is irrelevant. This conclusion is consistent with Renouf's reference to the 'irrebuttable presumption of trade effect attached to prohibited subsidies'.[214]

Article 22.6 arbitrators have interpreted footnote 9 rather differently. As adverse effects need not be demonstrated to establish the existence of a prohibited subsidy in violation of Article 3 of the SCM Agreement,[215] the arbitrators in *US – FSC (Article 22.6 – US)* suggested that countermeasures may exceed what is necessary to counter any such effects.[216] Instead, in all three arbitrations on this point, the arbitrators have started or ended their proportionality analysis with the amount of the prohibited subsidy,[217] which can be seen as representing the extent of the 'wrongful act'[218] or culpability of the subsidising Member. Harm caused by the prohibited subsidy (including its effects on the complainant's trade) has been relegated to the role of a potentially relevant factor rather than a necessary consideration.[219] In order to justify their approach, arbitrators have relied heavily on the text of Article 4.10 of the SCM Agreement, which makes no reference to the concept of nullification and impairment, in comparison to articles such as Article 7.9, where the drafters used 'specific language to install a strict requirement of proportionality between the countermeasure and the detrimental effects of the subsidy'.[220] However, this approach ignores an important element of the text of Article 4.10, the use of the term 'appropriate', which is considered by Sebastian to embody a proportionality requirement.[221] In *Brazil – Aircraft (Article 22.6 – Canada)* the arbitrators concluded that a countermeasure is 'appropriate' if 'it effectively induces compliance'.[222] Yet there was no explanation by the arbitrators of why countermeasures that were equal to the value of the subsidy would be able to effectively induce compliance.

214 Renouf, 'Brief Introduction', 80.

215 Decision by the Arbitrators, *US – FSC (Article 22.6 – US)*, [5.39].

216 Ibid. [5.41], [5.49], [5.61].

217 Decision by the Arbitrators, *Brazil – Aircraft (Article 22.6 – Brazil)*, [3.60]; Decision by the Arbitrators, *US – FSC (Article 22.6 – US)*, [6.10]–[6.11]; Decision by the Arbitrators, *Canada – Aircraft (Article 22.6 – Canada)*, [3.51]. See also Renouf, 'Brief Introduction', 80.

218 Decision by the Arbitrators, *US – FSC (Article 22.6 – US)*, [6.11].

219 Ibid. [5.23], [6.10], [6.33]–[6.35]. 220 Sebastian, 'World Trade Organization', 358–9.

221 Ibid. 222 Decision by the Arbitrators, *Brazil – Aircraft (Article 22.6 – Canada)*, [3.44].

This interpretation of footnote 9 is not merely at odds with the principle of proportionality, which is informed by notions of justice and fairness. It also raises serious problems given that the WTO is a multilateral agreement in which numerous WTO Members may challenge a prohibited subsidy. If harm does not play a limiting role in assessing the proportionality of countermeasures, this means that the first complainant may retaliate beyond the level it has suffered and up to the full amount of the subsidising Member's culpability. Later complainants will either have to rely on the first complainant's decision about whether to impose countermeasures as authorised by the DSB, or they will be granted an additional right to impose countermeasures, meaning that the subsidising Member must pay several times over for its violation. Article 22.6 arbitrators have suggested that this problem can be avoided and the countermeasures authorised will depend on the number of complainants.[223] However, this assumes that all challenges to a particular prohibited subsidy will be brought at the same time. It also seems strange that the question of whether a given countermeasure proposed by a WTO Member complies with the proportionality requirement will depend on other Members' complaints about the same measure.

In *Canada – Aircraft (Article 22.6 – Canada)*, the arbitrators determined that countermeasures amounting to 120 per cent of the amount of the prohibited subsidy were not disproportionate.[224] The arbitrators might have chosen to base this decision on a finding that Canada's culpability in granting the prohibited subsidy, and the harm caused by that subsidy, went beyond the amount of the subsidy. This would have been consistent with the principle of proportionality. However, this was not their rationale. Rather, the arbitrators added the additional 20 per cent 'to take into account the fact that Canada, until now, has stated that it does not intend to withdraw the subsidy at issue and the need to reach a level of countermeasures which can reasonably contribute to induce compliance'.[225] All Article 22.6 arbitrators have suggested that the purpose of countermeasures under Article 4.10 of the SCM Agreement is to induce compliance through the withdrawal of the prohibited subsidy.[226]

223 Decision by the Arbitrators, *Brazil – Aircraft (Article 22.6 – Brazil)*, [3.59]; Decision by the Arbitrators, *US – FSC (Article 22.6 – US)*, [6.27]–[6.28], [6.62].

224 Decision by the Arbitrators, *Canada – Aircraft (Article 22.6 – Canada)*, [3.121].

225 Ibid. [3.119].

226 Ibid. [3.59]; Decision by the Arbitrators, *US – FSC (Article 22.6 – US)*, [5.57]; Decision by the Arbitrators, *Brazil – Aircraft (Article 22.6 – Brazil)*, [3.44].

In this context, I agree with Palmeter and Alexandrov that the arbitrators went too far.[227] Even assuming that the purpose of countermeasures for prohibited subsidies is to induce compliance, to use this as a justification for increasing countermeasures beyond the degree of culpability or harm is plainly contrary to the principle of proportionality. As I suggested earlier in relation to proportionality as a general principle of law, non-comparative proportionality sets an absolute ceiling on the amount of the penalty imposed for a given offence, based on the seriousness of the offence and the injury it causes. The arbitrators in *Canada – Aircraft (Article 22.6 – Canada)* had discretion to identify this ceiling and, below this ceiling, to adjust the amount of the countermeasures according to comparative proportionality (that is, countermeasures allowed in similar cases, which the arbitrators did consider)[228] and other factors such as utilitarian objectives, including deterrence and inducing compliance.

6.5.2 *Interpreting provisions on unilateral remedies*

A. Proportionality and anti-dumping

Given my conclusion that proportionality has certain characteristics that could suggest it is a general principle of law, a principle of customary international law, and a principle of WTO law, how might Panels and the Appellate Body make use of proportionality in interpreting WTO trade remedy provisions? As mentioned earlier, the allowance for anti-dumping or countervailing measures beyond the level of harm caused is not consistent with proportionality in general or international law. However, this does not mean that the principle of proportionality is irrelevant to the interpretation of the WTO provisions on unilateral remedies. The practice of 'zeroing' in anti-dumping investigations provides a useful example.

Before a Member may impose anti-dumping duties on imports of a product from a particular country, the Member's investigating authorities must establish, among other things, that imports of that product from that country are being dumped. Put simply, dumping occurs where the export price of a product is less than its normal value.[229] Some Members' investigating authorities have used zeroing in calculating dumping margins, as follows. The authorities divide the

[227] Palmeter and Alexandrov, '"Inducing Compliance"', 653–4.
[228] Appellate Body Report, *Canada – Aircraft*, [3.40]–[3.41].
[229] Anti-Dumping Agreement, art. 2.1.

product into different models and calculate the extent of dumping for each model by subtracting the weighted average export price from the weighted average normal value. They then determine the dumping margin for the product as a whole by adding the results from each model. However, where the result for a model is negative (meaning that model has not been dumped), they count the degree of dumping for that model as zero instead of the relevant negative number.

In *EC – Bed Linen*, the Appellate Body found that the form of zeroing practised by the European Communities, as applied in a particular investigation, was inconsistent with Article 2.4.2 of the Anti-Dumping Agreement.[230] That provision states that dumping margins 'shall normally be established on the basis of a comparison of a weighted average normal value with a weighted average of prices of all comparable export transactions'. In making its decision, the Appellate Body emphasised the words 'all comparable export transactions' in Article 2.4.2, indicating that the European Communities 'did *not* take fully into account the entirety of the prices of *some* export transactions, namely, those export transactions involving models' that had not been dumped.[231] It supported its conclusion by reference to Article 2.4 of the Anti-Dumping Agreement, which requires Members to make a 'fair comparison . . . between the export price and the normal value'.[232]

As the Appellate Body explained, Article 2.4.2 is expressed to apply '[s]ubject to the provisions governing fair comparison' in Article 2.4. Article 2.4 therefore provides relevant context for interpreting Article 2.4.2. However, Article 2.4 is directed towards a comparison of normal value and export price 'at the same level of trade . . . and in respect of sales made at as nearly as possible the same time', making '[d]ue allowance . . . for differences which affect price comparability', such as 'conditions and terms of sale, taxation, levels of trade, quantities, [and] physical characteristics'. This suggests that the requirement of a 'fair comparison' in Article 2.4 and the reference to 'all comparable export transactions' in Article 2.4.2 relate to the comparability of export transactions in view of these features. They do not seem to speak to the practice of zeroing, which the authorities use only after they have identified all the comparable export transactions.

Moreover, the Appellate Body's reliance on the words 'all comparable export transactions' in finding that Article 2.4.2 prohibits zeroing when

230 Appellate Body Report, *EC – Bed Linen*, [66]. 231 Ibid., [55] (original emphasis).
232 Ibid. [59]–[60].

authorities use a weighted average to weighted average methodology raises the question of whether zeroing is permitted when authorities use one of the other methodologies described in Article 2.4.2, namely 'a comparison of normal value and export prices on a transaction-to-transaction basis' or a comparison between 'normal value established on a weighted average basis [and] prices of individual export transactions'. The words 'all comparable export transactions' do not specifically appear in relation to these two methodologies.

The Appellate Body addressed zeroing more recently in *US – Softwood Lumber V*. In that case, the Appellate Body found that the United States acted inconsistently with Article 2.4.2 of the Anti-Dumping Agreement by using a similar practice of zeroing to calculate dumping margins using a weighted average to weighted average methodology.[233] However, this time the Appellate Body did not rely on the words 'all comparable export transactions' in Article 2.4.2; nor did it suggest that the requirement to make a 'fair comparison' under Article 2.4 influenced its decision. Instead, the Appellate Body's assessment of zeroing focused on its conclusion, based on certain other provisions, that the dumping margins to be determined under Article 2.4.2 are dumping margins for the product as a whole, rather than for individual models.[234] Its conclusion that the United States' use of zeroing was inconsistent with Article 2.4.2 appeared to hinge on its view that zeroing 'inflates the margin of dumping for the product as a whole'.[235]

The Appellate Body's approach in *US – Softwood Lumber V* may be preferable to its earlier approach in *EC – Bed Linen*, because it does not rely on the wording of Articles 2.4 and 2.4.2 regarding comparability. However, in the absence of express textual guidance regarding whether zeroing is acceptable in calculating dumping margins, it is unclear why zeroing should be prohibited. The use of the proportionality principle could have helped explain why inflation of the dumping margin is problematic. Anti-dumping duties are essentially a penalty that Members are allowed to impose in response to unfair conduct – dumping. Anti-dumping duties that exceed the degree of dumping are disproportionate to dumping – that is, the penalty is disproportionate to the

233 Appellate Body Report, *US – Softwood Lumber V*, [63], [117].

234 Ibid., [96]–[99]. In para. 96, the Appellate Body pointed out that it had reached the same conclusion in Appellate Body Report, *EC – Bed Linen*, [53].

235 Appellate Body Report, *US – Softwood Lumber V*, [101]. The Appellate Body made the same point in Appellate Body Report, *EC – Bed Linen*, [55].

culpability of the Member whose products are being dumped. If zeroing were allowed, this would enable Members to ignore the extent of non-dumped transactions and, therefore, overstate the degree of dumping. In turn, Members would be able to impose anti-dumping duties beyond the level of dumping.

Thus, the proportionality principle could be used to interpret Article 2.4.2 so as to prohibit zeroing. The legal basis for using proportionality in this way would be that the principle of proportionality is a relevant rule of international law under Article 31(3)(c) of the VCLT and that it also reflected (as a principle of WTO law) in the context and object and purpose of the Anti-Dumping Agreement, as discussed in Chapter 3. The example of zeroing also shows how principles may be used to evaluate decisions of WTO Tribunals even where those decisions do not mention such principles.

B. Proportionality and safeguards

In two trade remedy disputes, the Appellate Body has recognised the principle of proportionality as a principle of customary international law.[236] First, it did so implicitly in *US – Cotton Yarn* in 2001, based on Article 51 of the ILC Articles (then in draft form).[237] Next, it did so explicitly in *US – Line Pipe* in 2002, based not only on Article 51 but also on two ICJ decisions.[238] In that case, the Appellate Body also 'observed' that the United States itself had recognised the existence of such a principle in customary international law in its comments on the draft ILC Articles and in an international arbitral tribunal.[239] Of itself, the Appellate Body's recognition of the proportionality principle may not be particularly remarkable. However, in both cases the Appellate Body used the principle of proportionality in an unusual way.

In *US – Cotton Yarn*, the Appellate Body was examining the 'specific transitional safeguard mechanism'[240] provided under Article 6 of the

[236] Appellate Body Report, *US – Cotton Yarn*, [120]–[122]; Appellate Body Report, *US – Line Pipe*, [259].

[237] Appellate Body Report, *US – Cotton Yarn*, n. 90.

[238] Appellate Body Report, *US – Line Pipe*, [259] and n. 256 (citing *Military and Paramilitary Activities in and against Nicaragua (Nicaragua* v. *United States of America)* [1986] ICJ Rep 14, [249] and *Gabčíkovo-Nagymaros Project (Hungary / Slovakia)* [1997] ICJ Rep 7, 220).

[239] Appellate Body Report, *US – Line Pipe*, [259] and n. 257 (referring to the Arbitral Tribunal established by the Compromise of 11 July 1978 in the *Air Services Agreement of 27 March 1946 (United States* v. *France))*.

[240] ATC, art. 6.1.

now defunct Agreement on Textiles and Clothing (ATC).[241] This mechanism enabled a Member to impose a safeguard if a product was being imported into its territory in such increased quantities as to cause serious damage to the domestic industry producing like or directly competitive products.[242] Article 6.4 of the ATC stated that Members had to apply safeguard measures 'on a Member-by-Member basis', such that 'Members to whom serious damage is attributed . . . shall be determined on the basis of a sharp and substantial increase in imports . . . from such . . . Members individually'. This contrasts with the MFN rule in Article 2.2 of the Agreement on Safeguards, which states that safeguards imposed under that agreement 'shall be applied to a product being imported irrespective of its source'. Based primarily on Article 6.4, the Appellate Body concluded that 'the part of the total serious damage attributed to an exporting Member' (and, hence, the level of the safeguard applied to that Member) 'must be proportionate to the damage caused by the imports from that Member'.[243] This seems to follow from the text of the provision, particularly when read in context.

The Appellate Body could well have ended its analysis here. However, it went on to support its interpretation of Article 6.4 of the ATC by reference to the proportionality principle. The Appellate Body suggested that Article 22.4 of the DSU incorporates this principle by requiring suspension of concessions to be equivalent to the level of nullification or impairment.[244] I came to a similar conclusion above. But what does that have to do with the transitional safeguard under the ATC? Noting that safeguards are not imposed in response to unfair trade, the Appellate Body stated:

> It would be absurd if the breach of an international obligation were sanctioned by proportionate countermeasures, while, in the absence of such breach, a WTO Member would be subject to a disproportionate and, hence, 'punitive', attribution of serious damage not wholly caused by its exports. In our view, such an exorbitant derogation from the principle of proportionality in respect of the attribution of serious damage could be justified only if the drafters of the *ATC* had expressly provided for it, which is not the case.[245]

Although the Appellate Body did not refer to the principle of proportionality in the context of anti-dumping or countervailing measures, the principle it applied was similar to that existing under the

[241] This agreement was terminated, in accordance with its Article 9, on 1 January 2005.
[242] ATC, art. 6.2. [243] Appellate Body Report, *US – Cotton Yarn*, [119].
[244] Ibid. [120]. [245] Ibid.

Anti-Dumping Agreement and Part V of the SCM Agreement. Put simply, it concluded that textile safeguards could not be applied to a Member from whom imports had not increased (just as anti-dumping duties cannot generally be imposed against a company whose exports have not been dumped, and countervailing duties cannot generally be imposed against a company whose exports have not been subsidised). Intuitively, this seems like a fair and sensible result, and it may well flow from a proper reading of Article 6.4 of the ATC, as mentioned earlier. However, it seems to me that the Appellate Body's invocation of the proportionality principle in this context was not only unnecessary but also inappropriate.

It would have been one thing for the Appellate Body to reason that anti-dumping duties cannot exceed the dumping margin, and countervailing duties cannot exceed the amount of the subsidy (reflecting the principle of proportionality), and therefore it would not make sense for safeguards to exceed the increase in imports justifying their application. It was quite another for the Appellate Body to apply the proportionality principle in interpreting Article 6.4 of the ATC, which is what it did, stating that this provision 'is to be seen in the light of the principle of proportionality as the means of determining the scope or assessing the part of the total serious damage that can be attributed to an exporting Member'.[246] Culpability plays an essential role in the principle of proportionality, as shown in Table C of this chapter, where every instance involves culpability through an unlawful or undesirable act. In the absence of culpability, sanctions can have no retributive purpose or effect. The Appellate Body expressly recognised that safeguards are not responses to unfair or culpable conduct, but it applied the principle of proportionality anyway. It is not clear what meaning that principle can have when divorced from one of its core elements and rationales.

The second case in which the Appellate Body recognised the principle of proportionality in connection with safeguards was *US – Line Pipe*. In that case, the Appellate Body was examining Article 5.1 of the Agreement on Safeguards, which requires Members to impose safeguards 'only to the extent necessary to prevent or remedy serious injury and to facilitate adjustment'.[247] The Appellate Body characterised the question before it as 'whether the permissible extent of a safeguard measure is limited to the injury that can be attributed to increased imports, or

[246] Ibid. [122]. [247] Appellate Body Report, *US – Line Pipe*, [237].

whether a safeguard measure may also address the injurious effects caused by other factors'.[248] In answering this question, the Appellate Body first noted that Article 4.2(b) of the Agreement on Safeguards states that, '[w]hen factors other than increased imports are causing injury to the domestic industry at the same time, such injury shall not be attributed to increased imports'. It suggested that this provision 'informs the permissible extent to which the safeguard measure may be applied pursuant to Article 5.1'.[249]

The Appellate Body quoted certain passages relating to proportionality in *US – Cotton Yarn* and stated that 'the same reasoning applies here'.[250] In addition to comparing the imposition of safeguards to the suspension of concessions, as it had done in *US – Cotton Yarn*, the Appellate Body compared the imposition of safeguards to the imposition of anti-dumping or countervailing measures:

> If the pain inflicted on exporters by a safeguard measure were permitted to have effects beyond the share of injury caused by increased imports, this would imply that an exceptional remedy, which is not meant to protect the industry of the importing country from unfair or illegal trade practices, could be applied in a more trade-restrictive manner than countervailing and anti-dumping duties. On what basis should the *WTO Agreement* be interpreted to limit a countermeasure to the extent of the injury caused by unfair practices or a violation of the treaty but not so limit a countermeasure when there has not even been an allegation of a violation or an unfair practice?[251]

The Appellate Body therefore read Article 5.1 as requiring safeguards to be limited to the extent necessary to prevent or remedy serious injury attributed to increased imports.[252] It is interesting to note that the Appellate Body here referred to countermeasures, even though the Agreement on Safeguards does not refer to safeguards as countermeasures. Indeed, the only reference to countermeasures in the WTO agreements is, as described above, in connection with subsidies that have been found inconsistent with Part II or III of the SCM Agreement (in connection with prohibited and actionable subsidies respectively),[253] and not in connection with trade remedies.

[248] Ibid. [241] (emphasis omitted). [249] Ibid. [252]. [250] Ibid. [254]–[257].
[251] Ibid. [257]. [252] Ibid. [260].
[253] Article 9.4 of the SCM Agreement also refers to countermeasures in connection with 'non-actionable subsidies'. Article 9.4 (and the category of non-actionable subsidies in Part IV of the SCM Agreement) expired at the end of 1999 in accordance with Article 31 of the SCM Agreement.

The Appellate Body's use of proportionality in the context of the Agreement on Safeguards suffers from the same deficiency as its use of proportionality in the context of the ATC – the absence of culpability renders the principle almost meaningless. However, the deficiency is even greater under the Agreement on Safeguards. As already explained, if a Member decides to apply safeguards under this agreement because a 'product is being imported into its territory in such increased quantities . . . and under such conditions as to cause . . . serious injury to the domestic industry',[254] the Member must apply safeguards to each import of that product 'irrespective of its source'.[255] In *US – Line Pipe*, the Appellate Body was therefore not addressing the attribution to different Members of increased imports. Rather, it was addressing the attribution to 'increased imports' (as opposed to other factors) of injury suffered by the domestic industry.[256] A safeguard imposed under the Agreement on Safeguards is therefore even less like a penalty than the transitional safeguard under the ATC that the Appellate Body addressed in *US – Cotton Yarn*.

It seems clear from the terms of Article 5.1 itself that safeguards can go beyond what is needed to prevent or remedy serious injury – they can be used also to the extent necessary 'to facilitate adjustment'.[257] Putting this to one side, the Appellate Body is probably correct that the 'serious injury' described in Article 5.1 is serious injury caused by increased imports. Yet, as in *US – Cotton Yarn*, it did not need to rely on the proportionality principle to reach this conclusion. As the Appellate Body correctly pointed out,[258] Article 4.2(b) of the Agreement on Safeguards confirms that the serious injury that is relevant is that caused by increased imports. Furthermore, Article XIX:1(a) of GATT 1994, from which the Agreement on Safeguards derives, provides:

> If . . . any product is being imported into the territory of [a Member] in such increased quantities and under such conditions as to cause or threaten serious injury to domestic producers in that territory of like or directly competitive products, the Member shall be free [to impose a safeguard] in respect of such product . . . to the extent and for such time as may be necessary to prevent or remedy such injury.

[254] Agreement on Safeguards, art. 2.1. [255] Agreement on Safeguards, art. 2.2.

[256] Appellate Body Report, *US – Line Pipe*, [241] (emphasis omitted).

[257] The Appellate Body does not appear to account for the words 'to facilitate adjustment' in its reading of Article 5.1 in ibid. [260].

[258] Ibid. [252].

Evidently, the term 'such injury' in this provision refers to the serious injury described earlier in the passage, confirming that the injury relevant to the inquiry is serious injury caused by increased imports.

The United States' particularly vehement reaction to *US – Line Pipe*[259] may have stemmed from the Appellate Body's recognition of the principle of proportionality or, more specifically, its use of that principle in interpreting the WTO agreements. In this section, I have highlighted several difficulties with the Appellate Body's use of the proportionality principle in *US – Line Pipe*, as well as *US – Cotton Yarn*. This provides an example of the dangers of using principles with insufficient precision.

6.6 Conclusion

This chapter has provided certain evidence to suggest that proportionality could be characterised as a general principle of law, a principle of customary international law, and a principle of WTO law. More importantly, it has demonstrated how the principle of proportionality could be used in relation to WTO disputes, particularly in evaluating the level and type of multilateral and unilateral remedies that WTO Members may have in response to a WTO violation or other conduct that is classified as unfair in the WTO agreements.

Proportionality could be used in a non-interpretative manner, for example, as the basis for a claim that a Member proposes to suspend concessions in response to a WTO-inconsistency in an amount that goes beyond the level of nullification or impairment caused by the inconsistent measure. It could also be used in a non-interpretative manner as part of the applicable law, to the extent that it is incorporated in certain WTO provisions such as footnote 9 of the SCM Agreement. But the most obvious way in which the principle of proportionality could be used is in interpreting the WTO agreements. In this regard, it confirms the purpose of suspension of concessions as inducing compliance, as well as the limit on retaliation established by the harm caused by and culpability associated with the WTO violation in question. Proportionality could also help resolve ambiguity in the text of certain WTO provisions, such as Article 2.4.2 of the Anti-Dumping Agreement in relation to zeroing.

[259] See DSB, *Minutes of the DSB Meeting Held on 8 March 2002*, WT/DSB/M/121, [35].

This chapter has also revealed that principles such as proportionality should be used with caution in WTO disputes. Where the text of a WTO provision is clearly contrary to a general principle of law or a principle of customary international law, the principle cannot be used to interpret this distinction away. Thus, proportionality cannot be used in an interpretative manner to change the clear intention of the drafters of the Anti-Dumping Agreement and the SCM Agreement that Members should be entitled to impose anti-dumping or countervailing measures beyond the level of harm caused by the challenged dumping or subsidisation (provided that the measures comply with the other conditions of the agreements). Finally, if WTO Tribunals are to use principles to inform their interpretation of particular provisions, they must ensure that they have secure grounds for doing so. As explained in this chapter, I regard proportionality as having no relevance to the imposition of safeguards, because safeguards are not imposed in response to any illegal or unfair act, and proportionality in general and international law centres on both harm and culpability. Accordingly, WTO Tribunals have erred in their use of the principle of proportionality in this context.

7 Special and differential treatment

7.1 Introduction

Development has always played an important role in GATT/WTO. The Preamble to GATT 1947 recognised the objective of 'raising standards of living'. The Preamble to the Marrakesh Agreement signed in 1994 reiterated and expanded this concept, recognising the 'need for positive efforts designed to ensure that developing countries, and especially the least developed among them, secure a share in the growth in international trade commensurate with the needs of their economic development'. In 2001, upon the launch of the Doha Round, the Ministerial Conference stated: 'The majority of WTO members are developing countries. We seek to place their needs and interests at the heart of the Work Programme adopted in this Declaration'.[1] Hence the name 'Doha Development Agenda'.

Central to the recognition of development needs in the WTO is the notion of 'special and differential treatment' (S&D) for developing countries. In contrast to the strong thread of non-discrimination running through the WTO agreements, S&D involves discrimination in favour of developing countries. This discrimination takes the form of both differential rights or obligations mandated by the WTO agreements themselves, and differential treatment accorded to developing countries by other Members. An example of the former is a WTO provision providing longer transition times (that is, time to implement a particular WTO obligation) to developing than to developed country Members. An example of the latter is preferential tariff treatment accorded by a developed country Member to a developing country Member. Both are based on the belief that the trade needs of developing

[1] Doha Declaration, [2].

countries are substantially different from those of developed countries and therefore that the two types of economies should not be subject to the same trade rules.[2]

In this chapter, I first examine the development of S&D within GATT and the WTO, before considering certain potential difficulties with S&D as a unified principle. The fourth section of the chapter considers whether a sufficiently well-defined and well-accepted principle of S&D now exists for WTO Tribunals to use it in disputes, either to resolve procedural matters in the exercise of inherent jurisdiction, or to assist in interpreting the WTO agreements. I conclude that the various S&D provisions in the WTO are not coherent enough to provide a principle to guide interpretation of the WTO agreements in a general sense. This may be due in part to the different and sometimes conflicting interests of developing country Members, the limited experience of the dispute settlement system with S&D as a principle, and the absence of a corresponding general principle of law or customary international law principle. This chapter will not discuss S&D as a general principle of law because S&D cannot exist at the domestic level, since it concerns developing states. This chapter will also not discuss S&D as a principle of customary law since S&D has only been recognised in the international sphere in specific circumstances in some multilateral treaties.[3] This limited recognition is clearly insufficient to make S&D a principle of customary international law.

7.2 Special and differential treatment as a principle of WTO law

In one form or another, special and differential treatment (S&D) has been a defining feature of the multilateral trading system for most of the post-war period. The battle to establish the principle that a set of uniform multilateral

[2] Endre Ustor, 'Most-Favoured-Nation Clause' in Rudolf Bernhardt (ed.), *Encyclopaedia of Public International Law* (2003) vol. 3, 468, 471. The notion of S&D has also been reflected in other legal regimes. In international environmental law, it is reflected in the principle of 'common but differentiated responsibility', which takes into account differentiated degrees of responsibility for and capacity to redress environmental problems in searching for a global solution. See Nina E. Bafundo, 'Compliance with the Ozone Treaty: Weak States and the Principle of Common but Differentiated Responsibility' (2005) 21 *American University International Law Review* 461.

[3] See, e.g., *Vienna Convention for the Protection of the Ozone Layer*, opened for signature 22 March 1985, 1513 UNTS 323, art. 4(2) (entered into force 22 September 1988); *Montreal Protocol on Substances that Deplete the Ozone Layer*, opened for signature 16 September 1987, 1522 UNTS 3, art. 5 (entered into force 1 January 1989).

rights and obligations among a deeply diverse set of nations could not serve the best interests of all parties was won a long time ago.[4]

7.2.1 *Special and differential treatment in GATT/WTO*

The WTO agreements refer to developing countries in numerous provisions, often using different terminology. The different ways in which the agreements describe developing countries, and the different types of S&D provisions contained in the agreements, reflect the changing role and perception of developing country concerns and consequent amendments to GATT throughout the first seven rounds of negotiations, as well as the Uruguay Round leading to the WTO. Since the WTO came into force in 1995, the significance of development in the WTO and the attitudes of developing country Members have continued to evolve, albeit without formal amendments to the agreements. Others have already examined extensively the treatment of developing countries in GATT and the WTO, including the relevant history and economic considerations.[5] In this section, I provide a brief synopsis of these matters as a background for understanding the potential for use of S&D as a principle in WTO disputes today. This background may play a role in interpreting WTO provisions, to the extent that it falls within the meaning of 'preparatory work' under Article 32 of the VCLT, as discussed in Chapter 3.

When GATT 1947 entered into force, the term 'underdeveloped countries' had fallen out of favour,[6] and the first S&D provision (Article XVIII) referred instead to 'contracting parties the economies of which can only support low standards of living and are in the early stages of development' and contracting parties 'the econom[ies] of which [are] in the process of development'.[7] This provision, which was contained in the original GATT and revised and expanded in the 1950s,[8] allows

[4] Alexander Keck and Patrick Low, 'Special and Differential Treatment in the WTO: Why, When and How?' (Working Paper No ERSD-2004-03, WTO, 2004) 3.

[5] See, e.g., Robert E. Hudec, *Developing Countries in the GATT Legal System* (1987); Faizel Ismail, 'Mainstreaming Development in the World Trade Organization' (2005) 39 *Journal of World Trade* 11; Kym Anderson, 'Setting the Trade Policy Agenda: What Roles for Economists?' (2005) 39 *Journal of World Trade* 341, 346–9, 353–4; Raj Bhala, *Modern GATT Law: A Treatise on the General Agreement on Tariffs and Trade* (2005) chs. 37–8.

[6] A. A. Fatouros, 'Developing States' in Rudolf Bernhardt (ed.), *Encyclopaedia of Public International Law* (2003) vol. I, 1017.

[7] GATT 1994, arts. XVIII:1, XVIII:4(b).

[8] Article XVIII:B was added in 1957: Panel Report, *India – Quantitative Restrictions*, [5.28].

developing country Members to withdraw or modify certain WTO obligations in order to protect infant industries or address balance of payments problems. However, these exceptions are subject to several conditions, including in some cases the need to consult with Members affected by the withdrawal or modification. Also during the 1950s review session, a new Article XXVIII*bis* introduced the notion of non-reciprocity in tariff negotiations (or, in Hudec's words, 'governments agreed to a rather vague relaxation of the "reciprocity" principle').[9] Paragraph 3(b) of that provision recognises 'the needs of less-developed countries for a more flexible use of tariff protection to assist their economic development and the special needs of these countries to maintain tariffs for revenue purposes'. According to Hudec, 'probably th[e] most significant impact' of these amendments 'was at the level of principle – the fuller and now almost enthusiastic endorsement of the idea that legal freedom "helps" developing countries'.[10]

In 1964, an entire new part (Part IV) entitled 'Trade and Development' was added to the end of GATT 1947, containing S&D provisions for 'less-developed contracting parties'.[11] The non-reciprocity principle is expressed in concrete terms in Article XXXVI:8 as follows: 'The developed contracting parties do not expect reciprocity for commitments made by them in trade negotiations to reduce or remove tariffs and other barriers to the trade of less-developed contracting parties'. This provision is now elaborated as meaning that developing countries 'should not be expected, in the course of trade negotiations, to make contributions which are inconsistent with their individual development, financial and trade needs, taking into consideration past trade developments'.[12] Part IV also contains several provisions endorsing S&D treatment by developed country Members in favour of developing country Members, although these all fall short of binding, enforceable obligations. For example, developed country Members 'shall, to the fullest extent possible – that is, except when compelling reasons, which may include legal reasons, make it impossible' – reduce barriers to products of particular export interest to developing country Members[13] and shall 'give active consideration to the adoption of other measures designed to provide greater scope for the development of imports' from developing country Members.[14] Again, in view of the fact that '[t]he

[9] Hudec, *Developing Countries*, 27. [10] Ibid. 28. [11] See, e.g., GATT 1947, art. XXXVI:1(a).
[12] GATT 1994, ad art. XXXVI:8. [13] GATT 1994, art. XXXVII:1.
[14] GATT 1994, art. XXXVII:3(b).

drafting reached new heights in suggesting commitment where there was none', Hudec suggests that '[t]he major significance of Part IV was its force as an agreed statement of principle'.[15]

Part IV also refers to collaboration with the United Nations Conference on Trade and Development (UNCTAD).[16] In fact, the establishment of UNCTAD as a permanent institution in 1964 reflected growing demands of developing country GATT contracting parties and gave GATT a competitor, hence increasing the bargaining power of developing countries. Other developments that may have added to developing countries' power were the growing proportion of developing relative to developed country contracting parties in GATT and the creation of the 'Group of 77' developing countries.[17] This informal negotiating group now contains 132 countries and 'provides the means for the countries of the South to articulate and promote their collective economic interests and enhance their joint negotiating capacity on all major international economic issues within the United Nations system'.[18]

In 1971, GATT contracting parties agreed to a temporary (ten-year) waiver from the MFN obligation in Article I for the GSP, directed towards voluntary tariff preferences granted by developed country to developing country Members on a fairly uniform basis (as opposed to the selective provision of preferences to former colonies by, for example, the European Communities). This temporary waiver was replaced by a permanent ministerial decision to exempt GSP schemes from Article I in 1979. The 1979 Enabling Clause is now part of GATT 1994, by virtue of paragraph 1(b)(iv) of the introductory wording to GATT 1994, which states that GATT 1994 incorporates 'decisions of the CONTRACTING PARTIES to GATT 1947'. Among other things, this allows developed country Members to establish GSP schemes granting tariff preferences to developing country Members. I discuss the Enabling Clause further below in relation to the dispute *EC – Tariff Preferences*.[19]

The agreements negotiated in the Uruguay Round not only retained the existing S&D provisions in GATT but also introduced many more such provisions and recognition of the special needs of developing

[15] Hudec, *Developing Countries*, 56–8. [16] GATT 1994, art. XXXVIII:2(b).

[17] Hudec, *Developing Countries*, 40; *Joint Declaration of the Seventy-Seven Developing Countries Made at the Conclusion of the United Nations Conference on Trade and Development* (Geneva, 15 June 1964); *First Ministerial Meeting of the Group of 77: Charter of Algiers* (Algiers, 10–25 October 1967).

[18] The Group of 77 at the United Nations, *About the Group of 77*, www.g77.org/doc.

[19] See below, section 7.3.2.

countries in the new agreements. The WTO Secretariat has compiled summaries of the many S&D provisions in the WTO agreements.[20] Typically, these provisions refer to 'developing countries' and 'the least developed among them'.[21] Nevertheless, from a substantive perspective, developing countries may have got less than they bargained for. Given the 'unbalanced outcome' of the Uruguay Round, including the introduction of TRIPS in the absence of real concessions in textiles/clothing or agriculture, developing country Members have continued to press for more.[22]

Paragraph 44 of the Doha Declaration states that the Ministerial Conference 'agree[s] that all special and differential treatment provisions shall be reviewed with a view to strengthening them and making them more precise, effective and operational'. The Doha Declaration also endorses the S&D work programme contained in the Doha Implementation Decision.[23] The Doha Implementation Decision instructs the Committee on Trade and Development to 'identify those [S&D] provisions that are ... mandatory ... and those that are non-binding ... [and] to consider the legal and practical implications for developed and developing Members of converting special and differential treatment measures into mandatory provisions'.[24] Members also 'reaffirm' in the Doha Implementation Decision that GATT Article XVIII 'is a special and differential treatment provision for developing countries and that recourse to it should be less onerous than to

[20] See, e.g., WTO Committee on Trade and Development, 'Implementation of Special and Differential Treatment Provisions in WTO Agreements and Decisions: Note by the Secretariat', WT/COMTD/W/77 (25 October 2000); 'Developing Countries and the Multilateral Trading System: Past and Present – Background Note by the Secretariat' (WTO High Level Symposium, 17–18 March 1999) Annex II.

[21] See, e.g., Marrakesh Agreement, Preamble.

[22] Michael Finger and Julio Nogués, 'The Unbalanced Uruguay Round Outcome: The New Areas in Future WTO Negotiations' (2002) 25 *World Economy* 321, 326, 336; T. N. Srinivasan, 'Developing Countries in the World Trading System: From GATT, 1947, to the Third Ministerial Meeting of the WTO, 1999' (1999) 22 *World Economy* 1047, 1053–4; Bernard Hoekman, Constantine Michalopoulos and Alan Winters, 'Special and Differential Treatment of Developing Countries in the WTO: Moving Forward After Cancún' (2004) 27 *World Economy* 481, 482; Rubens Ricupero, 'Rebuilding Confidence in the Multilateral Trading System: Closing the "Legitimacy Gap"' in Gary Sampson (ed.), *The Role of the World Trade Organization in Global Governance* (2001) 37, 49–50; Bernard Hoekman and Carlos Braga, 'Special and Differential Treatment and the Doha Development Agenda: Beyond Tariff Preferences' (Paper presented at the OECD Global Forum on Trade, *Special and Differential Treatment: Thinking Outside the Box*, Bridgetown, Barbados, 28–29 June 2005) 11.

[23] Doha Declaration, [44]. [24] Doha Implementation Decision, [12.1(i)].

Article XII',[25] which is the general safeguard provision for Members with balance of payment difficulties. Perhaps this statement would fall within the terms of Article 31(3)(a) of the VCLT as a 'subsequent agreement between the parties' on the interpretation of Article XVIII and therefore influence the interpretation of that provision. However, the broad terms of the Doha Implementation Decision provide little guidance as to how exactly they are intended to affect the reading of Article XVIII.

7.2.2 Non-discrimination and special and differential treatment

While Howse describes S&D as 'a basic tenet of the international economic legal order',[26] the WTO Director-General's Consultative Board sees it as a 'significant source of discrimination in the world trading system'.[27] This raises an important point about S&D. It is a temporary, second-best solution, or a 'necessary evil'.[28] Ideally, the MFN rule, which is an embodiment of the overarching principle of non-discrimination in the WTO as mentioned in Chapter 1, would apply across the board.[29] Until that becomes feasible, some departures from MFN are permitted, and S&D is one of them. However, it is not in the interests of either developed or developing country Members to maintain S&D indefinitely. The transitory nature of S&D[30] is reflected in the facts that certain S&D provisions apply for only a fixed period,[31] GSP donors typically exclude beneficiaries once they reach a certain

[25] Doha Implementation Decision, [1.1].

[26] Robert Howse, 'India's WTO Challenge to Drug Enforcement Conditions in the European Community Generalized System of Preferences: A Little Known Case with Major Repercussions for "Political" Conditionality in US Trade Policy' (2003) 4 *Chicago Journal of International Law* 385, 390.

[27] WTO Consultative Board, *The Future of the WTO: Addressing Institutional Challenges in the New Millennium* (2004) [88]. In June 2003, WTO Director-General Supachai Panitchpakdi established a Consultative Board of eight distinguished individuals to examine the WTO and its future. Former Director-General Peter Sutherland chaired the Consultative Board.

[28] William Kerr, 'Special and Differential Treatment: A Mechanism to Promote Development?' (2005) 6 *Estey Centre Journal of International Law and Trade Policy* 84, 88.

[29] See Bernard Hoekman and Susan Prowse, 'Policy Responses to Preference Erosion: From Trade as Aid to Aid for Trade' (Paper presented at the OECD Global Forum on Trade, *Special and Differential Treatment: Thinking Outside the Box*, Bridgetown, Barbados, 28-29 June 2005) [5], [15], [28]-[29].

[30] Keck and Low, 'Special and Differential Treatment', 8.

[31] See, e.g., SCM Agreement, art. 27.

stage of development,[32] and the value of preferences is in any case gradually being eroded as MFN tariffs decrease as envisaged in the WTO agreements.[33]

If one were to identify a hierarchy of principles of WTO law, the principle of non-discrimination would almost undoubtedly rise above the principle of S&D. This follows from the discussion in the previous paragraph, as well as the nature of the WTO as a trade organisation rather than a development organisation.[34] The conflict between S&D and non-discrimination suggests that some balancing is required to determine when the objectives of S&D outweigh those of non-discrimination. The drafters themselves spelled out the appropriate balance in many provisions. One question addressed in this chapter is whether WTO Tribunals could use a principle of S&D to determine the necessary balance in the absence of clear indications in the text of the WTO agreements.

In the following section, I explain some of the more concrete difficulties that may arise in using S&D as a procedural or interpretative principle in WTO disputes.

7.3 Potential difficulties with special and differential treatment

7.3.1 *Value of S&D to developing countries*

For the principle of S&D to be used in WTO disputes, it is not enough that it be reflected in a series of WTO provisions and in the structure of the WTO agreements. It should also have internal coherence and validity, as evidenced by the objects and purposes of the WTO. S&D is intended to provide benefits to developing country Members so that they may 'share in the growth in international trade commensurate with the needs of their economic development'.[35] But S&D does not operate effectively in the interests of developing countries in all circumstances.

32 Gene Grossman and Alan Sykes, 'A Preference for Development: the Law and Economics of GSP' (2005) 4 *World Trade Review* 41, 61; Keck and Low, 'Special and Differential Treatment', 12.

33 Hoekman and Prowse, 'Policy Responses', [2], [7]–[21], [54]; Frank Garcia, 'Beyond Special and Differential Treatment' (2004) 27 *Boston College International & Comparative Law Review* 291, 304.

34 Bernard Hoekman, 'Operationalizing the Concept of Policy Space in the WTO: Beyond Special and Differential Treatment' (2005) 8 *Journal of International Economic Law* 405, 423.

35 Marrakesh Agreement, Preamble.

In some cases this is because the principle itself is inconsistent with the needs of developing countries; in others, it is because the principle is not powerful enough to ensure results favourable to developing countries.

As mentioned earlier, under Article XXXVI:8 of GATT 1994, developed country Members 'do not expect reciprocity for commitments made by them in trade negotiations to reduce or remove tariffs and other barriers to the trade of less-developed Members'. This means that developing country Members are not expected, 'in the course of trade negotiations, to make contributions which are inconsistent with their individual development, financial and trade needs'.[36] This notion is reiterated in paragraph 5 of the Enabling Clause. Because of the principle of MFN treatment in the WTO, developing country Members should nevertheless enjoy the benefits of commitments negotiated between other Members, often on a bilateral basis. However, the ability of a developing country to secure MFN benefits through the WTO may not be as valuable as the potential to obtain benefits in areas of specific interest by negotiating reciprocal commitments.[37] In addition, developing country Members that refrain from making commitments may foreclose the advantages and opportunities of autonomous liberalisation,[38] as well as the benefits of multilateral obligations in withstanding domestic opposition to market opening from minority interest groups.[39] Hence, insisting on the right of non-reciprocity could prove prejudicial to developing countries' own interests.

Another implication of S&D in the context of negotiations is found in Article XXXVI:4 of GATT 1994, which recognises the 'continued dependence' of many developing country Members on export of 'a limited range of primary products' and provides that Members should devise measures 'to attain stable, equitable and remunerative prices' for those products. Developed country Members should also 'accord high priority to the reduction and elimination of barriers to products currently or potentially of particular export interest' to developing

36 GATT 1994, ad art. XXXVI:8.

37 See Hudec, *Developing Countries*, 180–203; Keck and Low, 'Special and Differential Treatment', 9.

38 Hoekman, 'Operationalizing the Concept of Policy Space', 409. See generally Michael Hart and Bill Dymond, 'Special and Differential Treatment and the Doha "Development" Round' (2003) 37 *Journal of World Trade* 395.

39 Hudec, *Developing Countries*, 160–3; Keck and Low, 'Special and Differential Treatment', 9.

country Members.[40] Unfortunately, many of the products of particular export interest to least-developed countries (LDCs) and other developing country Members also happen to be particularly sensitive for developed country Members, such as cotton, sugar, and other agricultural products. In the face of domestic opposition, a non-binding principle of S&D may not stand much chance. Nevertheless, the potential for liberalising markets for these products is increased through dispute settlement to enforce obligations under the SCM Agreement and the Agreement on Agriculture,[41] as well as initiatives such as the Sub-Committee on Cotton.[42]

The value of tariff preferences to developing countries, one form of S&D, has also been questioned. As already mentioned, these preferences are invariably temporary. They are also voluntary and often subject to policy-motivated conditions and costly implementation requirements.[43] Moreover,

> preferences generate interests opposed to non-discriminatory liberalization . . . Vested interests in both the export and import-competing sectors are created that resist change to the status quo, in particular further multilateral trade liberalization . . . When beneficiary countries are 'too successful', they may be dropped from schemes and left with overcapacity or a production structure that is not based on comparative advantage.[44]

All in all, the value of tariff preferences to developing countries may be quite small.[45]

One of the most obvious forms of S&D is the provision of 'technical assistance' (euphemistically termed 'technical cooperation') by the WTO Secretariat, developed country Members, and other organisations (such as the joint UNCTAD/WTO International Trade Centre) to developing country Members. This is typically conducted through seminars and workshops, held in Geneva or locally, on WTO law and practice. Yet even something as seemingly straightforward as this has given rise to numerous problems. While many developing countries have significant technical assistance needs, developed countries may be

[40] GATT 1994, art. XXXVI:1(a).

[41] See e.g., Appellate Body Report, *US – Upland Cotton*; Appellate Body Report, *EC – Sugar Exports*.

[42] July Package, Annex A [4].

[43] Keck and Low, 'Special and Differential Treatment', 11–13, 24; Hoekman and Prowse, 'Policy Responses to Preference Erosion: From Trade as Aid to Aid for Trade', [1].

[44] Keck and Low, 'Special and Differential Treatment', 13, 29–30.

[45] Grossman and Sykes, 'Preference for Development', 63.

prepared to provide such assistance only on an ad hoc basis and without accepting legal obligations to contribute specified amounts. In addition, developed countries may tend to construct technical assistance programs to pursue their own interests, such as the 'Singapore issues' and geographical indications, regardless of the direction of the negotiations.[46] Finally, some commentators emphasise that technical assistance needs to cover more than just the narrow WTO rules; it should extend to matters such as technology transfer, adjustment assistance, and capacity building.[47]

7.3.2 Distinguishing between developing countries

Another problematic aspect of S&D as a principle to be used in WTO disputes is that it does not currently provide a clear and defensible means of distinguishing between developing countries at different levels of development.[48]

The WTO agreements recognise three main categories of WTO Members: developed country Members, developing country Members, and LDC Members.[49] LDCs form a sub-category of developing countries, and are identified by the United Nations according to a low-income criterion, a human resource weakness criterion, and an economic vulnerability criterion.[50] At present, fifty LDCs exist, most of which are WTO Members or are in the process of WTO accession.[51] Other WTO Members (that is, non-LDCs) wishing to take advantage of special WTO provisions for developing countries are left to identify themselves as such, subject to challenge by other Members. This means not only that no clear criteria apply for establishing developing country status, but also that the development status of Members lacks transparency. The

[46] Olivier Cattaneo, 'Has the WTO Gone Too Far or Not Far Enough? Some Reflections on the Concept of "Policy Space"' in Andrew Mitchell (ed.), *Challenges and Prospects for the WTO* (2005) 55, 82–3. See also Mari Pangestu, 'Special and Differential Treatment in the Millennium: Special for Whom and How Different?' (2000) 23 *World Economy* 1285, 1298.

[47] Hoekman, Michalopoulos and Winters, 'Special and Differential Treatment', 501–2.

[48] On distinguishing between developing countries to determine eligibility for S&D, see Peter Kleen and Sheila Page, *Special and Differential Treatment of Developing Countries in the World Trade Organization* (2005) 79–95.

[49] A fourth category could be described as 'economies in transition'. See, e.g., GATS, art. XII:1; TRIPS Agreement, art. 65.3; SCM Agreement, art. 29.

[50] UN Economic and Social Council, *Committee for Development Policy: Report on the Sixth Session*, E/2004/33 (29 March – 2 April 2004) 15.

[51] WTO, *Least-Developed Countries*, www.wto.org/english/thewto_e/whatis_e/tif_e/org7_e.htm.

WTO Secretariat has described the membership as comprising approximately two-thirds developing countries (when there were 150 Members),[52] but it does not publish a list identifying those Members. In any case, it goes without saying that these developing countries represent an extremely wide spectrum of economies and interests.[53]

Paragraph 50 of the Doha Declaration specifically recognises the 'principle' of S&D, stating:

> The negotiations and the other aspects of the Work Programme shall take fully into account the principle of special and differential treatment for developing and least-developed countries embodied in: Part IV of the GATT 1994; the [Enabling Clause]; the Uruguay Round Decision on Measures in Favour of Least-Developed Countries; and all other relevant WTO provisions.

Some practical applications of S&D in the Doha Round of negotiations, or in WTO negotiations more generally, are expressly mandated. This round includes a specific work programme on issues relating to the trade of 'small economies'. The small economies work programme is intended to promote the 'fuller integration of small, vulnerable economies into the multilateral trading system, and not to create a subcategory of WTO Members'.[54] Thus, it is not intended to introduce a new category in addition to the recognised (although somewhat amorphous) categories of developed countries, developing countries, and LDCs. Submissions under the work programme include suggested criteria for identifying small economies[55] (a controversial matter in itself), and a proposal that small economies be granted duty and quota-free access to the markets of developed country Members[56] (which such Members 'should' already provide for agricultural products from

[52] WTO, *Understanding the WTO* (3rd edn, 2007) 93. As at 27 July 2007, 151 countries are WTO Members: WTO, *Members and Observers*, www.wto.org/english/thewto_e/whatis_e/tif_e/org6_e.htm.

[53] Jean-Christophe Bureau, Sébastien Jean and Alan Matthews, 'The Consequences of Agricultural Trade Liberalization for Developing Countries: Distinguishing between Genuine Benefits and False Hopes' (Discussion Paper No 73, Institute for International Integration Studies, April 2005) 14.

[54] Doha Declaration, [35]. See also July Package, [1(d)].

[55] WTO Committee on Trade and Development, *Work Programme on Small Economies: Communication from Antigua and Barbuda, Barbados, Bolivia, Cuba, Dominican Republic, El Salvador, Fiji, Guatemala, Honduras, Jamaica, Mauritius, Mongolia, Nicaragua, Paraguay, Sri Lanka, Trinidad and Tobago*, WT/COMTD/SE/W/12 (21 February 2005) 2.

[56] WTO Committee on Trade and Development, *Proposals Submitted by the Landlocked Developing Countries: Work Programme on Small Economies*, WT/COMTD/SE/W/10 (27 April 2004) 2.

LDCs).[57] In addition to the separate work on 'small economies', several groups of developing countries seek recognition for the special difficulties they face as, for instance, 'landlocked developing countries',[58] 'small island developing states',[59] 'newly acceded Members',[60] or 'net food-importing developing countries'.[61]

Although increasing classification of developing countries is controversial,[62] several leading economists are in favour of linking S&D more closely to the needs of individual countries. This would not necessarily require classifying each Member in one particular way for the purposes of the WTO agreements as a whole. To do so, for example on the basis of some of the groups mentioned above, might disadvantage certain developing countries that do not fit into such groups but, for example, are heavily dependent on particular products, such as Venezuela (oil)[63] and Sri Lanka (textiles and clothing).[64] Choosing a single classification might also be too arbitrary, excluding some countries that deserve to be included and including some that should be excluded.[65] Thus, classification according to specific criteria might better operate at the level of individual WTO agreements or even at the level of specific provisions, such that the criteria chosen reflect the development implications of each provision.[66] Keck and Low point to the example of Article 27.2(a)

[57] July Package, Annex A [45].

[58] WTO General Council, Committee on Trade and Development, *Communiqué of the Fifth Annual Ministerial Meeting of Landlocked Developing Countries (LLDCs)*, WT/L/585, WT/COMTD/SE/2 (7 October 2004); WTO General Council, Committee on Trade and Development, *Proposals Submitted by the Landlocked Developing Countries: Work Programme on Small Economies*, WT/COMTD/SE/W/10 (27 April 2004).

[59] WTO Committee on Agriculture, *WTO Negotiations on Agriculture: Proposals by Small Island Developing States (SIDS)*, G/AG/NG/W/97 and Corr.1 (29 December 2000).

[60] Negotiating Group on Market Access, *Market Access for Non-Agricultural Products – The Issue of Newly-Acceded Members: Submission by the Separate Customs Territory of Taiwan, Penghu, Kinmen and Matsu*, TN/MA/W/19/Add.1 (16 May 2003); July Package, Annex B [11] (see also Annex A [47]).

[61] WTO Ministerial Conference, *Decision on Measures Concerning the Possible Negative Effects of the Reform Programme on Least-Developed and Net Food-Importing Developing Countries*, LT/UR/D-1/2 (15 March 1994); WTO Committee on Agriculture, *WTO African Group: Joint Proposal on the Negotiations on Agriculture*, G/AG/NG/W/142 (23 March 2001) [7], [19]–[20].

[62] Hoekman, 'Operationalizing the Concept of Policy Space', 413, 415.

[63] WTO Committee on Trade and Development, *Trade and Economic Performance: The Role of Economic Size? Note by the Secretariat*, WT/COMTD/SE/W/5 (23 October 2002) [32].

[64] WTO Committee on Trade and Development, *Note on the Meeting of 12 May 2004*, WT/COMTD/SE/M/7 (16 July 2004) [28].

[65] Keck and Low, 'Special and Differential Treatment', 25, 27.

[66] Ibid. 9–10, 24; Hoekman, 'Operationalizing the Concept of Policy Space', 413; Hoekman and Braga, 'Special and Differential Treatment', 13.

and Annex VII of the SCM Agreement, which impose a '$1,000 GDP per capita criterion that determines whether non-LDCs can continue to apply export subsidies to manufactures'.[67]

Given that developing countries have different needs and interests, who should determine the criteria for distinguishing them? Ideally, the Members would undertake this task.[68] This has not yet occurred, although perhaps it is a possibility in the Doha Round. In the absence of an agreement on such criteria, in the context of tariff preferences it is left to developed country GSP donors to determine who to include as beneficiaries and on what grounds. Perhaps this is a better result than having WTO Tribunals establish the necessary criteria, but it presents 'the danger of a return to the pre-UNCTAD days of widespread discrimination'[69] and hence a further incursion into the greater principle of non-discrimination in the WTO. More worryingly, the Appellate Body has endorsed this situation.

EC – Tariff Preferences concerned preferential arrangements that the European Communities provided to twelve countries, to assist in combating drug trafficking, as part of its GSP scheme.[70] The main issue in dispute was whether the European Communities was entitled to grant the 'drug arrangements' to only a subset of its GSP beneficiaries. India, the complainant, was a beneficiary of the European Communities' general GSP scheme but not the drug arrangements. Pakistan was a beneficiary of both.[71] This dispute proved understandably controversial, with one of the three panelists issuing a rare dissenting opinion, and the Appellate Body reversing key aspects of the majority Panel reasoning while upholding the result.

Paragraphs 1 and 2(a) of the Enabling Clause allow developed country Members to provide '[p]referential tariff treatment . . . to products originating in developing countries in accordance with the Generalized System of Preferences'. Footnote 3 to paragraph 2(a) states: 'As described in the Decision of the CONTRACTING PARTIES of 25 June 1971, relating to the establishment of "generalized, non-reciprocal and non discriminatory preferences beneficial to the developing countries"

67 Keck and Low, 'Special and Differential Treatment', 10. 68 See ibid. 30.

69 Grossman and Sykes, 'Preference for Development', 66.

70 Panel Report, *EC – Tariff Preferences*, [2.7]; Appellate Body Report, *EC – Tariff Preferences*, [3].

71 Appellate Body Report, *EC – Tariff Preferences*, [3]–[4]. See also Panel Report, *EC – Tariff Preferences*, [7.228]–[7.235].

(BISD 18S/24)'.[72] Based in particular on the term 'non discriminatory' in this footnote, the majority of the Panel found that 'preference-giving countries [must] provide the GSP benefits to *all* developing countries without differentiation, except for the implementation of a priori limitations in GSP schemes'.[73] The majority held that the drug arrangements were inconsistent with the MFN obligation in Article I of GATT 1994 and not justified by the Enabling Clause because they were not granted to all GSP beneficiaries (nor only to LDCs).[74]

In contrast, the Appellate Body concluded that 'preference-granting countries must make available identical tariff preferences to all *similarly-situated* beneficiaries',[75] and that additional preferences may be granted to respond positively to a particular 'development, financial [or] trade need', provided that they are 'made available to all beneficiaries that share that need'.[76] The existence of the need in question should also be established objectively, for example through '[b]road-based recognition . . . set out in the *WTO Agreement* or in multilateral instruments adopted by international organizations'.[77] The Appellate Body nevertheless upheld the Panel's findings that the drug arrangements were not justified by the Enabling Clause because the European Communities granted them to a 'closed list' of beneficiaries and set out 'no criteria or standards to provide a basis for distinguishing beneficiaries under the Drug Arrangements from other GSP beneficiaries'.[78]

To a lawyer, permitting this kind of differentiation among GSP beneficiaries may seem reasonable in the abstract. However, Grossman and Sykes explain that additional preferences such as the drug arrangements are likely to divert trade away from GSP beneficiaries that are not entitled to these preferences (such as India, in this dispute) and towards those that are (such as Pakistan).[79] As a result, the gains of the latter group of developing countries will often come at the expense of the former, with the developed, preference-granting country (the European Communities) furthering its political goals at little cost.[80] On the other hand, a blanket prohibition on discrimination of this kind

[72] In paragraph 12.2 of the Doha Implementation Decision, the Ministerial Conference '[r]eaffirm[ed] that preferences granted to developing countries pursuant to the . . . Enabling Clause . . . should be generalized, non-reciprocal and non-discriminatory'.

[73] Panel Report, *EC – Tariff Preferences*, [7.144] (original emphasis). [74] Ibid. [7.177].

[75] Appellate Body Report, *EC – Tariff Preferences*, [154] (emphasis added). [76] Ibid. [165].

[77] Ibid. [163]. [78] Ibid. [187]–[188].

[79] Grossman and Sykes, 'Preference for Development', 60, 64.

[80] Ibid. 65. See also Keck and Low, 'Special and Differential Treatment', 29.

might cause developed countries to scale down their GSP schemes or withdraw them altogether. Law alone can no more determine the best way of balancing these problems than can economics – the requisite 'empirical and political analysis'[81] to define the scope of allowable differentiation among developing countries is therefore better left to the Members than to WTO Tribunals. This throws further doubt on the utility of S&D as a principle in WTO disputes.

7.3.3 Conflicting developing country interests

A related concern with S&D as a principle of WTO law is that it may not be sufficiently mature or detailed to provide informative guidance in particular instances involving more than one developing country. Given that developing countries may have vastly different concerns and interests, it will frequently be impossible to identify the response that will best serve developing countries.[82] In the absence of textual specificity in the WTO agreements, S&D may therefore be something of an empty shell.

Article 12.10 of the DSU contains a fairly straightforward S&D provision, requiring Panels examining a complaint against a developing country Member to 'accord sufficient time for the developing country Member to prepare and present its argumentation'. Hence, in *India – Quantitative Restrictions*, which was a case brought by the United States against India, the Panel granted India an additional ten days to prepare its submission.[83]

Other S&D provisions are more ambiguous. For example, Article 21.2 of the DSU states that '[p]articular attention should be paid to matters affecting the interests of developing country Members with respect to measures which have been subject to dispute settlement'. However, it does not say who should pay particular attention (presumably Panels and the Appellate Body, but does it also include other Members?) or which developing country Members are relevant (only those party to the dispute, or only a Member whose measure is subject to challenge?).[84] The application of this broad provision may therefore

[81] Grossman and Sykes, 'Preference for Development', 65–6.

[82] For a discussion of the compliance problems caused by the failure to take into account the divergent needs of developing countries in applying the principle of S&D within an international environmental context, see Bafundo, 'Compliance with the Ozone Treaty'.

[83] Panel Report, *India – Quantitative Restrictions*, [5.10].

[84] Article 21.3(c) Arbitration Award, *EC – Tariff Preferences*, [59].

pull in opposite directions, as it did in the arbitration to determine the period of time for implementation in *Chile – Price Band System*, where the arbitrator (Appellate Body member John Lockhart) recognised that 'Chile may indeed face obstacles as a developing country in its implementation of the recommendations and rulings of the DSB, and that Argentina, likewise, faces continuing hardship as a developing country so long as the WTO-inconsistent PBS is maintained'.[85]

This example, found in the context of arbitrations under Article 21.3(c) of the DSU, reflects broader complicating factors in the use of S&D as a principle. Increasingly, WTO disputes are not between a developed country Member on one side and a developing country Member on the other. Even when disputes like this arise, they may involve developing country interests on both sides. For instance, in *EC – Tariff Preferences*, if the question had been merely whether the European Communities could grant tariff preferences to developing countries, then, even apart from the Enabling Clause, a principle of S&D might have indicated that it could do so. However, the case pitted the interests of one developing country (India, who did not benefit from the drug arrangements) against those of several others (namely the twelve beneficiaries of the drug arrangements, who might be disadvantaged if the drug arrangements were extended to all of the European Communities' GSP beneficiaries). Indeed, at the Panel stage, 17 developing country Members were third parties, supporting different sides of the dispute.[86] Other disputes, of course, involve developing country Members as both complainant and respondent, as occurred recently in *Dominican Republic – Import and Sale of Cigarettes* (involving a complaint by Honduras) and in *Korea – Paper* (involving a complaint by Indonesia).[87]

Preferences provided by the European Communities provide another example of conflicting developing country interests, not in connection with drug trafficking but in connection with bananas. At Doha, WTO Members granted the European Communities a limited waiver from its MFN obligations under Article I:1 of GATT 1994 in respect of its preferential tariff treatment for African, Caribbean and Pacific (ACP) countries, including for bananas imported from those countries.[88]

[85] Article 21.3(c) Arbitration Award, *Chile – Price Band System*, [56].
[86] Most of these countries were also third participants in the appeal.
[87] *Korea – Anti-Dumping Duties on Certain Imports of Paper from Indonesia: Communication from the Chairman of the Panel* (WT/DS312/4, 25 April 2005).
[88] WTO Ministerial Conference, *European Communities – the ACP–EC Partnership Agreement: Decision of 14 November 2001* (WT/MIN(01)/15, 14 November 2001) Annex. See also

According to the waiver, from 1 January 2006, a new 'tariff only' regime was to replace the current tariff quota regime.[89] On 31 January 2005, the European Communities notified the WTO of its intentions regarding the structure of the new tariff only regime.[90] Several non-ACP developing countries contested the European Communities' proposal. Pursuant to the terms of the waiver, the matter was subject to arbitration.[91] This involved a direct clash of the interests of the ACP countries and those of Brazil, Colombia, Costa Rica, Ecuador, Guatemala, Honduras, Nicaragua, Panama, and Venezuela.[92]

Another example of developing countries' interests being non-aligned is in relation to textiles and clothing. Article 9 of the ATC provided for that agreement to terminate on the first day of the 121st month that the Marrakesh Agreement is in effect – thus, it expired after ten years, on 1 January 2005. With the expiry of the ATC, textiles and clothing are now subject to the same WTO rules as other goods, and import quotas that were temporarily allowed under the ATC must be eliminated. Most of these quotas were imposed by developed countries on developing country imports, such that imports from developing countries like China and India with a comparative advantage in the sector were restricted by quotas, and imports from developing countries without a comparative advantage were encouraged through the opportunity of filling assigned quotas.[93] Some feared that the end of this trade distortion would lead to huge increases in the market shares of China and India, to the detriment of other developing countries in

WTO Ministerial Conference, *European Communities – Transitional Regime for the EC Autonomous Tariff Rate Quotas on Imports of Bananas: Decision of 14 November 2001*, WT/MIN(01)/16 (14 November 2001).

89 Commission of the European Communities, *Report from the Commission to the European Parliament and the Council on the Operation of the Common Organisation of the Market in Bananas* (Brussels, COM(2005) 50 final) 6.

90 European Commission, *Press Release – Banana Imports: Commission Announces Envisaged New Tariff for Bananas to the WTO*, IP/05/118 (31 January 2005).

91 WTO Ministerial Conference, *European Communities – the ACP–EC Partnership Agreement: Decision of 14 November 2001*, WT/MIN(01)/15 (14 November 2001) Annex.

92 Award of the Arbitrator, *European Communities – the ACP–EC Partnership Agreement – Recourse to Arbitration Pursuant to the Decision of 14 November 2001*, WT/L/616, 1 August 2005.

93 Hildegunn Kyvik Nordås, *The Global Textile and Clothing Industry Post the Agreement on Textiles and Clothing* (Discussion Paper No 5, WTO, 2004) 13, 34; Garcia, 'Beyond Special and Differential Treatment', 304.

particular.[94] When China became a Member of the WTO at the end of 2001, its accession protocol included a 'Transitional Product-Specific Safeguard Mechanism' to allow other Members to respond to remedy market disruption caused by increased Chinese imports.[95] In response to political pressure, China also voluntarily imposed export tariffs on certain textiles to coincide with the end of the ATC.[96]

These examples demonstrate the difficulty of applying any broad S&D principle not explicitly contained in the WTO agreements. Although it may be fairly uncontroversial that developing country Members are entitled to S&D relative to developed country Members, frequently what is good for one developing country Member will be detrimental to another. When developing country interests conflict, the S&D principle becomes less useful for resolving problems in interpreting WTO provisions. That is not to say that the principle of S&D has no place in the WTO agreements or that it should be abandoned, but it does caution against careless use of the principle.

7.4 Using special and differential treatment in WTO disputes

7.4.1 S&D and WTO Tribunals' inherent jurisdiction regarding procedural matters

Keeping in mind the difficulties of the principle of S&D outlined in the previous section, I now consider how S&D might be used in WTO disputes. One practical way in which S&D may be used in the WTO is in dispute settlement proceedings – not for the purpose of interpreting WTO provisions, but in the management of specific disputes. Only a few developing countries, such as Brazil and India, have extensive experience of WTO dispute settlement. The time and financial cost of being involved in a dispute, even as a third party, is too high for many developing countries.[97] Lack of experience, in turn, may prevent developing countries from pursuing their rights in disputes. The

[94] See, e.g., US International Trade Commission, *Textiles and Apparel: Assessment of the Competitiveness of Certain Foreign Suppliers to the U.S. Market* (Publication No 3671, January 2004) xi–xii.

[95] WTO Ministerial Conference, *Accession of the People's Republic of China: Decision of 10 November 2001*, WT/L/432 (23 November 2001) 9–10.

[96] 'China Announces Increased Export Tariffs on Textiles', *People's Daily Online*, 13 December 2004; 'Unquotable', *The Economist*, 28 December 2004.

[97] Bernard Hoekman and Petros Mavroidis, 'WTO Dispute Settlement, Transparency and Surveillance' (2000) 23 *World Economy* 527, 532, 535.

Advisory Centre on WTO Law (ACWL) now provides training and legal advice on WTO law to developing countries, and supports these countries in WTO disputes. The ACWL's fees are relatively low and vary according to the circumstances of the relevant country. This may be seen as one example of S&D in operation, albeit outside the formal ambit of the WTO agreements and the WTO Tribunals. However, few of the poorest WTO Members are ever likely to be involved in disputes, since their markets are too small to be of economic significance to other Members.

The WTO agreements are full of S&D provisions in relation to dispute settlement procedure. Under the DSU, a developing country Member in a dispute with a developed country Member may request that the Panel include at least one panelist from a developing country Member.[98] Where a developing country Member brings a complaint, the DSB, in considering what action to take, must take into account 'not only the trade coverage of measures complained of, but also their impact on the economy of developing country Members concerned'.[99] Under Article 24.1 of the DSU, 'particular consideration shall be given to the special situation of [LDCs]' at all stages in disputes involving LDC Members. In addition, Members are to 'exercise due restraint in raising matters under these procedures involving [an LDC]'.[100] These S&D provisions relate to material aspects of dispute settlement, although, like many such provisions in the WTO agreements, they may be difficult to enforce. Moreover, many of these provisions focus on disputes involving developing countries as parties, but issues related to development and developing countries may arise in other disputes. Thus, some contend that the requirement of a developing country panelist should extend to all disputes, and Appellate Body divisions as well.[101]

Panels and the Appellate Body have, in several disputes, accorded some leeway to developing countries in procedural matters, in view of applicable S&D provisions.[102] For example, Article 12.11 of the DSU requires that Panels 'explicitly indicate the form in which account has been taken of relevant [S&D provisions] that . . . have been raised by' a developing country Member that is a party to the dispute. Relying on this provision, the Panel in *US – Offset Act (Byrd Amendment)* addressed an

[98] DSU, art. 8.10. [99] DSU, art. 21.8. [100] DSU, art. 24.1.

[101] See Asif Qureshi, 'Interpreting World Trade Organization Agreements for the Development Objective' (2003) 37 *Journal of World Trade* 847, 860–1.

[102] See the cases discussed ibid. 857–9.

S&D provision in the Anti-Dumping Agreement despite the failure of the complainants (several of whom were developing countries) to mention this provision in their requests for establishment of a Panel.[103] Ordinarily, such an omission would have resulted in the provision falling outside the Panel's terms of reference.[104] Perhaps the Panel was relying on the principle of S&D to permit the consideration of S&D provisions in cases involving developing countries, whether or not the parties have raised such provisions.

The Panel in *India – Quantitative Restrictions* referred expressly to the 'principle' of S&D.[105] In response to Article 12.11 of the DSU, the Panel stated that Article XVIII:B of GATT 1994 'embodies' the 'principle of special and differential treatment',[106] and indicated that '[t]his entire part G [of the Panel report] reflects our consideration of relevant provisions on special and differential treatment, as does Section VII of our report (suggestions for implementation)'.[107] The Panel also referred to Article 21.2 of the DSU, which states that '[p]articular attention should be paid to matters affecting the interests of developing country Members with respect to measures which have been subject to dispute settlement'. It suggested that the 'principle of special and differential treatment' underscored the importance of certain factors related to India's development that should be taken into account in establishing the 'reasonable period of time' for India to implement its WTO obligations by bringing its inconsistent measure into conformity with the WTO agreements.[108] These factors included, for example, a recommendation by the IMF that the relevant measures be phased out rather than immediately removed, and bilateral agreements between India and other Members for gradual elimination of the measures.[109]

Several of the difficulties faced by developing countries in making effective use of the WTO dispute settlement system cannot be addressed through the current S&D provisions or assistance from the ACWL. Rather, they stem directly from fundamental aspects of the system such as the compliance procedure, under which suspension of concessions is the last resort. As developing countries may be unable to avail themselves of this ultimate remedy in many circumstances,[110] several more

[103] Panel Report, *US – Offset Act (Byrd Amendment)*, [7.87].
[104] Appellate Body Report, *EC – Bananas III*, [142].
[105] The Appellate Body did not address this aspect of the Panel's reasoning on appeal.
[106] Panel Report, *India – Quantitative Restrictions*, [5.157]. [107] Ibid. [5.157].
[108] Ibid. [7.6]. [109] Ibid. [7.5].
[110] Hoekman and Mavroidis, 'WTO Dispute Settlement', 531.

development-friendly proposals have been put forward in the negotiations on DSU reform – for example, requiring consideration of other forms of compensation.[111] Other proposals focus on the practical difficulties faced by LDCs in engaging in disputes, for example by mandating consultations in the LDC capital where an LDC is party to a dispute.[112]

Could WTO Tribunals exercise their inherent jurisdiction to resolve procedural matters in individual disputes taking into account the principle of S&D? Presumably they could, such that they could allow developing countries additional flexibility in the course of disputes even in the absence of a specific S&D provision. However, the potential for developing country interests to collide in a given dispute and the wide differences in the levels of development of developing countries mean that it may be difficult for WTO Tribunals to apply this principle in any meaningful way without textual direction. In addition, as explained in Chapter 3, WTO Tribunals should use principles in the exercise of inherent jurisdiction only where necessary to the maintenance of subject-matter jurisdiction and the judicial function. WTO Tribunals are likely to achieve a better and more legitimate result simply by exercising their discretion taking into account the particular circumstances before them rather than any preconceived notion of S&D. Finally, apart from the DSU provisions precluding the addition or diminution of rights or obligations by WTO Tribunals,[113] the procedural limits on inherent jurisdiction mean that WTO Tribunals could not use this method to rework the DSU framework of implementation and retaliation from a developing country perspective, even if they considered this part of their role.

7.4.2 S&D in interpreting the WTO agreements

A. Significance of S&D: a 'mere' exception?

If WTO Tribunals were to use S&D as a principle in interpreting any WTO provisions, this would need to be balanced against the principle of non-discrimination, as explained earlier in this chapter. The question therefore arises whether S&D is an 'exception' to non-discrimination (specifically the MFN rule) and, if so, whether this has any impact on its value as an interpretative principle. In the Doha Declaration,[114] the

[111] WTO Dispute Settlement Body, *Special Session of the Dispute Settlement Body: Report by the Chairman, Ambassador Péter Balás, to the Trade Negotiations Committee*, TN/DS/9 (6 June 2003) 14.

[112] Ibid. 3. [113] DSU arts. 3.2, 19.2. [114] Doha Declaration, [44].

Ministerial Conference specifically took note of the 'Proposal for a Framework Agreement on Special and Differential Treatment' made by Cuba, the Dominican Republic, Honduras, India, Indonesia, Kenya, Malaysia, Pakistan, Sri Lanka, Tanzania, Uganda and Zimbabwe in July 2001.[115] This proposal describes S&D as 'a fundamental building bloc[k] of the multilateral trading system' that is 'to be looked at not as [an] *exceptio[n]* to the general rules but . . . as an integral and inherent objective of the multilateral trading system'.[116]

The suggestion that S&D is not an exception to the MFN rule is countered by the Appellate Body decision in *EC – Tariff Preferences*. GSP schemes are allowed under the Enabling Clause '[n]otwithstanding' the MFN obligation imposed by Article I of GATT 1994. Before addressing the drug arrangements themselves, the Panel in this dispute examined the relationship between Article I of GATT 1994 and the Enabling Clause in order to determine who bore the burden of proof: that is, did India have to establish that the drug arrangements were inconsistent with the Enabling Clause, or did the European Communities have to establish that the drug arrangements were consistent with the Enabling Clause as a defence to inconsistency with Article I? The majority of the Panel found that the Enabling Clause was an exception to Article I, based, *inter alia*, on the optional nature of the Enabling Clause (in the sense that it does not oblige Members to adopt GSP schemes) and the use of the word '[n]otwithstanding' in paragraph 1 of the Enabling Clause. Therefore, according to the majority, after India had demonstrated inconsistency with Article I, it was up to the European Communities to establish that the Enabling Clause provided a defence to this inconsistency.[117]

The anonymous dissenter (United States Professor Marsha Echols, according to Howse)[118] found that the Enabling Clause is not an exception to the MFN rule in Article I. Rather, the Enabling Clause 'is the applicable WTO rule regarding tariff preferences for developing countries'.[119] India should therefore have brought its claim under the Enabling Clause rather than Article I, and its apparent failure to do so meant that the claim should be dismissed.[120] This conclusion was

[115] General Council, 'Preparations for the Fourth Session of the Ministerial Conference: Proposal for a Framework Agreement on Special and Differential Treatment', WT/GC/W/442 (31 July 2001).

[116] Ibid. [1] (emphasis added). [117] Panel Report, *EC – Tariff Preferences*, [7.39].

[118] Howse, 'India's WTO Challenge', 404. [119] Panel Report, *EC – Tariff Preferences*, [9.2].

[120] Ibid. [9.21].

based in part on reading the word '[n]otwithstanding' in paragraph 1 of the Enabling Clause as meaning that Members have the right to grant preferences within the terms of the Enabling Clause, 'despite' Article I and not as an 'exception' to Article I.[121] The dissenter also viewed the Enabling Clause as reflecting the GATT contracting parties' 'expect[ation] and desir[e] that the right to grant tariff preferences be exercised'.[122]

In surprisingly brief reasoning focusing on the word 'notwithstanding' in paragraph 1, the Appellate Body held that the Enabling Clause is an exception to the MFN principle in Article I:1.[123] Nevertheless, like the dissenting panelist, the Appellate Body reviewed the history of the Enabling Clause within GATT/WTO and concluded that it has a 'special status' and, unlike other WTO exceptions, it actually encourages Members to provide preferences within its terms.[124] On this basis, the Appellate Body held that India was required, in its claim, to raise the aspects of the Enabling Clause that it regarded as contrary to the European Communities' drug arrangements, and the European Communities was then required to establish that its measure fulfilled those aspects.[125] The Appellate Body found that India had, in fact, sufficiently raised the Enabling Clause in its claim.[126]

In defending its regulation in *EC – Tariff Preferences*, the European Communities emphasised the 'principle' of S&D,[127] but the Panel and the Appellate Body refrained from describing the concept in this way. In contrast, the Appellate Body referred twice to the 'MFN principle' embodied in Article I:1 of GATT 1994[128] and the Panel relied on the 'principle' of non-discrimination, not only as reflected in the Preamble and Articles I and III of GATT 1994, but also as reflected in the Enabling Clause itself.[129] One cannot assume that the Panel and Appellate Body deliberately shied away from the word 'principle' in the context of S&D. However, the context of the relevant pronouncements suggests that this omission was intended to have some meaning. The Appellate Body

[121] Ibid. [9.13]. [122] Ibid. [9.16].

[123] Appellate Body Report, *EC – Tariff Preferences*, [90].

[124] Ibid. [107], [111], [114]. However, developed country Members are not obliged to establish GSP schemes: see Lorand Bartels, 'The WTO Enabling Clause and Positive Conditionality in the European Community's GSP Program' (2003) 6 *Journal of International Economic Law* 507, 513.

[125] Appellate Body Report, *EC – Tariff Preferences*, [118]. [126] Ibid. [125].

[127] Ibid. [14], [27], [93]; Panel Report, *EC – Tariff Preferences*, [4.42].

[128] Appellate Body Report, *EC – Tariff Preferences*, [89], [101].

[129] Panel Report, *EC – Tariff Preferences*, [7.144], [7.157].

called the Enabling Clause 'an integral part of the GATT 1994' but then decided that the Enabling Clause was an exception to the MFN principle in Article I:1.[130] Perhaps the Appellate Body was of the view that something as important as a 'principle' could not be characterised as a mere 'exception', even though it hastened to add that 'the characterization of the Enabling Clause as an exception in no way diminishes the right of Members to provide or to receive "differential and more favourable treatment" '.[131]

This dispute illustrates the difficulties of using a principle such as S&D that directly contradicts another WTO principle in interpreting particular provisions. The hierarchy between non-discrimination and S&D that I posited earlier suggests that S&D is in fact an exception to the MFN rule. However, it is difficult to identify the implications of this conclusion. On the one hand, it could be said that the rule should have primacy in the case of doubt. On the other, it could be said that the exception by definition overrides the rule. The answer to this dilemma is probably that S&D should not be regarded as an independent interpretative principle.

B. S&D as an interpretative principle

The three WTO trade remedy agreements – the Anti-Dumping Agreement, the SCM Agreement, and the Agreement on Safeguards – contain specific provisions regarding the application of their provisions to developing country Members and the use of trade remedies against such Members. These provide an interesting case study of S&D provisions because they relate to the consideration of S&D treatment not only by Panels and the Appellate Body but also by domestic authorities of (typically, developed country) Members. I focus in particular on certain provisions of the Agreement on Safeguards and the Anti-Dumping Agreement.

The Agreement on Safeguards contains two main S&D provisions – one precluding the application of safeguard measures against products from developing country Members in certain circumstances, and one allowing developing country Members to impose safeguard measures for longer periods of time than other Members. Under Article 9.1, Members are not to apply safeguard measures against a product originating in a developing country Member 'as long as its share of imports of the product concerned in the importing Member does not exceed

[130] Appellate Body Report, *EC – Tariff Preferences*, [90]. [131] Ibid. [98].

3 per cent, provided that developing country Members with less than 3 per cent import share collectively account for not more than 9 per cent of total imports of the product concerned'. This is an exception to the general MFN rule as applied in the safeguards context, whereby safeguard measures are to apply to imports of the relevant product from all sources.[132]

A developing country's entitlement to the exemption under Article 9.1 of the Agreement on Safeguards depends not on an abstract measure of that country's development but on the impact of that country's exports on the importing Member, whether alone or together with imports from other developing country Members. Article 9.1 therefore sets out the boundary between S&D and the interests of all Members in protecting themselves from increased imports. Thus, WTO Tribunals need not refer to any broader S&D principle to interpret this provision. However, the precision of the boundary established in Article 9.1 contrasts with many other S&D provisions, where Members were unable to agree detailed rules.

The first sentence of Article 15 of the Anti-Dumping Agreement requires developed country Members, when considering whether to impose anti-dumping duties, to give 'special regard . . . to the special situation of developing country Members'. Like many S&D provisions, this is a fairly vague requirement, and a WTO Panel has found that it 'imposes no specific or general obligation on Members to undertake any particular action' because 'Members cannot be expected to comply with an obligation whose parameters are entirely undefined'.[133] This reading seems to render the first sentence of Article 15 inutile, as does the somewhat more generous suggestion that the 'operational modalities of the first sentence' are articulated in the second sentence.[134] Panels have also interpreted narrowly the second sentence of Article 15, which requires Members to 'explor[e]' the '[p]ossibilities of constructive remedies . . . before applying anti-dumping duties where they would affect the essential interests of developing country Members'. According to certain Panels, a Member cannot breach this obligation before it imposes definitive anti-dumping duties,[135] leaving developing country Members with no preventative measure in the interim. Moreover,

[132] Agreement on Safeguards, art. 2.2. [133] Panel Report, *US – Steel Plate*, [7.110].
[134] Panel Report, *EC – Tube or Pipe Fittings*, [7.68].
[135] See, e.g., ibid. [7.82]; Panel Report, *EC – Bed Linen (Article 21.5 – India)*, [6.258]–[6.260].

the verb 'explore' has also been narrowly interpreted,[136] such that Members need merely go through the motions of considering constructive remedies in order to comply with Article 15.

One commentator describes the non-mandatory nature of most S&D provisions as a 'birth defect'.[137] However, it is hard to justify the use of S&D as an interpretative principle to address this defect, particularly when Members are engaged in such a process themselves, as mentioned above. The Panel in *EC – Tube or Pipe Fittings* specifically noted that the Doha Implementation Decision directs the Committee on Anti-Dumping Practices to make recommendations on 'operationaliz[ing]' Article 15. The Panel did not consider it its 'task to presuppose the outcome of these discussions'.[138] Indeed, even to the extent that the S&D principle is reflected in relevant text, context, or object and purpose within the meaning of Article 31(1) of the VCLT, WTO Tribunals are rightly inclined to adopt a cautious approach to the interpretation of S&D provisions, since Members disagree on the benefits, meaning, and future of S&D.

The Appellate Body has found that S&D applies 'under the *Agreement on Agriculture*, only where and to the extent that it is specifically provided for in that Agreement', because Article 15 of the Agreement on Agriculture states that 'special and differential treatment in respect of commitments shall be provided as set out in the relevant provisions of this Agreement and embodied in the Schedules of concessions and commitments'.[139] Thus, the Appellate Body does not appear to preclude the possibility that S&D could apply more broadly in WTO agreements that do not specifically circumscribe the scope of S&D.

This door should be closed. If the principle of S&D may be of limited use in interpreting S&D provisions, it is even less likely to play a legitimate role in interpreting other WTO provisions. Thus, the Panel in *US – Upland Cotton* properly refused to alter its interpretation of WTO provisions on the grounds that no 'substantive' S&D provision applied in the particular circumstances of the case. Presumably, this Panel distinguished such provisions from merely 'procedural' S&D provisions specifically. The Panel declined to allow the status of Benin and Chad as LDCs to affect its interpretation of Articles 5(c) and 6.3(c) of the SCM

136 See, e.g., Panel Report, *US – Steel Plate*, [7.114]; Panel Report, *EC – Bed Linen*, [6.233].

137 Gustavo Olivares, 'The Case for Giving Effectiveness to GATT/WTO Rules on Developing Countries and LDCs' (2001) 35 *Journal of World Trade* 545, 551.

138 Panel Report, *EC – Tube or Pipe Fittings*, [7.85].

139 Appellate Body Report, *Chile – Price Band System*, [197].

Agreement,[140] and it also refused to interpret the word 'significant' in Article 6.3(c) (in the context of significant price suppression) having regard to the developing country status of the complainant, Brazil.[141]

Qureshi proposes the recognition of a 'development dimension' in interpreting the WTO agreements, including 'a focus on those aspects of the interpretative process that . . . lend themselves to . . . reduce or alleviate some of the burdens that accompany trade liberalization' and 'facilitate fair play between the different types of membership of the WTO'.[142] He contends that this approach is already reflected in the traditional technique of examining the object and purpose of the treaty, given that the development objective is reflected in several provisions, such as the Preamble to the Marrakesh Agreement.[143] Garcia calls on the WTO to replace the ideology of free trade with a focus on development and fairness.[144] This may be a valid approach for WTO Members to discuss in negotiations. However, an open-ended use of S&D as an interpretative principle cannot be justified by either the strict terms of Articles 31 and 32 of the VCLT or the nature of S&D. The value and scope of S&D is contested among WTO Members, and the WTO Tribunals are not well-placed to draw distinctions between different developing countries or to select 'development-friendly' outcomes.

7.5 Conclusion

S&D has a long history in GATT/WTO. Several aspects of S&D make it a less than ideal example of a useful 'principle' in WTO dispute settlement. First, its content is uncertain. Although some S&D provisions are quite detailed, many are vague and amorphous, reflecting the absence of agreement on more concrete application of the principle. Second, the different needs of developing countries in different situations and at different stages of development limit the utility of a general S&D principle. In interpreting the WTO agreements, such a principle may provide some guidance where it is reflected in an applicable provision or directly relevant context or object and purpose, but it will often be unable to resolve questions where developing country interests are opposed. Nor can a coherent S&D principle be established to direct

[140] Panel Report, *US – Upland Cotton*, [7.1409]–[7.1413]. [141] Ibid. [7.1331].

[142] Asif Qureshi, 'Interpreting World Trade Organization Agreements for the Development Objective' (2003) 37 *Journal of World Trade*, 847, 851.

[143] Ibid. 854. [144] Garcia, 'Beyond Special and Differential Treatment', 300–1.

WTO Tribunals in their exercise of inherent jurisdiction regarding procedural matters affecting developing country Members. Finally, the fact that S&D is a temporary derogation from the key principle of non-discrimination in the WTO means that the two principles must be carefully balanced. To the extent possible, it is for WTO Members and not WTO Tribunals to determine the appropriate trade-off between these principles.

8 Conclusion

8.1 A principled approach

The use of principles in WTO dispute settlement as proposed in this book would not mark a radical break with the tradition of WTO Tribunals. However, it would involve a clearer articulation of the legal basis and justification for using principles, and a more precise investigation of the nature and scope of principles used. In this book I have identified three types of principles that are capable of reasonably clear definition, have a recognised basis in international law, and are suitable for examination in the specific context of the WTO, namely: principles of WTO law; principles of customary international law; and general principles of law. In many cases, these types of principles can and should be used by WTO Tribunals to interpret WTO provisions. In a narrower set of circumstances, WTO Tribunals should be prepared to use certain principles in non-interpretative ways, for example to resolve procedural issues.

The need for principles in interpreting the WTO agreements is inevitable, given the inherent uncertainty of language and gaps in treaties. Moreover, an important objective of the WTO dispute settlement system is certainty: in particular, the 'security and predictability to the multilateral trading system'. As Lord Mansfield stated in *Vallejo* v. *Wheeler*:

> [i]n all mercantile transactions the great object should be certainty: and therefore, it is of more consequence that a rule should be certain, than whether the rule is established one way or the other. Because speculators in trade then know what ground to go upon.[1]

[1] (1774) 1 Cowp 143, 153; 98 ER 1012, 1017.

By contributing to the clarification of WTO provisions and the coherence of WTO Tribunals' decisions, principles can assist in achieving security and predictability in multilateral trade.

WTO Members frequently refer to 'principles' in connection with WTO disputes. The following extracts from the minutes of certain DSB meetings reflect some Members' concerns about the way WTO Tribunals have used principles in resolving disputes to date:

> 'General principles of international law' were not listed in the covered agreements set forth in Appendix 1 of the DSU, and a WTO adjudicatory body had no authority to enforce those principles.[2]

> There was a distinction between the rules of interpretation and the rights and obligations under customary international law. Members agreed to be subject to dispute settlement proceedings to deal with disputes which involved their rights and obligations under the covered agreements. Members did not intend the WTO to be the arbiter of their rights and obligations under customary international law.[3]

> The United States believed it was inappropriate for the Appellate Body to develop a new 'principle' not based in the text ... Proportionality had no relevance when the duration, magnitude, and scope of the remedy was prescribed in the agreement.[4]

> Nowhere in Appendix 1 to the DSU, which defined the covered agreements for purposes of the DSU, was there listed an international law principle of good faith ... A finding that a Member had not acted in 'good faith' would clearly and unambiguously exceed the mandate of dispute settlement panels and the Appellate Body set forth in Articles 7, 11 and 19 of the DSU, to confine their findings to the question of conformity with the covered agreements cited in a panel request, and not to add to or diminish the rights and obligations under those agreements.[5]

The framework for principles set out in this book addresses these concerns. It establishes the particular circumstances in which WTO

[2] DSB, *Minutes of the Dispute Settlement Body Meeting Held on 18 March 2003*, WT/DSB/M/145 (7 May 2003) [49] (United States).

[3] DSB, *Minutes of the Dispute Settlement Body Meeting Held on 19 June 2000*, WT/DSB/M/84 (24 July 2000) [64] (Philippines).

[4] DSB, *Minutes of the Dispute Settlement Body Meeting Held on 5 November 2001*, WT/DSB/M/112 (4 December 2001) [34] (United States).

[5] DSB, *Minutes of the Dispute Settlement Body Meeting Held on 27 January 2003*, WT/DSB/M/142 (27 January 2003) [57] (United States).

Tribunals may use different types of principles, the ways in which they may use principles, and the concrete legal basis for doing so.

WTO Tribunals are to interpret WTO provisions in accordance with Articles 31 and 32 of the VCLT, even if the resulting interpretation involves a departure from a general principle of law, a principle of customary international law, or a principle of WTO law. Thus, for example, certain WTO provisions, properly interpreted, depart from the principle of proportionality in international law outside the WTO. Nevertheless, the scope for using principles in interpreting WTO provisions is certainly larger than that for using principles as the basis for claims or as applicable law. If the WTO Tribunals are to apply a general principle of law such as good faith as an independent source of substantive rights or obligations in WTO disputes, they must identify the grounds for doing so in WTO law. Turning to the example of the principle of due process, WTO Tribunals are correct in using this principle to resolve procedural matters in the exercise of their inherent jurisdiction. When these requirements are respected, there is no question of adding to or diminishing the rights and obligations of WTO Members. Furthermore, if a principle is too vague or its value too contested (as is the case with S&D), it should be set aside until its content is more reliable and definable.

8.2 Summary of the book

In the introduction (Chapter 1), I explained the necessity of going beyond the explicit rules contained in the WTO agreements in dispute settlement, specifically the need to utilise principles that underlie the WTO system or derive from sources of law outside the WTO. Although the term 'principles' is frequently employed, many of the most fundamental aspects of principles are taken for granted. Therefore, this chapter discussed the distinction between rules and principles and the normative and descriptive theories of principles. It then considered the concept of interpretation of legal texts and its relationship to principles, establishing a definition of 'interpretation' for the rest of the book. The chapter then explained the important interpretative and evaluative role that principles may play in WTO disputes, taking into account the position of the WTO within the broader field of international law and the possible concerns of Members and commentators about such a role.

Part I of the book established a framework for the use of principles in WTO disputes, which provided a backdrop for the case studies of individual principles in Part II.

In Chapter 2, I identified three broad types of principles that are of particular relevance to WTO disputes: principles of WTO law, principles of customary international law, and general principles of law. I also gave several examples of principles that could be used in WTO disputes, demonstrating the variety of potentially relevant principles, even though only four are taken up in Part II. In the course of this chapter I considered certain possible criticisms that could be made of customary international law and general principles of law in particular, as it is necessary to face these criticisms in order to determine whether the types of principles chosen have solid legal foundations. The principles introduced in Chapter 2 illustrated how WTO Tribunals have used certain principles and some potential difficulties in their definition and use.

Chapter 3 explained the most important ways in which WTO Tribunals could use principles of WTO law, principles of customary international law, and general principles of law. Broadly, WTO Tribunals can use principles drawn from these categories to interpret WTO provisions, based on Article 3.2 of the DSU, and Articles 31 and 32 of the VCLT. This follows most directly from a teleological approach to interpretation, but principles also feature under subjective and textual approaches to interpretation. WTO Tribunals may also use certain principles in a non-interpretative manner. Indeed, this may be a necessity, particularly to address procedural issues. Precisely how a principle may be used depends on its type, content and status.

Part II of the book examined in detail four principles that could be used in WTO dispute settlement.

The principle of good faith was the focus of Chapter 4. The definition of good faith in international law has been largely elusive, and its indefinite boundaries complicate its use in the WTO. Nevertheless, good faith is almost certainly a general principle of law and a principle of customary international law. It is also a principle of WTO law that is reflected in several provisions of the DSU. WTO Tribunals may use the principle of good faith not merely to interpret WTO provisions, but also in the exercise of their inherent jurisdiction, for example in employing the doctrine of estoppel, which is one particularisation of good faith. However, the use of good faith in WTO dispute settlement entails three important considerations and qualifications. First, the principle should not be used to overwhelm WTO provisions that appear to be based on concepts similar to those underlying the principle of good faith, such as non-violation complaints, which are subject to detailed rules. Second, the principle should not be confused with other principles that may appear to be related, in particular due process. Third, in my view, WTO Tribunals have no legal basis for finding that a Member has violated a principle of good faith independent of a WTO provision. Some existing reports err in this regard.

In Chapter 5, I addressed the principle of due process. This is a necessarily broad concept, but it is capable of more concrete definition in particular circumstances, despite the difficulties WTO Tribunals have had in using it correctly. WTO Tribunals have confidently exercised their inherent jurisdiction to resolve procedural matters, without generally acknowledging that they were using due process in the exercise of inherent jurisdiction. The Appellate Body has been less adept in its approach to reviewing Panel proceedings for due process compliance. Because of its apparent uncertainty about principles and the validity and scope of its inherent jurisdiction, the Appellate Body has stretched the boundaries of Article 11 of the DSU instead of liberating the due process obligations on Panels from the WTO agreements. Its jurisprudence constitutes an unsteady guide as to the standard required of Panels in making an objective assessment under that provision, and a more open application of the principle of due process could assist in guiding and explaining future decisions. Due process obligations are imposed not only on WTO Tribunals but also on WTO Members. Although due process could be used to improve the interpretation of GATT Article X:3(a), it seems to have been used in connection with GATT Article XX with little forethought.

Chapter 6 considered the principle of proportionality. This principle can usefully be applied in relation to WTO disputes in two key ways. First, I considered how proportionality can be used in determining the level and type of remedies available to Members for WTO violations or certain other undesirable or unfair conduct. The most obvious means of applying the principle of proportionality is in an interpretative manner. As an aid to interpretation, proportionality confirms the purpose of suspension of concessions as inducing compliance and could help clarify the meaning of ambiguous WTO provisions. However, the principle of proportionality can also be applied in a non-interpretative manner, for example, as the basis for a claim that a Member proposes to suspend concessions in response to a WTO-inconsistency in an amount that goes beyond the level of nullification or impairment caused by the inconsistent measure. Second, I considered the use of proportionality in relation to exceptions to rules and objectives of the WTO agreements. This chapter also cautioned that principles must yield to the relevant text of the WTO agreements, where that text is unambiguous, and that WTO Tribunals must carefully investigate the meaning and scope of a principle before using it in the WTO. Contrary to certain past decisions, the principle of proportionality is not relevant to the imposition of safeguards in the WTO.

The principle of special and differential treatment was explored in Chapter 7, the final chapter of Part II. Despite the importance of development and the need for continued technical assistance and consideration for developing countries, S&D is not particularly useful as a principle in WTO dispute settlement for a number of reasons. First, many of the S&D provisions in the WTO agreements are extremely vague. Moreover, unlike the other principles examined in Part II, the content of the principle is not informed by any general principle of law or principle of customary international law. Second, using the principle in an interpretive manner, pursuant to the object and purpose of the WTO agreements, is rendered extremely difficult due to the heterogenous needs of developing countries and the contested economic implications of S&D. Finally, as S&D involves a derogation from the key principle of non-discrimination (and in particular MFN), it involves a delicate balancing that is better left to WTO Members.

8.3 The future of principles

Despite the rapidly expanding volume of literature on the WTO, the use of principles in WTO dispute settlement remains relatively unexplored. In some ways, this is surprising, given the heated discussions during DSB meetings about WTO Tribunals' use or misuse of principles, the growing number of references to principles in the submissions of Members to WTO Tribunals, and reports of WTO Tribunals that suggest some confusion about how to deal with principles. On the other hand, the use of principles in dispute settlement remains under-explored in international law generally.

Principles raise a large number of issues in the context of the WTO, and in this book I have had to be selective. There is enormous potential for future research. In Chapter 2, I briefly discussed several principles that are relevant to the WTO but not covered in Part II of the book. An examination of additional principles, perhaps using the framework established in Chapter 3, would improve understanding about the complex relationships between principles and how conflicts between principles might be resolved in the WTO. It would also be interesting to see whether principles of WTO law that lack public international law counterparts could play a more significant role than S&D was found to play in Chapter 7. Finally, principles could also be explored outside the context of dispute settlement. For example, principles might be relevant in analysing potential new areas for inclusion in the WTO framework, in guiding the accession process for new Members, or in WTO negotiations generally.

Principles are essential in dispute settlement systems, and the WTO is no exception. However, at present WTO Tribunals are too timid in their use of principles. This is understandable, given the attractiveness of justifying decisions on textual grounds. However, it is not desirable, for two reasons. First, WTO Tribunals sometimes avoid using principles when they could and should do so. For example, they have shown an unusual reluctance towards estoppel, which should be recognised as falling within their inherent jurisdiction. Related to this, WTO Tribunals may be inclined to distort provisions of the WTO agreements in order to find a textual basis for a particular norm rather than acknowledging that the norm derives from a principle that is not necessarily recorded explicitly in the agreements. Second, when WTO Tribunals do use principles, and they are finding it increasingly necessary to do so, they do not fully acknowledge their use and may employ them in a flippant or inaccurate manner. In particular, WTO Tribunals tend to overlook key questions such as the legal basis for using a given principle, whether the principle is being used in an interpretative manner or as applicable law, and the meaning of the principle in international law. This book has established a framework for addressing these questions. The use of such a framework should allay fears and misconceptions about the use of principles and ensure that they are used in a justifiable manner. Principles are indispensable. WTO Tribunals should employ them with confidence and rigour.

Bibliography

ARTICLES, BOOKS, CHAPTERS, AND PAPERS

Abi-Saab, Georges, 'The WTO Dispute Settlement and General International Law' in Rufus Yerxa and Bruce Wilson (eds.), *Key Issues in WTO Dispute Settlement: The First Ten Years* (Cambridge: Cambridge University Press, 2005)

Adede, A. O., 'A Fresh Look at the Meaning of Denial of Justice under International Law' (1976) 14 *Canadian Yearbook of International Law* 73

Affolder, Natasha, 'Tadic, the Anonymous Witness and the Sources of International Procedural Law' (1998) 19 *Michigan Journal of International Law* 445

Akehurst, Michael, 'Custom as a Source of Law' (1974) 47 *British Yearbook of International Law* 1

Alavi, Amin, 'On the (Non-)Effectiveness of the World Trade Organization Special and Differential Treatments in the Dispute Settlement Process' (2007) 41 *Journal of World Trade* 319

Alexander, Larry, 'The Philosophy of Criminal Law' in Jules Coleman and Scott Shapiro (eds.), *The Oxford Handbook of Jurisprudence & Philosophy of Law* (Oxford: Oxford University Press, 2002) 815

Alexander, Larry and Kress, Ken, 'Against Legal Principles' (1997) 82 *Iowa Law Review* 739

Allars, Margaret, *Introduction to Australian Administrative Law* (Sydney: Butterworths, 1990)

American Law Institute, *Restatement of the Law Third: The Foreign Relations Law of the United States* (St Paul, MN: American Law Institute Publishers, 1987)

Restatement of the Law Second, Contracts (St Paul, MN: American Law Institute Publishers, 1981)

Andenas, Mads and Zleptnig, Stefan, 'Proportionality and Balancing in WTO Law: A Comparative Perspective' (2007) 20 *Cambridge Review of International Affairs* 71

'Proportionality: WTO Law: In Comparative Perspective' (2007) 42 *Texas International Law Journal* 371

Anderson, Kym, 'Peculiarities of Retaliation in WTO Dispute Settlement' (2002) 1 *World Trade Review* 123

'Setting the Trade Policy Agenda: What Roles for Economists?' (2005) 39 *Journal of World Trade* 341

Appleton, Arthur and Heiskanen, Veijo, 'The Sardines Decision: Fish without Chips?' in Andrew D. Mitchell (ed.), *Challenges and Prospects for the WTO* (London: Cameron May, 2005) 165

Atiyah, P. S., *Law and Modern Society* (Oxford: Oxford University Press, 1983)

Ávila, Humberto, *Theory of Legal Principles* (Dordrecht: Springer, 2007)

Bafundo, Nina E., 'Compliance with the Ozone Treaty: Weak States and the Principle of Common but Differentiated Responsibility' (2005) 21 *American University International Law Review* 461

Bagchi, Aditi, 'Compulsory Licensing and the Duty of Good Faith in TRIPS' (2003) 55 *Stanford Law Review* 1529

Bartels, Lorand, 'Applicable Law in WTO Dispute Settlement Proceedings' (2001) 35 *Journal of World Trade* 499

'The Separation of Powers in the WTO: How to Avoid Judicial Activism' (2004) 53 *International and Comparative Law Quarterly* 861

'The WTO Enabling Clause and Positive Conditionality in the European Community's GSP Program' (2003) 6 *Journal of International Economic Law* 507

Berlin, Isaiah, *Four Essays on Liberty* (Oxford: Oxford University Press, 1969)

Bermann, George, 'The Principle of Proportionality' (1977–78) 26 *American Journal of Comparative Law Supplement* 415

Beynon, Robert (ed.), *The Routledge Companion to Global Economics* (London: Routledge, 2001)

Bhala, Raj, *Modern GATT Law: A Treatise on the General Agreement on Tariffs and Trade* (London: Sweet & Maxwell, 2005)

Bix, Brian H., *A Dictionary of Legal Theory* (Oxford: Oxford University Press, 2004)

Blackshield, Tony, Coper, Michael and Williams, George (eds.), *The Oxford Companion to the High Court of Australia* (South Melbourne: Oxford University Press, 2001)

Bohanes, Jan, 'Risk Regulation in WTO Law: A Procedure-Based Approach to the Precautionary Principle' (2002) 40 *Columbia Journal of Transnational Law* 323

Bossche, Peter van den, *The Law and Policy of the World Trade Organization: Text, Cases and Materials* (New York: Cambridge University Press, 2005)

Bowett, Derek, 'Estoppel Before International Tribunals and Its Relation to Acquiescence' (1957) 33 *British Yearbook of International Law* 176

Bridge, M. G., 'Does Anglo-Canadian Contract Law Need a Doctrine of Good Faith?' (1984) 9 *Canadian Business Law Journal* 385

Briggs, H., 'The Incidental Jurisdiction of the International Court of Justice as Compulsory Jurisdiction' in F. A. Frhr vd Heydte et al. (eds.), *Völkerrecht und Rechtliches Weltbild: Festschrift für Alfred Verdross* (Vienna: Springer, 1960)

Bronckers, Marco, 'Better Rules for a New Millennium: A Warning against Undemocratic Developments in the WTO' (1999) 2 *Journal of International Economic Law* 547

Broude, Tomer, *International Governance in the WTO: Judicial Boundaries and Political Capitulation* (London: Cameron May, 2004)

Brown, L. Neville and Jacobs, Francis G., *The Court of Justice of the European Communities* (London: Sweet & Maxwell, 2nd edn, 1983)

Brownlie, Ian, *Principles of Public International Law* (Oxford: Oxford International Press, 5th edn, 1998)

Principles of Public International Law (Oxford: Oxford International Press, 6th edn, 2003)

Bureau, Jean-Christophe, Jean, Sébastien and Matthews, Alan, 'The Consequences of Agricultural Trade Liberalization for Developing Countries: Distinguishing between Genuine Benefits and False Hopes' (Discussion Paper No 73, Institute for International Integration Studies, April 2005)

Butler, Andrew and Butler, Petra, *The New Zealand Bill of Rights Act: A Commentary* (Wellington: LexisNexis New Zealand, 2005)

Byers, Michael, *Custom, Power, and the Power of Rules: International Relations and Customary International Law* (Cambridge: Cambridge University Press, 1999)

'Abuse of Rights: An Old Principle, A New Age' (2002) 47 *McGill Law Journal* 389

Cameron, James and Gray, Kevin, 'Principles of International Law in the WTO Dispute Settlement Body' (2001) 50 *International and Comparative Law Quarterly* 248

Cannizzaro, Enzo, 'The Role of Proportionality in the Law of International Countermeasures' (2001) 12 *European Journal of International Law* 889

Cass, Deborah Z., 'The "Constitutionalization" of International Trade Law: Judicial Norm-Generation as the Engine of Constitutional Development in International Trade' (2001) 12 *European Journal of International Law* 39

The Constitutionalization of the World Trade Organization: Legitimacy, Democracy, and Community in the International Trading System (Oxford: Oxford University Press, 2005)

Cassese, Antonio, 'The Contribution of the International Criminal Tribunal for the Former Yugoslavia to the Ascertainment of General Principles of Law Recognized by the Community of Nations' in Sienho Yee and Wang Tieya (eds.), *International Law in the Post-Cold War World: Essays in Memory of Li Haopei* (London: Routledge, 2001) 43

International Law (Oxford: Oxford University Press, 2nd edn, 2005)

Cattaneo, Olivier, 'Has the WTO Gone Too Far or Not Far Enough? Some Reflections on the Concept of "Policy Space"' in Andrew D. Mitchell (ed.), *Challenges and Prospects for the WTO* (London: Cameron May, 2005) 55

Chang, Ruth (ed.), *Incommensurability, Incomparability, and Practical Reason* (Cambridge, MA: Harvard University Press, 1997)

Charlesworth, Hilary and Chinkin, Christine, *The Boundaries of International Law: A Feminist Analysis* (Manchester: Manchester University Press, 2000)

Charnovitz, Steve, 'Should the Teeth Be Pulled? An Analysis of WTO Sanctions' in Daniel Kennedy and James Southwick, *The Political Economy of International Trade Law: Essays in Honor of Robert E. Hudec* (Cambridge: Cambridge University Press, 2002) 602

Cheng, Bin, *General Principles of Law: As Applied by International Courts and Tribunals* (Cambridge: Grotius, 1987)

Cheyne, Ilona, 'Gateways to the Precautionary Principle in WTO Law' (2007) 19 *Journal of Environmental Law* 155

'Risk and Precaution in World Trade Organization Law' (2006) 40 *Journal of World Trade* 837

'China Announces Increased Export Tariffs on Textiles', *People's Daily Online*, 13 December 2004

Choudhry, Sujit, 'Globalization in Search of Justification: Toward a Theory of Comparative Constitutional Interpretation' (1999) 74 *Indiana Law Journal* 819

Cohen, George, 'Implied Terms and Interpretation in Contract Law' in Boudewijn Bouckaert and Gerrit de Geest (eds.), *Encyclopedia of Law and Economics* (Northampton, MA: Edward Elgar Publishing, 2000) vol. III, 78.

Cohen, Morris R., *Reason and Law* (New York: Collier Books, 1961)

Consultative Board, WTO, *The Future of the WTO: Addressing Institutional Challenges in the New Millennium* (Geneva: WTO, 2004)

Cottier, Thomas, Oesch, Matthias and Fischer, Thomas, *International Trade Regulation: Law and Policy in the WTO, the European Union and Switzerland – Cases, Materials and Comments* (Berne: Staempfli Publishers, 2005)

Cottier, Thomas and Schefer, Krista, 'Good Faith and the Protection of Legitimate Expectations in the WTO' in Marco Bronckers and Reinhard Quick (eds.), *New Directions in International Economic Law: Essays in Honour of John H Jackson* (The Hague: Kluwer Law International, 2000) 47

'Non-Violation Complaints in WTO/GATT Dispute Settlement: Past, Present and Future' in Ernst-Ulrich Petersmann (ed.), *International Trade Law and the GATT/WTO Dispute Settlement System* (London: Kluwer Law International, 1997) 145

Crawford, James, *The International Law Commission's Articles on State Responsibility: Introduction, Text, and Commentaries* (Cambridge: Cambridge University Press, 2002)

D'Amato, Anthony A., *The Concept of Custom in International Law* (Ithaca, NY: Cornell University Press, 1971)

Davey, William, 'Has the WTO Dispute Settlement System Exceeded Its Authority? A Consideration of Deference Shown by the System to Member Government Decisions and Its Use of Issue-Avoidance Techniques' in Thomas Cottier and Petros C. Mavroidis (eds.), *The Role of the Judge in International Trade Regulation: Experience and Lessons for the WTO* (Ann Arbor, MI: University of Michigan Press, 2003) vol. IV, 43

de Búrca, Gráinne, 'Subsidiarity and Proportionality as General Principles of Law' in Joakim Nergelius and Ulf Bernitz (eds.), *General Principles of European Community Law: Reports from a Conference in Malmö, 27–28, August 1999* (The Hague: Kluwer Law International, 2000) 97

De Noronha Goyos, Durval, 'Brazil: Duty of Good Faith in International Services Negotiations' (2005) 11 *International Trade Law & Regulation* N15

Degan, Vladimir, *Sources of International Law* (The Hague: Kluwer Law International, 1997)

Delbridge, A. et al. (eds.), *The Macquarie Dictionary* (McMahons Point: Macquarie Library, 2nd edn, 1991)

Delbrück, Jost, 'Proportionality' in Rudolf Bernhardt (ed.), *Encyclopedia of Public International Law* (Amsterdam: North-Holland Publishing Co, 2003) vol. III, 1140

Delimatsis, Panagiotis, 'Due Process and "Good" Regulation Embedded in the GATS – Disciplining Regulatory Behaviour in Services through Article VI of the GATS' (2007) 10 *Journal of International Economic Law* 13

Desmedt, Axel, 'Proportionality in WTO Law' (2001) 4 *Journal of International Economic Law* 441

Dodge, William, 'Loewen Group, Inc *v.* United States. Modev International Ltd *v.* United States' (2004) 98 *American Journal of International Law* 155

Dominicé, Christian, 'Methodology of International Law' in Rudolf Bernhardt (ed.), *Encyclopaedia of Public International Law* (Amsterdam: North-Holland Publishing Co, 2003) vol. III, 354

Durling, James, 'Deference, but Only when Due: WTO Review of Anti-Dumping Measures' (2003) 6 *Journal of International Economic Law* 125

Dworkin, Ronald, *Law's Empire* (Cambridge, MA: Belknap Press, 1986)

Taking Rights Seriously (London: Duckworth, 1977)

Edmundson, William, 'The Antinomy of Coherence and Determinacy' (1996) 82 *Iowa Law Review* 1

Ehlermann, Claus-Dieter, 'Six Years on the Bench of the "World Trade Court" Some Personal Experiences as Member of the Appellate Body of the World Trade Organization' (2002) 36 *Journal of World Trade* 605

Ellinghaus, M. P. and Wright, E. W., 'The Common Law of Contracts: Are Broad Principles Better than Detailed Rules? An Empirical Investigation' (2005) 11 *Texas Wesleyan Law Review* 399

Ellis, Evelyn (ed.), *The Principle of Proportionality in the Laws of Europe* (Oxford: Hart, 1999)

Endicott, Timothy A. O., *Vagueness in Law* (Oxford: Oxford University Press, 2000)

Fallon, Richard, 'Foreword: Implementing the Constitution' (1997) 111 *Harvard Law Review* 54

Farnsworth, Allan, 'Duties of Good Faith and Fair Dealing under the UNIDROIT Principles, Relevant International Conventions, and National Laws' (1995) 3 *Tulane Journal of International and Comparative Law* 47

Fatouros, A. A., 'Developing States' in Rudolf Bernhardt (ed.), *Encyclopaedia of Public International Law* (Amsterdam: North-Holland Publishing Co, 2003) vol. I, 1017

Fenrick, William, 'The Rule of Proportionality and Protocol in Conventional Warfare' (1982) 98 *Military Law Review* 91

Finger, Michael, 'A Diplomat's Economics: Reciprocity in the Uruguay Round Negotiations' (2005) 4 *World Trade Review* 27

Finger, Michael and Nogués, Julio, 'The Unbalanced Uruguay Round Outcome: The New Areas in Future WTO Negotiations' (2002) 25 *World Economy* 321

Fitzmaurice, Gerald, 'Some Problems Regarding the Formal Sources of International Law' [1958] *Symbolae Verzijl* 153

'The General Principles of International Law Considered from the Standpoint of the Rule of Law' (1957-II) *Recueil des Cours* 1

'The Law and Procedure of the International Court of Justice, 1951–4: General Principles and Sources of Law' (1959) 30 *British Yearbook of International Law* 1

'The Law and Procedure of the International Court of Justice 1951–4: Treaty Interpretation and Other Treaty Points' (1957) 33 *British Yearbook of International Law* 203

Ford, Christopher, 'Judicial Discretion in International Jurisprudence: Article 38(1)(C) and "General Principles of Law"' (1994) 5 *Duke Journal of Comparative and International Law* 35

Fox, Richard, 'The Meaning of Proportionality in Sentencing' (1994) 19 *Melbourne University Law Review* 489

Franck, Thomas M., *Fairness in International Law and Institutions* (Oxford: Oxford University Press, 1995)

Freeman, Alwyn V., *The International Responsibility of States for Denial of Justice* (London: Longmans, Green & Co, 1938)

Friedmann, Wolfgang, 'The Uses of "General Principles" in the Development of International Law' (1963) 57 *American Journal of International Law* 279

Frischtak, Ana, 'Balancing Judicial Economy, State Opportunism, and Due Process Concerns in the WTO' (2005) 26 *Michigan Journal of International Law* 947

Gaffney, John, 'Due Process in the World Trade Organization: The Need for Procedural Justice in the Dispute Settlement System' (1999) 14 *American University International Law Review* 1173

Garcia, Frank, 'Beyond Special and Differential Treatment' (2004) 27 *Boston College International & Comparative Law Review* 291

Gardam, Judith, 'Proportionality as a Restraint on the Use of Force' (1999) 20 *Australian Yearbook of International Law* 161

Garner, Bryan A., *A Dictionary of Modern Legal Usage* (New York: Oxford University Press, 2nd edn, 1995)

Gerstetter, Christiane and Maier, Matthais Leonhard, 'Legalise It, or Criticise It? Debating the Precautionary Principle in and around the WTO' (Working Paper, Universität Bremen, 2004)

Goldsmith, Jack and Posner, Eric, 'A Theory of Customary International Law' (1999) 66 *University of Chicago Law Review* 1113

'Understanding the Resemblance between Modern and Traditional Customary International Law' (2000) 40 *Virginia Journal of International Law* 639

Gonthier, Charles, 'Liberty, Equality, Fraternity: The Forgotten Leg of the Trilogy, or Fraternity: The Unspoken Third Pillar of Democracy' (2000) 45 *McGill Law Journal* 567

Goode, Royston, *Commercial Law* (New York, NY: Penguin Books 2nd edn, 1995)

Goodwin-Gill, Guy, 'State Responsibility and the "Good Faith" Obligation in International Law' in Malgosia Fitzmaurice and Dan Sarooshi (eds.), *Issues of State Responsibility Before International Judicial Institutions* (Oxford: Hart, 2004) 75

Greenawalt, Kent, 'Constitutional and Statutory Interpretation' in Jules Coleman and Scott Shapiro (eds.), *The Oxford Handbook of Jurisprudence and Philosophy of Law* (Oxford: Oxford University Press, 2002) 268

Grieg, D. W., 'Reciprocity, Proportionality, and the Law of Treaties' (1994) 34 *Virginia Journal of International Law* 295

Grossman, Gene and Sykes, Alan, 'A Preference for Development: the Law and Economics of GSP' (2005) 4 *World Trade Review* 41

Gutteridge, H. C., 'Comparative Law and the Law of Nations' (1944) 21 *British Yearbook of International Law* 1

Comparative Law (Cambridge: Cambridge University Press, 2nd edn, 1949)

Hall, Kermit L (ed.), *The Oxford Companion to the Supreme Court of the United States* (New York: Oxford University Press, 1992)

Hart, H. L. A., *The Concept of Law* (Oxford: Oxford University Press, 1961)

Hart, Michael and Dymond, Bill, 'Special and Differential Treatment and the Doha "Development" Round' (2003) 37 *Journal of World Trade* 395

Harvard Research in International Law, 'Draft Convention on the Law of Treaties' (1935) 29 *American Journal of International Law (Supplement)* 697

'The Law of Responsibility of States for Damage Done in Their Territory to the Person or Property of Foreigners' (1929) 23 *American Journal of International Law (Supplement)* 131

Hilf, Meinhard, 'Power, Rules and Principles – Which Orientation for WTO/GATT Law?' (2001) 4 *Journal of International Economic Law* 111

Hilf, Meinhard and Goettsche, Goetz J., 'The Relation of Economic and Non-Economic Principles in International Law' in Stefan Griller (ed.), *International Economic Governance and Non-Economic Concerns: New Challenges for the International Legal Order* (New York: Springer, 2003)

Hilf, Meinhard and Puth, Sebastian, 'The Principle of Proportionality on its Way into WTO/GATT law' in Armin von Bogdandy, Petros Mavroidis and Yves Mény (eds.), *European Integration and International Co-Ordination: Studies in Transnational Economic Law in Honour of Claus-Dieter Ehlermann* (The Hague: Kluwer Law International, 2002) 199

Hiscock, Mary, 'The Keeper of the Flame: Good Faith and Fair Dealing in International Trade' (1996) 29 *Loyola of Los Angeles Law Review* 1059

Hoekman, Bernard, 'Operationalizing the Concept of Policy Space in the WTO: Beyond Special and Differential Treatment' (2005) 8 *Journal of International Economic Law* 405

Hoekman, Bernard and Braga, Carlos, 'Special and Differential Treatment and the Doha Development Agenda: Beyond Tariff Preferences' (Paper presented at the OECD Global Forum on Trade, *Special and Differential Treatment: Thinking Outside the Box*, Bridgetown, Barbados, 28–29 June 2005)

Hoekman, Bernard and Mavroidis, Petros, 'WTO Dispute Settlement, Transparency and Surveillance' (2000) 23 *World Economy* 527

Hoekman, Bernard, Michalopoulos, Constantine and Winters, Alan, 'Special and Differential Treatment of Developing Countries in the WTO: Moving Forward After Cancún' (2004) *World Economy* 481

Hoekman, Bernard and Prowse, Susan, 'Policy Responses to Preference Erosion: From Trade as Aid to Aid for Trade' (Paper presented at the OECD Global Forum on Trade, *Special and Differential Treatment: Thinking Outside the Box*, Bridgetown, Barbados, 28–29 June 2005)

Hogg, Peter W., *Constitutional Law of Canada* (Toronto: Carswell, student edn, 2002)

Honderich, Ted (ed.), *The Oxford Companion to Philosophy* (Oxford: Oxford University Press, 1995)

Horlick, Gary, 'Problems with the Compliance Structure of the WTO Dispute Resolution Process' in Daniel Kennedy and James Southwick, *The Political Economy of International Trade Law: Essays in Honor of Robert E Hudec* (Cambridge: Cambridge University Press, 2002) 636

Howse, Robert, 'Adjudicative Legitimacy and Treaty Interpretation in International Trade Law: The Early Years of WTO Jurisprudence' in Joseph Weiler (ed.), *The EU, the WTO and the NAFTA: Toward a Common Law of International Law* (Oxford: Oxford University Press, 2000) 35

'India's WTO Challenge to Drug Enforcement Conditions in the European Community Generalized System of Preferences: A Little Known Case with Major Repercussions for "Political" Conditionality in US Trade Policy' (2003) 4 *Chicago Journal of International Law* 385

'The Jurisprudential Achievement of the WTO Appellate Body: A Preliminary Appreciation' (Working Paper, University of Michigan, 2004)

'The Most Dangerous Branch? WTO Appellate Body Jurisprudence on the Nature and Limits of the Judicial Power' in Thomas Cottier and Petros C. Mavroidis (eds.), *The Role of the Judge in International Trade Regulation: Experience and Lessons for the WTO* (Ann Arbor, MI: University of Michigan Press, 2003) vol. I, 11

Howse, Robert and Nicolaïdis, Kalypso, 'Enhancing WTO Legitimacy: Constitutionalization or Global Subsidiarity?' (2003) 16 *Governance* 73

Hudec, Robert E., *Developing Countries in the GATT Legal System* (Aldershot, Hampshire, UK: Gower, for the Trade Policy Research Centre, London, 1987)

Ismail, Faizel, 'Mainstreaming Development in the World Trade Organization' (2005) 39 *Journal of World Trade* 11

Jacobs, Francis, 'Varieties of Approach to Treaty Interpretation: With Special Reference to the Draft Convention on the Law of Treaties Before the Vienna Diplomatic Conference' (1969) 18 *International and Comparative Law Quarterly* 318

Jaenicke, Günther, 'States, Equal Treatment and Non-Discrimination' in Rudolf Bernhardt (ed.), *Encyclopaedia of Public International Law* (Amsterdam: North-Holland Publishing Co, 2003) vol. IV, 660

Jalet, Frances, 'The Quest for the General Principles of Law Recognized by Civilized Nations – A Study' (1963) 10 *UCLA Law Review* 1041

Janis, Mark W., *An Introduction to International Law* (New York: Aspen Publishers, 4th edn, 2003)

Jennings, Robert, 'What is International Law and How Do We Tell It When We See It?' (1981) 37 *Schweizerisches Jahrbuch für Internationales Recht* 59

Jennings, Robert and Watts, Arthur (eds.), *Oppenheim's International Law* (Harlow, Essex, UK: Longman, 9th edn, 1992)

Johnstone, Ian, 'Treaty Interpretation: The Authority of Interpretive Communities' (1991) 12 *Michigan Journal of International Law* 371

Jung, Youngjin and Lee, Sun Hyeong, 'The Legacy of the Byrd Amendment Controversies: Rethinking the Principle of Good Faith' (2003) 37 *Journal of World Trade* 921

Jürgensen, Thomas, 'Crime and Punishment: Retaliation under the World Trade Organization Dispute Settlement System' (2005) 39 *Journal of World Trade* 327

Kaplow, Louis, 'General Characteristics of Rules' in Boudewijn Bouckaert and Gerrit de Geest (eds.), *Encyclopedia of Law and Economics* (Northampton, MA: Edward Elgar Publishing, 2000) vol. V, 502

'Rules versus Standards: An Economic Analysis' (1992) 42 *Duke Law Journal* 557

Keck, Alexander and Low, Patrick, 'Special and Differential Treatment in the WTO: Why, When and How?' in Simon Evenett and Bernard Hoekman (eds.), *Economic Development & Multilateral Trade Cooperation* (Washington DC: Palgrave Macmillan, World Bank, 2006) 147

Keily, Troy, 'Good Faith & the Vienna Convention on Contracts for the International Sale of Goods (CISG)' (1999) 3 *Vindobona Journal of International Commercial Law & Arbitration* 15

Kelly, Patrick, 'The Twilight of Customary International Law' (2000) 40 *Virginia Journal of International Law* 449

Kelsen, Hans, *Pure Theory of Law* (Berkeley: University of California Press, Max Knight trans, 2nd rev. edn, 1967)

Kennedy, David, 'Theses about International Legal Discourse' (1980) 23 *German Yearbook of International Law* 353

Kerr, William, 'Special and Differential Treatment: A Mechanism to Promote Development?' (2005) 6 *Estey Centre Journal of International Law and Trade Policy* 84

Kirgis, Fredric, 'Custom on a Sliding Scale' (1987) 81 *American Journal of International Law* 146

'Evolving Constitutions of International Organizations by Tetsuo Sato' (1998) 92 *American Journal of International Law* 153

Kirk, Jeremy, 'Constitutional Guarantees, Characterisation and the Concept of Proportionality' (1997) 21 *Melbourne University Law Review* 1

Kishoiyian, Bernard, 'The Utility of Bilateral Investment Treaties in the Formulation of Customary International Law' (1994) 14 *Northwestern Journal of International Law and Business* 327

Kiss, Alexandre, 'Abuse of Rights' in Rudolf Bernhardt (ed.), *Encyclopaedia of Public International Law* (Amsterdam: North-Holland Publishing Co, 2003) vol. I, 4

Knop, Karen, 'Reflections on Thomas Franck, Race and Nationalism (1960): "General Principles of Law" and Situated Generality' (2003) 35 *New York University Journal of International Law and Politics* 437

Kolb, Robert, 'Principles as Sources of International Law (with Special Reference to Good Faith)' (2006) 53 *Netherlands International Law Review* 1

Koskenniemi, Martii, *From Apology to Utopia* (Helsinki: Finnish Lawyers' Pub. Co., 1989)

General Principles: Reflexions on Constructivist Thinking in International Law (1985) XVIII *Oikeustiede-Jurisprudentia* 121.

Kuyper, Pieter, 'The Law of GATT as a Special Field of International Law: Ignorance, Further Refinement or Self-Contained System of International Law?' (1994) 25 *Netherlands International Law Review* 227

Lauterpacht, Hersch, 'De l'interprétation des traités' (1950) 43 *Annuaire de l'Institut de Droit International* 366

'Restrictive Interpretation and the Principle of Effectiveness in the Interpretation of Treaties' (1949) 26 *British Yearbook of International Law* 48

The Development of International Law by the International Court (London: Stevens, 1958)

The Function of Law in the International Community (Hamden, Conn.: Archon Books 1966)

Lee, Yong-Shik, 'Destabilization of the Discipline on Safeguards? Inherent Problems with the Continuing Application of Article XIX after the Settlement of the Agreement on Safeguards' (2001) 35 *Journal of World Trade* 1235

Lennard, Michael, 'Navigating by the Stars: Interpreting the WTO Agreements' (2002) 5 *Journal of International Economic Law* 17

Lieber, Francis, *Legal and Political Hermeneutics, or Principles of Interpretation and Construction in Law and Politics, with Remarks on Precedents and Authorities* (Boston: C.C. Little and J. Brown, 1839)

Lockhart, Nicolas and Mitchell, Andrew, 'Regional Trade Agreements Under GATT 1994: An Exception and Its Limits' in Andrew D. Mitchell (ed.), *Challenges and Prospects for the WTO* (London: Cameron May, 2005) 217

Lucy, William, 'Adjudication' in Jules Coleman and Scott Shapiro (eds.), *The Oxford Handbook of Jurisprudence & Philosophy of Law* (Oxford: Oxford University Press, 2002) 206

MacCormick, Neil, *Legal Reasoning and Legal Theory* (Oxford: Clarendon Press, 1994)

Malanczuk, Peter, *Akehurst's Modern Introduction to International Law* (London: Routledge, 7th edn, 1997)

Mann, F. A., 'Reflections on a Commercial Law of Nations' (1957) 33 *British Yearbook of International Law* 20

'British Treaties for the Promotion and Protection of Investments' (1982) 52 *British Yearbook of International Law* 241

Marceau, Gabrielle, 'A Call for Coherence in International Law - Praise for the Prohibition against "Clinical Isolation" in WTO Dispute Settlement' (1999) 33 *Journal of World Trade* 87

'Conflicts of Norms and Conflicts of Jurisdictions: The Relationship between the WTO Agreement and MEAs and other Treaties' (2001) 35 *Journal of World Trade* 1081

'La jurisprudence sur le principe de précaution dans le droit de l'OMC' (Paper presented at the Inaugural Professorial Lecture, Faculty of Law, University of Geneva, 19 May 2005)

Margue, Georges, 'Abuse of Rights and Luxembourg Law' in Council of Europe (ed.), *Abuse of Rights and Equivalent Concepts: The Principle and Its Present Day Application* (Strasbourg: Council of Europe, Pub. and Documentation Service 1990) 58

Martin, Elizabeth, *A Dictionary of Law* (Oxford: Oxford University Press, 5th edn, 2002)

Matsushita, Mitsuo, Schoenbaum, Thomas and Mavroidis, Petros, *The World Trade Organization: Law, Practice, and Policy* (Oxford: Oxford University Press, 2003)

Mavroidis, Petros, 'Remedies in the WTO Legal System: Between a Rock and a Hard Place' (2000) 11 *European Journal of International Law* 763

McGinnis, John, 'The Appropriate Hierarchy of Global Multilateralism and Customary International Law: The Example of the WTO' (2003) 44 *Virginia Journal of International Law* 229

McLachlan, Campbell, 'The Principle of Systemic Integration and Article 31(3)(c) of the Vienna Convention' (2005) 54 *International and Comparative Law Quarterly* 279

McNair, Arnold, 'The Functions and Differing Legal Character of Treaties' (1930) 11 *British Yearbook of International Law* 100

The Law of Treaties (Oxford: Clarendon Press, 1961)

McRae, Donald, 'Reflections on the Appellate Body of the World Trade Organization (WTO): Comments on Dr Claus-Dieter Ehlermann's Lecture' (2003) 97 *American Society of International Law Proceedings* 87

'What is the Future of WTO Dispute Settlement?' (2004) 7 *Journal of International Economic Law* 3

Mendelson, Maurice, 'The International Court of Justice and the Sources of International Law' in Vaughan Lowe and Malgosia Fitzmaurice (eds.), *Fifty Years of the International Court of Justice* (Cambridge: Grotius/Cambridge University Press, 1996) 63

'Reservations to the Constitutions of International Organizations' (1971) 45 *British Yearbook of International Law* 137

Merrills, J., *International Dispute Settlement* (Cambridge: Cambridge University Press, 3rd edn, 1998)

Mitchell, Andrew, 'Does One Illegality Merit Another? The Law of Belligerent Reprisals in International Law' (2001) 170 *Military Law Review* 155

Mitchell, Andrew and Griffith, Gavan, 'Contractual Dispute Resolution in International Trade: The UNCITRAL Arbitration Rules (1976) and the UNCITRAL Conciliation Rules (1980)' (2002) 3 *Melbourne Journal of International Law* 184

Müller, Jörg and Cottier, Thomas, 'Estoppel' in Rudolf Bernhardt (ed.), *Encyclopaedia of Public International Law* (New York: North-Holland, 2003) vol. 2, 116

Müller, Jörg and Kolb, Robert, 'Article 2(2)' in Bruno Simma (ed.), *The Charter of the United Nations: A Commentary* (Oxford: Oxford University Press, 2nd edn, 2002) vol. 1, 91

Neumann, Jan and Türk, Elisabeth, 'Necessity Revisited: Proportionality in World Trade Organization Law After *Korea – Beef*, *EC – Asbestos* and *EC – Sardines*' (2003) 37 *Journal of World Trade* 199

Ngangjoh, Yenkong, '*Pacta Sunt Servanda* and Complaints in the WTO Dispute Settlement' (2004) 1 *Manchester Journal of International Economic Law* 76

Nordås, Hildegunn Kyvik, *Discussion Paper No 5: The Global Textile and Clothing Industry post the Agreement on Textiles and Clothing* (Geneva: WTO, 2004)

Note, 'Looking It Up: Dictionaries and Statutory Interpretation' (1994) 107 *Harvard Law Review* 1437

Nygh, Peter and Butt, Peter (eds.), *Australian Legal Dictionary* (1997)

O'Connell, Daniel, *International Law* (London: Stevens, 2nd edn, 1970)

O'Connor, J., *Good Faith in International Law* (Aldershot, Hants, England: Dartmouth, 1991)

Olivares, Gustavo, 'The Case for Giving Effectiveness to GATT/WTO Rules on Developing Countries and LDCs' (2001) 35 *Journal of World Trade* 545

Orakhelashvili, Alexander, 'Questions of International Judicial Jurisdiction in the LaGrand Case' (2002) 15 *Leiden Journal of International Law* 105

Ortino, Federico, *Basic Legal Instruments for the Liberalisation of Trade: A Comparative Analysis of EC and WTO Law* (Portland: Hart Publishing, 2004)

'From "Non-Discrimination" to "Reasonableness": A Paradigm Shift in International Economic Law?' (Working Paper No 01/05, Jean Monnet Centre for International and Regional Economic Law & Justice, 2005)

Osiro, D. A., 'GATT/WTO Necessity Analysis: Evolutionary Interpretation and its Impact on the Authority of Domestic Regulation' (2002) 29 *Legal Issues of Economic Integration* 123

Page, Sheila and Kleen, Peter, *Special and Differential Treatment of Developing Countries in the World Trade Organization* (Stockholm: Norstedts Tryckeri AB, 2005)

Palmeter, David, 'The Need for Due Process in WTO Proceedings' (1997) 31 *Journal of World Trade* 51.

Palmeter, David and Alexandrov, Stanimir, ' "Inducing Compliance" in WTO Dispute Settlement' in Daniel Kennedy and James Southwick, *The Political Economy of International Trade Law: Essays in Honor of Robert E. Hudec* (Cambridge: Cambridge University Press, 2002) 646

Palmeter, David and Mavroidis, Petros C., *Dispute Settlement in the World Trade Organization: Practice and Procedure* (New York: Cambridge University Press, 2nd edn, 2004)

'The WTO Legal System: Sources of Law' (1998) 92 *American Journal of International Law* 398

Pangestu, Mari, 'Special and Differential Treatment in the Millennium: Special for Whom and How Different?' (2000) 23 *World Economy* 1285

Panitchpakdi, Supachai, 'Why Cancún Matters', Second International Conference on Globalisation, Leuven, 26 November 2002, www.wto.org/english/news_e/spsp_e/spsp08_e.htm

Panizzon, Marion, *Good Faith in the Jurisprudence of the WTO* (Oxford: Hart, 2006)

Park, Kyung, 'Korean Principle of Proportionality, American Multi-Leveled Scrutiny, and Empiricist Elements in US-Korean Constitutional Jurisprudence' (2001) 1 *Journal of Korean Law* 105

Pater, Joshua, 'Struck out Looking: Continued Confusion in Eighth Amendment Proportionality Review after Ewing *v.* California, 123 S. Ct. 1179 (2003)' (2003–04) 27 *Harvard Journal of Law & Public Policy* 399

Pauwelyn, Joost, *Conflict of Norms in Public International Law: How WTO Law Relates to Other Rules of International Law* (Cambridge: Cambridge University Press, 2003)

'Enforcement and Countermeasures in the WTO: Rules are Rules – Toward a More Collective Approach' (2000) 94 *American Journal of International Law* 335

'The Nature of WTO Obligations' (Working Paper No 1/02, Jean Monnet Centre for International and Regional Economic Law & Justice, 2002)

'The Puzzle of WTO Safeguards and Regional Trade Agreements' (2004) 7 *Journal of International Economic Law* 109

'The Role of Public International Law in the WTO: How Far Can We Go?' (2001) 95 *American Journal of International Law* 535

Perez-Aznar, Facundo, *Countermeasures in the WTO Dispute Settlement System: An Analysis of Their Characteristics and Procedure in the Light of General International Law* (Geneva: Graduate Institute of International Studies, 2006)

Perry, Stephen, 'Two Models of Legal Principles' (1997) 82 *Iowa Law Review* 787

Petersmann, Ernst-Ulrich, *The GATT/WTO Dispute Settlement System: International Law, International Organizations and Dispute Settlement* (London: Kluwer Law International, 1997)

'Trade Policy as a Constitutional Problem: On the Domestic Policy Functions of International Rules' (1996) 41 *Aussenwirtschaft* 405

Petrova, Irina, '"Stepping on the Shoulders of a Drowning Man": The Doctrine of Abuse of Right as a Tool for Reducing Damages for Lost Profits: Troubling Lessons from the Patuha and Himpurna Arbitrations' (2004) 35 *Georgetown Journal of International Law* 455

Pound, Roscoe, *An Introduction to the Philosophy of Law* (New Haven: Yale University Press, 1922)

Powers, Paul, 'Defining the Undefinable: Good Faith and the United Nations Convention on the Contracts for the International Sale of Goods' (1999) 18 *Journal of Law and Commerce* 333

Qureshi, Asif, 'Interpreting World Trade Organization Agreements for the Development Objective' (2003) 37 *Journal of World Trade* 847

Randelzhofer, Albrecht, 'Article 2' in Bruno Simma (ed.), *The Charter of the United Nations: A Commentary* (Oxford: Oxford University Press, 2nd edn, 2002) vol. I, 63

Raz, Joseph, *Practical Reason and Norms* (Princeton, NJ: Princeton University Press, rev. edn, 1999)

The Morality of Freedom (Oxford: Oxford University Press, 1986)

Redfern, Alan et al., *Law and Practice of International Commercial Arbitration* (London: Sweet & Maxwell, 4th edn, 2004)

Regan, Donald, 'Do WTO Dispute Settlement Reports Affect the Obligations of Non-Parties?' (2003) 37 *Journal of World Trade* 883

Renouf, Yves, 'A Brief Introduction to Countermeasures in the WTO Dispute Settlement System' in Rufus Yerxa and Bruce Wilson (eds.), *Key Issues in WTO Dispute Settlement: The First Ten Years* (Cambridge: Cambridge University Press, 2005) 75

Report of the International Law Commission on the Work of Its Fifty-third Session, UN GAOR, 56th sess, Supp No 10, UN Doc A/56/10 (2001)

Ricupero, Rubens, 'Rebuilding Confidence in the Multilateral Trading System: Closing the "Legitimacy Gap" ' in Gary Sampson (ed.), *The Role of the World Trade Organization in Global Governance* (Tokyo: United Nations University Press, 2001) 37

Roberts, Anthea, 'Traditional and Modern Approaches to Customary International Law: A Reconciliation' (2001) 95 *American Journal of International Law* 757

Robinson, Davis, 'Expropriation in the Restatement (Revised)' (1984) 78 *American Journal of International Law* 176

Roessler, Frieder and Gappah, Petina, 'A Re-Appraisal of Non-Violation Complaints under the WTO Dispute Settlement Procedures' in Patrick F. J. Macrory et al. (eds.), *The World Trade Organization: Legal, Economic and Political Analysis* (New York: Springer, 2005) vol. I, 1371

Rosenne, Shabtai, *Developments in the Law of Treaties 1945–1986* (Cambridge: New York, 1989)

Sacerdoti, Giorgio, 'Bilateral Treaties and Multilateral Instruments on Investment Protection' (1997) 269 *Recueil des Cours* 251

Sartorius, Rolf, 'The Justification of the Judicial Decision' (1968) 78 *Ethics* 184

Sato, Tetsuo, *Evolving Constitutions of International Organizations* (The Hague: Kluwer Law International, 1996)

Schlesinger, Rudolf, 'Research on General Principles of Law Recognized by Civilized Nations' (1957) 51 *American Journal of International Law* 734

Schreuer, Christoph, 'Fair and Equitable Treatment in Arbitral Practice' (2005) 6 *Journal of World Investment and Trade* 357

Schwarzenberger, Georg, *The Inductive Approach to International Law* (London: Stevens, 1965)

Schwarzenberger, Georg and Brown, E. D., *A Manual of International Law* (Milton, UK: Professional Books, 6th edn, 1976)

Schwebel, Stephen, 'The Effect of Resolutions of the UN General Assembly on Customary International Law' (1979) 73 *American Society of International Law Proceedings* 301

Sebastian, Thomas, 'World Trade Organization Remedies and the Assessment of Proportionality: Equivalence and Appropriateness' (2007) 48 *Harvard International Law Journal* 337

Sim, Disa, *The Scope and Application of Good Faith in the Vienna Convention on Contracts for the International Sale of Goods* (Cambridge: Law School, Harvard University, 2000)

Simpson, John and Weiner, Edmund (eds.), *The Oxford English Dictionary* (Oxford: Oxford University Press, 2nd edn, 1989)

Sinclair, Ian, *The Vienna Convention on the Law of Treaties* (Manchester, UK: Manchester University Press, 2nd edn, 1984)

Srinivasan, T., 'Developing Countries in the World Trading System: From GATT, 1947, to the Third Ministerial Meeting of the WTO, 1999' (1999) 22 *World Economy* 1047

'Nondiscrimination in GATT/WTO: Was There Anything to Begin with and Is There Anything Left?' (2005) 4 *World Trade Review* 69

Stack, David, 'The Two Standards of Good Faith in Canadian Contract Law' (1999) 62 *Saskatchewan Law Review* 201

Steger, Debra, 'Jurisdiction of the WTO' (2004) 98 *American Society of International Law Proceedings* 142

Steinberg, Richard and Josling, Timothy, 'When the Peace Ends: The Vulnerability of EC and US Agricultural Subsidies to WTO Legal Challenge' (2003) 6 *Journal of International Economic Law* 369

Stone, Julius, 'Fictional Elements in Treaty Interpretation – A Study in the International Judicial Process' (1953–55) 1 *Sydney Law Review* 344

Sykes, Alan, 'The Least Restrictive Means' (2003) 70 *University of Chicago Law Review* 403

Tasioulas, John, 'In Defence of Relative Normativity: Communitarian Values and the Nicaragua Case' (1996) 16 *Oxford Journal of Legal Studies* 85

Taylor, G. D. S., 'The Content of the Rule against Abuse of Rights in International Law' (1972–73) 46 *British Yearbook of International Law* 323

Tetley, William, 'Good Faith in Contract: Particularly in the Contracts of Arbitration and Chartering' (2004) 35 *Journal of Maritime Law and Commerce* 561

Thirlway, Hugh, 'The Law and Procedure of the International Court of Justice 1960–1989: Part Two' (1990) 61 *British Yearbook of International Law* 1

'The Law and Procedure of the International Court of Justice' (1998) 69 *British Yearbook of International Law* 1

Trachtman, Joel 'Book Review of Joost Pauwelyn, Conflict of Norms in Public International Law' (2004) 98 *American Journal of International Law* 855

'Jurisdiction in WTO Disputes' in Rufus Yerxa and Bruce Wilson (eds.), *Key Issues in WTO Dispute Settlement* (Cambridge: WTO/Cambridge University Press, 2005)

'The Domain of WTO Dispute Resolution' (1999) 40 *Harvard International Law Journal* 333

'The Jurisdiction of the World Trade Organization' (2004) 98 *American Society of International Law Proceedings* 139

'United States: Tax Treatment for "Foreign Sales Corporations" ', *European Journal of International Law: Survey of Decisions of the Appellate Body of the World Trade Organization*, available at www.ejil.org/journal/curdevs/sr8.html

Trebilcock, Michael J. and Howse, Robert, *The Regulation of International Trade* (London: Routledge, 3rd edn, 2005)

Trumble, William and Stevenson, Angus (eds.), *Shorter Oxford English Dictionary on Historical Principles* (Oxford: Oxford University Press, 5th edn, 2002)

'Unquotable', *The Economist*, 28 December 2004

US International Trade Commission, *Textiles and Apparel: Assessment of the Competitiveness of Certain Foreign Suppliers to the US Market* (Publication No 3671, January 2004)

Ustor, Endre, 'Most-Favoured-Nation Clause' in Rudolf Bernhardt (ed.), *Encyclopaedia of Public International Law* (Amsterdam: North-Holland Publishing Co, 2003) vol. III, 468

Vagts, Detlev and Varges, Gabe, 'Book Review: Good Faith in International Law' (1992) 86 *American Journal of International Law* 841

Van Alstine, Michael P., 'The Death of Good Faith in Treaty Jurisprudence and a Call for Resurrection' (2005) 93 *Georgetown Law Journal* 1885

Vandevelde, Kenneth, *United States Investment Treaties: Policy and Practice* (Deventer, Netherlands: Kluwer Law and Taxation, 1992)

Verosta, Stephan, 'Denial of Justice' in Rudolf Bernhardt (ed.), *Encyclopaedia of Public International Law* (Amsterdam: North-Holland Publishing Co, 2003) vol. I, 1007

Virally, Michael, 'Review Essay: Good Faith in Public International Law' (1983) 77 *American Journal of International Law* 130

von Hirsch, Andrew, 'Proportionality in the Philosophy of Punishment' (1992) 16 *Crime & Justice* 55

Voyame, Joseph et al., 'Abuse of Rights in Comparative Law' in Council of Europe (ed.), *Abuse of Rights and Equivalent Concepts: The Principle and Its Present Day Application* (Strasbourg: The Council, 1990) 23

Waincymer, Jeff, *WTO Litigation: Procedural Aspects of Formal Dispute Settlement* (London: Cameron May, 2002)

Waldock, Humphrey, 'General Course on Public International Law' (1962-II) 106 *Recueil Des Cours* 1

Walker, David M., *The Oxford Companion to Law* (Oxford: Oxford University Press, 1980)

Wallace, Rebecca M. M., *International Law* (London: Sweet & Maxwell, 4th edn, 2002)

Weiler, Joseph, 'The Rule of Lawyers and the Ethos of Diplomats – Reflections on the Internal and External Legitimacy of WTO Dispute Settlement' (2001) 35 *Journal of World Trade* 191

Weiss, Wolfgang, 'Security and Predictability under WTO Law' (2003) 2 *World Trade Review* 183

White, Gillian, 'The Principle of Good Faith' in Vaughan Lowe and Colin Warbrick (eds.), *The United Nations and the Principles of International Law: Essays in Memory of Michael Akehurst* (London: Routledge, 1994) 230

White, N. D. and Abass, A., 'Countermeasures and Sanctions' in Malcolm Evans (ed.), *International Law* (Oxford: Oxford University Press, 2003) 505

Whittington, Keith E, *Constitutional Interpretation: Textual Meaning, Original Intent, and Judicial Review* (Lawrence: University Press of Kansas, 1999)

Winckel, Anne, 'The Contextual Role of a Preamble in Statutory Interpretation' (1999) 23 *Melbourne University Law Review* 184

Woolman, Stu and Botha, Henk, 'Limitations' in *Constitutional Law of South Africa* (2nd edn, Original Service 07–06)

WTO, *Understanding the WTO* (Geneva: WTO, 3rd edn, 2003)

Yanovich, Alan and Voon, Tania, 'What Is the Measure at Issue?' in Andrew D Mitchell (ed.), *Challenges and Prospects for the WTO* (London: Cameron May, 2005) 115

Zeitler, Helge, '"Good Faith" in the WTO Jurisprudence – Necessary Balancing Element or an Open Door to Judicial Activism' (2005) 8 *Journal of International Economic Law* 721

Zoller, Elisabeth, *La Bonne Foi en Droit International Public* (Paris: Editions A Pedone, 1977)

PCIJ AND ICJ CASES

Aerial Incident of 10 August 1999 (Pakistan v. *India)* (Jurisdiction) [2000] ICJ Rep 12

Aerial Incident of July 27, 1955 (Preliminary Objections) (Israel v. *Bulgaria)* [1959] ICJ Rep 127

Application for Review of Judgment No 158 of the United Nations Administrative Tribunal (Advisory Opinion) [1973] ICJ Rep 166

Article 3, Paragraph 2, of the Treaty of Lausanne (Frontier between Turkey and Iraq) (Advisory) [1925] PCIJ Series B, No 12, 6

Asylum Case (Colombia v. *Peru)* [1950] ICJ Rep 266

Barcelona Traction, Light and Power Company Ltd (Belgium v. *Spain) (Merits)* [1970] ICJ Rep 3

Border and Transborder Armed Actions (Nicaragua v. *Honduras) (Jurisdiction and Admissibility)* [1988] ICJ Rep 69

Certain Norwegian Loans (France v. *Norway) (Jurisdiction)* [1957] ICJ Rep 9

Conditions of Admission of a State to Membership in the United Nations (Advisory Opinion) [1948] ICJ Rep 57

Continental Shelf (Tunisia v. *Libyan Arab Jamahiriya) (Application by Malta for Permission to Intervene)* [1981] ICJ Rep 3

Delimitation of the Maritime Boundary in the Gulf of Maine Area (Canada v. *United States of America) (Merits)* [1984] ICJ Rep 246

Effect of Awards of Compensation Made by the United Nations Administrative Tribunal (Advisory Opinion) [1954] ICJ Rep 47

Factory at Chorzów (Claim for Indemnity) (Jurisdiction) [1927] PCIJ (ser A) No 9, 4

Factory at Chorzów (Claim for Indemnity) (Merits) [1928] PCIJ (ser A) No 17, 4

Fisheries (United Kingdom v. *Norway)* [1951] ICJ Rep 116

Free Zones of Upper Savoy and the District of Gex Case (*France* v. *Switzerland*) (*Merits*) [1932] PCIJ Reports Ser A/B, No 46
Gabčíkovo-Nagymaros Project (*Hungary* v. *Slovakia*) (*Merits*) [1997] ICJ Rep 7
German Interests Case (*Merits*) [1926] PCIJ (ser A) No 7, 4
Interpretation of the Agreement of 25 March 1951 between the WHO and Egypt (Advisory Opinion) [1980] ICJ Rep 73
Interpretation of the Greco-Turkish Agreement of December 1st, 1926 (Advisory Opinion) [1928] PCIJ (ser B) No 31, 5
Judgments of the Administrative Tribunal of the ILO upon Complaints Made against the UNESCO (Advisory Opinion) [1956] ICJ Rep 77
Land and Maritime Boundary between Cameroon and Nigeria (*Cameroon* v. *Nigeria*) (*Preliminary Objections*) [1998] ICJ Rep 275
Land, Island and Maritime Frontier Dispute (*El Salvador* v. *Honduras*) (*Application by Nicaragua for Permission to Intervene*) [1990] ICJ Rep 92
Legal Consequences for States of the Continued Presence of South Africa in Namibia (*South West Africa*) *Notwithstanding Security Council Resolution 276 (1970)* (*Advisory Opinion*) [1971] ICJ Rep 16
Legal Status of Eastern Greenland (*Denmark* v. *Norway*) [1933] PCIJ Series A/B, No 53, 22
Legality of the Threat or Use of Nuclear Weapons [1996] ICJ Rep 226
Military and Paramilitary Activities in and against Nicaragua (*Nicaragua* v. *United States of America*) (*Merits*) [1986] ICJ Rep 14
North Sea Continental Shelf (*Federal Republic of Germany* v. *Denmark; Federal Republic of Germany* v. *Netherlands*) [1969] ICJ Rep 3
Northern Cameroons (*Cameroons* v. *United Kingdom*) [1963] ICJ Rep 15
Nuclear Tests (*Australia* v. *France*) (Merits) [1974] ICJ Rep 253
Oil Platforms (*Islamic Republic of Iran* v. *United States of America*) (Merits) [2003] ICJ Rep 161
Reparation for Injuries (*Advisory Opinion*) [1949] ICJ Rep 174
Right of Passage over Indian Territory (*Portugal* v. *India*) (*Merits*) [1960] ICJ Rep 6
SS Lotus (*France* v. *Turkey*) [1927] PCIJ (ser A) No 10
Temple of Preah Vihear (*Cambodia* v. *Thailand*) (*Merits*) [1962] ICJ Rep 6
United Kingdom v. *Iceland* (*Merits*) [1974] ICJ Rep 3

OTHER ARBITRATIONS AND CASES

Agreement to Arbitrate the Boundary Dispute concerning the Taba Beachfront, Egypt–Israel (1986) text in (1987) 26 ILR 1
Allen v. *Wood* (1897) 1898 App Cas 1
Arafura Seafood Products Pty Ltd v. *Landos* (1988) 16 ALD 519
Australian Broadcasting Tribunal v. *Bond* (1990) 170 CLR 321
Azinian, Davitian and Baca v. *United Mexican States*, Award, 1 November 1999, 5 ICSID Reports 269
Boundary Dispute concerning the Taba Area, Arbitration Award (1998) text in (1988) 27 ILM 1421

Bremer Vulkan v. *South India Shipping* [1981] AC 909
Bugmy v. *The Queen* (1990) 169 CLR 525
Cabell v. *Markham*, 148 F.2d 737, 739 (2d Cir, 1945)
Case C-104/75 de Peijper [1976] ECR 613, [16]–[29]
Case C-120/78, Cassis de Dijon [1979] ECR 649
Case C-169/91, Stoke-on-Trent [1992] ECR I-6625, [15]
Cave v. *Mills* (1862) 7 Hurlstone & Norman 913
Chief Constable of North Wales Police v. *Evans* [1982] 3 All ER 141
Claro v. *Minister for Immigration, Local Government & Ethnic Affairs* (1993) 46 FCR 494
Coker v. *Georgia*, 433 US 584 (1977)
de Freitas v. *Permanent Secretary of Ministry of Agriculture, Fisheries, Lands and Housing* [1999] 1 AC 69, 80, quoting *Nyambirai* v. *National Social Security Authority* [1996] 1 LRC 64, 75
Earl of Iveagh v. *Minister of Housing and Local Government* [1962] 2 QB 147
Enmund v. *Florida*, 458 US 782 (1982)
Ewing v. *California*, 538 US 11 (2003)
Goldblatt v. *Town of Hempstead*, 369 US 590, 594–5 (1962)
Golder v. *United Kingdom* (1975) 18 Eur Court HR (ser A)
Handyside v. United Kingdom (1979) 1 EHRR 737
Harmelin v. *Michigan*, 501 US 957 (1991)
Hoare v. *The Queen* (1989) 167 CLR 348
Huang v. *Secretary of State for the Home Department*; *Kashmiri* v. *Same* [2007] UKHL 11. [2007] 2 AC 167, [19]
ICTY Decision, Decision of the Prosecutor's Appeal on Admissibility of Evidence, *Prosecutor* v. *Aleksovski*, Case No I-95–14/1-A, Appeals Chamber International Tribunal for the Former Yugoslavia, 16 February 1999
Indo-Pakistan Western Boundary (Rann of Kutch) Case (*India* v. *Pakistan*) (1968) 50 ILR 2
Interfoto Picture Library Ltd v. *Stiletto Visual Programmes Ltd* [1988] 1 All ER 348
Kupreskic et al. Case (IT-95–16), International Criminal Tribunal for the former Yugoslavia, Judgment of 14 January 2000
Lake Lanoux (*France* v. *Spain*) (Award of 16 November 1957) (1957) 18 RIAA 415
Lockyer v. *Andrade*, 538 US 63 (2003)
Loewen Group, Inc and Raymond L. Loewen v. *United States of America*, ICSID Case No ARB(AF)/98/3 (Award dated 26 June 2003)
Mahon v. *Air New Zealand Ltd* [1984] AC 808
Matthews v. *Eldridge*, 424 US 319 (1976)
Minister for Immigration & Ethnic Affairs v. *Pochi* (1980) 44 FLR 41
Mondev International Ltd v. *United States of America*, ICSID Case No ARB(AF)/99/2 (Notice of Arbitration dated 1 September 1999)
Mondev International Ltd v. *United States of America*, ICSID Case No ARB(AF)/99/2 (Award dated 11 October, 2002)
Murray's Lessee v. *Hoboken Land & Improvement Co*, 59 US (18 How) 272 (1856)

"Naulilaa" (Responsibility of Germany for Damage Caused in the Portuguese Colonies in the South of Africa) (1928) II Reports of International Arbitral Awards 1013
North Atlantic Coast Fisheries Arbitration (*United States* v. *Great Britain*) (1910) 11 RIAA 167
Prosecutor v. *Blaskic* Case No. IT-95-14 (Trial Chamber, ICTY, 3 March 2000)
Prosecutor v. *Tadic*, Case No IT-94-I-T (Trial Chamber, ICTY, 10 August 1995)
R (Daly) v. *Secretary of State for the Home Department* [2001] 2 AC 532, [27] (Lord Steyn)
R (Daly) v. *Secretary of State for the Home Department* [2001] 2 AC 532, [28] (Lord Steyn)
Re Poyser and Mills' Arbitration [1964] 2 QB 467
Schweiker v. *McClure*, 456 US 188 (1982)
Solem v. *Helm*, 463 US 277 (1983)
Tacna-Arica (*Chile* v. *Peru*) (1925) II RIAA 921
The Queen v. *Shrestha* (1991) 173 CLR 48
Trial Smelter Arbitration (*USA* v. *Canada*) (1949) 3 RIAA 1905
Westminster City Council v. *Great Portland Street Estates plc* [1985] AC 661

WTO DOCUMENTS

Award of the Arbitrator, *European Communities – the ACP-EC Partnership Agreement – Recourse to Arbitration Pursuant to the Decision of 14 November 2001*, WT/L/616, 1 August 2005
DSB, *Minutes of Meeting Held on 20 May 1996*, WT/DSB/M/17 (6 June 1996)
Minutes of Meeting Held on 11 February 2000, WT/DSB/M/75 (1 February 2000)
Minutes of Meeting Held on 19 June 2000, WT/DSB/M/84 (24 July 2000)
Minutes of Meeting Held on 5 November 2001, WT/DSB/M/112 (4 December 2001)
Minutes of Meeting Held on 27 January 2003, WT/DSB/M/142 (6 March 2003)
Minutes of Meeting Held on 18 March 2003, WT/DSB/M/145 (7 May 2003)
DSB, Special Session, 'Negotiations on Improvements and Clarifications of the Dispute Settlement Understanding on Improving Flexibility and Member Control in WTO Dispute Settlement', TN/DS/W/52 (14 March 2003)
'Report by the Chairman, Ambassador Péter Balás, to the Trade Negotiations Committee', TN/DS/9 (6 June 2003)
Contribution by the United States, TN/DS/W/74 (15 March 2005)
General Council, 'Preparations for the Fourth Session of the Ministerial Conference: Proposal for a Framework Agreement on Special and Differential Treatment', WT/GC/W/442 (31 July 2001)
Korea – Anti-Dumping Duties on Certain Imports of Paper from Indonesia: Communication from the Chairman of the Panel, WT/DS312/4 (25 April 2005)
Negotiating Group on Market Access, Market Access for Non-Agricultural Products – The Issue of Newly-Acceded Members: Submission by the Separate Customs Territory of Taiwan, Penghu, Kinmen and Matsu, TN/MA/W/19/Add.1 (16 May 2003)

WTO Committee on Agriculture, *WTO Negotiations on Agriculture: Proposals by Small Island Developing States (SIDS)*, G/AG/NG/W/97 and Corr.1 (29 December 2000)

WTO African Group: Joint Proposal on the Negotiations on Agriculture, G/AG/NG/W/142 (23 March 2001)

WTO Committee on Trade and Development, *Implementation of Special and Differential Treatment Provisions in WTO Agreements and Decisions: Communiqué of the Fifth Annual Ministerial Meeting of Landlocked Developing Countries (LLDCs)*, WT/L/585, WT/COMTD/SE/2 (7 October 2004)

Note by the Secretariat, WT/COMTD/W/77 (25 October 2000)

Note on the Meeting of 12 May 2004, WT/COMTD/SE/M/7 (16 July 2004)

Proposals Submitted by the Landlocked Developing Countries: Work Programme on Small Economies, WT/COMTD/SE/W/10 (27 April 2004)

Trade and Economic Performance: The Role of Economic Size? Note by the Secretariat, WT/COMTD/SE/W/5 (23 October 2002)

Work Programme on Small Economies: Communication from Antigua and Barbuda, Barbados, Bolivia, Cuba, Dominican Republic, El Salvador, Fiji, Guatemala, Honduras, Jamaica, Mauritius, Mongolia, Nicaragua, Paraguay, Sri Lanka, Trinidad and Tobago, WT/COMTD/SE/W/12 (21 February 2005)

WTO Ministerial Conference, *Accession of the People's Republic of China: Decision of 10 November 2001*, WT/L/432 (23 November 2001)

Decision on Measures Concerning the Possible Negative Effects of the Reform Programme on Least-Developed and Net Food-Importing Developing Countries, LT/UR/D-1/2 (15 March 1994)

European Communities – The ACP–EC Partnership Agreement: Decision of 14 November 2001, WT/MIN(01)/15 (14 November 2001)

European Communities – The ACP–EC Partnership Agreement: Decision of 14 November 2001, WT/MIN(01)/15 (14 November 2001) Annex

European Communities – Transitional Regime for the EC Autonomous Tariff Rate Quotas on Imports of Bananas: Decision of 14 November 2001, WT/MIN(01)/16 (14 November 2001).

WTO Secretariat, 'Developing Countries and the Multilateral Trading System: Past and Present – Background Note by the Secretariat' (WTO High Level Symposium, 17–18 March 1999) Annex II.

'The Fundamental WTO Principles of National Treatment, Most-Favoured-Nation Treatment and Transparency', WT/WGTCP/W/114 (14 April 1999)

Update of WTO Dispute Settlement Cases, WT/DS/OV/31 (22 August 2007)

Index

CAMBRIDGE STUDIES IN INTERNATIONAL AND COMPARATIVE LAW

Books in the series

Legal Principles in WTO Disputes
ANDREW D. MITCHELL

War Crimes in Internal Armed Conflicts
EVE LA HAYE

Humanitarian Occupation
GREGORY H. FOX

The International Law of Environmental Impact Assessment: Process, Substance and Integration
NEIL CRAIK

The Law and Practice of International Territorial Administration: Versailles, Iraq and Beyond
CARSTEN STAHN

Cultural Products and the World Trade Organization
TANIA VOON

United Nations Sanctions and the Rule of Law
JEREMY FARRALL

National Law in WTO Law Effectiveness and Good Governance in the World Trading System
SHARIF BHUIYAN

The Threat of Force in International Law
NIKOLAS STÜRCHLER

Indigenous Rights and United Nations Standards
ALEXANDRA XANTHAKI

International Refugee Law and Socio-Economic Rights
MICHELLE FOSTER

The Protection of Cultural Property in Armed Conflict
ROGER O'KEEFE

Interpretation and Revision of International Boundary Decisions
KAIYAN HOMI KAIKOBAD

Multinationals and Corporate Social Responsibility: Limitations and Opportunities in International Law
JENNIFER A. ZERK

Judiciaries within Europe: a Comparative Review
JOHN BELL

Law in Times of Crisis: Emergency Powers in Theory and Practice
OREN GROSS AND FIONNUALA NÍ AOLÁIN

Vessel-Source Marine Pollution: The Law and Politics of International Regulation
ALAN TAN

Enforcing Obligations Erga Omnes in International Law
CHRISTIAN J. TAMS

Non-Governmental Organisations in International Law
ANNA-KARIN LINDBLOM

Democracy, Minorities and International Law
STEVEN WHEATLEY

Prosecuting International Crimes: Selectivity and the International Law Regime
ROBERT CRYER

Compensation for Personal Injury in English, German and Italian Law: a Comparative Outline
BASIL MARKESINIS, MICHAEL COESTER, GUIDO ALPA, AUGUSTUS ULLSTEIN

Dispute Settlement in the UN Convention on the Law of the Sea
NATALIE KLEIN

The International Protection of Internally Displaced Persons
CATHERINE PHUONG

Imperialism, Sovereignty and the Making of International Law
ANTONY ANGHIE

Necessity, Proportionality and the Use of Force by States
JUDITH GARDAM

International Legal Argument in the Permanent Court of International Justice: the Rise of the International Judiciary
OLE SPIERMANN

Great Powers and Outlaw States: Unequal Sovereigns in the International Legal Order
GERRY SIMPSON

Local Remedies in International Law
C. F. AMERASINGHE

Reading Humanitarian Intervention: Human Rights and the Use of Force in International Law
ANNE ORFORD

Conflict of Norms in Public International Law: How WTO Law Relates to Other Rules of Law
JOOST PAUWELYN

Transboundary Damage in International Law
HANQIN XUE

European Criminal Procedures
Edited by MIREILLE DELMAS-MARTY AND JOHN SPENCER

The Accountability of Armed Opposition Groups in International Law
LIESBETH ZEGVELD

Sharing Transboundary Resources: International Law and Optimal Resource Use
EYAL BENVENISTI

International Human Rights and Humanitarian Law
RENÉ PROVOST

Remedies Against International Organisations
KAREL WELLENS

Diversity and Self-Determination in International Law
KAREN KNOP

The Law of Internal Armed Conflict
LINDSAY MOIR

International Commercial Arbitration and African States: Practice, Participation and Institutional Development
AMAZU A. ASOUZU

The Enforceability of Promises in European Contract Law
JAMES GORDLEY

International Law in Antiquity
DAVID J. BEDERMAN

Money Laundering: a New International Law Enforcement Model
GUY STESSENS

Good Faith in European Contract Law
REINHARD ZIMMERMANN AND SIMON WHITTAKER

On Civil Procedure
J. A. JOLOWICZ

Trusts: a Comparative Study
MAURIZIO LUPOI

The Right to Property in Commonwealth Constitutions
TOM ALLEN

International Organizations Before National Courts
AUGUST REINISCH

The Changing International Law of High Seas Fisheries
FRANCISCO ORREGO VICUÑA

Trade and the Environment: a Comparative Study of EC and US Law
DAMIEN GERADIN

Unjust Enrichment: a Study of Private Law and Public Values
HANOCH DAGAN

Religious Liberty and International Law in Europe
MALCOLM D. EVANS

Ethics and Authority in International Law
ALFRED P. RUBIN

Sovereignty Over Natural Resources: Balancing Rights and Duties
NICO SCHRIJVER

The Polar Regions and the Development of International Law
DONALD R. ROTHWELL

Fragmentation and the International Relations of Micro-States: Self-determination and Statehood
JORRI DUURSMA

Principles of the Institutional Law of International Organizations
C. F. AMERASINGHE

www.ingramcontent.com/pod-product-compliance
Lightning Source LLC
LaVergne TN
LVHW101457200926
848483LV00001B/151

* 9 7 8 0 5 2 1 8 7 3 2 6 0 *